Using Microsoft Dynamics AX 2012

Andreas Luszczak

Using Microsoft Dynamics AX 2012

Updated for Version R2

3rd Edition

Dr. Andreas Luszczak
Vienna, Austria

ISBN 978-3-658-01708-8   ISBN 978-3-658-01709-5 (eBook)
DOI 10.1007/978-3-658-01709-5

The Deutsche Nationalbibliothek lists this publication in the Deutsche Nationalbibliografie; detailed bibliographic data are available in the Internet at http://dnb.d-nb.de.

Library of Congress Control Number: 2013946307

Springer Vieweg
© Springer Fachmedien Wiesbaden 2009, 2012, 2013

Springer Vieweg is a brand of Springer DE.
Springer DE is part of Springer Science+Business Media.
www.springer-vieweg.de

Preface

When looking for a business management solution supporting business processes in mid-sized and large companies, Microsoft Dynamics AX is likely to be your favorite. Because of its deep functional and technological integration, it is also a good choice for universities teaching ERP systems.

Reading this Book

The primary purpose of this book is to provide you with a good knowledge of the standard application concept and functionality, enabling you to run business processes in Microsoft Dynamics AX 2012. This book applies to you, if you are an end user, student, or consultant interested in learning how to use Dynamics AX.

Going beyond the operations on the user interface, you will also learn how the different parts of the application work together. As a result, you will also take advantage from learning the end-to-end application concept, if you are a system administrator, developer, IT executive or experienced consultant not knowing the complete application already.

Actually working in an application is the best way to learn it. This book therefore includes exercises building up on each other in a comprehensive case study. If you need support for the exercises, a free download of sample solutions is available.

The current edition of this book is based on Microsoft Dynamics AX 2012 R2 and includes the core changes of Dynamics AX 2012 in the initial version and in R2. It is an update of the previous edition "Using Microsoft Dynamics AX 2012" published in 2012.

Since Dynamics AX is a very comprehensive business solution, it is not possible to cover all parts of the application in a single book. In order to provide a profound understanding of the core application, this book addresses the primary functionality in supply chain (including trade, logistics and production control) and finance management. It shows the application, but does not cover tasks in system administration and development. If you want to learn more about the concepts and options for implementing Dynamics AX, the book "Implementing Microsoft Dynamics AX 2012 with Sure Step 2012" by Keith Dunkinson and Andrew Birch might be interesting for you.

Applicable Settings

In Dynamics AX, you can individually choose the language of your user interface. Descriptions and illustrations in this book refer to the language "EN-US". Whereas it is obvious that the Dynamics AX client displays different labels when choosing languages like Spanish or Russian, there are also differences when selecting British English. For example, the label for the field "Sales tax" is "VAT" in British English. Other differences between your application and the descriptions in the book are possibly caused by your permissions, by applicable local features, or by specific modifications and features implemented in your Dynamics AX system.

In order to benefit from the explanations, it is recommended to access a Dynamics AX application. A separate test application for executing the exercises minimizes the risk of affecting actual company data.

The exercises and illustrations refer to a sample company "Anso Technologies Ltd.", which shows a simple setup limited to the described functionality. In order to grant flexibility for selecting the training environment, the tasks in the exercises are specified in a way that you can also use the Microsoft standard demo environment ("Contoso") or any other test environment.

This book has been updated for Microsoft Dynamics AX 2012 R2. If you are using the initial version of Dynamics AX 2012 or the Dynamics AX 2012 Feature Pack, a limited number of features and settings work different. Notes in the book show the differences between the initial version and R2, enabling you to use this book in all versions of Dynamics AX 2012. If you want to know in which version you are working, click the button *Help* / *About Microsoft Dynamics AX* in the command bar of the Dynamics AX client – if you are in the Feature Pack or R2, it is displayed.

Available Support

In order to download solutions to the exercises in this book and other applicable resources, please access the online service of the publisher or following web site:

http://axbook.addyn.com

If you have comments or questions regarding the book or the exercises, please contact me through the web site mentioned above or via e-mail to *lua@addyn.com*.

Acknowledgements

Many people have been involved in finalizing this book, directly and indirectly, from the first edition in German to the current English edition. I want to thank all of them. In particular, I would like to mention:

➢ Matthias Gimbel (Senior Consultant at STZ IT-Business Consulting)
➢ Ingo Maresch (Solution Architect at Semantax Business Consulting)
➢ Keith Dunkinson (Owner at ERP advisers)

Thank you also to editorial team Bernd Hansemann and Maren Mithöfer. Finally, my special thanks go to my family – Sonja, Felix and Caroline.

Andreas Luszczak

Table of Contents

    8.1   Principles of Ledger Transactions 305
          8.1.1 Basic Approach 305
          8.1.2 At a glance: Ledger Journal Transactions 306
    8.2   Setting up Finance 307
          8.2.1 Fiscal and Ledger Calendars 307
          8.2.2 Currencies and Exchange Rates 309
          8.2.3 Financial Dimensions 312
          8.2.4 Account Structures and Charts of Accounts 314
          8.2.5 Customer, Vendor and Bank Accounts 321
          8.2.6 VAT / Sales Tax Settings 322
          8.2.7 Case Study Exercises 325
    8.3   Business Processes in Finance 326
          8.3.1 Basics Setup for Journal Transactions 326
          8.3.2 General Journals 328
          8.3.3 Invoice Journals 333
          8.3.4 Payments 337
          8.3.5 Reversing Transactions 341
          8.3.6 Case Study Exercises 342
    8.4   Ledger Integration 343
          8.4.1 Basics of Ledger Integration 344
          8.4.2 Ledger Integration in Inventory 345
          8.4.3 Ledger Integration in Production 349

9   Core Setup and Essential Features 351

    9.1   Organizational Structures 351
          9.1.1 Data Partitions 352
          9.1.2 Organization Model Architecture 353
          9.1.3 Organization Units 353
          9.1.4 Organization Hierarchy Structures 356
          9.1.5 Legal Entities (Company Accounts) 357
          9.1.6 Virtual Company Accounts 359
          9.1.7 Sites 360
    9.2   Security and Information Access 362
          9.2.1 Access Control 362
          9.2.2 User Management 362
          9.2.3 Role-based Security 366
          9.2.4 Securing the Global Address Book 370

1 What is Microsoft Dynamics AX?

Dynamics AX is Microsoft's core business management solution, designed to meet the requirements of mid-sized companies and multinational organizations. Based on state-of-the-art architecture and deep integration, Dynamics AX shows comprehensive functionality while ensuring high usability at the same time.

In version Dynamics AX 2012, it shows a vast number of innovations including a new user interface consequently applying the role tailored user experience across the application, increased capabilities in administration, finance and product data management, and an enhanced industry foundation.

The R2 version of Microsoft Dynamics AX 2012 additionally provides data partitions, country-specific features for additional key countries like Brazil, China, India, Japan and Russia – included in a single layer for all country localizations – and several functional enhancements, improving the option for multinational organizations to run Dynamics AX in one global instance.

1.1 Axapta and the History of Dynamics AX

Dynamics AX in its origin has been developed under the name *Axapta* by Damgaard A/S, a Danish software company. The first version released to market has been published in March 1998. At that time, the founders of Damgaard – Erik and Preben Damgaard – have already had more than ten years of experience designing ERP systems. Among others, they have been co-founders of PC&C, where they joined the development of Navision (now Dynamics NAV).

Version 1.0 of Axapta has been available in Denmark and the USA only. Version 1.5, published in October 1998, included support for several European countries. Releasing version 2.0 in July 1999 and version 3.0 in October 2002, Axapta provided continuously increasing application functionality and support of additional countries. Until releasing Axapta under the new brand Dynamics AX in version 4.0, improvements have been deployed in a number of service packs.

After signing a merger agreement in November 2000, Damgaard A/S united with the local rival Navision A/S, a successor of PC&C. Finally, Microsoft acquired Navision-Damgaard in May 2002 and accepted their main products, Navision and Axapta, as the core business solutions of Microsoft. Whereas Dynamics NAV (Navision) in functional and technological aspect applies to small companies, Dynamics AX (Axapta) is the product for mid-sized and large companies.

When releasing version 4.0 in June 2006, Microsoft rebranded Axapta to Dynamics AX. Microsoft Dynamics AX 4.0 differs from previous versions not only by functional enhancements but also by a new user interface, showing a complete redesign with a Microsoft Office-like look and feel.

In June 2008, Dynamics AX 2009 has been published including role centers, workflow functionality and an improved user interface. Dynamics AX 2009 also provided enhanced functionality, including the multisite foundation and additional modules ensuring an end-to-end support for the supply chain requirements of global organizations.

Dynamics AX 2012 has been published in August 2011, showing an updated user interface with an action pane in all forms and applying list pages for replacing the Overview tab on forms. Role-based security, the new accounting framework with segmented account structures, the enhanced use of shared data structures and other features facilitate collaboration across legal entities and operating units within the application, also suitable to large multinational enterprises.

Updated versions of Dynamics AX 2012 have been released later – in February 2012 the Dynamics AX 2012 Feature Pack (adding industry features for retail and process manufacturing) and in December 2012 the version Dynamics AX 2012 R2 (adding data partitions, functionality for additional countries and support for the latest Microsoft platform including Windows 8).

1.2   Dynamics AX 2012 Product Overview

Microsoft Dynamics AX is an adaptable business management solution, which is easy to use and nevertheless supports the complex requirements of multinational companies. Another characteristic is the deep integration to Microsoft technologies and applications like Microsoft SQL Server, SharePoint Services and BizTalk Server.

When accessing Dynamics AX for the first time, most people feel comfortable from the very beginning because the user interface is already known from Microsoft Windows and Microsoft Office. The intuitive user experience helps to start working in Dynamics AX easily and efficiently, supported by a tight integration to other Microsoft software. Role centers grant an easy and fast overview of information required by individuals.

1.2.1   Functional Capabilities

The end-to-end support of business processes across the whole organization allows integrating external business partners like customers and vendors on the one hand and internal organization units on the other hand.

Multi-language, multi-country and multi-currency support, the organization model for managing multiple hierarchies of operating units and legal entities, and the option to manage several sites within one legal entity enable managing complex global organizations in a common database.

The basic ERP capabilities of Dynamics AX include following main areas:

➢ Sales and marketing
➢ Supply chain management
➢ Production
➢ Procurement and sourcing
➢ Service management
➢ Financial management
➢ Project management and accounting
➢ Human capital management
➢ Business intelligence and reporting

Supplementing the basic ERP solution, industry specific capabilities for manufacturing, distribution, retail, services and the public sector included in the core standard application provide a broad industry foundation.

The workflow system in Dynamics AX (see section 9.4) provides configurable workflows to support routine procedures like the approval process for a purchase requisition. The workflow infrastructure in Dynamics AX is based on the Windows Workflow Foundation enabling workflow messages in Microsoft Outlook, the Enterprise Portal or the regular Dynamics AX Windows client.

High scalability and adaptability make it easy to manage changes in the organization and in business processes. If applicable for example, only deploy finance at the beginning and simply add new functional areas like production or warehouse management later. Enhancing Dynamics AX with additional users or legal entities is also possible at any time.

Local features are available in order to comply with country-specific requirements. In Dynamics AX 2012, they are controlled by the country/region of the primary address of your company (legal entity).

1.2.2   Business Intelligence

In order to access data for analysis, integrated functionality for reporting and business intelligence grants a fast and reliable presentation of business data. Business intelligence features are not only available for analysis in finance, but also for users in all other areas of Dynamics AX who need to analyze their data. Depending on the requirements, different types of reporting tools including structured and ad-hoc reports are required.

In Dynamics AX, business intelligence is based on the platform of the Microsoft SQL Server. The basis for structured Dynamics AX standard reports is provided by SQL Server Reporting Services (SSRS). Business intelligence components like Key Performance Indicators apply OLAP cubes, which are provided by SQL Server Analysis Services (SSAS).

1.2.3   Collaboration Features

Collaboration functionality for connecting external partners is available in two ways:

➢ Enterprise Portal
➢ Application Integration Framework

The Enterprise Portal as the first option provides direct access to Dynamics AX through a regular Internet browser like the Microsoft Internet Explorer. Limiting access to role-specific data, the Enterprise Portal is not only applicable to internal employees but also to external customers and vendors.

The Application Integration Framework (AIF) as the second option supports automatic data exchange with other business applications inside and outside your company. It enables receiving and sending documents like invoices, packing slips or price lists in XML format. An external converter then may convert the documents to any other format like EDIFACT if necessary.

For legal entities within a common Dynamics AX database and partition, the intercompany functionality enables automatic purchase and sales processes between companies.

1.2.4   Implementation

Microsoft does not directly sell Dynamics AX to customers, but offers an indirect sales channel. Customers may purchase licenses from certified partners, which also offer their services to support the implementation of Dynamics AX. This support includes application training and consulting as well as system installation and the development of enhancements to the core functionality.

In order to assist the implementation of Dynamics applications, Microsoft provides a standardized implementation methodology for partners – Microsoft Dynamics Sure Step. The Microsoft Dynamics Sure Step Methodology is a comprehensive approach to implement Microsoft Dynamics solutions including project management principles and solution-specific guidelines and tools.

Additional resources including product information, customer stories and online demos are available in a global version on the Microsoft Dynamics AX web page *http://www.microsoft.com/en-us/dynamics/erp-ax-overview.aspx* or in a local version accessible through the Microsoft homepage of your country.

The Microsoft web pages also provide support for finding an implementation partner or accessing the Microsoft Dynamics Marketplace with an overview of partner add-on solutions.

1.3   Technology and System Architecture

The development of Dynamics AX (formerly Axapta) from the very start aimed to support international implementations and to provide a deep integration of components. Integration is not limited to components within Dynamics AX – it also includes the Microsoft software stack with Windows operating systems, SQL Server, SharePoint, Internet Information Server and other applications.

Three core technological characteristics are essential in Dynamics AX:

➢ Development environments
➢ Model driven layered technology
➢ Three-tier architecture

1.3.1 Development Environments

Dynamics AX 2012 stores the application objects (like tables and forms) within a SQL database. The Application Object Tree (AOT) shows a tree structure of these application objects.

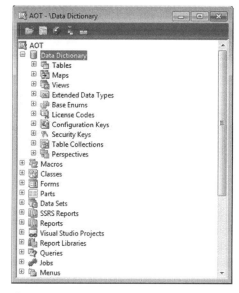

Figure 1-1:   The Application Object Tree (AOT) containing programmable objects

For modifying application objects, choose between different development environments:

➢ **Microsoft Visual Studio**
➢ **MorphX IDE** – Integrated development environment in Dynamics AX

The MorphX IDE in the developer workspace directly within the Dynamics AX Windows client provides access to the AOT for designing, editing, compiling and debugging code.

The Visual Studio development environment, which is closely integrated with MorphX, supports managed code and is required for some tasks like creating reports. Reports in Dynamics AX 2012 are only delivered by SQL Server Reporting Services (SSRS).

The programming language in the MorphX development environment is X++, an object-oriented, proprietary language similar to C# and Java. Since application objects in MorphX show an open source code, you can adjust and enhance Dynamics AX functionality in the development environment.

1.3.2   Layer Technology

Applying a layer structure, Dynamics AX provides a hierarchy of levels in the application source code separating the standard application from modifications. Different application object layers make sure that customer-specific modifications do not interfere with standard objects stored in other layers. The layering system therefore facilitates release upgrades on the one hand and the implementation of industry or generic solutions on the other hand.

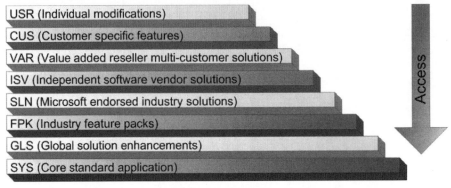

Figure 1-2:   Hierarchy of application object layers in Dynamics AX 2012

The lowest object level in Dynamics AX is the SYS layer, which together with the GLS layer contains the core Dynamics AX standard objects. The FPK layer containing industry solutions and features is the third layer of the base solution reserved for Microsoft. The layers SLN, ISV and VAR are available for partners and independent software vendors (ISV) to provide industry, vertical or multi-customer solutions. The highest object level is the USR layer, which contains installation specific modifications.

In addition, each layer refers to a patch layer with a name ending with "P" (e.g. "USP" for the USR layer). The patch layers are reserved for application updates to the related regular layer.

When accessing the Dynamics AX application, the kernel looks for a version of every object required. The version search starts from the highest layer, the USR layer. If no object version is available in the USR layer, the kernel will go through the lower layers until finding the object – locating it in the SYS layer if no modifications apply.

If you have modified the vendor list page for example, Dynamics AX applies the form *VendTableListPage* which you have modified in the USR layer – and not the standard object with the same name in the SYS layer.

1.3.3   Three-Tier Architecture

In order to support large implementations with a high number of users, Dynamics AX consequently applies a three-tier architecture. The three-tier architecture is characterized by separating database, application and client.

Data managed in Dynamics AX 2012 are stored in a relational Microsoft SQL Server database. A database cluster may be used in large installations.

The application tier contains the business logic of Dynamics AX, executing the code designed in the development environment. It may run on a single Application Object Server (AOS) or on a server cluster.

The client tier contains the graphical user interface, which is required for processing data input and output. Apart from the regular Dynamics AX Windows client, web browsers (applying the Enterprise Portal), Microsoft Office (applying the Office add-ins) and other applications (e.g. for mobile devices) are further options for accessing restricted areas of Dynamics AX.

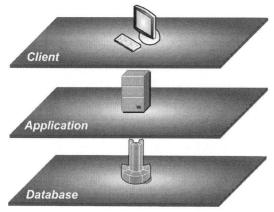

Figure 1-3:   The three-tier architecture in Dynamics AX

Database, application (AOS) and client usually run on different computers. In case of small implementations, optionally install database and application together on a single server. For testing purposes, all three tiers may run on a common device.

1.3.4   Data Structure

When working in Dynamics AX (or any other business software), you are accessing and creating data describing processes (e.g. item transactions). As a prerequisite for transactions, you need to manage data describing objects (e.g. customers).

Three data types group the different kinds of data:

➢ Setup data
➢ Master data
➢ Transaction data

Setup data determine the way business processes work in Dynamics AX. For example, choose in the setup whether to apply warehouse locations, pallets or serial numbers. Apart from modifying programmable objects, setup is the second way to adapt the application according to the requirements of an enterprise. Setup data are entered when initially setting up the system. Later modifications of core setup data need to be checked carefully.

Master data describe objects like customers, main accounts or products. They do not change periodically, but only at the time related objects change – for example when a customer gets a new address. Master data are entered or imported initially before a company starts working in the application. Later on, you need to insert or edit master data occasionally depending on your business.

Transaction data are continuously created when processing business activities. Examples for transaction data are sales orders, invoices or item transactions. In Dynamics AX, the application generates transaction data for every business activity. Registration and posting of transaction data complies with the voucher principle.

1.3.5   Voucher Principle

If you want to post a transaction, you have to register a voucher containing a header and one or more lines first. Every voucher is processed in two steps then:

➢ **Registration** – Registering the voucher (creating a non-posted document)
➢ **Posting** – Posting the voucher (creating a posted document)

Vouchers are based on master data like main accounts, customers or products. It is not possible to post a voucher as long as it does not comply with the rules defined by setup data and the Dynamics AX-internal business logic. Once a voucher is posted, it is not possible to change it any more.

Examples for vouchers in Dynamics AX are orders in sales or purchasing as well as journals in finance or inventory management. After posting, the posted documents are available as packing slips, invoices, ledger transactions or inventory transactions.

Note: Some minor vouchers like quarantine orders show an exception regarding the voucher structure – they do not contain a separate header and lines part.

2 Getting Started: Navigation and General Options

One of the core principles of Microsoft Dynamics AX is to grant a familiar look and feel to people, who are used to Microsoft software. However, business software has to adapt to business processes, which may be quite complex.

2.1 User Interface and Common Tasks

Before we start to go through business processes and case studies, we want to take a look at the general functionality in this chapter.

2.1.1 Logon and Authentication

Microsoft Dynamics AX logon is Active Directory based, applying Windows authentication. You do not need to log on to Dynamics AX with separate credentials as a result. After selecting the Dynamics AX icon on the Windows desktop or in the Start menu, you are automatically connecting to the Dynamics application using your Windows account.

The Dynamics AX user-ID, company (legal entity) and language derive from your user options, which you can change within the client. In Dynamics AX 2012 R2, data partitions (see section 9.1.1) apply additionally – the appropriate default partition is specified in the user management or in the client configuration.

Figure 2-1: Icon for Microsoft Dynamics AX on the Windows desktop

Sometimes you want to use different user accounts within Dynamics AX – e.g. if you have to check user permissions. In this case, you have to make sure that the user you want to apply is set up in Active Directory administration. In order to start Dynamics AX with a user which is different from your current Windows account, choose the option *"Run as different user"* in the pop-up menu (available if pressing the *Shift* key while doing a right-hand click) of the Dynamics AX- icon.

If you want to close your session and to logoff from Dynamics AX, proceed the same way as you do in any other Windows program: Push the shortcut key *Alt+F4*, choose the command *File/Exit* or click the button ⊠ on the top right-hand corner of the Dynamics AX workspace. If you have opened several workspace windows, you are logging off when closing the last workspace.

2.1.2   User Interface

The Dynamics AX workspace is the first page visible when accessing Microsoft Dynamics AX. The content of the workspace is depending both on the system configuration and on your permissions and individual settings.

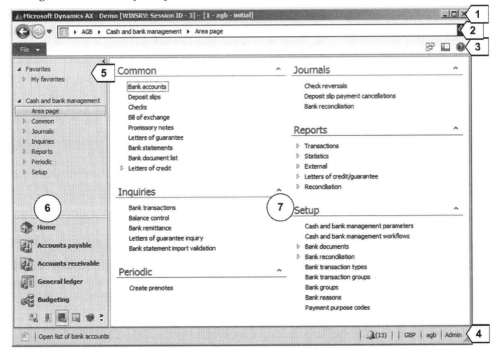

Figure 2-2:   Dynamics AX workspace, showing an area page in the content pane

The workspace of Microsoft Dynamics AX 2012 consists of following areas as shown in Figure 2-2:

➢ Title bar [1]
➢ Address bar [2]
➢ Command bar and jewel menu [3]
➢ Status bar [4]
➢ Favorites [5]
➢ Navigation pane [6]
➢ Content pane [7]

2.1.2.1   Title Bar

The title bar shows the name of the application ("Microsoft Dynamics AX"), the name of the organization holding the Dynamics AX license, the server name, the session ID, and the current company.

In Dynamics AX 2012 R2, the title bar additionally shows the current data partition if the Dynamics AX database contains multiple partitions.

2.1.2.2 Address Bar

The address bar (breadcrumb bar) provides navigation options known from the Windows Explorer and present-day Internet browsers. It shows a "breadcrumb" trail of the pages which you have opened in the content pane, enabling you to go back and forward by clicking the travel buttons *Forward* and *Back*.

The address field shows the path of the current page and allows navigation to other companies, modules and pages.

Figure 2-3: Navigating Dynamics AX in the address bar

If the Enterprise search (see section 2.1.6) is enabled in Dynamics AX, a search box shows on the right-hand side of the address bar. This search box provides access not only to Dynamics AX data but also to the Dynamics AX help content.

2.1.2.3 Command Bar and Jewel Menu

The jewel menu contains commands, which are available globally within Dynamics AX. This includes common Windows commands like *Copy* and *Paste* as well as specific Dynamics AX commands like *Filter* and *Document handling*. Depending on the content page, some commands are not active. If a particular command is also accessible through a shortcut key, it shows on the right-hand side of the applicable option.

Figure 2-4: The jewel menu in Dynamics AX

In the command bar, there are following buttons on the right:

➢ **Windows** ▦ – For switching between forms.
➢ **View** ▣ – For changing workspace settings.
➢ **Help** ◉ – For showing the online help.

The options for changing workspace settings are not only available in the *View* button, but also in the jewel menu (choosing the command *File/View* there).

2.1.2.4 Status Bar

The status bar at the bottom of the Dynamics AX workspace contains the document handling button, a short help text on the active element (field or menu item) and several other fields. If you want to change the elements included in the status bar, choose appropriate settings in your user options (see section 2.3.1). If all elements are displayed in the status bar of the workspace window, it shows following fields:

➢ **Document handling** [1] – See section 9.5.1
➢ **Help text** [2]
➢ **Notifications** [3] – Alerts and workflow status
➢ **Currency** [4] – Controls currency of displayed amounts
➢ **Application object model** [5]
➢ **Application object layer** [6]
➢ **Current company** [7]
➢ **Current partition** [8] – Data partition in Dynamics AX 2012 R2
➢ **Caps Lock status** [9]
➢ **Num Lock status** [10]
➢ **Current user** [11]
➢ **Session date** [12]
➢ **Session time** [13]
➢ **AOS name** [14] – Server name
➢ **Operation progress indicator** [15] – Shows database activity

Figure 2-5: The status bar in the Dynamics AX workspace (all elements displayed)

The status bar does not only display information, it also offers additional functionality started by clicking following status bar fields:

➢ **Notifications** – Opens the notifications form.
➢ **Currency** – Opens the currency converter, which gives you the possibility to show currency amounts in different currencies.
➢ **Current company** – Switch between companies (legal entities).
➢ **Session date** – Default for the posting date in the current session.

In detail forms, the status bar looks a little different from the way it looks in the Dynamics AX workspace by additionally providing the option to scroll between records and to switch between the view mode and the edit mode. More details are available in the section on master detail forms below.

2.1.2.5 Navigation Pane

The navigation pane on the left hand side of the workspace provides access to all list pages and forms. List pages and detail forms are the place for working in the modules of Dynamics AX as described in section 2.1.3 and 2.1.5 of this book.

If you want to hide the navigation pane, click the button *View/Navigation Pane* in the command bar. If you just want to prevent the navigation pane to show completely all the time, activate automatic collapsing to a left-hand sidebar by pushing the shortcut key *Alt+Shift+F1* (or by clicking the button *View / Auto-Hide Navigation* or the arrow [<] in the top right corner of the navigation pane). If the Auto-Hide feature is enabled, the navigation pane shows completely whenever moving the mouse pointer to the navigation sidebar.

2.1.2.6 Favorites

Whereas the module buttons with the related menu items in the navigation pane show a uniform structure, the favorites pane (see section 2.1.3) allows arranging menu items the way preferred for personal use. Therefore, the favorites pane is used for easily accessing list pages, forms, inquiries and reports needed frequently. The functionality of favorites in Dynamics AX is similar to the favorites in Microsoft Outlook or in the Internet Explorer.

2.1.2.7 Content Pane

The content pane shown in the center of the Dynamics AX workspace contains following types of pages:

➢ **List pages** – See description below
➢ **Area pages** – See section 2.1.3
➢ **Role centers** – See section 2.1.4

2.1.2.8 Workspace

If requiring a second Dynamics AX workspace, open a new workspace within the current session by pushing the shortcut key *Ctrl+W* or clicking the button *Windows/ New workspace* in the command bar. Clicking the button *New Workspace* in the dialog box displayed when changing the company account is another way for opening a new workspace.

2.1.2.9 List Page

A list page like the customer page shown in Figure 2-6 provides a list of records of a particular table. List pages are available for viewing records, in addition providing the option to complete daily tasks on these records by clicking the appropriate button in the action pane.

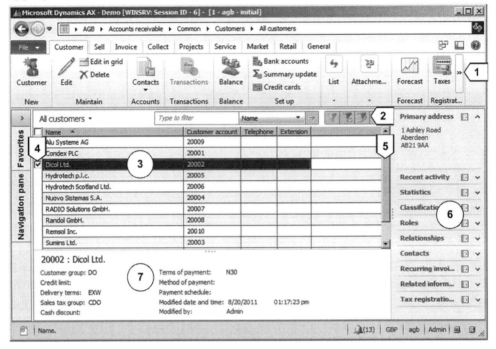

Figure 2-6: List page *Customers* (*Auto-Hide Navigation* enabled)

List pages show a common structure, but some elements and functions depend on the table displayed. This structure includes following basic elements:

➢ **Action pane** [1] – Contains the action buttons (similar to the Microsoft Office ribbon). You may distinguish buttons for executing activities related to the selected record (like placing an order) on the one hand and buttons for opening related detail forms (displaying more information) on the other hand. The number and functionality of buttons is depending on the particular page. Depending on available actions, buttons show on several tabs (e.g. the action pane tabs *Customer* or *Sell* in Figure 2-6).

➢ **Filter pane** [2] – Allows entering filter criteria (see section 2.1.6).

➢ **Grid** [3] – Displays the list of records.

➢ **Grid check boxes** [4] – Enable selecting multiple or – if selecting the checkbox in the header line – all records.

➢ **Scroll bar** [5] – Available to scroll through the records. A pop-up menu accessed by right-hand clicking on the scroll bar supports scrolling. Alternatively, push the shortcut keys *PgUp*, *PgDn*, *Ctrl+Home* and *Ctrl+End*.

> **FactBoxes** [6] – Show a summary of additional information referring to the selected record (e.g. the primary address of a selected customer).
> **Preview pane** [7] – Below the grid, showing more detailed information on the selected record (e.g. additional fields of the customer record).

If you do not want to show all elements, hide the FactBoxes and the preview pane through the appropriate option in the button *View* 🖳 of the command bar. A general setting for activating or deactivating the FactBox pane and the preview pane is available in the system administration menu (*System administration> Setup> System> Client performance options*).

List pages do not automatically refresh, if data displayed on the screen change in the database (e.g. if somebody is working on the records concerned). After editing a record in a detail form, refresh the related list page by pushing the *F5* key (or by clicking the button *Refresh* 🔄 on the right-hand side of the breadcrumb bar).

2.1.2.10 Detail Form for Master Data

Unlike list pages, which are there for viewing a list of records, detail forms are there for inserting and modifying individual records. By double-clicking a record in a list page, Dynamics AX opens the related detail form.

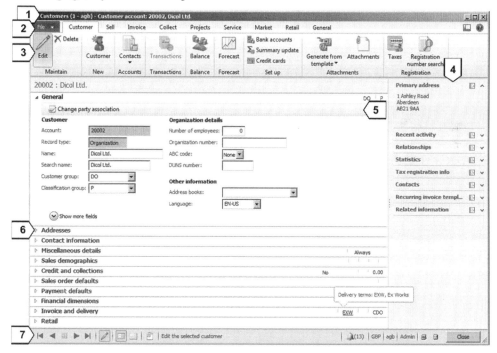

Figure 2-7:   Elements of a detail form on the example of the customer detail form

Alternatively, access a detail form by clicking the button *Edit* on the first tab of the action pane in a list page.

Whereas list pages display within the Dynamics AX workspace, detail forms open separate windows which you may move or resize on your Windows desktop.

Detail forms got a common structure similar to list pages, with some elements and functions depending on the particular form. Figure 2-7 shows the customer detail form (accessible through the list page *Accounts receivable> Common> Customers> All customers*) as an example for the structure of detail forms.

The common structure of detail forms includes the following basic elements:

➢ **Title bar** [1] – Showing the form name, the current company (if selected in the users options) and the identification of the record. For illustration, the example in Figure 2-7 shows the number and name of customer "20002" in the company account "AGB".

➢ **Command bar** [2] – Including jewel menu, *View* and *Help* button.

➢ **Action pane** [3]

➢ **FactBoxes** [4]

➢ **Action pane strips** [5] – Providing access to actions in case there are only a few options available. On the one hand, there are action pane strips related to fast tabs as shown in Figure 2-7. On the other hand, there are action pane strips replacing the full action pane on the top of forms, which only contain a few actions – e.g. in the customer groups form (*Accounts receivable> Setup> Customers> Customer groups*).

➢ **Fast tabs** [6] – Grouping fields according to their functional area. In comparison to regular tabs, fast tabs additionally show summary fields displaying core data directly on the tab. In Figure 2-7, the fast tab *Invoice and delivery* for example shows the delivery terms "EXW". You may expand fast tabs by clicking the particular tab. A right-hand click on a tab provides the option to expand or collapse all tabs at the same time.

➢ **Status bar** [7] – Containing options to move between records (in addition to the options in the status bar of the workspace). Apart from the button *Ctrl+Home* ◄, *Ctrl+PgUp* ◄, *Ctrl+PgDn* ►, *Ctrl+End* ►I for switching the selected record (e.g. moving to another customer in Figure 2-7), there is the button *Grid View* for viewing a list of records.

Another option available in the status bar is to switch between the view mode and the edit mode clicking the button *Edit* .

Section 2.1.5 later in this book contains more information on editing records, working with fast tabs and other options available in list pages and detail forms.

2.1.2.11 Grid View

The grid view in detail forms is an option for managing a list of records. Compared to list pages, which are read-only, the grid view additionally enables editing records.

In detail forms, switch to the grid view by clicking the button *Grid View* ⬜ in the status bar. In a list page, directly access the grid view of the detail form by clicking the button *Edit in grid* on the first tab of the action pane.

After selecting a record in the grid view, you can view the details of this record in the related details view by clicking the button *Details View* ▦ in the status bar.

2.1.2.12 Detail Form for Transaction Data

In addition to the detail forms for master data described above, Dynamics AX also contains detail forms for transaction data like the sales order form (see Figure 2-8).

You can access a transaction detail form from the related list page (e.g. the sales order list page *Sales and marketing> Common> Sales orders> All sales orders*) similar to accessing a master data detail form in a master data list page. When accessing transaction detail forms, the fast tab *Lines* expands providing the option to enter lines immediately.

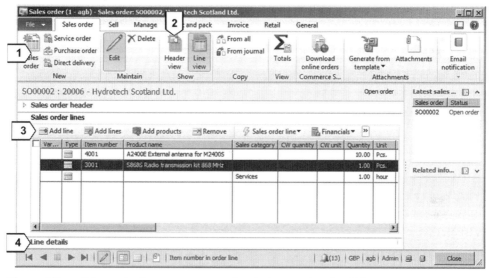

Figure 2-8:   Sales order form as an example of a transaction detail form

In the **action pane strip** [3] of the *Lines* tab there are buttons for executing actions on the selected line – for example deleting a line by clicking the button *Remove*. The **action pane** [1] at the top of the form is there to perform actions at header level – for example deleting a complete order by clicking the button ✖ *Delete*.

If you want to edit details not available in the line grid, expand the fast tab **Line details** [4]. In order to structure the field display, the line details fast tab contains several sub-tabs at the bottom.

If you want to view header data, expand the *Header* tab. In addition, clicking the button **Header view** [2] in the action pane grants access to all fields of the header record. In the header view, the button *Line view* in the action pane takes you back to the lines.

2.1.2.13 Setup Forms

In comparison to detail forms for master data and transactions, setup forms show a simple layout. Dynamics AX 2012 contains the following kinds of setup forms:

> **Simple list** – Editable grid with an action pane strip, e.g. the customer groups (*Accounts receivable> Setup> Customers> Customer groups*).
> **Simple list & Details** – Two pane form showing the list of records on the left side and editable detail fields on the right side, e.g. the terms of payment (*Accounts receivable> Setup> Payment> Terms of payment*).
> **Parameter form** – Showing a table of contents (similar to the tab structure) on the left and related fields on the right, e.g. the accounts receivable parameters (*Accounts receivable> Setup> Accounts receivable parameters*).

2.1.2.14 New in Dynamics AX 2012 and in AX 2012 R2

Based on the new design principles for the user interface (initially available in Dynamics AX 2009 list pages), the Dynamics AX client has completely changed in Dynamics AX 2012. List pages and detail forms with FactBoxes, fast tabs and action panes now completely replace the forms available in Dynamics AX 2009.

Compared with the initial version of Dynamics AX 2012, the R2 version in addition includes options for accessing and viewing data partitions.

2.1.3   Navigation

There are four ways for accessing pages and forms in Microsoft Dynamics AX:

> Navigation pane
> Area pages
> Address bar
> Favorites pane

2.1.3.1   Navigation Pane

Whereas the favorites pane usually contains a limited number of menu items which you want to use frequently, the other options (navigation pane, area pages and address bar) show all items for which you have appropriate permissions.

For adapting the navigation pane, click the button *View* 🔲 in the command bar. Apart from hiding or showing the favorites and the navigation pane, optionally hide or move particular module buttons through the *Navigation Pane Options*.

If all areas of the workspace are available and shown, the Dynamics AX application window consists of following navigation items as shown in Figure 2-9:

> Module buttons [1]
> Menu items [2]
> Common tasks [3]
> Journals [4]
> Inquiries [5]

> Reports [6]
> Periodic activities [7]
> Setup [8]

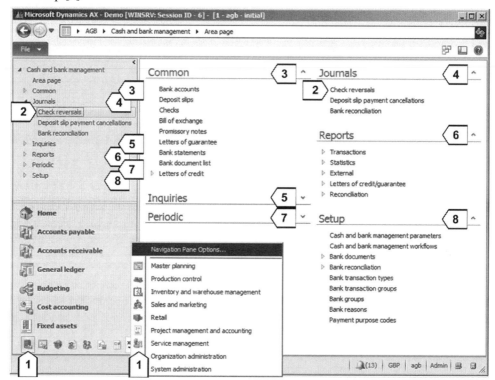

Figure 2-9:   Navigation in Dynamics AX 2012 (Favorites pane not shown)

2.1.3.2 Modules

The structure of the navigation pane complies with functional areas like *Accounts payable*, *Budgeting* or *Production control* referring to the different standard roles in the industry.

By default, the first module button is the *Home* menu (see section 2.1.4), followed by functional modules. The module buttons *Organization administration* and *System administration* refer to basic settings and tasks in the system and its companies.

Depending on the available space, the first module buttons show with the module name on the right, followed by modules only displaying module icons. If you want to access further modules, click the button ⁝ right next to the module icons.

After clicking a module button, the workspace shows the menu items of the selected module in the navigation pane and in the area page. The name of the module displays in the title bar of the navigation pane. Whereas the basic structure for navigation is common to all modules as shown below, the subfolders and menu items are different in every module.

2.1.3.3 Menu Structure

The options in the folder **Common** (daily tasks) provide access to list pages for frequent tasks in the particular module, e.g. sales order management in the *Sales and marketing* module.

The folder **Journals** contains forms which are required for entering and posting transactions.

The folder **Inquiries** contains forms for reporting and analysis, which show the result directly on the screen.

The menu items in the folder **Reports** generate a printout on paper. If you do not actually require a hard copy, alternatively display a print preview or save the report to a file.

The folder **Periodic** contains items, which are not required frequently. In this folder, there are menu items for tasks like month end closing or summary updates.

The folder **Setup** grants access to configuration data of the particular module. Configuration data are entered when a company (legal entity) is set up initially. Later you will usually change configuration only if an alteration in business processes causes new functional requirements for Dynamics AX.

Some settings should not be changed without a deep knowledge of the Dynamics AX functionality to ensure data integrity in line with correct data in finance. In general, system administrators set the permissions for the *Setup* folder in a way that regular users may not edit sensible configuration data.

2.1.3.4 Area Page

The first option in the navigation pane of each module is the area page. The structure of the area page shown in the content pane of the Dynamics AX workspace complies with the structure of related menu items in the navigation pane. You may open folders and menu items in the area page like you do in the navigation pane.

2.1.3.5 Address Bar

Navigating the address bar provides access to the list pages and folders, which are also shown in the navigation pane. After selecting a menu folder or subfolder in the address bar, the workspace shows related menu items.

In addition to the options available in the navigation pane and in the area page, the address bar also provides the option to switch companies.

2.1.3.6 Favorites

The favorites pane provides the option of setting up personal folders and menu items according to your individual requirements. If you want to add a form or a list page to your favorites, select the particular menu item in the navigation pane or in the area page and choose the option *Add to favorites* in the pop-up menu, which opens by doing a right-hand click.

If you want to hide the favorites pane (or show it, if it is hidden), click the button *View/Show Favorites in Navigation Pane* in the command bar of the workspace.

You may edit your favorites choosing the command *File/Favorites/Organize favorites* in the jewel menu. As shown in Figure 2-10, favorites management displays a dialog box known from other Microsoft applications. In order to establish a structure for your favorites, optionally create folders and subfolders and move the menu items as needed.

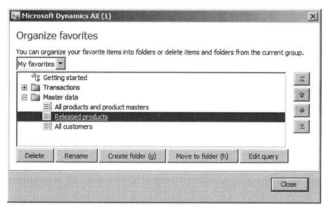

Figure 2-10:   Favorites administration dialog box

In addition to folders, favorites groups are another option to structure favorites. You may create groups by choosing the command *File/Favorites/Create group* in the jewel menu or by right-clicking on the header *Favorites* in the navigation pane

A feature not available for regular menu items in the navigation pane is accessible by clicking the button *Edit query* in the favorites administration. This button allows assigning a filter to a form or a list page, which applies whenever opening the particular favorites item. You may also choose the query feature if you want to show two separate favorites for one menu item – e.g. one for domestic and one for foreign customers. Section 2.1.6 explains how to enter and apply such filters.

2.1.3.7 Switching the Current Company

If you want to switch from one legal entity to another, open the dialog for switching companies. You may access this dialog by choosing the command *File/Tools/Select company accounts* or by clicking the company field of the status bar. After selecting a company in the dialog box, open it by double-clicking or by clicking the button *OK*. If clicking the button *New workspace* in the dialog, the selected company opens in a second Dynamics AX workspace.

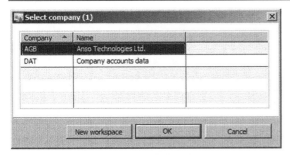

Figure 2-11:   Dialog box for switching the current company

Alternatively, switch companies through the address bar of the Dynamics AX Windows client by selecting the new company in first node of the menu path.

2.1.3.8 New in Dynamics AX 2012

In Dynamics AX 2012, the module structure has changed to better comply with role tailored navigation. Examples are the module *Product information management* holding *Products* (former *Items* in *Inventory management*) and *Product builder* or the modules *System administration* and *Organization administration* replacing *Basic* and *Administration*.

Since detail forms are only accessible through the related list page, there is no direct link to detail forms in the navigation pane or area pages.

2.1.4   Home Menu

The home menu, which usually is the first menu in the navigation pane, contains items referring to general tasks. Except for the role center, the home menu therefore shows options and menu items not related to a specific functional role.

2.1.4.1 Items in the Home Menu

The first item in the home menu is the role center. The other items in the home menu show the regular structure of a module, including area page, common tasks, inquiries, reports, periodic activities and setup.

The options in the area page of the home menu compile menu items from all functional areas, which are relevant for any kind of user. These items include:

➢ **Global address book** – See section 2.4
➢ **Work items** – Referring to workflow management, see section 9.4.3
➢ **Cases** – Referring to case management, see section 9.5.2
➢ **Activities** - Referring to sales and marketing
➢ **Absences** – Referring to human resources
➢ **Time and attendance** – Referring to human resources
➢ **Timesheets** – Referring to project management and accounting
➢ **Questionnaires**
➢ **Document management** – See section 9.5.1

2.1.4.2 Role Center

Role centers are customizable role-based homepages, showing an overview of data frequently required. Elements available in role centers include task lists, reports, alerts and analysis views. You may view your role center both in the Enterprise Portal (web interface) and in the regular Dynamics AX Windows client, where it is the homepage of your workspace.

The standard application of Dynamics AX 2012 contains multiple role centers supporting different roles like purchasing agent, sales manager or controller. If you have access to the development environment, optionally set up additional role centers.

Role centers do not directly refer to the security roles in the role based security model (see section 9.2.3). The applicable role center of a user is determined by the assigned user profile – and not by assigned security roles.

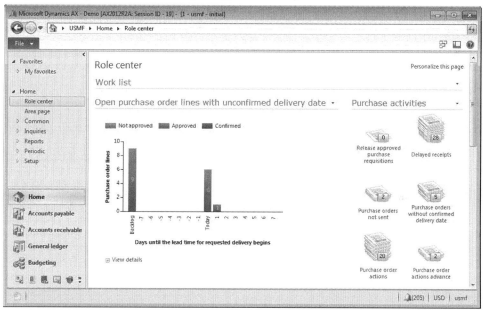

Figure 2-12: Role center for a purchasing agent in the Dynamics AX Windows client

User profiles represent specific roles in the organization, grouping users with a common role center. If you want to know which user profiles are assigned to a specific user, view the FactBox *Profiles for selected user* in the user list page (*System administration> Common> Users> Users*) after selecting the particular user.

In order to set up user profiles, choose the menu item *System administration> Common> Users> User profiles*. If you want to add a user to a user profile, click the button *Add user* after selecting the appropriate profile line. A user may be linked to the same user profile for all companies, or to a different profile per company.

Cues are a unique element in role centers. Their main purpose is to show remaining work tasks graphically – in Figure 2-12 for example the number of purchase orders not sent. In addition to a graphic sign, each cue also displays a selected key figure representing the workload for the responsible person. A mouse click on a cue opens the related form in Dynamics AX, where you can do your work.

As a preparation for creating a cue, save a filter as a cue in a list page or detail form (see section 2.1.6). If you have appropriate permissions in Microsoft SharePoint, add the new cue to a Web part of your role center page then.

As a prerequisite for using role centers, Microsoft SharePoint and the Enterprise Portal Framework have to be available.

2.1.4.3 New in Dynamics AX 2012

In Dynamics AX 2012, the home menu not only contains the role center but compiles menu items relevant for all users.

2.1.5   Working with Records

When accessing a menu item for master data or transactions, Dynamics AX shows the appropriate list page. List pages therefore are the starting point for working on items, giving you the possibility to search and filter records you want to view.

Buttons in the action pane of the list page provide the option to edit, delete and insert data according to your permissions. It is not possible to edit data in a list page itself, however. Clicking the button *Edit* in the action pane after selecting a line takes you to the related detail form.

2.1.5.1 Viewing Records

Whereas a list page only shows a limited number of fields, the detail form shows all available fields of the record. For accessing the detail form after selecting a line in the list page, double-click the line or by press the *Enter* key.

Fast tabs on detail forms expand by clicking them or by pushing the shortcut key *"Ctrl"* + *"+"*. If you want to collapse an individual fast tab, click on the fast tab header again or push the shortcut key *"Ctrl"* + *"-"*. Further options are available by a right-hand click on tab headers. Selecting to expand all tabs enables scrolling through the complete record information (e.g. using your mouse wheel).

Some tabs contain less important fields, which are not shown immediately when expanding the tab. In this case, the expanded tab shows the button ⊗ *Show more fields* for displaying those fields.

2.1.5.2 Edit/View Mode

Depending on the settings of the form, a detail form usually opens in view mode, which prevents data to be changed unintentionally. If you are in view mode and want to edit a record, you have got several options to switch to the edit mode: The button ✎ *Edit* in the status bar and in the action pane, the command *File/Edit record* or the shortcut key *Ctrl+Shift+E*.

If you want to start a particular form always in edit mode, click the button *View/Default Form/View Edit Mode* in the command bar of the form. If you want to set your general default mode to *Edit* or *View*, choose the appropriate setting in the section *General* of your user options.

2.1.5.3 Inserting Data

In order to insert a record, alternatively push the shortcut key *Ctrl+N*, click the button *New* in the action pane, or choose the command *File/New* in the jewel menu.

In many list pages, a *Quick create* dialog (see Figure 2-13) displays then. The quick create dialog contains the core fields of a record, making it possible to insert records in a fast way. If you need to enter additional data, click the button *Save and open* at the bottom of the dialog to switch to the related detail form. Depending on the page, the *Save and open* button includes additional options – e.g. to switch to the sales quotation form immediately when creating a customer.

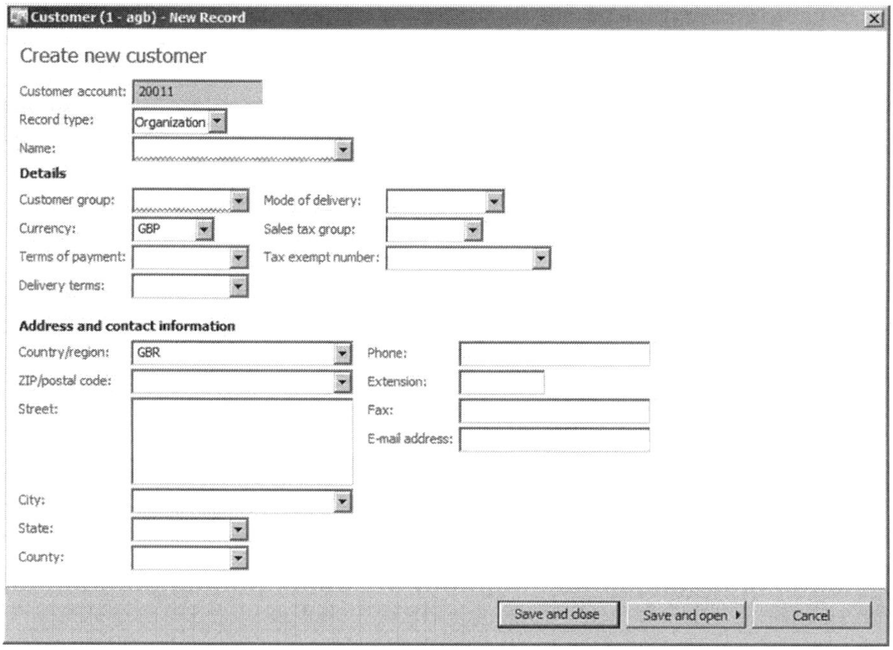

Figure 2-13:   Quick create dialog for entering new customer

If no quick create dialog is available in a particular list page, Dynamics AX takes you to the related detail form showing an empty record (presuming no templates apply, see section 2.3.2) for entering data. If you are already in a detail form and decide to insert a record there, the detail form also starts an empty record.

If a mandatory field, which is left empty, is included on a collapsed fast tab, the fast tab shows the *required field indicator* (✱).

In the lines of a transaction form (e.g. the sales order lines), insert a new record by simply pushing the key *PgDn* (or the *Down Arrow*) in the last line of the grid.

2.1.5.4 Editing Data

Before you may edit a record in a detail form (detail view or grid view), make sure you are in the edit mode. In order to switch between the fields of the form then, alternatively choose the mouse, the *Enter* key, the *Tab* or the *Shift+Tab* shortcut key.

Once you have finished entering or viewing record data in a detail form, close it by clicking the button *Close* at the bottom (the command *File/Close* and Windows standard options like the shortcut key *Alt+F4* or the ![X] top right work as well).

If you are by mistake inserting a record which contains a mandatory field, you might have to delete it as described below if you want to cancel registration – even if you did not enter record data. Alternatively, close the form without saving by pushing the *Esc* key. In a quick create dialog, click the button *Cancel* at the bottom.

There are options available for saving a record in detail forms manually – the command *File/Save* or the shortcut key *Ctrl+S*. Usually you do not apply them, because Dynamics AX saves every change of a record automatically when you leave the record. If you close a form pushing the *Esc* key, Dynamics AX will ask if you want to save the changes. The confirmation dialog for saving changes always shows, if it is selected in your user options (see section 2.3.1).

The *Undo*-function, available by choosing the command *File/Edit/Undo* or pushing the shortcut key *Ctrl+Z*, refers to the content of individual fields. It is only available as long as you do not leave the input field to which the changes apply.

After leaving a field – if not selecting another record or manually saving – you can restore the record from the database by pushing the shortcut key *Ctrl+F5* or through the command *File/Command/Restore*. Another option not to save changes is to close the form pushing the *Esc* key or the shortcut key *Ctrl+Q* (as long as you did not leave the particular record in the form).

2.1.5.5 Deleting Data

In order to delete the content of an input field, push the *Delete* key. If you want to delete a complete record, alternatively choose the command *File/Delete Record*, or push the shortcut key *Alt+F9*, or click the button *Delete* in the action pane after selecting the particular record.

In some cases, Dynamics AX shows an error message preventing you from deleting a record – e.g. if there are open transactions.

2.1.5.6 Elements in a Detail Form

When registering data in a form, you have to distinguish between following elements as shown in Figure 2-14 on the example of the bank accounts detail form (*Cash and bank management> Common> Bank accounts*):

➢ Field group [1]
➢ Checkbox [2]
➢ Mandatory field [3]
➢ Date field [4]
➢ Lookup field with a fixed list of values [5]
➢ Lookup field with a related main table [6]

Other field types are textboxes and number fields. If a field is locked for data input in edit mode, it shows in gray.

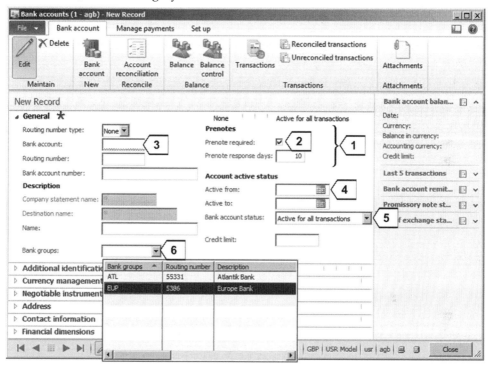

Figure 2-14:   Types of fields in a form (*Bank accounts* detail form in edit mode)

Field groups link fields to increase display clearness.

Mandatory fields show a wavy red line and require data input before you can save the record. In case data input is missing, the particular fast tab shows the required field indicator (✱) at the same time.

If you want to select a **checkbox** (e.g. *Prenote required* in Figure 2-14), click it with the left mouse button or push the *Space bar* once the cursor is on the checkbox.

Settings for **date fields** and number fields come from your Windows settings. You know date fields from the calendar icon (▦), which is available for selecting a particular date. If entering a date manually, you don't have to type date separators like "." or "/". For a date in the current month, simply enter the day (e.g. "23"). In order to insert the current date, enter "t" (or "d" for the session date).

If you want to enter a number in a numeric field, optionally use basic arithmetical operations. An amount of "GBP 55.00 plus 10 %" for example is easily entered by typing "55 * 1.1" instead of "60.50".

2.1.5.7 Lookup fields

Lookup fields are another important field type. They only allow entering of predefined values and may be grouped in two different types:

➢ **Lookup fields with a related main table**, which contains permitted values – e.g. *Bank groups* in Figure 2-14.
➢ **Lookup fields with a fixed list of values**, which is given by Dynamics AX enumerable types (*Enums*) – e.g. *Bank account status* in Figure 2-14.

In **Edit mode**, lookup fields show the lookup button ▾ in the right part of the field. In **View mode**, lookup fields show as a link (similar to Internet links).

When editing or inserting a record in a form, click the lookup button ▾ or push the shortcut key *Alt + Down Arrow* for executing a value lookup in a lookup field. Another option to start the value lookup is to enter the first characters of the field content followed by an asterisk (*). If entering "E*" in a lookup field for example, the lookup form automatically pops up showing all records starting with "E" in the key field.

In the lookup form, select a record for inserting into the lookup field by clicking it. If a value lookup contains multiple lines, limit the number of displayed lines by applying the functions *Filter*, *Find*, and *Sort* as shown in section 2.1.6. But you should not click the left mouse button for selecting a column (this would select a record for the lookup field). In order to select a column, do a right-hand click or push the *Tab* key (or *Shift+Tab*).

If required, sort by any column in the lookup form (for example clicking on the column header *Description*).

A specific feature lookup forms is the option of accessing a line by typing the first characters of the required value. As shown in Figure 2-15, you can select the first statistics group starting with "03" by typing "03" in the statistics group lookup form. This works in the *Statistics group* column as well as in the *Description* column. If you want to select a record in the *Description* column, push the *Tab* key to activate this column. While typing, the recorded characters appear in the status line for some time.

2.1.5.8 Table reference

Apart from value lookup, the table reference also provides the possibility to open the administration form referring to a lookup field. If you want to insert a new statistics group in the form shown in Figure 2-15 for example, access the statistics group form directly from the *Statistics group* field.

In edit mode, the administration form referring to a lookup field is accessible by choosing the option *View details* in the pop-up menu (which opens by doing a right-hand click) or the command *File/Command/View details* (or *Ctrl+Alt+F4*).

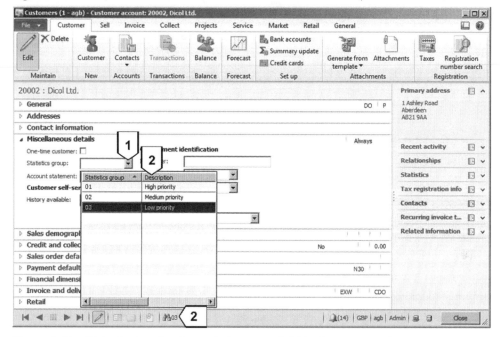

Figure 2-15: Value lookup for the statistics group field in the customer form

In view mode or in non-editable fields, the table reference displays as a link providing the option to access the related administration form through a simple mouse click.

After opening a referenced table form, edit records there the same way as if accessed from the navigation pane. Therefore, you can use the table reference for directly inserting and editing related master data. In addition, you can apply the table reference for viewing details of related records. For example, choosing the option *View details* in the column *Sales order* directly opens the related sales order from the invoice inquiry (*Accounts receivable> Inquiries> Journals> Invoice journal*).

2.1.5.9 Segmented Entry Control

A special kind of lookup is available in ledger account fields, for example in the lines of financial journals. Since the ledger account is one field with several segments (the main account and applicable financial dimensions), a specific control for the lookup and data entry applies – the segmented entry control (see section 8.3.2).

2.1.5.10 Infolog

If there is a problem with the operation you are executing in Dynamics AX, a warning or error message shows up in a separate window – the *Infolog*. It is possible to disable warnings and error messages in the user options.

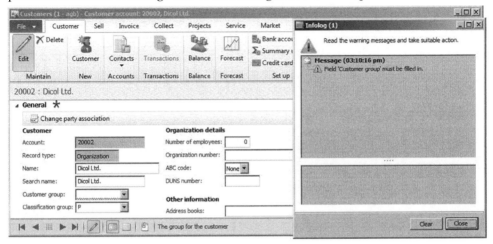

Figure 2-16: Infolog, displaying an error message in the customer form

You may copy or print the message displayed in the *Infolog* through a pop-up menu, which displays when doing a right-hand click on the message text.

2.1.5.11 Transaction Progress

If a transaction – e.g. running a report – is taking a long time, Dynamics AX shows a notification in the taskbar of your Windows desktop. If you do not want to wait until the transaction is finished, cancel the operation by pushing the shortcut key *Ctrl+Break*. After confirming a dialog box – which is sometimes displayed belatedly – Dynamics AX cancels the transaction.

2.1.5.12 Basic Operations

As shown, Dynamics AX provides four different elements for executing basic operations in a list page or detail form:

➢ **Command bar** and **Jewel menu** – Showing options for various commands
➢ **Action pane**
➢ **Shortcut keys**
➢ **Pop-up menus** – Display after doing a right-hand click

Whereas the command bar and the action pane contain all available functions, the shortcut keys and the pop-up menus only provide access to frequently used operations. An overview of shortcut keys for executing basic operations in Dynamics AX is included in the appendix of this book.

Note: In some forms, there are no buttons for standard activities like filtering. Therefore it is a good idea to memorize core shortcut keys (e.g. for filtering).

2.1.5.13 New in Dynamics AX 2012

Based on the design principles for the user interface in Dynamics AX 2012, new elements like fast tabs, FactBoxes, the edit mode, the grid view or the quick create dialogs are available in detail forms. In edit mode, the former option *Go to the Main Table Form* is now called *View details*, in view mode it shows as a link.

Another new element is the segmented entry control, which refers to the new financial dimension framework (see section 8.2.4).

2.1.6   Filter, Find and Sort

In order to work in a table with numerous records efficiently, it is crucial to quickly find the records in demand. For this purpose, the functions *Filter*, *Find* and *Sort* are available in list pages and forms. In Microsoft Dynamics AX, the *Filter* and the *Find* features are similar.

2.1.6.1   Filter Pane

The filter pane in list pages provides the easiest way for filtering records. After entering characters into the filter field as needed, apply the filter by pushing the *Enter* key or by clicking the arrow button 🔁 on the right next to the filter field.

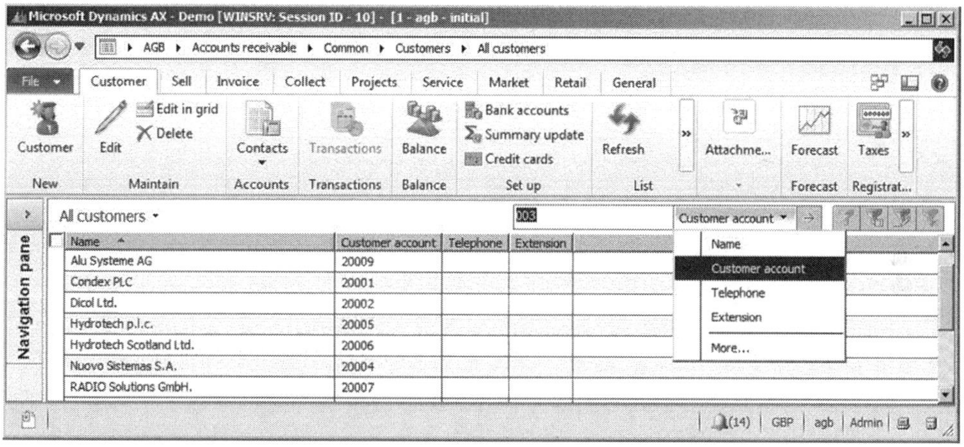

Figure 2-17:   Filter pane in a list page, selecting the column for the filter

In the right-hand part of the lookup field, select the column to which the filter applies. In addition to the fields displayed in the grid, the option *More* at the bottom of the lookup grants access to all fields available for the list page. Selecting an additional field adds the appropriate column to the grid and to the fields available for filtering.

Figure 2-17 shows an example for entering a filter in the filter pane. In the example, the filter for customers containing the characters "003" in the customer account field is not yet executed.

If you need to enter more complex filter criteria, apply advanced filter options as described below. Unlike the filter pane, advanced filter options are not only available in list pages, but also in the grid view of detail forms.

2.1.6.2 Filter Criteria

When entering characters in the filter field of the filter pane, Dynamics AX shows records containing those characters.

All other filter options – e.g. the filter by grid – allow selecting filter criteria in order to apply more precise filtering definitions. The table below shows an overview of the most important filter criteria:

Table 2-1: Important filter criteria

Meaning	Sign	Example	Explanation
Equal	=	EU	Field content to match "EU"
Not equal	!	!GB	Field content not to match "GB"
Interval	..	1..2	Field content from "1" to "2" (incl.)
Greater	>	>1	Field content more than "1"
Less	<	<2	Field content less than "2"
Connection	,	1,2	Field content to match "1" OR "2"; criteria "Not equal" (e.g. "!1,!2") connect with *AND*
Wildcard	*	*E*	Field content containing "E"
	?	?B*	First character unknown, followed by a "B", other characters unknown

2.1.6.3 Filter by Selection

If you want to display a list of records showing a common value in a particular column, apply the *Filter by selection*. In order to make use of this filter in a list page, first click a field which contains the value you want for filtering. After pushing the shortcut key *Alt+F3*, or clicking the icon ▇ in the filter pane, or selecting the option *Filter by selection* in the pop-up menu, the filter applies.

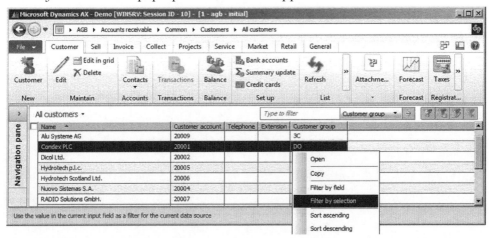

Figure 2-18: Filter by selection (chosen in the pop-up menu)

The example in Figure 2-18 shows how to apply a *Filter by selection* for the *Customer group* "3C" in the customer list page (*Accounts receivable> Common> Customers> All customers*).

2.1.6.4 Filter by Grid

Another option for setting a filter in list pages is the *Filter By Grid*. This filter displays after pushing the shortcut key *Ctrl+G* or clicking the icon ▓.

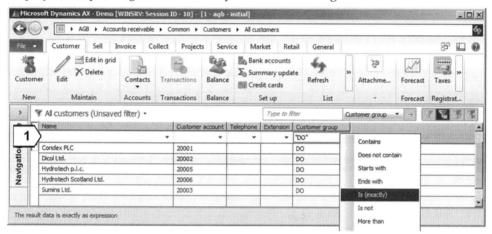

Figure 2-19:   Filter by grid

In your user options (see section 2.3.1), optionally choose to display the filter by grid whenever accessing a list page or value lookup.

After selecting the *Filter By Grid*, it shows a separate line for filter criteria at the top of the grid. If you need support for entering a criterion in the filter line, click the arrow ▼ on the right of a specific filter field. If you have already entered filter criteria before showing the filter line (e.g. in a filter by selection), the filter by grid displays them.

2.1.6.5 Advanced Filter

If you have to enter complex filter criteria, apply the advanced filter in list pages by pushing the shortcut key *Ctrl+F3* or by clicking the icon ▓.

The advanced filter opens a separate form, which displays a different view of the criteria entered in the filter by selection and the filter by grid. In addition, the advanced filter provides the option to set a filter on fields, which do not show on the list page.

If you need to enter an additional criterion in the advanced filter, insert a record in the filter form by pushing the shortcut *Ctrl+N* or clicking the button *Add*. In the new filter line, enter the criterion in the columns *Table, Derived table, Field* and *Criteria*. The fields *Table* and *Derived table* of a new line by default contain the basic table of the filtered list page. In case of simple criteria, you don't have to change it.

A lookup (⯆) in the column *Field* helps to select the field name of the table field. Next to the column *Field*, the column *Criteria* is available for entering the filter criterion. If the field for the filter is a lookup field, optionally open a value lookup.

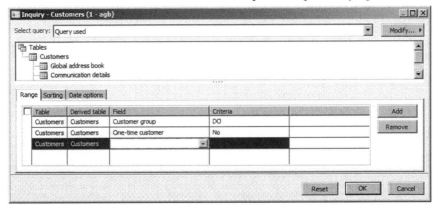

Figure 2-20:   Entering filter criteria in the advanced filter form

Once you have finished entering filter criteria, close the advanced filter form by clicking the button *OK*. The filter then applies and the list page only shows matching records.

2.1.6.6   Related Tables

The *Structure* pane in the upper part of the advanced filter form enables entering of filter criteria on tables, which are linked to the basic table of the list page or detail form. In order to apply this option, select the related table choosing the option *1:n* or *n:1* in the pop-up menu (doing a right-hand click) on the appropriate basic table in the *Structure* pane.

Since it is possible to select different tables in the filter lines of the advanced filter form, you have to make sure to select the right table in the column *Table* then.

Displaying only customers in the customer list page, which have got transactions in the current year, is an example for a filter on related tables. The appropriate selection for this filter would be a *1:n*-relation from the customer table to the customer transactions, where the advanced filter contains a filter line on the field *Date* of the table *Customer transactions*.

When applying a filter on related tables, you have to keep in mind that the structure of the filter has to comply with the database and program structure – especially for filters in reports – in order to show correct results. To make sure, you should apply a quick check of the result when choosing a new filter combination of related tables.

2.1.6.7   Clearing a Filter

If you do not want to apply a selected filter any longer, clear it by pushing the shortcut key *Ctrl+Shift+F3*, or by choosing the command *File/Edit/Filter/Remove*

Filter/Sort in the jewel menu, or by clicking the icon ![icon]. After clearing the filter, the list page shows all records again.

2.1.6.8   Active Filter and Filter Button

The icon ![icon] for clearing a filter indicates whether a filter is active in a particular list page. If the icon is active and you can click it, a filter is in use. In order to display this filter, open the advanced filter form (*Ctrl+F3*).

A funnel in the filter button (e.g. ![All customers (Unsaved filter)]) on the left side of the filter pane in list pages additionally indicates an active filter. The filter button also provides an alternative access to all filtering options mentioned above.

2.1.6.9   Filtering in Detail Forms (Grid View)

In setup forms and in the grid view of detail forms, the filter pane is not available and accessing filter features is only possible through shortcuts keys or a right-hand click. As an alternative, choose the jewel menu (command *File/Edit/Filter*).

2.1.6.10 Saving a Filter

If you frequently need particular filter criteria or if you want to apply them in your favorites, you can save them. The button *Modify/Save as* in the advanced filter form allows saving filter criteria. A dialog box then requires entering a filter name.

Saved filters are stored in your *Usage data*, which means that nobody else can use your saved filters. In order to select a saved filter, choose it in the lookup of the field *Select query* in the advanced filter form as shown in Figure 2-21.

In addition to the filters saved manually, the filter you have used the last time is available in every page by selecting the option *Previously used query* in the *Select query* lookup.

Figure 2-21:   Selecting a saved filter in the advanced filter form

As an alternative to the advanced filter form, the filter button in the filter pane of list pages also allows saving and selecting filters.

2.1.6.11 Saving a Cue

Save a filter as a cue, if you need the cue in your role center. Similar to the way of regularly saving a filter, click the button *Modify/Save as Cue* in the advanced filter form (or the filter button in the filter pane of list pages) to save a filter as a cue.

After saving a filter as a cue, it is available for cues in the Web Parts of role centers (see section 2.1.4).

2.1.6.12 Sorting

Sorting in list pages or in the grid view of detail forms is available by simply clicking the appropriate column header. A second click on the column header switches between ascending and descending sorting. Alternatively, sort in the advanced filter form or choose the option *Sort ascending* or *Sort descending* in the pop-up menu (doing a right-hand click on the appropriate column in the grid).

If choosing the advanced filter form, access the tab *Sorting* in order to enter applicable sorting criteria. Like entering a filter criterion, register sorting criteria with table and field name in one or more lines.

2.1.6.13 Search Functionality

Apart from filtering, Dynamics AX offers two additional options to search for records: The *Find* function and the *Enterprise search*.

Whereas the find function is similar to a filter, the Enterprise search resembles the functionality of search engines.

2.1.6.14 Find Function

You may access the *Find* dialog by pushing the shortcut key *Ctrl+F* or by choosing the command *File/Edit/Find*. When applying the find function, you should be aware that finding always refers to the selected column or field. Therefore you have to click the appropriate column or field before opening the find dialog. The name of the selected field displays in the header of the find dialog box as shown in Figure 2-22. The rules for entering find criteria are the same as for filter criteria.

The function *Filter by field* is similar to the find function, except that it opens with the shortcut key *Ctrl+K* (or the option *Filter by field* in the pop-up menu) and by default already shows the content of the selected field in the dialog box. Since the *Filter by field* is a filter function, it enables coupling of criteria – e.g. selecting an additional filter by applying the *Filter by field* on a second field.

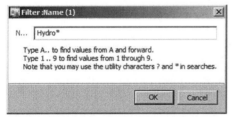

Figure 2-22:   The find dialog box (for the column *Customer name* as an example)

2.1.6.15 Distinguish Value Lookup

When choosing the *Filter* or *Find* function, you should not confuse it with the value lookup shown in section 2.1.5. Whereas the value lookup is available for entering a value into a field, the *Filter* and *Find* feature select records from the table displayed in the grid.

2.1.6.16 Enterprise Search

Unlike find and filter functions, which are applied to the current list page or form, the Enterprise search performs a full search through all Dynamics AX data, documents and help topics according to the system configuration.

Before you can start using the Enterprise search, the administrator has to specify which tables and fields should be included in the search (*System administration> Setup> Search> Search configuration*). The setup for the Enterprise search affects search options for all users – both in the Dynamics AX Windows client and in the Enterprise portal. Therefore, Dynamics AX administration has to be responsible for the search settings.

Once the setup is finished and the search is started, the Enterprise search is available through the *Search* field in the Dynamics AX address bar. Like in the filter pane of list pages, there is no need to enter wild cards in the *Search* field.

2.1.6.17 New in Dynamics AX 2012

In Dynamics AX 2012, the Enterprise search with enhanced functionality replaces the *Global Search* in Dynamics AX 2009.

2.1.7 Help System

If you need help for functional questions, access the Microsoft Dynamics AX Help system available throughout the whole application. In the help system, there are three areas of help content:

➢ Application user help
➢ System administrator help
➢ Developer help

The help system is based on a help server, which ensures a common and up-to-date content for all users. The content on the help server is focused on application users. For system administrators and developers, the help viewer in Dynamics AX shows links to the appropriate web-based help content.

2.1.7.1 Getting Help

In order to access help, press the *F1* key or click the button ⦿/Help in every list page or form. The help viewer displays help information referring to the particular form, and includes the help text, the option to print, a table of contents, and an enhanced search functionality (see Figure 2-23).

Since the help system is form-based, choose the local search in the help viewer (*Ctrl+F* or *Options/Find on this page*) when looking for the help text on a particular field.

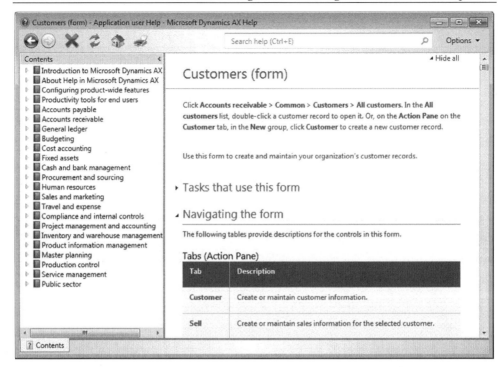

Figure 2-23:   Dynamics AX help referring to the customer form

In the text, there are three different types of links:

➢ Links referring to other help content (pressing the *Shift* key while clicking the link opens it in a new window)
➢ Links referring to menu items in the Dynamics AX client, showing the menu path (clicking the link opens the related Dynamics AX form)
➢ Links to web resources

The search field at the top of the help viewer provides options similar to the options in search engines on the web, showing abstracts in the search results to easily recognize relevant text.

2.1.7.2 Customizing Help Content

The help server also provides an option to publish individual help content for your organization by simply writing help content in Microsoft Word.

The easiest way to start publishing content is to search for "help template" in the help system. The help viewer then shows a link to a Word template containing Macros necessary for publishing, and a description on how to proceed.

Using the template, you want to start Microsoft Word, write the content as needed and enter required document properties on the tab *Microsoft Dynamics Help* in the Word ribbon. These properties include:

➤ **Topic ID** – Enter *"Forms.FormName"* to link help content to a particular form, e.g. *"Forms.CustTable"* for the customer form. You may view the form name on the tab *Information* of the *Personalization* form (see section 2.3.1).

➤ **Publisher ID** – Enter your organization name to distinguish your help content from the content of Microsoft, ISVs and partners.

In order to prepare publishing, save the document as a Webpage (file format *mht*). In parallel, the template saves an Html file. For publishing the content, copy both files to a subfolder of the folder *C:/Inetpub/wwwroot/<HelpServerName>/Content* on the help server.

2.1.7.3 New in Dynamics AX 2012

The architecture of the help system has completely changed in Dynamics AX 2012, providing a help server with the option to easily update and customize help content.

2.1.8   Case Study Exercises

Exercise 2.1 – Logon
Your first task is to log on to a Dynamics AX training system, where you should access a company different to your default company. Then open a second workspace, choose the *Accounts payable* menu in the navigation pane and access the list page *All vendors*. Finally, log out and close the Dynamics AX session.

Exercise 2.2 – Favorites
Start a client session in Dynamics AX, select the training company and open the favorites pane. Add the list page *Released products*, which you may find in the menu *Product information management*, to your favorites.

Afterwards, create a new favorites folder "Invoicing". This folder should contain the list pages *All sales orders* and *All free text invoices* in the menu *Accounts receivable* as well as the form *Payment journal* in the menu *Accounts receivable> Journals*.

Exercise 2.3 – Detail Forms
As an example of detail forms in Dynamics AX, access the vendor detail form through the vendor list page (*Accounts payable> Common> Vendors> All vendors*). When accessing the form, you want to view the vendor in the third line of the list page. Show an example of a field group and a lookup with and without main table.

Then show an example of a checkbox field. What can you tell about fast tabs and FactBoxes? How do you proceed if you want to edit the vendor? Is there an option to edit several vendors in the form?

Exercise 2.4 – Inserting Records
Create a new vendor without applying record templates. For the beginning, you only have to register the vendor with the name "##-Exercise 2.4 Inc." (## = your user ID) and a vendor group.

Notes: If the number sequence for vendor accounts is set to "Manual", you have to enter the vendor number manually. If the *Accounts payable parameters* require entering a tax-exempt number (VAT registration number), access the fast tab *Invoice and delivery* and enter a *Tax exempt number* (*VAT number*), which you create through the *View details* feature before.

Exercise 2.5 – Lookup Fields

You want to update the vendor of exercise 2.4. Searching a *Buyer group* in the lookup of the appropriate field on the tab *Miscellaneous details* of the vendor form, you notice that the required group is not available. Create a new buyer group ##-P (## = your user ID) using the *View details* option. Then select the new group for your vendor.

Exercise 2.6 – Filtering

In order to get some exercise with filtering, enter a few filters in the vendor list page as given below. For the first filter you should apply the filter field in the filter pane, for the second filter choose a *Filter by selection*. For the other filter exercises, apply the *Filter By Grid* and the *Advanced Filter/Sort*.

For filtering, choose following criteria one after the other and clear the filter after each task:

➢ All vendors containing "inc" in the name
➢ All vendors assigned to the vendor group you selected in exercise 2.4
➢ All vendors with a name starting with "T"
➢ Vendors with a number from 30003 to 30005 or higher than 30008
➢ Vendors with a number ending with "5" and an "i" in the name
➢ Vendors with an "e" on the second character of the name
➢ Vendors with a name not starting with "C"

Once you have finished the filtering tasks above, open the advanced filter window and select vendors, who do not have *Terms of payment* "Net 30 days".

Note: If working in the Microsoft standard demo environment ("Contoso"), apply similar filter criteria for filters not showing a result with the given criteria.

2.2   Printing and Reporting

Depending on your requirements, there are several options available for viewing and analyzing data. Apart from Business Intelligence tools, printing structured reports is one of the most common ways for presenting data.

2.2.1   Printing Reports

Dynamics AX applies Microsoft SQL Server Reporting Services (SSRS) for printing reports. You may start printing of reports from several places in Microsoft Dynamics AX:

➤ **Menu path** – *Reports* in the navigation pane, address bar and area pages
➤ **Buttons** – In list pages and detail forms
➤ **Post and print** – Checkbox *Print* in posting forms
➤ **Auto-reports** – In list pages and forms

2.2.1.1 Standard Reports

In each module, there are standard reports in the folder *Reports* – in most cases containing subfolders. In addition, some list pages and detail forms also provide the option to run a standard report by clicking an appropriate button – e.g. a customer account statement by clicking the button *Collect/Statements* in the customer list page (*Accounts receivable> Common> Customers> All customers*).

2.2.1.2 Post and Print

When posting an external document like an invoice or a packing slip, you also want to print the document in most cases. Posting forms therefore contain a checkbox for printing the related document – e.g. the checkbox *Print invoice* when posting an invoice. The buttons *Select* (filter selection) and *Printer setup* (printer selection) in posting forms enable specifying filter criteria and print destinations as described for standard reports below.

If the printout of a posted document is required at a later date (e.g. if you missed to select the checkbox *Print)*, print it in the inquiry of the particular posted document. For (re-)printing a sales invoice for example, access the invoice journal (e.g. by clicking the button *Journals/Invoice* on the action pane tab *Invoice* of the sales order form) and click the button *Preview/Print* there.

2.2.1.3 Auto-report

Auto-reports are available in every list page and detail form by pushing the shortcut key *Ctrl+P* or choosing the command *File/Print/Print*. They show a report containing main fields of the particular table.

2.2.1.4 Report Form

In order to explain how printing works in Dynamics AX, the description below shows the example of printing a standard report.

After selecting the menu item for a standard report, Dynamics AX shows the report form where you may enter filter criteria and print destinations. Figure 2-24 for example shows the report form of the customer list (*Accounts receivable> Reports> Customer> Customers*) after a filter on the group "10" has been entered.

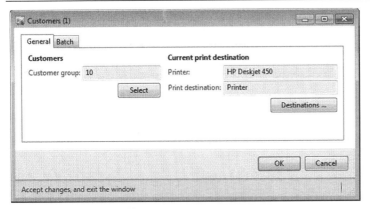

Figure 2-24: Report form for the customer list

2.2.1.5 Print Destination (Printer Selection)

The button *Destinations* in the report form opens the print destination settings, where you can select the destination for the printout choosing between the different options show in Table 2-2.

Table 2-2:   Print destinations for reports

Destination	Explanation
Print archive	Saves the report selection to the print archive
Screen	Shows a report preview on the screen
Printer	Prints the report to the selected printer
File	Saves the report content to a CSV, Excel, HTML, XML or PDF file or to an image (JPEG or other format)
E-mail	Saves the report content to a file and sends it to an e-mail recipient (the recipient has to be entered manually)

2.2.1.6 Filter in Reports

The button *Select* in the report form opens an advanced filter form, where you may enter filter criteria. The filter form for reports works in the same way as the advanced filter in list pages and forms (see section 2.1.6). You may enter filter criteria on the tab *Range* as well as sorting criteria on the tab *Sorting*.

After closing the filter form, the selected filter shows in the report form.

2.2.1.7 Report Form Defaults

Once you have finished entering the filter criteria and the print destination in the report form, run the report by clicking the button *OK* in the report form. The settings applied for running the report are automatically stored in the user options.

They show by default when starting the report the next time again. You can change the filter criteria and the print destination as required then.

2.2.1.8 Print Archive

The print archive allows saving a report within Dynamics AX. In the print destination settings, choose the archive either by directly selecting the print archive as print destination or – if choosing a different print destination – by selecting the checkbox *Save in print archive*.

The report selection is stored in the print archive in this case, making it possible to reprint the report later. For accessing your print archive, choose the command *File/Tools/Print archive*. In order to access the print archives of all users, open the form *Organization administration> Inquiries> Print archive*.

Printing to the archive during the regular operation time and applying a batch job to finally print the archive on a printer at night time might be an option to deal with high-volume printing.

2.2.1.9 Print Preview

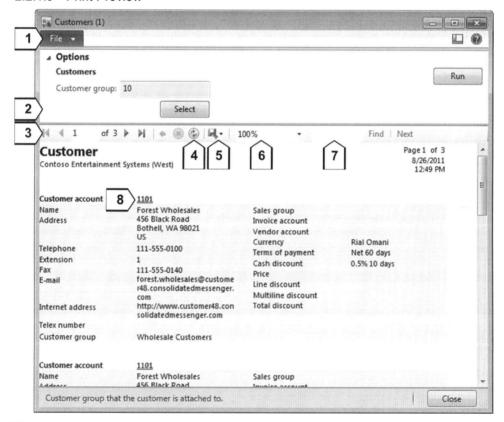

Figure 2-25:   Print preview options

If selecting the screen as print destination, Dynamics AX shows a print preview on the screen. The preview includes following options (see Figure 2-25):

> **Print** [1] the preview (command *File/Print/Print* or shortcut *Ctrl+P*)
> **Apply or change filter** [2] selections (button *Select* in the section *Options*)
> **Scroll** [3] between pages entering the page number or applying one of the available shortcut keys and buttons (*Ctrl+Home/*◀, *Page Up/*◁, *Page Down/*▷ and *Ctrl+End/*▶)
> **Refresh** [4] the preview to retrieve current data (button ⟳)
> **Export** [5] the preview to different file formats like XML, CSV, PDF, HTML, TIFF, Excel or Word (button ▦▾)
> **Zoom** [6] in and out
> **Find** [7] text in the report
> **Link** [8] to access the detail form of fields concerned

2.2.1.10 Batch Processing

If you do not immediately need the results of a particular report, switch to the tab *Batch* in the report form for submitting the report to a batch process. After selecting the checkbox *Batch processing* and – if required – a *Batch group*, specify the starting time and repetitions for the batch job by clicking the button *Recurrence*.

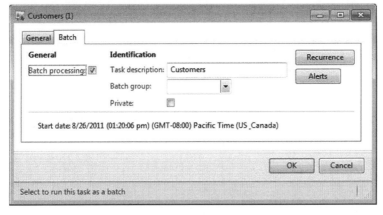

Figure 2-26:   Batch processing selection in a report form

As a prerequisite for applying batch processing, a batch server has to be set up and started. For setting up the batch server, access the menu item *System administration> Setup> System> Server configuration*.

Batch processing is performed in the background on the batch server except for client and private tasks, which require running the periodic activity *Organization administration> Periodic> Batch processing* on a client.

If you want to check and to edit the status of batch jobs, access the form *System administration> Inquiries> Batch jobs> Batch jobs*.

2.2.1.11 Printing and Modifying Auto-reports

Auto-reports are another kind of report. You may start them in every list page or detail form choosing the command *File/Print/Print* or pushing the shortcut key

Ctrl+P. Auto-reports show a list containing the main data (field group *Auto-report*) of the particular table shown in the form. Apart from the additional button *Modify* enabling to create personal reports, they work similar to regular reports.

Clicking the button *Modify/New* in the auto-report form starts a report wizard for creating a personal report. This report is stored in your usage data. Once you have finished the report wizard, the new auto-report is available in the lookup field *Select report* of the auto-report form.

Compared to reports in the development environment, the wizard for auto-reports has only got limited functionality.

2.2.1.12 New in Dynamics AX 2012

The technical basis of reports has completely changed in Dynamics AX 2012, now applying SSRS reports instead of the MorphX reports in earlier releases. Among other advantages, SSRS reports provide the options to apply filters in the preview, refresh data, search for text within the preview and generate multiple export formats including Word and Excel.

2.2.2   Copy/Paste and Microsoft Office Add-Ins

Whereas copying data from Dynamics AX and pasting them to another program works with any Windows application, the Office add-ins are designed to work specifically with Microsoft Office.

2.2.2.1 Copy and Paste

A comfortable way for retrieving data from Dynamics AX is the data export through the clipboard. For this purpose, select lines by marking the appropriate grid check boxes leftmost in the grid of list pages (or in the grid view of detail forms). Alternatively, select lines by clicking them directly in the grid while holding the *Ctrl* key. The *Shift* key selects several consecutive lines, the shortcut key *Ctrl+A* (or the grid check box in the header line) selects all lines of the grid.

For copying the selected records to the clipboard, push the shortcut key *Ctrl+C*, or choose the command *File/Edit/Copy*, or the option *Copy* in the pop-up menu (doing a right-hand click). Finally, insert the records into another Windows application (like Microsoft Excel) by pushing the shortcut key *Ctrl+V*.

Copying in a Dynamics AX list page only includes columns displayed in the list page. In the original release of Dynamics AX 2012 (not in AX 2012 R2), copying in the grid view of detail forms does not only copy fields of the grid but also fields shown on the other tabs of the form.

2.2.2.2 Microsoft Office Add-Ins

Microsoft Office add-ins in Dynamics AX enable data interaction with Microsoft Office. This data interaction includes:

➤ **Exporting** data from Dynamics AX to Microsoft Excel
➤ **Refreshing and editing** AX-data in Microsoft Office
➤ **Importing** data from Microsoft Excel into Dynamics AX

In the general section of your user options (*File/Tools/Options*), there are two settings for the *Export to Microsoft Excel*, which are relevant for the Office add-ins:

➤ **Workbook support refresh** – Apply either static or refreshable exports (choose *Never* for static exports when sharing reports with external people)
➤ **Remote desktop session exports to** – Applicable for Remote Desktop Clients (Terminal Services), making it possible to export data directly to Microsoft Office on the local PC.

Changes of Office add-in settings in the user options apply after restarting the Dynamics AX client session.

2.2.2.3 Export to Excel and Refresh

On list pages and in the grid view of detail forms, the command *File/Export to Microsoft Excel* (and the appropriate button on the first tab of the action pane) is available to export the list to Microsoft Excel.

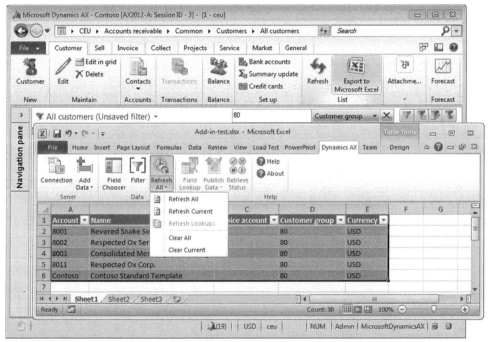

Figure 2-27: Using the Office add-ins (Excel export in the customer list page)

Depending on your user options, the Dynamics AX export to Excel generates a static or refreshable Excel sheet, where you may find the tab *Dynamics AX* in the ribbon (see Figure 2-27). When saving a refreshable sheet, you can open it later and retrieve current data from Dynamics AX including new lines for new records by simply clicking the button *Refresh* in the Excel sheet.

The button *Field Chooser* in Excel enables adding Dynamics AX data columns. In addition, include regular Excel columns as required – e.g. using Excel formulas for calculation.

The button *Filter* in Excel enables applying a query filter for retrieving Dynamics AX data. If a filter applies in Dynamics AX when starting the Excel export, this filter also applies in Excel by default (e.g. customer group "80" in Figure 2-27).

2.2.2.4 Edit Data in Excel and Dynamics AX Import Options

When exporting to Excel, Dynamics AX generates a read-only query. For editing Dynamics AX data directly in Excel, a Web service for the specific use of the Dynamics AX Office add-ins has to be registered in the Organization management module (*Organization management> Setup> Document management> Document data sources*).

In order to edit data in Excel, click the button *Add Data/Add Data* in Excel. A dialog then displays, showing installed queries and services which are available for you according to your permissions. After selecting a data source (e.g. *Budget register entries*), Microsoft Excel shows the available fields in the task pane. Indicators show key and required fields, making sure they are entered when editing Dynamics AX data. Clicking the button *Publish Data* transfers the data from Excel to Dynamics AX.

2.2.2.5 New in Dynamics AX 2012

In addition to the static Excel export available already in Dynamics AX 2009, Excel integration now includes options for refreshing, editing and importing (presuming you have got access to the appropriate Web services).

2.2.3   Case Study Exercise

Exercise 2.7 – Printing
Print a vendor list (*Accounts payable> Reports> Vendors> Vendors*), selecting a print preview for the print destination. Then print the vendor list again, filtering on any vendor group of your choice and choosing a PDF-file as print destination.

2.3   Advanced Options

Before you can access the Microsoft Dynamics AX workspace, system administration has to set up a Dynamics AX user with appropriate permissions for you. In some areas of the application, a worker record (see section 9.2.2) assigned to your user is required in addition.

After accessing the Dynamics AX workspace, individual settings enable adjusting the user interface to your needs.

2.3.1   User Options and Personalization

Options for personally adjusting the Dynamics AX user interface are available in the user options. In addition, personalization provides enhanced features for individually configuring every single form.

2.3.1.1   User Options

The user options are a form controlling core personal settings in Dynamics AX. You may access your user options choosing the command *File/Tools/Options* in the jewel menu, if you have got appropriate permissions. In addition, the user management form (*System administration> Common> Users> Users*, button *Options*) allows administrators to access your user options as well.

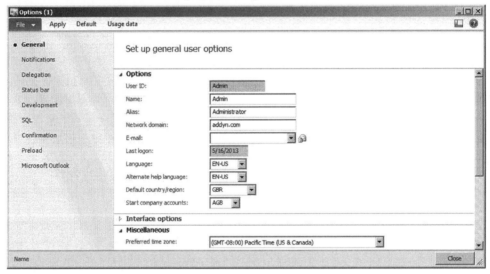

Figure 2-28:   Managing preferences in the user options form

Main settings in the user option form as shown in Figure 2-28 include following preferences for your workspace:

> **Language** – Language of the user interface
> **Alternate help language** – Language of the help system
> **Default country/region** – Default for the country/region when entering a postal address
> **Start company accounts** – Default-company when logging on
> **Autocomplete** – Characters entered in a field apply as default for the next record when starting to enter the same characters in the same field
> **Infolog / Detail level** – Show warnings and error messages
> **Automatic shutdown** – Minutes of inactivity, after which your session is closed
> **Filter by grid on by default** – Show filter line (see section 2.1.6)

➢ **Default global view/edit mode** – Start all detail forms in view or edit mode
➢ **Document handling** – See section 9.5.1
➢ **Notifications** tab – Alerts and workflow-notifications (see section 9.4.1)
➢ **Status bar** tab – Fields shown in the status bar
➢ **Confirmation** tab – Show a confirmation dialog in forms before deleting or saving modified records

2.3.1.2 Usage Data

The button *Usage data* in the action pane strip of user options form opens a form, which shows detailed settings of a user. These settings include filter settings, auto-reports, form settings and record templates (user templates), which have been stored automatically or manually.

In the usage data, switch from the tab *General* to the other tabs for showing a list of usage data lines in the particular area. Clicking the button *Data* after selecting a usage data record shows the record details. It is not possible to modify usage data records, but you can delete usage data lines by pushing the shortcut key *Alt+F9* or choosing the command *File/Delete Record*. Clicking the button *Reset* on the tab *General* deletes all your usage data.

If your administrator implements modifications or updates in your Dynamics AX application, it may happen that your usage data do not fit to the form settings required by the new application status. In this case, you have to delete the affected usage data records (or reset all usage data) in order to display the new form content correctly.

2.3.1.3 Form Configuration

Apart from modifications in the development environment, which apply to all users, changes of the user interface in list pages and forms are also available at personal level. For this purpose, each user with appropriate permissions in Dynamics AX may adapt forms according to his personal requirements.

The first option to adjust a form individually is to configure it. The button *View* 🖳 in the command bar provides access to the form configuration. In the form configuration, optionally choose to hide or show FactBoxes and preview panes separately for every form.

For hiding or showing columns on list pages (and fields or fast tabs on detail forms), select the option *Hide* or *Show* in the pop-up menu accessed by a right-hand click on the appropriate column.

In list pages, change the width and position of columns with your mouse (drag and drop in the header column). In addition, add columns by choosing the option *More* in the lookup of the filter field if required (see section 2.1.6). In order to remove an additional column, access the personalization form.

2.3.1.4 Personalization

If you need enhanced options for individual form settings, access the *Personalization* form available in every list page or detail form by choosing the command *File/Command/Personalize* or the option *Personalize* in the pop-up menu., Figure 2-29 for example shows a personalization form, which has been opened from the vendor list page (*Accounts payable> Common> Vendors> All vendors*) for personalizing the vendor page.

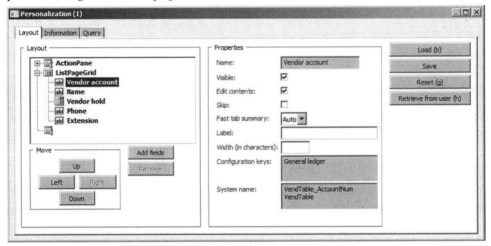

Figure 2-29: Form settings in the personalization form for the vendor page

On the tab *Layout* of the personalization form, hide or move fast tabs, field groups and fields as well as button groups and buttons in the action pane as required. You can move elements within and between tabs by pushing the buttons *Up, Down, Left* and *Right* or using your mouse (drag and drop). If required, click the button *Add fields* for adding additional table fields to the form.

After selecting an element in the *Layout* pane of the personalization form, settings in the *Properties* pane show if it is visible and editable.

Once closing the personalization form, the modified settings apply. Clicking the button *Save* in the personalization form enables storing different versions for displaying a particular form. When saving a version, enter a name for identifying the version later. Selecting a saved version requires clicking the button *Load* in the personalization form. If you want to apply the standard form again, click the button *Reset*.

All individual form settings are stored in your usage data. If applicable, it is possible to restrict access to form settings by appropriate user permissions.

2.3.2   Record Information and Templates

The record information dialog in Dynamics AX provides access to data and general features not directly shown on a list page or detail form.

2.3.2.1 Options in the Record Information Dialog

After selecting the appropriate record line, open the record information dialog in a list page or detail form by choosing the command *File/Command/ Record info* or the option *Record info* in the pop-up menu.

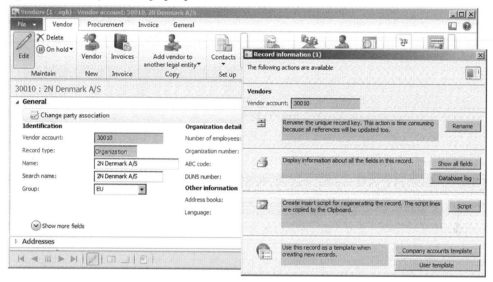

Figure 2-30:   The record information dialog in the vendor detail form

The *Record information* dialog provides following options for the selected record:

➢ **Rename key field** – Agree with system administration before using this option
➢ **Fill utility** – Modify multiple records (not available in AX 2012 R2)
➢ **Show all fields** and **Database log** – Information on the selected record
➢ **Script** – Create an insert script
➢ **Company accounts template** and **User template** – Create a record template (only available in detail forms)

<u>Notes</u>: Depending on your permissions and the Dynamics AX configuration, some options might not be available.

2.3.2.2 Renaming

You may rename the key field of a record by clicking the button *Rename* in the record information dialog. Renaming then opens a second dialog box for entering the new field content.

Processing a request for renaming may be a time-consuming activity, because Dynamics AX has to update all references. If you want to modify a vendor number for example, the vendor number also changes in vendor transactions, purchase orders and all other tables where it is used. You have to take into account, that references are only updated within Dynamics AX. Other applications and external partners like customers or vendors have to receive appropriate information separately.

Therefore, renaming usually is an exceptional activity with restricted access, secured by appropriate permission settings.

2.3.2.3 Fill Utility

The fill utility in the original release of Dynamics AX 2012 (not in R2) provides the option to change the content of a field in multiple records – similar to the *Find and Replace* feature in Microsoft Office.

If you want to change the payment terms for a number of vendors for example, open the vendor detail form (through *Accounts payable> Common> Vendors> All vendors*) and choose the fill utility for the *Terms of payment* after selecting the option *Record info* in the pop-up menu for this field. The fill utility then displays a form where you may select a filter identifying the vendors to be modified. Once you have finished entering the filter, click the button *OK* in the filter form. Dynamics AX then displays a separate form with the result of your filter. After confirming the selection with *OK*, enter the new payment terms in the next dialog.

Unlike *Find and Replace* in Microsoft Office, the fill utility in Dynamics AX does not only provide the option to change the content of a field from one value to another. The selection of records for the update is independent from the previous content in the field.

The fill utility is available for most fields in master data tables and in non-posted financial journals. As a prerequisite for applying the fill utility, it has to be activated in the license configuration (*System administration> Setup> Licensing> License configuration*, folder *Administration*). In addition, you need appropriate user permissions to run the fill utility.

2.3.2.4 Show All Fields and Database Log

The button *Show all fields* in the record information dialog displays the content of all fields of the selected record. You may choose this option if you want to know the content of fields not shown in a particular list page or detail form. The *Show all fields* form also displays field groups – e.g. the field group *Auto-report* containing the fields of the default auto-report.

The button *Database log* in the record information dialog shows a log file of all changes to the selected record. As a prerequisite, logging for the particular table has to be enabled in the form *System administration> Setup> Database> Database log setup* or in the development environment.

2.3.2.5 Record Templates

Record templates help creating new records by copying the content of fields from a template created before. As an example, it might be useful for a European company to provide templates in the vendor table for domestic vendors, for vendors within the EU, and for foreign vendors, to make sure that correct posting groups apply when inserting a new vendor.

When working with record templates, you have to distinguish between two types of templates:

➤ User templates
➤ Company accounts templates

2.3.2.6 User Templates

A user template is only available to the user who has created it. You may create a user template by clicking the button *User template* in the record information dialog. A second dialog then opens where you can enter the name and description of the template. The template is a copy of the record you have selected when opening the record information dialog.

User templates are stored in your usage data, where it is not possible to modify them later. If a user template is not required any more, you can delete it in the usage data (command *File/Tools/Options*> button *Usage data*> tab *Record templates*). Alternatively, delete a user template pushing the shortcut key *Alt+F9* in the template selection dialog as shown in Figure 2-31.

2.3.2.7 Company Accounts Templates

Unlike user templates, company accounts templates are available to all users. You may create a company accounts template by clicking the button *Company accounts template* in the record information dialog.

If you want to edit a company accounts template, open the form *Home*> *Setup*> *Record templates*. On the tab *Overview* of the record templates form, select the table to which the template belongs. Then switch to the tab *Templates* and select the particular template. Finally click the button *Edit* to modify it.

2.3.2.8 Using Templates

Once templates are available for a table, they display in a template selection dialog when inserting a new record in the particular table. Figure 2-31 for example shows the dialog displayed when creating a new vendor in the vendor detail form (*Accounts payable*> *Common*> *Vendors*> *All vendors*) if at least one template is available.

In the dialog, apply a template by clicking the button *OK* after selecting it or by double-clicking the appropriate line. Company account templates show the icon ▥, and user templates the icon ▥. In the far right column, optionally select one line for specifying the default template.

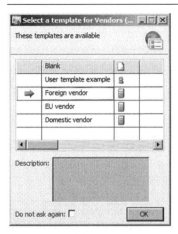

Figure 2-31:   The dialog for template selection

If selecting the checkbox *Do not ask again* at the bottom of the template selection dialog, Dynamics AX applies the default template without showing the dialog when inserting further records. If you want to show the template dialog when creating new records again, click the button *Show template selection* which then displays in the record information dialog.

2.3.2.9   New in Dynamics AX 2012 R2

The fill utility is only available in the first releases of Dynamics AX 2012, not in Dynamics AX 2012 R2.

2.3.3   Case Study Exercises

Exercise 2.8 – User Options and Worker Record

You want to access your user options in order to make sure your name and e-mail address is correct. In addition, select the training company to be the *Start company accounts* to avoid opening a different company when you log on the next time. Your settings for the status bar should include showing the user ID.

Since you need a worker assignment in some of the later exercises, create a new worker W-## (## = your user ID) with your name in the worker form. Your employment in the training company starts at the current date. Then assign the new employee to your Dynamics AX user ID in the user relations.

Note: If an automatic number sequence for personnel numbers applies, you don't have to enter a personnel number.

Exercise 2.9 – Record Templates

Create a new user template based on the vendor which you have entered in exercise 2.4. To get to know how to use templates, insert a new vendor applying this template afterwards.

2.4   Global Address Book

Dynamics AX has got a common table for all business relationships of your enterprise – companies and persons, internal and external. This common table is the global address book, applying the label "parties" for the business relationships. Parties in the global address book are shared across companies and include customers, sales leads, vendors, organization units, employees and other contacts.

2.4.1   Parties and Addresses

When creating a new customer, vendor or any other kind of party, Dynamics AX inserts a record in the global address book. A party may show one or more (postal) addresses and contact information data. Therefore, a party is not the same as an address – a party is an organization or person characterized by its name.

Depending on permission settings, you can access all parties in the global address book (*Home> Common> Global address book*). The party detail form accessed from the global address book shows record details like name, addresses and contact data.

2.4.1.1   Directly Creating Parties

You may insert a new party directly in the global address book by clicking the button *New/Party* in the action pane. In the new party record, the *Party ID* usually derives from the appropriate number sequence. The lookup field *Record type* then provides the alternative options "Organization" or "Person", controlling which fields display (e.g. the field *First name* only shows for a person).

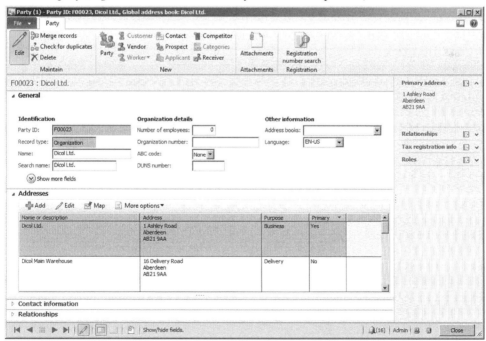

Figure 2-32:   Managing a party with multiple addresses in the party detail form

After entering the party name in the field *Name* (for an organization) or in the fields *First name* and *Last name* (for a person), register additional data including the postal address on the tab *Addresses* and contact data like e-mail address and phone number on the tab *Contact information*. Section 3.2.1 shows managing postal addresses and contact information in more detail on the example of vendor management.

2.4.1.2 Indirectly Creating Parties

Apart from directly creating a party in the global address book, alternatively create a party indirectly by entering a customer, a vendor, or any other kind of party in any module.

In forms indirectly creating parties, the field *Name* is a lookup providing the option to search an existing party. If selecting an existing party in this lookup, the party receives a new role. If not selecting an existing party, but typing a new name, Dynamics AX automatically creates a new party with this name.

If inserting a new customer in the customer form (*Accounts receivable> Common> Customers> All customers*) for example, a new party is created if a name is entered in the lookup field *Name* of the *Create new* form. If selecting an existing party in the lookup field *Name*, the new role "Customer" is assigned to the party.

Since a party may already exist in the global address book – e.g. a customer being a vendor in your own or an affiliated company within a common Dynamics AX database and partition – you should check existing parties before creating a party record in order to avoid duplicate parties. As a last resort when entering a duplicate party name, a confirmation dialog displays if duplicate check is selected in the global address book parameters (see below).

2.4.1.3 Internal Organizations

Apart from external parties (organizations and persons), internal organizations like operating units and legal entities (see section 9.1.3) are also parties in the global address book. You may know internal organizations from the *Record type* (e.g. "Legal entities"). Record types of internal organizations are not available when manually inserting a party directly in the global address book.

2.4.2   Address books

An address book is a collection of party records. You may set up one or more address books in the form *Organization administration> Setup> Global address book> Address books*, e.g. one for sales and one for purchasing.

In order to link a party to one or more address book, put a checkmark in front of the address books which display when accessing the lookup of the field *Address books* on the tab *General* of the party detail form (see Figure 2-32).

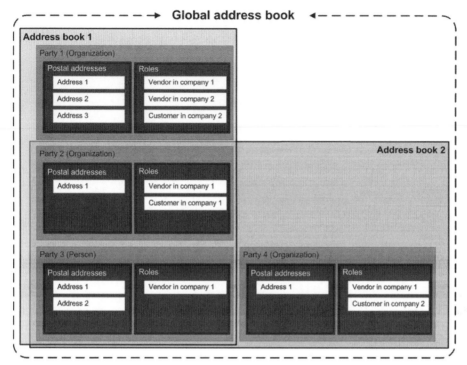

Figure 2-33:   Conceptual structure of the global address book

You can use address books for filtering addresses – e.g. in the filter field *Address books* in the global address book list page. But different address books may also apply as a basis for setting access permissions (see section 9.2.4).

The global address book then is the collection of all parties in all companies of a Dynamics AX system (see Figure 2-33).

2.4.2.1   Roles

A role (e.g. "Vendor" or "Customer") describes the kind of relationship between a party and your enterprise. A party may refer to one or more roles in one or more companies. There are two ways of assigning a role to a party:

> **Indirectly** – Entering a record in other areas like the customer list page automatically creates a party with the appropriate role.
> **Directly** – Clicking the appropriate button in the action pane (e.g. *New/Customer*) of the party detail form creates a record in the selected area (e.g. customer record) and assigns the specific role.

The roles of a party are shown in the FactBox *Roles* of the global address book list page. If you want to switch from a form like the customer detail form to the related party record, choose the option *View details* on the field *Name* there.

2.4.2.2 Address Book Parameters

If duplicate check is selected in the global address book parameters (*Organization administration> Setup> Global address book> Global address book parameters*, checkbox *Use duplicate check*), a dialog shows duplicate party records whenever you try to create a party (directly or indirectly) with a name of an already existing party. In the dialog you may choose whether to use the existing party or to create a new party, which by chance has got the same name.

Other global address book parameters include the default party type (*Organization* or *Person*), the name sequence for persons (first/last name), and security policy options (see section 9.2.4).

Settings regarding the format of postal addresses and available ZIP/postal codes or cities are specified in the address setup (*Organization administration> Setup> Addresses> Address setup*).

2.4.2.3 New in Dynamics AX 2012

The concept of the global address book has been enhanced in Dynamics AX 2012, now easily sharing parties and addresses across several companies.

2.4.3   Case Study Exercise

Exercise 2.10 – Global Address Book
In order to check the functionality of the global address book, check if you can find the party record of your vendor from exercise 2.4.

Next you want to insert a new party in the global address book. Fields to be entered include the name "##-Exercise 2.10" (## = your user ID) and a postal address in London. This new party becomes a vendor in your company. What do you do in Dynamics AX?

3 Purchasing

The primary responsibility of purchasing is to provide your company with goods and services from suppliers. This task requires following activities:

➤ Determine material requirements in operations planning
➤ Process purchase requisitions, requests for quotations and purchase orders
➤ Post item arrivals and purchase invoices

3.1 Business Processes in Purchasing

Before we start to go into details, the lines below give an overview of business processes in purchasing.

3.1.1 Basic Approach

Starting point for procurement are correct master data, especially vendor and product data. Instead of products, alternatively choose procurement categories for purchasing services or non-inventoried commodities.

3.1.1.1 Master Data and Transactions in Purchasing

As for all master data, vendor and product records (item records) are usually entered once and do not change frequently. In the course of purchase processing, master data are copied to transaction data. Planning records and purchase orders therefore retrieve defaults from item and vendor data. You may modify these default data in transactions, for example if you agree on different payment terms in a specific purchase order.

Changing data in a transaction does not change related master data. If you generally agree to change the payment terms with a particular vendor for example, you have to update the payment terms in the vendor record therefore.

Starting from correct master data, we may split the purchasing business process into six steps as shown in Figure 3-1.

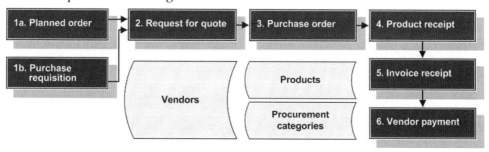

Figure 3-1: Purchase order processing in Dynamics AX

3.1.1.2 Material Requirements, Purchase Requisition and Request for Quotation

The identification of material requirements usually is the first step in the purchasing process. Depending on the particular product and the preconditions in the company, there are two different ways for processing material requirements:

➢ **Automatically** – Generating planned orders
➢ **Manually** – Entering purchase requisitions

The basis for generating planned orders within operations planning (master scheduling, see section 6.3) are accurate figures on inventory, sales orders, purchase orders and forecasts on the one hand, and appropriate item coverage settings on the other.

Purchase requisitions – unlike planned orders, which are created automatically by master scheduling – are manually entered, internal documents asking the purchase department to obtain particular items (like consumables and office supplies). A purchase requisition runs through an approval process workflow, before it is released as a purchase order.

Requests for quotation are sent to vendors in order to receive information on prices and delivery times. The purchasing department may either enter requests for quotation manually, or generate them in planned purchase orders and purchase requisitions.

3.1.1.3 Purchase Order

You may create purchase orders either manually or by transferring planned orders, purchase requisitions, or requests for quotation. A purchase order consists of a header, containing fields which are common to the whole order (e.g. vendor data), and one or more lines, containing the required items.

Once order entry is completed, start the approval process if change management is activated. After approval – or without approval if change management does not apply – you have to post a purchase order confirmation before you may continue order processing. Posting a confirmation means to store it, optionally sending it to the vendor electronically or in a printed document. The purchase order confirmation is available with its original content, no matter if there is a modification on the current purchase order afterwards.

The status of a purchase order is indicated by the order status and the document status in the header, and by the posted quantities in the lines. In addition to periodic reports and inquiries, alerts provide the option to receive a warning of problems like late shipments in order processing.

3.1.1.4 Product Receipt, Invoice Receipt and Vendor Payment

Once goods or services actually arrive, register the product receipt related to the purchase order in Dynamics AX. Posting the product receipt increases the physical quantity in inventory and reduces the open quantity in the purchase order.

Together with the item or some time later, the vendor submits an invoice. When registering the invoice in the vendor invoice form, Dynamics AX supports invoice control by matching the invoice with the purchase order and the product receipt. If receiving an invoice not referring to a purchase order, enter it either in the vendor invoice form or in an invoice journal (see section 8.3.3).

Based on posted invoices, you can register payments to vendors either manually or by running a payment proposal. Payment proposals include due date and cash discount period calculation. Payment processing is independent from purchase orders and usually a responsibility of the finance department. You can find a description on vendor payments in section 8.3.4 later in this book.

3.1.1.5 Ledger Integration and Voucher Principle

Because of the deep integration of Dynamics AX, all inventory and vendor transactions in purchasing are posted to ledger accounts depending on the setup as described in section 8.4.

In order to keep record of the whole business process, Dynamics AX comprehensively applies the voucher principle to transactions: You have to register a document (voucher), before you can post it. After posting, it is not possible to modify the document any more.

Figure 3-2 shows an overview of the documents in purchase order processing.

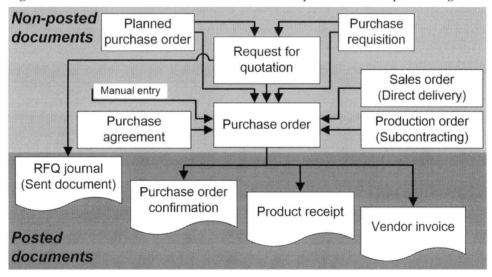

Figure 3-2: Posted and non-posted documents in purchasing

3.1.2   At a Glance: Purchase Order Processing

In order to provide an overview of the main steps in purchase order processing, this section shows the basics. For convenience, we create the order starting in the vendor list page and post all transactions directly in the purchase order form. Of course, you may alternatively enter the order in the *Purchase Orders* list page and access the specific posting forms through the menu.

When creating a new purchase order in the vendor list page (*Procurement and sourcing> Common> Vendors> All vendors*), apply a filter for selecting the particular vendor first. Clicking the button *New/Purchase order* on the action pane tab *Procurement* opens the line view of the purchase order form in *Edit* mode, creating a new purchase order header with default data like language or currency from the selected vendor.

After clicking the button *Add line* on the tab *Purchase order line*, or clicking on a new line there, start entering a purchase order line with item number (or procurement category), quantity, and price. When selecting the item, Dynamics AX applies appropriate defaults for quantity, price, and other fields like site or warehouse. Clicking the button *Header view* (or *Line view*) in the action pane switches between the line view shown in Figure 3-3 and the header view.

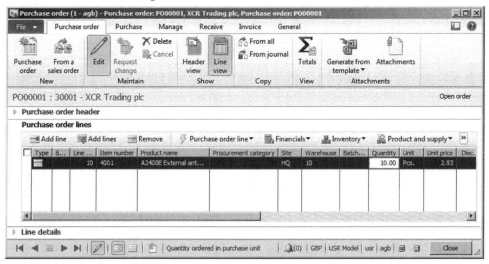

Figure 3-3:   Registering a purchase order line (Line view, in edit mode)

If change management applies, a yellow workflow message bar displays. In this case, click the button *Submit* there after registering all order lines. After approval – or without change management immediately – the order shows the *Approval status* "Approved".

In the next step, post the purchase order confirmation by clicking the button *Generate/Purchase order* (or *Confirm*) on the action pane tab *Purchase*. If you want to print the purchase order, select the checkboxes *Posting* and *Print purchase order* in the posting form. The button *Printer setup* enables selecting a printer for the printout as described in section 2.2.1.

Note: If registering only one line or if waiting for approval, you might need to press the *F5* key refreshing the form before you can confirm the order.

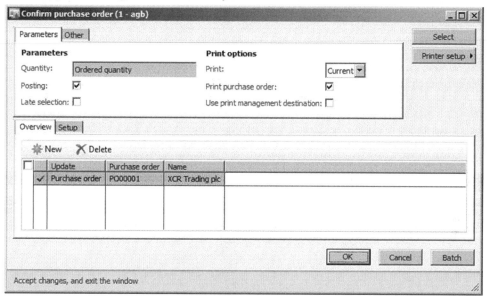

Figure 3-4: Confirming and printing the purchase order

When receiving the item, post the product receipt by clicking the button *Generate/Product receipt* on the action pane tab *Receive* of the purchase order form. Posting the product receipt is similar to purchase order posting as described above. But unlike purchase order posting, the product receipt usually does not include printing. If no previous item registration applies, select the option "Ordered quantity" in the lookup field *Quantity*. In the column *Product receipt* you have to enter the vendor's packing slip number. The product receipt increases the physical quantity in inventory and changes the order status to "Received".

If you want to post the invoice receipt directly in the purchase order form, click the button *Generate/Invoice* on the action pane tab *Invoice* of the order form. Showing an action pane and FactBoxes, the form for vendor invoice posting is different from the other posting forms. In order to check the totals there, view the appropriate FactBox on the right of the form or click the button *Totals*. After entering the vendor invoice number in the field *Number* (*Invoice identification*), post the invoice by clicking the button *Post/Post* in the action pane. Invoice posting generates an open vendor transaction to be paid and changes the order status to "Invoiced".

Note: If you want to quit the vendor invoice form without saving, click the button *Cancel* in the action pane – not the button *Close* at the bottom.

3.2   Vendor Management

Vendor records are required both in purchasing and in finance. According to the
deep integration of Dynamics AX, there is only one data record for each vendor,
which then applies to all areas of the application. Setting appropriate permissions,
you can limit access to fields and field groups of the vendor form.

3.2.1   Vendor Records

For checking existing or creating new vendors, access the vendor list page in the
procurement module (*Procurement and sourcing> Common> Vendors> All vendors*) or
in the accounts payable module (*Accounts payable> Common> Vendors> All vendors*).
According to the general structure of list pages, the vendor page shows the list of
available vendors.

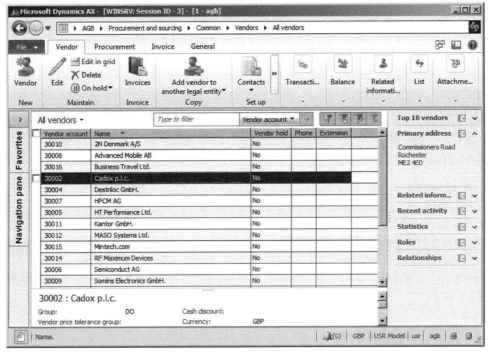

Figure 3-5:   Selecting a vendor in the vendor list page

If you want to view the details of a vendor in the list page, double-click the line of
the particular vendor for accessing the vendor detail form. In the vendor detail
form, you can switch to the edit mode by clicking the button *Edit* in the action pane
or the button ✎ in the status bar. Alternatively, access the vendor detail form in
edit mode by clicking the button *Edit* in the action pane of the list page after
selecting the vendor concerned.

The vendor detail form contains numerous fields representing default values for
purchase orders. Below you may find a description of core settings. Additional
information is available in the online help.

3.2.1.1 Creating a Vendor

If you want to register a new vendor, insert a record in the vendor list page or detail form by pushing the shortcut key *Ctrl+N* or by clicking the button *New/Vendor* on the action pane tab *Vendor*. If there are templates for vendors in your company (see section 2.3.2), optionally populate fields of the new record by choosing a template.

Depending on the settings of the number sequence, a unique vendor number in the field *Vendor account* is assigned automatically or has to be entered manually.

3.2.1.2 Global Address Book Integration

In the vendor detail form, the *Record type* determines if the vendor is a company (organization) or a person. Depending on the record type, the *General* tab shows different fields – e.g. *First name* and *Last name* for the record type "Person".

Vendors in parallel are parties in the global address book. When creating a new vendor, the field *Name* therefore is a lookup field providing the option to select an existing party from the global address book. If manually entering a name of a new vendor, a dialog displays in case an existing party has got exactly the same name and duplicate check is selected in the global address book parameters (see section 2.4.2). This dialog provides the option to link the vendor to an existing party or to create a new party, which by chance has got the same name.

After saving the vendor record, you can access the related party in the global address book applying the table reference (*View details*) on the vendor name field.

As an alternative to the vendor form, create new vendors in the global address book (*Home> Common> Global address book*, see section 2.4) in order to reduce the probability of duplicate party records. In the global address book, it is easy to check before creating a new vendor if this vendor is already a party – e.g. being a vendor in an affiliated company. If the vendor is a party, convert the party to a vendor in your company. If not, create the party record before converting it to a vendor.

3.2.1.3 General Data

The search name in the vendor record copies from the vendor name, but you may modify it. Mandatory fields in the vendor form apart from the name are the vendor group in the lookup field *Group* (usually controlling ledger integration, see section 3.2.3), and the currency on the tab *Purchasing demographics* (by default obtaining the company currency).

Further core fields on the tab *General* are the *Language*, specifying the language for printing purchase orders or other documents, and – in case address books are used, especially for access control – the *Address books* linked to the vendor.

The display field *Vendor hold* on the tab *Miscellaneous details* shows whether the vendor is blocked. If you want to change the hold status, click the button *On hold* on the action pane tab *Vendor*. After selecting the status "All" it is not possible to enter or to post any purchase order or other transaction for the vendor. The options "No" and "Never" enable all transactions, with "Never" showing that the vendor should not be blocked after a period of inactivity.

3.2.1.4   Input Tax

Tax settings are available on the tab *Invoice and delivery*, where you should enter a *Sales tax group* (*VAT group*) specifying the tax duty depending on the vendor location. A correct sales tax group is necessary to distinguish between domestic vendors, who charge sales tax or VAT, and foreign vendors, who do not.

The setup of sales tax groups and tax calculation depends on your company and its location. Section 8.2.6 contains more information on tax setup in Dynamics AX.

If your company is located within the European Union and you need to record the VAT registration number of vendors for tax purposes, enter it in the *Tax exempt number* (*VAT number*) field below the sales tax group. Since it is a lookup field, you have to insert a new tax-exempt number in the main table (*View details* in the pop-up menu, or *General ledger> Setup> Sales tax> External> Tax exempt numbers*) before selecting it in a vendor record. The setting *Tax exempt number requirement* in the accounts payable parameters (*Accounts payable> Setup> Accounts payable parameters*, the tab *General*) determines if you have to enter a tax exempt number when creating a vendor.

3.2.1.5   Settings for Delivery and Payment

The field *Delivery terms* on the tab *Invoice and delivery* of the vendor detail form specifies the usual delivery terms of the particular vendor. You may access the setup of required delivery terms including text in foreign languages in the form *Procurement and sourcing> Setup> Distribution> Terms of delivery*.

The tab *Payment* of the vendor detail form contains settings for payment terms and cash discount. You may find more details on these settings in section 3.2.2.

3.2.1.6   Postal Address

Address data are available on the tab *Addresses* of the vendor detail form, where you may enter multiple addresses per vendor. Addresses and contact data are shared with the party in the global address book linked to the particular vendor.

If you want to enter a new postal address of a vendor, click the button ⬛Add in the action pane strip of the tab *Addresses*. In the *New address* dialog, enter the identification (*Name or description*) of the address then – for the primary address usually the vendor name.

The *Purpose* in the address dialog determines the transactions, for which the address applies as default. For the primary address, choose the purpose "Business". If entering a second address, choose the appropriate purpose for this address – for example the option "Payment" identifying an alternative payee. One postal address can have several purposes at the same time. If no specific address is specified for a particular purpose, the primary address applies.

For setting up individual address purposes in addition to the standard purposes, access the form *Organization administration> Setup> Global address book> Address and contact information purpose*.

In the primary address of a vendor, make sure the checkbox *Primary* is and the checkbox *Private* is not selected.

Another important setting of a postal address is the *Country/region*, which is the basis for the address format on the one hand and for reports to the authorities – like sales tax and Intrastat reports – on the other.

After selecting the country code, only postal codes of this country show in the lookup of the *ZIP/postal Code* field. When entering a postal code, it is validated in the ZIP/postal code table depending on the settings in the address setup form (*Organization administration> Setup> Addresses> Address setup*). If ZIP/postal code validation is activated in the address setup, you have to insert a new postal code in the ZIP/postal code table before you can enter it in an address. You may access postal codes on the tab *ZIP/postal codes* of the address setup form, or applying the table reference (*View details*) on the ZIP/postal code field.

The tab *Contact information* in the address dialog contains contact data, which are specific to the particular address (e.g. the phone number of the alternate payee), not general contact data of the vendor.

3.2.1.7   Contact Information

On the tab *Contact information* of the vendor detail form, click the button 　Add　 in the action pane strip for entering general contact data as applicable (e.g. the vendor telephone number or the general e-mail address).

On the tab *Purchasing demographics* of the vendor detail form, select the main contact person in the field *Primary contact*. If you want to enter a new main contact, register data of this person by clicking the button *Set up/Contacts/Add contacts* on the action pane tab *Vendor* of the vendor form first.

3.2.1.8   Features in the Vendor Form

Clicking the buttons in the action pane of the vendor list page or detail form provides access to various inquiries and activities on the selected vendor:

➢ Action pane tab *Vendor*:
   o *Contacts* – Managing vendor contact persons
   o *Bank accounts* – Managing vendor bank accounts for payment
   o *Transactions* – Showing vendor invoices and payments
   o *Balance* – Showing the total of open liabilities

➤ Action pane tab *Procurement*:
  ○ *New/Purchase order* – Entering an order, see section 3.4.5
  ○ *Related information/Purchase orders* – Viewing existing orders
  ○ *Agreements/Trade agreements, Purchase prices, Discounts* –
    Viewing purchase prices and discounts, see section 3.3.3
  ○ *Agreements/Purchase agreements* – Blanket orders, see section 3.4.9
➤ Action pane tab *Invoice*:
  ○ *New/Invoice* – Entering a vendor invoice, see section 8.3.3
  ○ *Settle/Settle open transactions* – Settling invoices, see section 8.2.5
  ○ *Related information/Invoice* – Viewing posted invoices

3.2.1.9 One-time Vendor

One-time vendors provide the option to keep master data of regular suppliers separate from vendors, which supply items rarely or only once.

The accounts payable parameters (*Accounts payable> Setup> Accounts payable parameters*, tab *General*) include the vendor number of a vendor used as template for one-time vendors. In addition, a separate number sequence for one-time vendors is available on the tab *Number sequences* of the parameters.

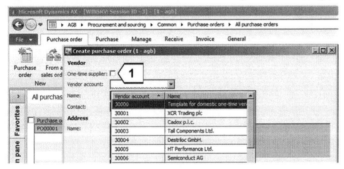

Figure 3-6:   Creating a one-time vendor in a new purchase order

If these parameters are set up for one-time vendors, select the checkbox *One-time supplier* in the dialog as shown in Figure 3-6 (instead of choosing an existing vendor) when creating a purchase order from a one-time vendor in the list page *Procurement and sourcing> Common> Purchase orders> All purchase orders*. Every new order with a selected checkbox *One-time supplier* automatically generates a new vendor. In the vendor record of these vendors, the vendor account number derives from the number-sequence for one-time vendors and the checkbox *One-time supplier* (tab *Vendor profile* on the vendor form) is selected. Clearing the checkbox *One-time supplier* in the vendor record transforms a one-time vendor to a regular vendor (keeping the original one-time vendor number).

3.2.1.10 New in Dynamics AX 2012 and in AX 2012 R2

In Dynamics AX 2012, items new to vendor management refer to the deeper integration of the global address book and to the new user interface design.

Unlike Dynamics AX 2012 R2, the original version of Dynamics AX 2012 requires clicking the button *Change name* in the action pane strip of tab *General* in the vendor detail form for changing the vendor name.

3.2.2   Payment Terms and Cash Discount

Unlike other business applications, which include cash discount settings in the payment terms, Dynamics AX clearly distinguishes payment terms and cash discount providing two different fields for these settings.

Payment terms and cash discounts in Dynamics AX are shared between vendors and customers. The appropriate administration forms therefore are available in both menus – the accounts payable menu and the accounts receivable menu.

The calculation of due date and cash discount date starts from the document date, which you may enter when registering an invoice. If you leave the document date empty, Dynamics AX applies the posting date as the start date for due date calculation. Especially in purchase invoices, the document date may deviate from the posting date.

You may modify the due date and cash discount date when posting the invoice or when settling it in the settle open transactions form (see section 8.2.5).

3.2.2.1   Terms of Payment

In order to manage payment terms, access the form *Accounts payable> Setup> Payment> Terms of payment* in the accounts payable menu or *Accounts receivable> Setup> Payment> Terms of payment* in the accounts receivable menu. The left-hand side of this form shows the list of payment terms with IDs and descriptions. The settings for due date calculation of a particular payment term are available on the right-hand side then.

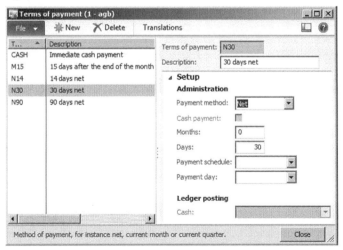

Figure 3-7:   Specifying due date calculation in the terms of payment

The lookup field *Payment method* on the tab *Setup* determines the start date for due date calculation. The payment method "Net" means starting from the document date, "Current month" means starting from month end. The period length for due date calculation is specified by the number of *Days* and *Months*. If required, there is the option to choose a payment schedule.

The button *Translations* provides the option of entering a longer text in own and foreign languages. If entered in the language of the particular document, this text will be printed on external documents (e.g. the printed purchase order) instead of the content in the field *Description* of the payment terms.

3.2.2.2 Cash on Delivery

If you want to enter a record for terms of payment applying cash on delivery, choose the *Payment method* "COD", select the checkbox *Cash payment*, and enter the main account number of the appropriate petty cash account in the field *Ledger posting/Cash*. When posting an invoice referring to this term of payment, Dynamics AX immediately posts the payment and settles the invoice applying the petty cash account of the payment term.

3.2.2.3 Cash Discount

As with payment terms, the cash discount setup is available in the accounts payable menu as well as in the accounts receivable menu (*Accounts payable> Setup> Payment> Cash discounts and Accounts receivable> Setup> Payment> Cash discounts*).

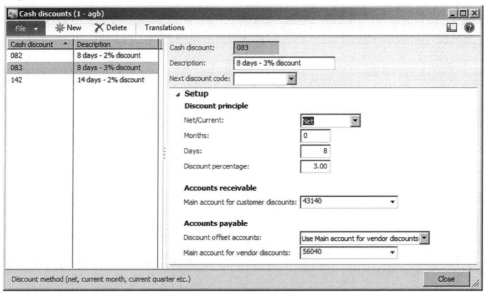

Figure 3-8:   Setting up a cash discount

Setting up new cash discounts works like setting up payment terms, except that you have to add a cash discount percentage and settings for posting the cash discount to the general ledger. Since cash discounts do not only apply to accounts payable but also to accounts receivable, different settings for vendors and customers are required:

> **Accounts receivable** – *Main account for customer discounts*
> **Accounts payable** – The main account applicable for posting the cash discount when posting the vendor payment is depending on the lookup *Discount offset accounts* in the cash discount settings, providing following options:
>   o *Use main account for vendor discounts* – Posting to the *Main account for vendor discounts* entered in the field below
>   o *Accounts on the invoice lines* – Posting to the accounts of the invoice lines (offsetting part of the invoiced expense accounts with the cash discount)

3.2.2.4 New in Dynamics AX 2012 R2

Compared with the initial version of Dynamics AX 2012, the R2 version in addition provides the option of posting the vendor cash discount to the accounts of the invoice lines (if the *Public sector* configuration key is activated).

3.2.3   Ledger Integration

Whenever posting an invoice in purchasing, the invoice automatically posts in finance in parallel. These postings in finance refer to two different areas: The general ledger on the one hand and subledgers for accounts payable, accounts receivable, inventory and others on the other hand.

3.2.3.1 Subledger

As mentioned, there is no separate form for vendors in purchasing and in the accounts payable (finance administration). Data of both areas are available in a common vendor form. When posting vendor invoices, credit notes, or payments, Dynamics AX also posts vendor transactions in the accounts payable.

3.2.3.2 General Ledger

In parallel to subledger posting, Dynamics AX posts transactions in the general ledger as described in section 8.4. There are two different settings relevant for assigning main accounts to purchasing transactions:

> **Assignment of products (items) to main accounts** – Settings for main accounts, applicable when receiving or invoicing items (or procurement categories), are available in the inventory posting setup depending on the vendor and the item or category (see section 8.4.2).
> **Assignment of vendors to main accounts** – Settings for applicable summary accounts are available in the posting profiles.

Both assignments – item and vendor transactions – are not only available at the level of individual items and vendors, but also at group level.

3.2.3.3   Settings for Vendor Transactions

Vendor groups in the form *Accounts payable> Setup> Vendors> Vendor groups* are the primary setting for vendor transactions. In addition to the ID and the description, optionally enter a *Default tax group* for the input tax in the vendor group. When creating a vendor, the default tax group applies as default for the sales tax group in the vendor record.

Vendor posting profiles, which control the assignment of vendors to summary accounts, are available in the form *Accounts payable> Setup> Vendor posting profiles.* As a prerequisite for posting purchase transactions, at least one posting profile has to be specified in your company. In addition, the posting profile defaulting regular purchase transactions has to be entered in the accounts payable parameters (*Accounts payable> Setup> Accounts payable parameters*, tab *Ledger and sales tax/Posting*).

The column *Summary account* on the tab *Setup* in the posting profile form contains the main accounts used as summary accounts for vendors.

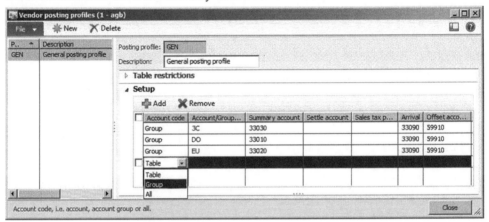

Figure 3-9:   The vendor posting profiles form

As shown in Figure 3-9, the assignment of summary accounts is available at three different levels. The specification level of a line shows in the column *Account code*:

➢ **Table** – Assigning a summary account to a particular vendor (enter the vendor number in the column *Account/Group number*)
➢ **Group** – Assigning a summary account to a vendor group (enter the vendor group in the column *Account/Group number*)
➢ **All** – Assigning a general summary account (*Account/Group number* remains empty)

If settings are available on multiple specification levels, Dynamics AX applies the most appropriate setting starting the search with the vendor number. The specification level "All" has the lowest priority.

If you have to use different profile settings for transactions like prepayment, set up additional posting profiles containing account assignments which are different to the general posting profile. In order to apply one of these additional posting profiles to a specific transaction, choose it in the particular transaction (e.g. for a purchase order on the *Setup* tab of the purchase order form header view). For prepayment, the posting profile is included in the accounts payable parameters.

3.2.4 Case Study Exercises

Exercise 3.1 – Terms of Payment

Your company wants to establish new terms of payment "60 days net", which you have to enter in Dynamics AX with a code P-## (## = your user ID). In addition, a new cash discount D-## for "14 days with 3 percent discount" is required.

Be sure to enter the values for due date and cash discount date calculation correctly. When registering the cash discount in Dynamics AX, choose main accounts similar to the accounts in existing cash discounts.

Exercise 3.2 – Create Vendor

The responsible department accepts a new domestic vendor, who wants to ship items to your company. Enter a new record for this vendor in Dynamics AX without applying a template. Register a name (starting with you user ID) and a primary address, select an appropriate vendor group and sales tax group. For this vendor, the terms of payment and the cash discount entered in exercise 3.1 apply.

Note: If a *Balancing financial dimension* is specified in the ledger form (*General ledger> Setup> Ledger*), enter a default value for this dimension on the tab *Financial dimensions* of the vendor detail form.

Exercise 3.3 – Ledger Integration

You want to find out about ledger integration. To which summary account in the general ledger will an invoice from your new vendor post?

3.3 Product Management for Purchasing

Goods received in purchasing include on the one hand stocked products and on the other hand intangible items like services, fees and licenses. Before purchasing any item, you have to ensure correct and complete master data. These item master data serve two different purposes:

➢ **Identification** – Clearly describing the item to make sure the vendor sells the right product
➢ **Internal settings** – Multiple settings in the item master data like the item group, which determines applicable main accounts in finance, control the way the particular item works in Dynamics AX

Item master data in Dynamics AX 2012 show two levels – the shared and the released products. Whereas item records are required for purchasing inventoried items, procurement categories are an alternative for purchasing intangible items.

Along with a short introduction to the basics of product management, this section primarily contains an explanation of product data necessary for purchasing. A more general description of product management is available in section 7.2.

3.3.1 Procurement Category Management

Product categories are groups of similar products and services, creating a simple or multilevel structure in category hierarchies. Depending on the hierarchy type, a category hierarchy contains procurement categories, sales categories, or other categories.

Linking products to product categories enables setting up a hierarchical structure of products. Depending on the requirements, set up multiple hierarchies in parallel and assign every item to a different category in each hierarchy.

In addition, you can enter a product category instead of an item number in purchase and sales order lines, simplifying the management of services and intangible items not tracked on stock.

3.3.1.1 Category Hierarchies

You may access category hierarchies in the list page *Product information management> Setup> Categories> Category hierarchies*. If you want to set up a new hierarchy, click the button *New/Category hierarchy* in the action pane and enter a name and a description for the new hierarchy. Dynamics AX then shows the category hierarchy detail form, where you may enter the categories of the new hierarchy.

For assigning a category hierarchy to a type, open the form *Product information management> Setup> Categories> Category hierarchy types*. You may assign one hierarchy to each *Category hierarchy type* – for purchasing applying the type "Procurement category hierarchy", and for sales the type "Sales category hierarchy". Depending on your requirements, choose the same or different hierarchies.

Purchasing-related detail data of categories included in the procurement category hierarchy (category hierarchy assigned to the hierarchy type "Procurement category hierarchy") are available in the *Procurement categories* form as described further down this section.

3.3.1.2 Product Categories

If you want to view the structure of an existing hierarchy, double-click the line of the particular hierarchy in the category hierarchy list page for accessing the category hierarchy detail form. Clicking the button *Edit* in the action pane then allows editing the structure.

In order to add a new category or a new category folder, select the parent node in the tree structure on the left and click the button *New category node* in the action pane (or do a right-hand click on the parent node). In the new category, you should at least enter the *Name, Code* and *Friendly name* (see Figure 3-10).

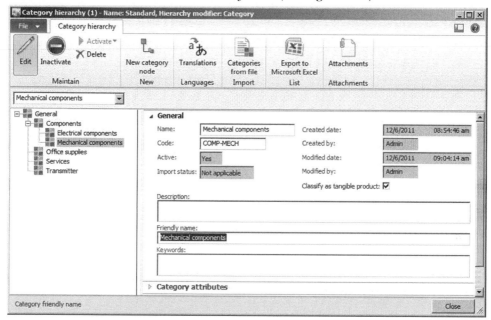

Figure 3-10:   Editing a product category in the category hierarchy detail form

3.3.1.3 Procurement Categories

Product categories belonging to the "Procurement category hierarchy" are available in the lines of purchase transactions, including purchase orders, purchase requisitions, and purchase agreements. When entering a line in these forms, optionally select a procurement category instead of a product number.

Purchasing-related settings for product categories are available in the procurement categories (*Procurement and sourcing> Setup> Categories> Procurement categories*), where the item sales tax group shows on the tab *Item sales tax groups*. Clicking the button *Edit category hierarchy* in the action pane strip of the procurement categories form provides an alternative access to the product category hierarchy assigned to purchasing.

As another prerequisite for using procurement categories in purchase transactions, the inventory posting setup (see section 8.4.2) has to include settings for the categories concerned (*Inventory and warehouse management> Setup> Posting> Posting,* tab *Purchase order*, option *Purchase expenditure for expense*).

3.3.2   Product Master Data for Purchasing

In order to support large enterprises with a multi-company structure, the data structure of product master data in Dynamics AX shows two levels:

> ➢ **Shared products** – Common to all companies
> ➢ **Released products** – Holding company-specific item data

The data structure of shared products applies to all implementations. But in a small enterprise with only one company, it is possible to access product management directly in the released product form. When creating a new released product there, Dynamics AX automatically generates a related shared product in the background.

3.3.2.1   Shared Products

The aim of shared product records is to link the products (items) of companies working in a common Dynamics AX database and partition. Apart from product number and name/description, shared products do not contain extensive information.

You may check existing products or create new products in the menu item *Product information management> Common> Products> All products and product masters*. The all products list page shows all items, including regular products, configurable products, and service items.

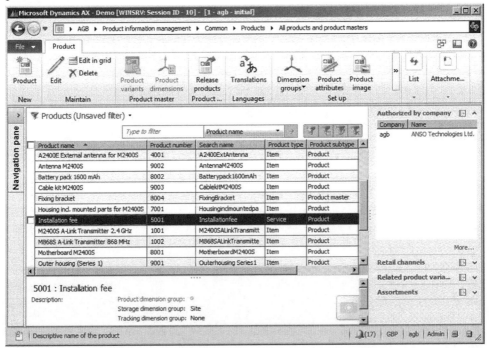

Figure 3-11:   Selecting an item in the all products list page

If you want to enter a new product, click the button *New/Product* in the action pane of the all products list page. In the *Create product* dialog, you want to enter following data:

➤ **Product type** – "Item" for stocked products, "Service" optional for services
➤ **Product subtype** – "Product" for regular items, "Product master" for configurable items with variants (see section 7.2.1)
➤ **Product number** – Manually, if no automatic number applies from the number sequence
➤ **Product name**
➤ **Search name**

Further fields in the dialog include the *Retail category*, applicable for retail business, and the checkbox *CW product* for catch weight products (see section 7.2.1).

In order to create a regular stocked item, choose the *Product type* "Item" and the *Product subtype* "Product". For intangible items like services, choose the *Product type* "Service". Alternatively, you can also choose the *Product type* "Item" for an intangible item if linking it to an item model group for non-inventoried items (see section 7.2.1) in the released product.

In addition to the fields in the create dialog, the shared product detail form contains optional settings – e.g. for linking the product to categories clicking the button *Set up/Product categories* in order to create hierarchical product structures.

Clicking the button *Dimension groups* in the action pane of the shared product form provides access to the assignment of inventory dimensions. Available inventory dimensions are divided into three dimension groups:

➤ **Product dimension group** – Only for the subtype "Product master"; specifying if the item is available in different configurations, sizes, colors, or styles
➤ **Storage dimension group** – Specifying if you track inventory of the item by site, warehouse, location, or pallet
➤ **Tracking dimension group** – Specifying if batch or serial numbers apply

You may leave dimension groups in the shared product empty. In this case, dimension groups not entered in the shared product have to be entered in the related released products. You may want to specify dimension groups in the released product, if different dimension settings are required at company level – for example if only one company in your enterprise applies pallet management.

3.3.2.2 Releasing a Product

Before you can actually register transactions for a new product, you have to release it by clicking the button *Release products* in the action pane of the shared product. The selected product then shows on the tab *Select products* in the release products dialog. After switching to the tab *Select companies* on the left pane of the dialog, put a checkmark in front of all companies which use the product and confirm the selection by clicking the button *OK*.

3.3.2.3 Managing Released Products

Released products (*Product information management> Common> Released products*),
also labeled "Item" in some areas of Dynamics AX, contain the item details. For
directly accessing a released product from the shared products, click the link *More*
in the FactBox *Authorized by company* and then apply the table reference (*View
details*) on the column *Item number* in the dialog.

After releasing a new product, you have to populate the following mandatory
fields in the released product from:

> **Item group** (tab *Manage costs*) – Linking main accounts for ledger integration
> **Item model group** (tab *General*) – Specifying item handling and inventory
>   valuation
> **Dimension groups** (button *Product/Dimension groups*) – If not specified on the
>   shared product

In addition, you should enter the *Item sales tax group* for purchasing on the tab
Purchase, and for sales on the tab *Sell*. Another important setting is the *Unit*
(inventory unit of measure, defaulting from inventory parameters) on the tab
Manage inventory. In the lookup field *Production type* on the tab *Engineer*, you
should select the option "None" if the item is only supplied through purchase
orders, but you can also purchase a BOM or formula item.

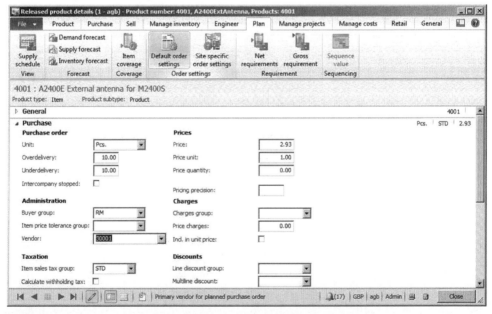

Figure 3-12:   Released order detail form, showing the action pane tab *Plan*

In the field *Price* on the tab *Manage costs*, enter a general cost price for the item as
applicable. The button *Item price* on the action pane tab *Manage costs* is provides the
option to enter a cost price per site as described in section 7.2.4.

If applicable (e.g. in a single-company implementation), optionally skip creating a shared product and immediately create a new product in the released products page by clicking the button *New/Product* on the action pane tab *Product*. If creating a released product this way, the *New released product* dialog creates a shared product in parallel.

3.3.2.4 Purchasing Related Data and Default Order Settings

The tab *Purchase* in the action pane of the released product form contains core purchasing information, including the item sales tax group already mentioned. The *Buyer group* there provides the option to specify purchasing responsibility for the item. Additional data required for purchasing the released product include purchase prices as well as item coverage and order settings.

The lookup field *Approved vendor check method* in AX 2012 R2, receiving its default from the corresponding field in the item model group, controls if the item may only be purchased from approved vendors. You may alternatively enforce approved vendors with a warning or an error message. For entering allowed vendors, click the button *Approved vendor/Setup* in the action pane tab *Purchase*.

Clicking the button *Default order settings* on the action pane tab *Plan* of the released product form provides access to the order settings for the product at company level. An important field in the default order setting form is the *Default order type* on the tab *General*. If the default order type is "Purchase order", the item is to be purchased from vendors (if no different settings apply from item coverage).

The tab *Purchase order* in the default order settings contains settings specific for purchasing – including defaults for lot size (field *Multiple*), order quantity (field *Standard order quantity*), and purchase site. Selecting the checkbox *Stopped* on this tab blocks the item to purchase transactions.

The second order settings button on the released product form – *Site specific order settings* – enables overriding the default order settings at site level (Sites represent subsidiaries within a company, see section 9.1.7). After creating a line with the particular site, register a default warehouse for purchasing, inventory transfer and sales as applicable. For overriding the default order settings for quantity defaults and lead time, select the checkbox *Override* in the site-specific order settings.

When entering an order, defaults like the order quantity from the order settings apply. You can override the defaults in the order line then (except item blocking).

3.3.2.5 Item Coverage

The primary setting for item coverage is the *Default order type* in the default order settings (see above). On the tab *Purchase* of the released product detail form, the field *Vendor* determines the main vendor for purchasing the item.

Coverage groups contain settings for requirements planning (see section 6.3.3). The basic default coverage group is specified in the master planning parameters

(*Master planning> Setup> Master planning parameters*, lookup field *General coverage group*). On the tab *Plan* of the released product detail form, optionally assign specific coverage groups to the particular items.

After clicking the button *Item coverage* on the action pane tab *Plan* in the released product form, further settings for the item – including a minimum and a maximum quantity – are available in the item coverage form. In addition, the item coverage contains a *Planned order type* (overriding the default order type) and a *Vendor account* (overriding the main vendor in the released product form). Depending on the dimension groups, coverage settings are required at inventory dimension level (e.g. per warehouse).

3.3.2.6   New in Dynamics AX 2012 and in AX 2012 R2

Dynamics AX 2012 introduces the concept of shared products and product masters containing basic item data common to all companies. The released product form replaces the item form, and the former single inventory dimension group splits to three separate dimension groups. The item type "BOM" is removed – default item replenishment is specified by the default order type now.

Compared with the initial version of Dynamics AX 2012, the R2 version contains additional settings in the product records like the *CW product*, the *Production type*, approved vendors and further settings for process industries and for retail.

3.3.3   Purchase Price and Discount

In Dynamics AX, the base functionality for pricing is the same in purchasing and in sales. Pricing includes a multi-stage calculation of prices and discounts, which starts at the base price in the released product form and continues with trade agreements for vendor groups and individual vendors.

Since sales uses discount calculation to a greater extent than purchasing in many companies, the section below focuses on price calculation. Details on discount calculation are available in section 4.3.2.

3.3.3.1   Purchase Base Price

The purchase base price shows in the field *Price* on the tab *Purchase* of the released product form. The *Price unit* specifies the quantity which is the basis for the price. A price unit "100" for example applies a price for hundred units (e.g. for inexpensive screws).

If you want to record different purchase base prices per subsidiary (site), click the button *Item price* on the action pane tab *Manage costs*. In the item price form, register and activate a price per site as shown in section 7.2.4 then (applying the *Price type* "Purchase price").

Purchase order lines apply the base price, if no trade agreement is applicable for the vendor and the item concerned. Since prices (and price charges) in the released product form are in the currency of your company, Dynamics AX converts the prices to the currency of the order if the order is in a foreign currency.

3.3.3.2 Price Charges

In order to record charges (like fees and freight), which are added to the base price, optionally enter *Price charges* on the tab *Purchase* of the released product form.

If the checkbox *Incl. in unit price* is cleared, the amount entered in the field *Price charges* adds to the total of an order line independent from the quantity. With this setting, purchasing for example 10 units of an item with a *Price* of GBP 3.00 and *Price charges* of GBP 1.00 gives a unit price in the purchase order line of GBP 3.00 and a line amount of GBP 31.00. The price charges do not show in a separate field on printed purchasing documents.

If the checkbox *Incl. in unit price* is selected, Dynamics AX adds the price charges to the unit price. In this case, the field *Price quantity* is the quantity basis for allocating the price charges to the unit price. With this setting, purchasing for example 10 units of an item with a *Price* of GBP 3.00, a *Price quantity* of 0.00 (or 1.00), and *Price charges* of GBP 1.00 gives a unit price in the purchase order line of GBP 4.00 and a line amount of GBP 40.00.

In addition to the general price charges in the released product form, site-specific price charges are available in the item price form (accessible by clicking the button *Item price* on the action pane tab *Manage costs* of the released product form).

When working with charges, do not confuse price charges specified in the item record (released product form) with charges transactions assigned to charges codes, which are managed in orders separately. Details on charges management in orders are available in section 4.4.5.

3.3.3.3 Trade Agreements for Purchase Prices

You may view the trade agreements for purchase prices of a particular product by clicking the button *View/Purchase prices* on the action pane tab *Purchase* of the released product form. Trade agreements, available for specifying detailed settings for prices and discounts, show following levels:

➤ **Period of validity** – From date and to date, depending on the procurement parameter *Date type* (on the tab *Prices*) referring to order entry or delivery date
➤ **Quantity** – From and to quantity
➤ **Unit of measure**
➤ **Currency**
➤ **Vendor dimension level** (column *Account code*) – Individual vendor, vendor group, or all vendors

In addition to the options listed above, trade agreements also include prices at inventory dimension level. You need this option if prices are different per site, or per warehouse, or depending on product dimensions like size or color. In order to control the dimension columns displayed in the purchase prices form, click the button *Inventory/Dimensions display* in this form. As a prerequisite for applying dimensions in pricing, the dimension group of the particular item has to include the selected dimensions in the price search (see section 7.2.2).

3.3.3.4 Search Priority

The price search in Dynamics AX runs from the most specific to the general agreement, in other words from vendor prices to vendor group prices and finally to general prices.

If the checkbox *Find next* in the right-most column of the trade agreements is selected, Dynamics AX searches for the lowest price in trade agreements – a lower group price overrides a higher vendor-specific price. You may stop this search by clearing the checkbox *Find next* in the appropriate trade agreements.

3.3.3.5 Registering New Trade Agreements

If you want to set up a new agreement for purchase prices, you have to register and post a journal in the form *Procurement and sourcing> Journals> Price/discount agreement journals*. As an alternative to the particular menu item, access price/discount agreement journals by clicking the button *Create trade agreements* on the action pane tab *Purchase* of the released product form.

Like all journals (compare inventory journals in section 7.4.2), price/discount agreement journals consist of a header and at least one line. The lookup field *Show* at the top of the price/discount agreement journal form enables to view only open journals or to include posted journals. In order to register a new journal, click the button *New* and select a journal name.

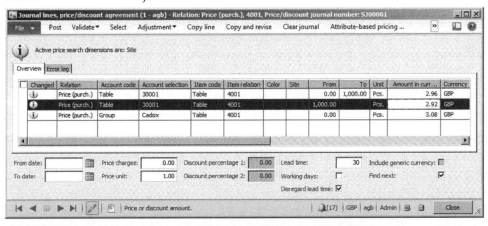

Figure 3-13:   Registering purchase prices in a price/discount journal

After clicking the button *Lines*, start inserting the first journal line. When recording a purchase price, make sure the option "Price (purch.)" is selected in the column *Relation*. The *Account code* specifies if the price is for a vendor ("Table"), for a vendor price group ("Group") or for all vendors. For prices, the column *Item code* has to show the option "Table" along with the product number in the *Item relation*.

In addition to the columns in the grid, fields for the validity dates, the price unit and the lead time are available at the bottom of the form. Price, price unit, and lead time of an applicable trade agreement override the defaults from the item record when entering an order line.

In order to view available inventory dimensions pricing, check the information text in the header part of the journal. In Figure 3-13, this header information tells that price agreements for the selected item may be entered at site level.

After entering the journal lines, click the button *Post* to activate the agreement. Other buttons available in the journal lines facilitate price management, providing the option to select and adjust existing agreements.

3.3.3.6 Updating or Deleting Existing Trade Agreements

If you want to edit or delete a purchase price agreement in Dynamics AX 2012 R2, open the trade agreements for example by clicking the button *View/Purchase prices* (or the button *Trade agreement/View trade agreements*) on the action pane tab *Purchase* of the released product form. After selecting the applicable trade agreement, click the button *Edit selected lines* in the action pane strip. Then choose the journal name, which applies to the new agreement journal used for updating, in the confirmation dialog and click the button *OK*.

The new price/discount agreement journal contains a line connected to the selected trade agreement, which you may edit before clicking the button *Post* to update the trade agreement. If you want to delete the existing trade agreement instead of updating, click the button *Select all agreements to be deleted* in the price/discount agreement journal and then post the journal.

3.3.3.7 Required Setup for Pricing

As a prerequisite for applying trade agreements, the appropriate price options in the price/discount setup (*Procurement and sourcing> Setup> Price/discount> Activate price/discount*) have to be selected.

If you want to enter prices at group level, you have to set up the required vendor price groups (*Procurement and sourcing> Setup> Price/discount> Vendor price/discount groups, Show* "Price group"). In the vendor detail form (*Procurement and sourcing> Common> Vendors> All vendors*), select the appropriate price group on the tab *Purchase order defaults*. When selecting a vendor in a purchase order, the vendor price group defaults the order. You can override the price group in the purchase order detail form then (*Procurement and sourcing> Common> Purchase orders> All purchase orders*, tab *Price and discount* in the header view).

3.3.3.8   New in Dynamics AX 2012 and in AX 2012 R2

In Dynamics AX 2012, you have to post price/discount agreement journals in order to update in trade agreement prices and discounts. In the trade agreement form itself, an additional column for the to-quantity is available.

Compared with the initial version of Dynamics AX 2012, where you can only edit existing trade agreements by choosing the *Select* option in price/discount agreement journals, the R2 version contains the additional button *Edit selected lines* in trade agreements for creating appropriate journals.

3.3.4   Case Study Exercises

Exercise 3.4 – Procurement Categories

Your company purchases a new kind of services, for which you want to set up appropriate product categories in the procurement hierarchy. Enter a new category node "##-services" containing the categories "##-assembling" and "##-fees" (## = your user ID). In addition, make sure the procurement categories receive the item sales tax group referring to the standard tax rate.

Exercise 3.5 – Product Record

In order to accomplish purchase order processing in the following exercises, you need to set up a new product. This first product is a trade item, later on we will continue with the more complex structures of BOM items.

Enter a new shared product with the product number I-## and the name "##-merchandise" (## = your user ID). It should be a regular stocked product without variants, serial or batch numbers. You want to track inventory per site and warehouse. Choose appropriate dimension groups in the shared product.

Then you want to release the product to your test company. In the released product, select an appropriate item group for merchandise and an item model group with FIFO-valuation. The item does not require approved vendors.

The item sales tax group for sales and for purchasing should refer to the standard tax rate. The unit of measure for the item is "Pieces" in all areas, and the main vendor is the vendor of exercise 3.2. The base purchase price and the base cost price are 50 pounds, the base sales price is 100 pounds.

In the *Default order settings* for purchasing and sales, you should enter the main site as well as default quantities (*Multiple* 20, *Min. order quantity* 40, *Standard order quantity* 100). In the *Site specific order settings*, you should enter the main warehouse of the main site for purchasing and sales.

Notes: If a *Balancing financial dimension* applies, enter a default value for this dimension on the tab *Financial dimensions* of the released product. If the number sequence for product numbers is set up for automatic numbering, you don't have to enter a product number.

Exercise 3.6 – Trade Agreement
You agree upon a lower price for the new item with your main vendor. Enter a trade agreement for the vendor of exercise 3.2, which specifies a purchase price of 45 pounds for the item of exercise 3.5. There is no minimum quantity and no end date for this price.

3.4   Purchase Orders

An order is a definite promise to deliver goods or services on agreed terms. Orders therefore have to include at least following details:

➤ Vendor with name and address
➤ Currency, Payment terms, Terms of delivery
➤ Product
➤ Quantity, Unit of measure
➤ Price
➤ Delivery date, Delivery address

When entering a purchase order, Dynamics AX monitors these requirements before you may post and print the purchase order.

3.4.1   Basics of Purchase Order Processing

For creating a new purchase order, either insert or generate it as follows:

➤ Automatically create a purchase order as a result of a purchase requisition workflow or of master scheduling
➤ Transfer a request for quotation, a planned order, or a purchase requisition to a purchase order
➤ Transfer a purchase journal to a purchase order
➤ Create a release order based on a purchase agreement (see section 3.4.9)
➤ Create a purchase order in a sales order (direct delivery, see section 4.7)
➤ Create a purchase order in a production order (Subcontracting, see section 5.7)

Other ways for creating purchase orders in Dynamics AX are automatic transfers – both through the AIF-framework from external applications, and through the intercompany functionality from affiliated companies within a common Dynamics AX database and partition.

Purchase order processing related to projects is part of the project module, described in the relevant online help and training documentation.

3.4.1.1   Possible Documents prior to Purchase Orders

Within procurement, there are three different documents, which you may process before creating a purchase order:

➤ Planned orders
➤ Purchase requisitions
➤ Requests for quotation

A request for quotation is required, if you want to obtain and compare quotes from several vendors in Dynamics AX. You may create requests for quotation either automatically in a planned order or a purchase requisition, or enter them manually.

When purchasing common items in daily business, usually skip the request for quotation and create a purchase order directly from a planned order or a purchase requisition.

Planned purchase orders are a result of master scheduling. Depending on master planning setup, master scheduling may skip planned orders and directly create purchase orders. You may find details on the appropriate setup in section 6.3.3.

3.4.1.2 Approving and Processing Purchase Orders

After creating and – if required – approving a purchase order, you want to process it from the start to the end as shown in Figure 3-14.

If change management applies to a purchase order, you have to submit the order for approval. Depending on the order and the approval workflow, approval may be granted automatically or involve manual authorization. If change management does not apply, the approval status of the order immediately shows *Approved*.

The first step in processing an approved purchase order then is to confirm the order. Confirming may include sending a hardcopy or electronic document to the vendor. Depending on the setup, optionally skip all subsequent steps of order processing except posting the vendor invoice.

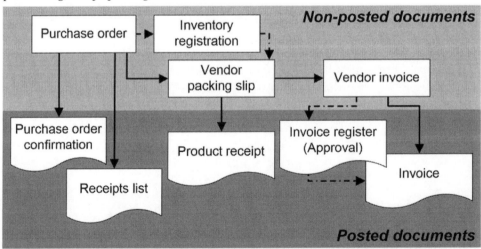

Figure 3-14:   Purchase order processing in Dynamics AX

3.4.1.3 Receipts List and Inventory Registration

If your warehouse requires a list of items for information purposes and for preparing item arrival, print a receipts list.

Unlike the receipts list, inventory registration as the next step actually updates the on-hand quantity in inventory. The inventory registration transaction, which contains all required inventory dimensions like warehouse, serial number and batch number, is an optional step before posting the product receipt. You may do this registration either by posting an item arrival journal in inventory, or through the registration form which is accessible by clicking the button *Update line/Registration* in the action pane strip of the purchase order line.

If the checkbox *Registration requirements* is selected in the item model group of the purchased product, you have to execute inventory registration before posting the product receipt.

3.4.1.4 Product Receipt

When posting a product receipt, Dynamics AX posts inventory transactions and – depending on the setup – general ledger transaction. You may access the product receipt posting form either from the related purchase order, or through the appropriate summary update in the procurement module, or from the posted item arrival journal in inventory.

3.4.1.5 Vendor Invoice

Once the invoice arrives, post it in the purchase order or in the pending vendor invoices. If applicable, you can't post the invoice before obtaining approval through a workflow.

Alternatively, record the vendor invoice in an invoice register and a subsequent invoice approval journal (see section 8.3.3).

3.4.1.6 Physical and Financial Transactions

The following sections contain more detailed explanations on purchase order processing. But when posting inventory transactions, be aware that there are two different kinds of transactions: Physical and financial transactions.

Generally speaking, physical transactions are packing slips (product receipts) and financial transactions are invoices. You have to distinguish between these transactions, in particular regarding inventory valuation and general ledger posting. Details on these topics are available in section 7.2.5.

3.4.2   Planned Purchase Orders

Planned purchase orders are based on the demand for a purchased item. The settings, whether item requirements calculation in master scheduling should include forecasts, available inventory on hand, sales quotes, sales orders, production orders, and purchase orders are available in the operations planning (master planning) setup.

The description below shows a simple procedure for generating planned orders in master scheduling. The item requirement in the example is triggered by a

minimum inventory quantity entered in the item coverage form, which exceeds the
quantity on hand.

3.4.2.1   Minimum Quantity

In order to enter a minimum inventory quantity for an item, open the item
coverage form by clicking the button *Item coverage* on action pane tab *Plan* in the
released product form (*Product information management> Common> Released products*)
after selecting the particular item.

Figure 3-15:   Entering a minimum inventory quantity in the item coverage form

In the item coverage, you can enter the minimum quantity in a new record.
Depending on the dimension groups of the item, the minimum quantity is to be
entered at dimension level, for example per site and warehouse.

3.4.2.2   Net Requirements and Master Scheduling

Item coverage settings and the item availability are displayed in the net
requirements form, accessible by clicking the button *Net requirements* on the action
pane tab *Plan* of the released product form.

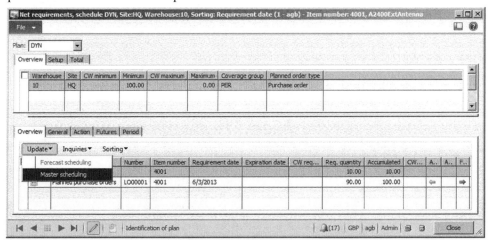

Figure 3-16:   Local master scheduling in the net requirements form

In the net requirements form, update master scheduling as required (see Figure
3-16). When updating the master schedule by clicking the button *Update/Master*

scheduling in the action pane strip of the lower pane in the net requirements form, Dynamics AX generates planned orders.

You can use multiple master plans in Dynamics AX, including a static master plan for current master scheduling and a separate dynamic master plan for simulation purposes (see section 6.3.1). When updating a master schedule, planned orders are only generated in the selected plan – the static, the dynamic, or any alternative master plan. If master planning parameters determine a two master plan strategy, the dynamic plan is the default for updating the master schedule in the net requirements form.

3.4.2.3 Planned Purchase Order

In order to access planned purchase orders generated in master scheduling, open the list page *Procurement and sourcing> Purchase orders> Planned purchase orders*. If the master planning setup includes a separate dynamic plan (two master plan strategy), choose the dynamic plan in the lookup field *Plan* above the grid in the planned order list page.

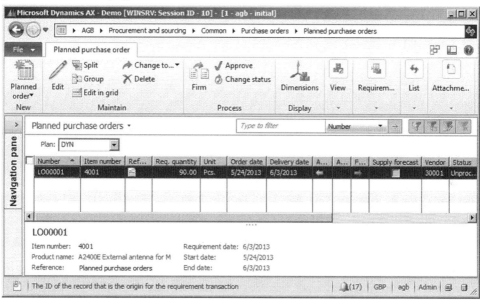

Figure 3-17: Processing a planned purchase order

After selecting the planned order concerned, modify it in the planned order detail form as necessary. If you want to know the origin of a requirement, check the tab *Pegging* on the detail form.

The field *Vendor* on the tab *Planned supply* shows the suggested vendor for the item, derived from the main vendor in the item record, from a trade agreement, or from item coverage. If there is no default for the vendor, you have to assign a vendor manually before you can transfer the planned order to an actual purchase order.

3.4.2.4 Creating a Purchase Order

Once you have finished updating planned orders, you can transfer them to purchase orders. Clicking the button *Process/Firm* in the action pane of the planned orders, Dynamics AX generates purchase orders for one or more planned orders.

As an alternative to directly creating purchase orders, change a planned purchase order to a request for quotation by clicking the button *Maintain/Change to…/Request for quotation* in the action pane (see section 3.4.4).

3.4.3   Purchase Requisitions

A purchase requisition is an internal document, asking the purchase department to buy requested goods or services. Unlike a planned order, which is created automatically because of an item requirement, a purchase requisition has to be entered manually by the person, who needs the item.

3.4.3.1 Prerequisites for Processing Purchase Requisitions

Before a purchase requisition is transferred to a purchase order, it has to run through an approval process. This approval process is based on the workflow system (see section 9.4).

In order to configure the purchase requisition workflow, you have to access the form *Procurement and Sourcing> Setup> Procurement and sourcing workflows*. When configuring a workflow for purchase requisitions, you want to choose the template "Purchase requisition review" (refers to the *Type* "PurchReqReview") or the template "Purchase requisition line review" (refers to "PurchReqLineReview").

As a prerequisite for specifying the items available for purchase requisitions, you have to set up and activate a procurement catalog (*Procurement and Sourcing> Common> Catalogs> Procurement catalog*) containing applicable categories and products. In the purchasing policies (*Procurement and Sourcing> Setup> Policies> Purchasing policies*), you want to make sure this catalog is selected in the policy rule *Catalog policy rule* of the policy applying to your organization.

3.4.3.2 Entering a Purchase Requisition

You may enter purchase requisitions both in the regular Dynamics AX Windows client and in the Enterprise Portal, which is the web access for occasional users.

If choosing the Dynamics AX Windows client, access the list page *Procurement and Sourcing> Common> Purchase Requisitions> All purchase requisitions*. When clicking the button *New/Purchase requisition* in the action pane, Dynamics AX shows a create dialog where you may enter a name for the requisition.

Depending on purchasing policy settings, optionally request a line on behalf of a different person or organization by selecting an appropriate *Requester, Buying legal entity*, or *Receiving operating unit* in the purchase requisition lines.

The way for entering requisition lines depends on the type of the particular item:

> ➤ **Internal catalog products** – Regular released products, linked to the current procurement catalog, may be selected in the *Item number* column.
> ➤ **Non-catalog products** – Services and new products may be registered entering a *Procurement category* and a *Product name* (description).
> ➤ **External catalog products** – Creating these requisition lines is only possible in the Enterprise Portal, navigating to an external vendor website.

Apart from entering lines directly on the tab *Purchase requisition lines* by choosing an item number or procurement category, alternatively click the button *Add items* in the action pane strip on this tab for opening the *Add items* form.

In the *Add items* form, click the button *Select* in the lower pane after selecting items on the upper tabs *Catalog items* and *Non-catalog items*. Clicking the button *OK* at the bottom of the form then transfers the items to the requisition lines.

3.4.3.3 Approval Workflow

As long as you are working on entering a purchase requisition, it shows the *Status* "Draft". Once you have finished and the purchase requisition is complete, click the button *Submit* in the in the yellow workflow message bar in order to start the requisition workflow. The requisition status switches to "In review" and the workflow system starts processing the submitted requisition in a batch process.

The further proceeding for approval depends on the workflow configuration of the purchase requisition workflow. Section 9.4 in this book contains a brief description of configuring and processing workflows.

As long as a purchase requisition shows the status "In review", you can create a related request for quotation by clicking the button *Create request for quotation* in the action pane tab of the purchase requisition.

3.4.3.4 Creating a Purchase Order

Once a purchase requisition is approved, it shows the *status* "Approved" and may be released for generating a purchase order.

In the purchasing policies (*Procurement and Sourcing> Setup> Policies> Purchasing policies*), there is the policy rule *Purchase order creation and demand consolidation*. This policy rule of the policy applying to your organization determines, if purchase orders are generated automatically or if they have to be released manually.

If manual releasing is necessary, click the button *New/Purchase order* in the action pane of the list page *Procurement and sourcing> Common> Purchase requisitions> Release approved purchase requisitions* for releasing a requisition to a purchase order.

3.4.3.5 New in Dynamics AX 2012

In Dynamics AX 2012, purchasing policies and organization hierarchies are new features applying to purchase requisitions.

3.4.4   Requests for Quotation

A request for quotation (RFQ) is an external document asking vendors to submit a quotation. In Dynamics AX, a single request for quotation may apply to multiple vendors. Once a quotation from a vendor arrives, register it in a "request for quotation reply" in order to prepare a comparison of quotes. If accepting a quote, transfer it to an order.

For creating a request for quotation, enter it manually in the request for quotations form or generate it from planned purchase orders and purchase requisitions.

3.4.4.1   Entering a Request for Quotation

In order to create a new request for quotations, click the button *New/Request for quotation* in the form *Procurement and sourcing> Common> Requests for quotations> All requests for quotations*. In the create dialog, choose the *Purchase type* "Purchase order" for a request referring to a regular purchase order. After entering the delivery and the expiration date, close the dialog clicking the button *OK*.

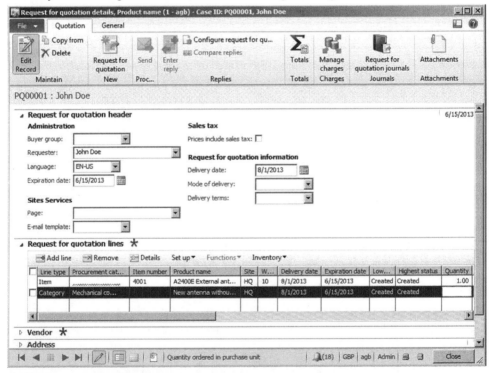

Figure 3-18:   Entering lines in the request for quotation form

Requests for quotation consist of a header part containing general data like delivery date and quotation deadline (*Expiration date*), and a lines part containing items and quantities. Both, the header and the lines, contain the fields *Lowest status* and *Highest status* showing the status ("Created", "Sent", "Accepted," or "Rejected") of the request and related quotations.

Like in the lines of purchase requisitions or purchase orders, a line in the request for quotation either refers to an item number or to a procurement category. In the request for quotation form, the column *Line type* controls whether an item or a procurement category applies. Data like delivery date and address in the lines retrieve appropriate defaults from the header. Applying document management (see section 9.5.1) allows adding details like data sheets or drawings to the request header or lines.

In order to specify the vendors receiving the request for quotation, switch to the tab *Vendor* and insert a new line for each vendor.

3.4.4.2 Sending the Request to Vendors

After registering the vendors concerned, click the button *Send* in the action pane to open the posting form for processing the request. When clicking the button *Print* in the action pane strip of the posting form, optionally select the checkbox *Print request for quotation*. Then click the button *OK* in the posting form for posting and printing the request.

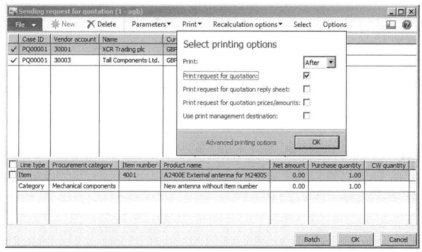

Figure 3-19: Printing a request for quotation

If you later want to know to which vendor you have sent the request for quotation, click the button *Journals/Request for quotation journals* in the request for quotation form for viewing the posted requests.

3.4.4.3 Request for Quotation Reply

In the action pane of the request for quotation form, click the button *Replies/Configure request for quotation reply* for specifying the fields to be included in a reply. These fields show on the request for quotation reply sheet, which you may print by selecting the appropriate checkbox in the printing options dialog when sending the request for quotation. The default for the reply field settings derives from the procurement parameters (*Procurement and sourcing> Setup> Procurement and sourcing parameters*, button *Default request for quotation reply fields* on the tab *Request for quotation*).

Once a vendor replies to a request by sending a quotation, register the quotation (reply) in the form *Procurement and sourcing> Common> Requests for quotations> Request for quotation replies*. Alternatively, access the replies by clicking the button *Replies/Enter reply* in the action pane of the request for quotation form, making sure to edit the reply of the right vendor in the reply form then.

In the reply form, enter details of the vendor quote on the tab *Purchase quotation lines* for the lines and on the tab *Quotation* for the header. In order to support data input, optionally click the button *Process/Copy data to reply* for copying data from the request into the reply fields.

Once you have finished entering the reply, the highest/lowest status of the request and the reply show the status "Received".

3.4.4.4   Approving and Rejecting Vendor Quotations

If you want to compare the different replies (quotes) from your vendors, click the button *Replies/Compare replies* in the action pane of the request for quotation form opening the *Compare request for quotation replies* form.

In the compare form, accept a quotation by selecting the checkbox in the column *Mark* of the reply and clicking the button *Accept* in the action pane. Alternatively, accept a quotation in the request reply form by clicking the button *Accept* there.

When posting the acceptance, Dynamics AX automatically creates a purchase order. If accepting all lines of a request in a reply, Dynamics AX suggests rejecting the other replies for the request. Alternatively reject a request by clicking the button *Process/Reject* in the reply.

3.4.5   Purchase Order Registration

Like all documents, purchase orders consist of a header and one or several lines. The header contains data, which are common to the whole order – e.g. the order number, vendor, language, currency, and payment terms. Other fields in the order header like the delivery date provide a default value for the order lines, where you can change them at line level.

The default for the *Purchase type* in the purchase order header derives from the procurement parameters (*Procurement and sourcing> Setup> Procurement and sourcing parameters*), usually showing the type "Purchase order" for creating regular purchase orders. You may choose any of the following options for the purchase type in the purchase order then:

➢ **Purchase order** – Regular purchase order
➢ **Journal** – Draft or template, not affecting inventory or finance
➢ **Returned order** – Credit note, see section 3.7

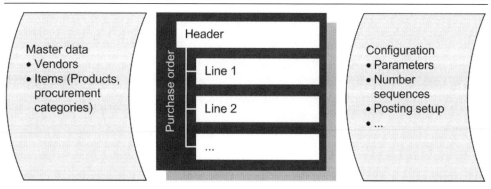

Figure 3-20:   Structure of purchase orders

Order lines contain data like item number or procurement category, description, quantity, price, discount, and delivery date. When ordering a stocked product, you have to select the item number of the released product. For non-inventoried items (e.g. services), either enter the item number of an intangible item or skip the item number and enter a procurement category.

3.4.5.1   Defaults for Purchase Orders

When inserting a new purchase order header or line, Dynamics AX retrieves defaults for numerous fields after selecting the vendor in the header or the item in a line. Depending on your permissions, change the content of fields in the purchase order subsequently.

If you agree with your vendor for example on different payment terms for a particular order, change the terms of payment in the order header. If the new payment terms apply to all future orders, you should also change the terms of payment in the vendor record for receiving the right default when entering the next order for this vendor.

3.4.5.2   Entering a New Purchase Order

Depending on how you want to proceed, there are two different ways for accessing purchase orders:

➢ **Vendor form** – Preferable, if first searching the vendor when accessing orders
➢ **Purchase order form** – Preferable, if the vendor is not the primary search key (e.g. if looking for all orders not yet approved)

When starting in the vendor list page (*Procurement and sourcing> Common> Vendors> All vendors*) or the related detail form, immediately create a new order after selecting a vendor by clicking the button *New/Purchase order* on the action pane tab *Procurement*. Dynamics AX creates a purchase order header applying defaults from the selected vendor and switches to the line view in the purchase order detail form, where you can enter the first order line.

If you are in the vendor list page and want to check existing purchase orders for a vendor, click the button *Related information/Purchase orders/All purchase orders* on the action pane tab *Procurement* of the vendor form. After clicking this button, Dynamics AX shows the purchase order list page filtered on the selected vendor.

When accessing the purchase order list page through the menu item *Procurement and sourcing> Common> Purchase orders> All purchase orders*, it shows the list of all purchase orders. If you want to view the details of a purchase order displayed in the list page, double-click the line concerned or click the button *Edit* on the action pane tab *Purchase order* for accessing the detail form.

If you want to register a new purchase order in the purchase order list page, push the shortcut key *Ctrl+N* or click the button *New/Purchase order* on the action pane tab *Purchase order*. In the *Create purchase order* dialog, you want to choose a vendor in the vendor lookup then (e.g. applying a *Filter by field* with a right-hand click in the column *Name* of the lookup).

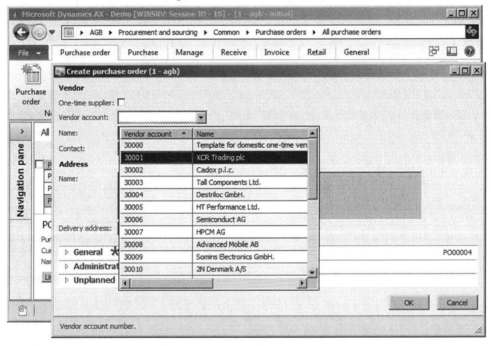

Figure 3-21:   Creating a new order in the purchase order list page

After selecting a vendor number, the create order dialog retrieves various defaults from the vendor record. Expanding the tabs *General* and *Administration* in the create order dialog provides access to additional fields of the new order header. If you want to change data like the vendor number, purchase type or currency, edit the appropriate fields in the dialog or – after closing the dialog – in the header view of the purchase order detail form.

After clicking the button *OK* in the *Create purchase order* dialog, Dynamics AX creates the purchase order header and switches to the purchase order detail form showing the line view.

3.4.5.3 Purchase Order Lines

In order to register an order line in the line view of the purchase order detail form, simply click the first line in the lines pane or click the button [Add line] in the action pane strip of the *Purchase order lines* tab and start selecting an item number (released product) or a purchase category. Item master data provide various defaults for fields like quantity, purchase unit, unit price, site or warehouse. If site and warehouse are entered in the order header, they take priority over the defaults from the item record.

Trade agreements may override the unit price from the released product, and provide a default for the discount fields (see section 4.3.2). The net amount of a line is calculated based on quantity, unit price, and discounts. If manually entering a net amount, Dynamics AX shows an empty unit price and discount.

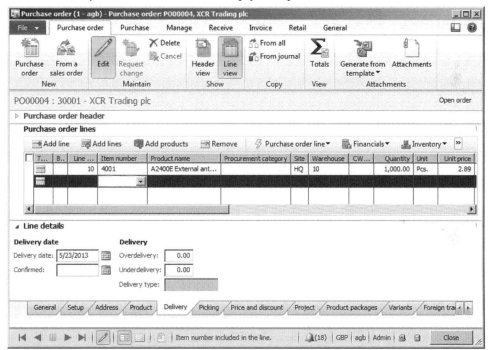

Figure 3-22:   Registering a purchase order line

The default for the *Line number* displays when saving the order line. The increment applicable for line numbering is specified in the system parameters (*System administration> Setup> System parameters*).

For viewing the delivery date and other extended line data, expand the fast tab *Line details* and switch to the appropriate sub-tab.

The delivery date available on the sub-tab *Delivery* receives the default value from the purchase order header, if this date is after the lead time of the item. Otherwise, the default for the delivery date of the line is the lead time added to the session date. You may specify the lead time for an item in the default or site-specific order settings of the item, in the purchase price trade agreements and in the item coverage form.

3.4.5.4   Intangible Items and Procurement Categories

If you want to order an intangible item (e.g. a particular service), select the item number of a non-inventoried product (item with product type "Service", or linked to an item model group for non-stocked items – see section 7.2.1) and enter the order line like you do for regular inventoried items.

As an alternative, skip the item number field in the order line and select a procurement category. The procurement category does not include as many details as the item record, however. Therefore you have to manually enter data including quantity, unit, unit price, line text (on the sub-tab *General*) and other details as applicable.

3.4.5.5   Inventory Transaction

When entering a line for an inventoried product in a regular purchase order, Dynamics AX creates a related inventory transaction. You can view this transaction by clicking the button *Inventory/Transactions* in the action pane strip of the order line. The transaction shows the receipt status "Ordered", and the fields *Physical date* and *Financial date* are empty. In the course of purchase order processing, posting the product receipt and the vendor invoice update the inventory transaction as shown in section 7.2.5.

3.4.5.6   Header View and Line View

When accessing the purchase order detail form, it shows in line view. In the upper part of the form, a header line between the action pane and the first tab displays the order number and the vendor on the left-hand side, and the order status on the right-hand side. After expanding the tab *Purchase order header* in the line view, it shows selected header fields like the delivery date.

If you want to access the complete header information, click the button *Header view* on the action pane tab *Purchase order* of the detail form. The header view enables editing data, which are common to the whole order – e.g. the vendor number, the sales tax group, or the payment terms. In addition, the order header contains other fields like the delivery date, which are only default values for the order lines. If you change header data after entering order lines, the procurement parameters (button *Update order lines* on the tab *Updates*) control whether to update existing order lines automatically.

In order to switch back from the header view to the line view, click the button *Line view* on the action pane tab *Purchase order*.

3.4.5.7 Delivery Address

You may select the delivery address for a purchase order on the tab *Address* in the purchase order header view. The default for this delivery address is your company address as specified on the tab *Addresses* in the legal entities form (*Organization administration> Setup> Organization> Legal entities*). If a delivery address is specified for a site or warehouse entered in the order header, the purchase order retrieves the site or warehouse address.

If you want to change the delivery address of a purchase order, choose between two options:

> **Select an existing address**, already available in the global address book
> **Insert a new address**

If you want to choose an existing address (e.g. a customer address), click the button ⊞ near the *Delivery address* lookup field on the *Address* tab. The address selection dialog enables selecting an address from all areas of the global address book.

If you want to enter a completely new address, click the button ⊞ near the *Delivery address* lookup field. In the *New address* dialog, enter the address for delivery (similar to entering a vendor address, see section 3.2.1). In the lookup field *Purpose*, select a purpose "Other" or "Alternative delivery" ("Delivery" if the address is the new main delivery address for your company), and additionally select the checkbox *One-Time* if applicable.

If different delivery addresses are required at line level, access the sub-tab *Address* on the *Line details* tab in the purchase order line view. In the lines, choose existing addresses or create new addresses (like in the header).

3.4.5.8 Charges

You may register additional costs like freight and insurance by entering charges at order header level or at line level. The functionality of charges in purchasing corresponds to charges in sales (see section 4.4.5).

In order to access charges referring to an order header, click the button *Charges/Maintain charges* on the action pane tab *Purchase*. For accessing line charges, click the button *Financials/Maintain charges* in the action pane strip of the tab *Purchase order lines* after selecting the line concerned.

3.4.5.9 Input Tax

Input tax (Sales tax/VAT) calculation is based on the relation of vendor and item:

> The vendor record contains the *Sales tax group* (VAT group) distinguishing between domestic and foreign vendors. For companies in the European Union, "EU vendors" usually is a third category.

➢ The item record contains the *Item sales tax group* (item VAT group) distinguishing between items with a regular tax rate and other items, for which a reduced rate applies (in many countries for example food).

Purchase order header and lines retrieve the tax groups from the vendor and the item. Based on these groups and related settings, the applicable tax is calculated automatically. You may edit the *Sales tax group* on the tab *Setup* in the header view. It is copied to the lines, where you may access the *Sales tax group* and the *Item sales tax group* in the line view on the sub-tab *Setup* of the *Line details* tab.

In order to view the calculated sales tax in the purchase order form, click the button *Tax/Sales tax* on the action pane tab *Purchase*.

3.4.5.10 Copying a Purchase Order

As an alternative to manually entering a new purchase order, copy an existing order. Since this existing order may include a different purchase type, there is the option to copy for example a journal into an order.

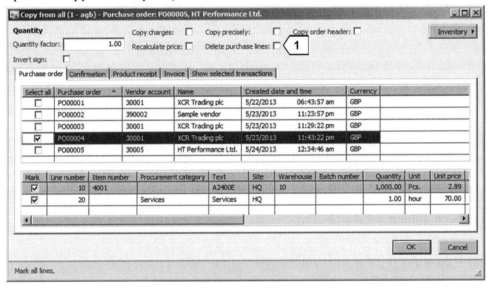

Figure 3-23: Selecting records in the *Copy from all* dialog

If you want to copy an order to a new purchase order, start with inserting a new order header which should receive the copied records. In the new order, click the button *Copy/Copy from all* on the action pane tab *Purchase order* for accessing the *Copy from all* dialog. In this dialog, which displays a list of orders available for copying, select the checkbox in the left-most column to mark the records to be copied as shown in Figure 3-23 – entire orders in the upper part or individual order lines in the lower part.

When copying an order, observe the checkbox *Delete purchases lines* [1]. If this checkbox is selected, all lines of the new order are deleted before inserting the lines selected for copying. Whereas this does not matter for a new order, it may be undesirable if you want to copy additional lines to an existing order.

Once you have finished selecting order headers and lines (lines may refer to different headers), close the copy dialog by clicking the button *OK*. Dynamics AX copies the selected lines, depending on the checkbox *Copy order header* including header data like payment terms (if copying header data, select only one header).

In addition to the *Copy from all* button, there is another button available for copying in the purchase order form – the button *Copy/Copy from journal*. You may apply this button if there is a purchase order with posted documents like vendor invoices, and you want to transfer the posted lines into the order again.

In addition to the copy buttons in the action pane, copy feature are also available as an option in the button *Purchase order line* of the action pane strip in the order lines.

3.4.5.11 Order Type Journal

Purchase orders of the order type "Journal" serve as draft or template. It is not possible to post documents like an order confirmation or a product receipt for this purchase type. Apart from copying a purchase journal to a regular purchase order, transferring a journal to a purchase order is also possible by simply changing the purchase type in the order header, or through the periodic activity *Procurement and sourcing> Periodic> Post the purchase journal*.

3.4.5.12 New in Dynamics AX 2012

Due to the new user interface including header and line view, purchase order management looks fundamentally different in Dynamics AX 2012. In addition, there are new features like procurement categories, delivery schedules and other improvements like the line numbers. The overview of posted line quantities is now available clicking the button *Line quantity* on the action pane tab *General*.

3.4.6 Change Management and Purchase Order Approval

Depending on the setting for change management, you have to run through an approval workflow after entering a purchase order before you can process it.

3.4.6.1 Change Management Settings

The primary setting for purchase order change management is available in the procurement parameters (*Procurement and sourcing> Setup> Procurement and sourcing parameters*, tab *General*). Selecting the checkbox *Activate change management* there activates approval workflows in all purchase orders.

If the checkbox *Allow override of settings per vendor* in the procurement parameters is selected, enter deviating settings for specific vendors as applicable. Selecting the checkbox *Override settings* in the vendor detail form (field group *Change management for purchase orders* on the tab *Purchase order defaults*) then enables overriding the general setting in both directions: Activating change management only for specific vendors while approval is not required in general, or the other way around.

The purchase order approval process is based on the workflow system (see section 9.4). Procurement workflows are available in the form *Procurement and Sourcing> Setup> Procurement and sourcing workflows*, where purchase order workflows refer to the template "Purchase order workflow" (*Type* "PurchTableTemplate") or the template "Purchase order line workflow" (*Type* "PurchLineTemplate").

3.4.6.2 Approval Status

The purchase order header contains the *Approval status*, displayed in a separate column in the purchase order list page. Depending on the approval workflow, a purchase order may show the following approval status:

➢ **Draft** – When registering the order, before submitting approval
➢ **In review** – While the approval workflow is executed
➢ **Approved** – After approval, making it possible to post a confirmation
➢ **Confirmed** – After posting the order confirmation, optionally sending a hardcopy or an electronic document to the vendor

If change management does not apply to a purchase order, the order immediately shows the approval status "Approved" and you may continue order processing by confirming the order.

3.4.6.3 Approval Workflow for Purchase Orders

If change management applies to a purchase order, a yellow workflow message bar displays above the grid providing the option to submit the order for approval. You have to submit for approval after entering a new order, or after modifying an order which has already been approved.

When submitting for approval, the approval status switches to "In review" and the workflow system starts processing the approval workflow in a batch process. Because of this batch process, it is not possible to post the order confirmation immediately for purchase orders applying change management. Even in case of workflow configurations applying automatic approval you have to wait until the workflow system has finished the batch process.

If manual approval applies, the responsible may grant approval to the purchase order in the work items assigned to him or his queues (see section 9.4.3).

3.4.6.4 Request Change

If you want to change a purchase order after approval, click the button *Maintain/ Request change* on the action pane tab *Purchase order*. After finishing the required changes on the purchase order, you have to submit the order for approval again.

When deciding on approving the modified order, the responsible may compare the current purchase order with the last confirmed version by clicking the button

History/Compare purchase order versions on the action pane tab *Manage* of the purchase order form. Clicking the button *History/View purchase order versions* you may view and compare all previous versions.

3.4.6.5 New in Dynamics AX 2012

Change management and purchase order approval workflows are new features in Dynamics AX 2012.

3.4.7   Canceling and Deleting Purchase Orders

In Dynamics AX, there is a difference between canceling and deleting a purchase order. Whereas canceling removes the remaining quantity available for product receipt, deleting completely eliminates an order line or the entire order.

In addition, deleting an order is not possible after posting the order confirmation or – if change management applies – after approval, whereas you may always cancel the order.

3.4.7.1 Canceling an Order or Order Line

You should cancel a purchase order line, if you want to keep the original order quantity while not expecting any further deliveries for the line.

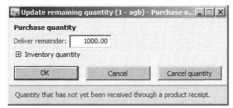

Figure 3-24:   The dialog box to change or cancel a remaining line quantity

In order to cancel a purchase order line or to change the open line quantity, click the button *Update line/Deliver remainder* in the action pane strip of the purchase order lines after selecting the line concerned. Dynamics AX then shows the dialog *Update remaining quantity*, where you may change or cancel the remaining quantity for deliveries. If you want to cancel the deliver remainder, click the button *Cancel quantity* in the dialog setting the deliver remainder to zero.

Clicking the button *OK* in the dialog adjusts the deliver remainder in the order line. You may cancel the remaining quantity of an order line no matter if there have been partial deliveries before.

If you want to cancel all lines of an order, cancel the order lines separately one after each other. If the purchase order confirmation has been posted already, alternatively cancel the complete order by clicking the button *Cancel* on the action pane tab *Purchase order* of the order form. After canceling all lines, the *Status* of the order shows "Canceled".

3.4.7.2 Deleting Purchase Orders and Order Lines

Unlike canceling, which reduces the open quantity of an order line, deleting a purchase order line completely removes it from Dynamics AX. In order to delete a purchase order line, select the record and click the button *Remove* in the action pane strip of the order lines, or push the shortcut key *Alt+F9*.

If you want to delete a complete order, click the button *Delete* in the action pane at the top of the detail form or – after selecting the order header – push the shortcut key *Alt+F9*.

Once you have posted the order confirmation or submitted approval, it is not possible to completely delete the order. If you want to delete order lines of an approved order to which change management applies, you have to request a change (button *Maintain/Request change*, see section 3.4.6).

<u>Note</u>: If you want to delete an order line, make sure to click the *Remove* button in the action pane strip – not the button *Delete*, which deletes the complete order.

3.4.7.3 New in Dynamics AX 2012

In Dynamics AX 2012, deleting a purchase order is not possible once processing has started (approval or confirmation).

3.4.8 Purchase Order Confirmation and Printing

Once entering and – if required – approving a purchase order is finished, you have to confirm it before you can continue order processing. Optionally, send the confirmation to the vendor.

Confirming a purchase order means to save it unchanging and separate from the current purchase order. The confirmation is evidence of the document which has been sent to the vendor. It does not create physical or financial transactions.

3.4.8.1 Posting Form for Purchase Order Confirmations

In order to confirm the purchase order, click the button *Generate/Purchase order* on the action pane tab *Purchase* of the purchase order form after selecting the particular order. Alternatively, click the button *Generate/Confirm* which executes the same functionality without showing the posting form.

When generating the purchase order confirmation, the posting form shows following options:

➢ **Parameters / Quantity** – „Ordered quantity" is the only option, posting the total quantity of all lines; in posting forms for other transactions like the receipts list described later, additional options are available

➢ **Parameters / Posting** – If selected, the order confirmation is posted; if cleared, the output is a pro forma document

➢ **Print options / Print** – When selecting several orders for summary update, the option "Current" prints documents individually while posting, whereas "After" prints after the last document has been posted

➢ **Print options / Print purchase order** – If selected, the order is printed; otherwise posting is without printing (reprinting is possible nevertheless)

➢ **Print options / Use print management destination** – If selected, print settings specified in the setup form *Procurement and sourcing> Setup> Forms> Form setup* (button *Print management*) or in the vendor form (button *Set up/Print management* on the action pane tab *General*) apply; otherwise, print settings accessible by clicking the button *Printer setup* in the posting form apply

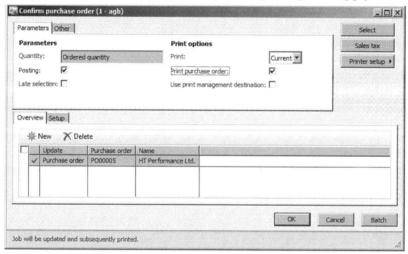

Figure 3-25: Selecting to print in the purchase order confirmation form

In order to finally execute posting the confirmation, click the button *OK* in the posting form. If the checkbox for printing in the posting form is selected, Dynamics AX prints to a printer or file depending on the printer selection.

3.4.8.2 Pro Forma Document

If the checkbox *Posting* in the posting form is cleared, Dynamics AX generates a pro forma document. A pro forma document, which may be required for purposes like customs declaration, is not a posted document. Therefore it is not possible to reprint or display the document independent from the purchase order once printing is finished.

You may alternatively print a pro forma document by clicking the button *Generate/ Pro forma purchase order* on the action pane tab *Purchase* of the purchase order form. In the posting form for pro forma documents, the checkbox *Posting* is not available.

3.4.8.3 Summary Update

Apart from posting by clicking the appropriate button in the order form, alternatively choose the periodic activity for summary update in order to post an order confirmation.

The summary order confirmation is available in the menu path *Procurement and sourcing> Periodic> Purchase orders> Confirm purchase orders*, showing the same posting form as the button in the purchase order. Whereas a filter selecting the current order automatically applies when accessing the posting form from a purchase order, the summary update requires manually entering a filter. You may do this by clicking the button *Select* in the posting form, which opens the advanced filter form for selecting purchase orders.

After closing the filter form, the selected orders show on the tab *Overview* of the posting form. If you do not want to post a particular order listed there, simply delete the appropriate line before posting by clicking the button *OK*.

3.4.8.4 Purchase Order Confirmation Inquiry

After confirming a purchase order, the posted document is available independent from modifications to the current order. For accessing the purchase order confirmation inquiry, choose the menu item *Procurement and sourcing> Inquiries> Journals> Purchase order confirmations* or click the button *Journals/Purchase order confirmations* on the action pane tab *Purchase* of the purchase order form.

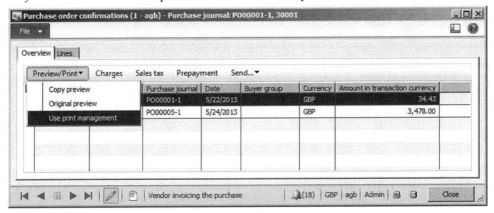

Figure 3-26:   Selecting to reprint in the purchase order inquiry form

The order confirmation inquiry form shows all purchase order confirmations on the tab *Overview*. The tab *Lines* displays the order lines of the order confirmation selected on the tab *Overview*.

3.4.8.5 Reprinting a Purchase Order

For displaying a print preview of the posted order confirmation, click the button *Preview/Print/Copy preview* or *Preview/Print/Original preview* in the inquiry form. The preview form then enables reprinting the document.

In order to print one or more posted order confirmations, alternatively click the button *Preview/Print/Use print management* printing to the printer specified in print management.

3.4.8.6 New in Dynamics AX 2012

In Dynamics AX 2012, posting the purchase order (now called "confirming") is compulsory.

3.4.9 Purchase Agreements

Purchase agreements in Dynamics AX provide the option to register and control blanket orders. Apart from purchase agreements at the level of product number and quantity, there are agreements not specifying the quantity, but only the value of a particular product, or agreements not referring to product numbers but to product categories.

3.4.9.1 Managing Purchase Agreements

For creating a purchase agreement, open the form *Procurement and sourcing> Common> Purchase orders> Purchase agreements* and click the button *New/Purchase agreement* in the action pane. When entering an agreement, you have to select a *Purchase agreement classification*. Agreement classifications (*Procurement and sourcing> Setup> Purchase agreements> Purchase agreement classification*) are for grouping and reporting purposes only, not controlling specific functionality.

The *Effective date* (start date of the contract) and the *Expiration date* (end date) in the agreement header serve as default for the agreement lines. Selecting the *Default commitment* in the header determines the level of the agreement:

➢ **Product quantity commitment** – Product number and quantity
➢ **Product value commitment** – Product number and value
➢ **Product category value commitment** – Value of a product category
➢ **Value commitment** – Total value for a vendor

After switching to the agreement lines by clicking the button *Line view* in the action pane, register line details including *Item number, Quantity, Unit price,* and *Discount percent* (or *Net amount* and *Procurement category*, depending on the option selected in the header field *Default commitment*). If you want to prevent, that the total quantity of related release order lines exceeds the quantity in the agreement, select the checkbox *Max is enforced* on the sub-tab *General* of the *Line details* tab.

Once you have finished entering the agreement lines, print the agreement by clicking the button *Generate/Confirmation* in the action pane. In the posting form for the agreement confirmation, select the checkbox *Print report* for actually printing the confirmation and optionally select the checkbox *Mark agreement as effective* for setting the *Status* in the agreement header to "Effective". If the agreement is not set as effective with the confirmation, you have to manually change the *Status* in the agreement header from "On hold" to "Effective" before you can generate a release order.

3.4.9.2 Release Orders

If you want to create a release order in the agreement form, click the button *New/Release order* after selecting the purchase agreement. Dynamics AX shows the *Create release order* form, where you may select items by entering the *Purchase quantity* and the *Delivery date* for the release order. Clicking the button *Create* creates the new release order, which is a regular purchase order of the type "Purchase order".

Instead of creating a release order in the purchase agreement form, alternatively start by creating a regular order in the purchase order form (*Procurement and sourcing> Common> Purchase orders> All Purchase orders*). On the tab *General* in the *Create purchase order* dialog, select a *Purchase agreement ID* in order to generate a release order to this agreement then. When entering an order line with an item covered by the agreement, Dynamics AX automatically generates a link. If you create a new purchase order in the vendor form (*Procurement and sourcing> Common> Vendors> All vendors*) and there is an applicable agreement, a dialog displays providing the option to select an agreement.

If you want to check the link to the purchase agreement in the purchase order line, click the button *Update line/Purchase agreement/Attached* in the action pane strip. At header level, click the button *Related information/Purchase agreement* on the action pane tab *General*.

In the release order, you have to post order confirmation, product receipt and vendor invoice like in any other purchase order. When posting the product receipt or the invoice, the related purchase agreement updates the order fulfillment (line view in the purchase agreement form, sub-tab *Fulfillment* on the tab *Line details*).

3.4.9.3 New in Dynamics AX 2012

In Dynamics AX 2012, purchase agreements replace the former purchase order type "Blanket order".

3.4.10 Case Study Exercises

Exercise 3.7 – Planned Order
In order to avoid processing purchase order approval, make sure change management does not apply to your vendor entered in exercise 3.2.

A minimum inventory quantity of 200 units on the main warehouse is required for the item entered in exercise 3.5. After registering this minimum quantity, you want to open the net requirements form for the item updating the master schedule. What is the result of this master scheduling update?

Open the planned purchase order form in the procurement and sourcing menu. If required, switch to the dynamic master plan which has applied when updating the net requirements. Select the planned order referring to your item and transfer it to a purchase order.

Exercise 3.8 – Request for Quotation

You want to receive vendor quotes for your item. For this purpose, enter a new request in the request for quotations form. This request should contain a line with your item from exercise 3.5. The RFQ reply configuration for the request should include the header field *Reply valid to* and the line fields *Quantity* and *Unit price*.

You want to send the request to your vendor from exercise 3.2 and another vendor of your choice. Once you have finished entering the request, choose the option *Send* in order to post and print the RFQ for these vendors.

After a while, you are receiving quotes with quantities and prices of your choice from both vendors. In order to track the quotes, enter them as request for quotation replies assigned to the original request. Your vendor from exercise 3.2 has submitted the better quote, which you want to accept transferring the RFQ reply to a purchase order. Then send a quote rejection to the other vendor.

Exercise 3.9 – Purchase Order

You want to order your item (entered in exercise 3.5) from your vendor (entered in exercise 3.2). You may start registering the purchase order in the vendor form. Which quantity and which price show in the order line by default, where do they come from? In a second order line, order two hours of the procurement category "##-assembling" (entered in exercise 3.4) for a price of GBP 100.

After closing the purchase order from, you want to display all orders referring to your vendor. How do you proceed and how many orders are available?

Exercise 3.10 – Order Confirmation

Post and print both purchase orders which you have created in the last two exercises. One time you should print to a PDF file, the other time you should display a print preview.

Then change the quantity in the first order line of exercise 3.9 to 120 units. How do you proceed?

3.5 Item Receipt

Once an ordered item arrives at your warehouse, you want to post an item receipt making the item available in inventory.

3.5.1 Basic Steps for Item Receipt

In order to make sure that required items arrive in time, optionally use following inquiries in Dynamics AX for displaying open purchase order lines:

➢ *Procurement and sourcing> Common> Purchase orders> Backorder purchase lines*: List page showing open order lines with a confirmed delivery date before the *Backorder date* entered in the filter area of the list page

> *Procurement and sourcing> Inquiries> Purchase orders> Open purchase order lines*: Inquiry form showing open order lines, where you may apply a filter – e.g. a filter by grid (*Ctrl+G*) – for selecting relevant records

3.5.1.1   Receipts List and Arrival Overview

Printing a receipts list supports preparing an expected item receipt. This list serves as information for the vendor and/or the responsible in your warehouse.

Independent of the receipts list, the warehouse responsible may choose the arrival overview form for viewing and preparing expected receipts.

3.5.1.2   Posting Item Receipts

Item receipt includes two different steps of posting:

> **Inventory registration** – You may record inventory registration, which preliminary increases the quantity on hand in inventory, directly in the order line or through an item arrival journal. When posting an arrival journal, depending on the setup pallet transactions in the warehouse may be required.
> **Product receipt** – The product receipt posts the physical inventory transaction and general ledger transactions for the item receipt finally. Inventory registration before the product receipt is optional, not compulsory.

Depending on the particular requirements, skip posting the item receipt (registration and product receipt) for a purchase order. In this case, Dynamics AX posts the item receipt together with the vendor invoice.

3.5.2   Receipts List

The functionality of the receipts list is similar to confirming and printing the purchase order: If you want a receipts list, you have to access a posting form for posting and printing. This posting does not create inventory or financial transactions.

In order to post and print a receipts list, access the purchase order form (*Procurement and sourcing> Common> Purchase orders> All purchase orders*) and click the button *Generate/Receipts list* on the action pane tab *Receive* after selecting the appropriate order. Alternatively, access the applicable posting form for summary update (*Procurement and sourcing> Periodic> Purchase orders> Posting receipts list*). In the posting form for summary update, enter a filter by clicking the button *Select*.

Printing of a receipts list is not very common, but you can apply it for information purposes regarding an expected item receipt.

3.5.3   Inventory Registration

Inventory registration is a preliminary step before posting the product receipt. There are three options for starting inventory registration:

> ➤ Registration form (purchase order line)
> ➤ Item arrival journal
> ➤ Arrival overview

Inventory registration only applies to products, not to order lines directly related to purchasing procurement categories.

3.5.3.1 Registration in a Purchase Order Line

If it is required to register the item quantity before posting the product receipt, the usual way is to post an item arrival journal. But you may also want to enter the inventory registration independent from the item arrival journal, for example if you need to split a single order line to different locations, batch or serial numbers.

In order to access the item registration form from the purchase order form, click the button *Update line/Registration* in the action pane strip of the tab *Purchase order lines* after selecting the appropriate order line.

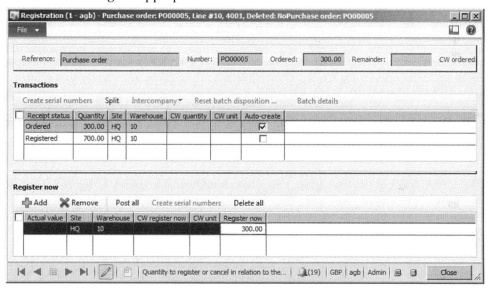

Figure 3-27:   Registering a receipt in the inventory registration form

The inventory registration form contains two parts: The upper pane (*Transactions*) shows the status of the inventory transaction(s) linked to the order line. The lower pane (*Register now*) is available for posting the registration.

Initially the upper pane shows a single inventory transaction, created when entering the order line. This transaction is split into several lines if you post partial deliveries or if you split the line manually. For registering inventory dimensions like different batch or serial numbers (if applicable), split a line by clicking the button *Split* or *Create serial numbers* in the registration form if necessary.

In order to record and post the inventory registration, insert appropriate lines in the *Register now* pane of the registration form. As an alternative to manually inserting a record by clicking the button *Add* there, select the checkbox in the column *Auto-create* of the *Transactions* pane as shown in Figure 3-27.

Before posting the registration by clicking the button *Post all*, change the warehouse, quantity and applicable inventory dimensions as required. If recording a partial registration by entering a smaller than the original quantity in the *Register now* pane before posting, the inventory transaction splits into two lines – one for the registered and one for the remaining quantity.

If you have already started a registration in the *Register now* pane and want to cancel it before posting, click the button *Delete all*. Clicking this button restores the registration as it has been before starting the current registration.

3.5.3.2   Registration Status

Once the inventory registration is posted, the recorded quantity shows the status "Registered" and is available in inventory. After registration, transfer, sell, or consume the registered quantity as required in your company.

Unlike product receipt and invoice posting, which generate voucher documents containing unchanging transactions, inventory registration is a preliminary transaction. If you reset an inventory registration, there is no posted transaction of the original registration any more. The only transaction you may view after resetting a registration is the posted item arrival journal, if registration has been posted through an item arrival journal.

3.5.3.3   Item Arrival Journal

If it is required to register item receipts in the warehouse separately from posting vendor packing slips (product receipts) in the office, use item arrival journals. Posting an item arrival journal generates the same transactions in inventory and purchasing as the registration directly in the purchase order line.

Item arrival journals are available in the form *Inventory and warehouse management> Journals> Item arrival> Item arrival*. Registering and posting an item arrival journal works similar to other inventory journals (see section 7.4.2).

After posting the item arrival journal, the inventory transaction shows the status "Registered" and the *Line quantity* form (button *Line quantity* on the action pane tab *General* of the purchase order) shows the posted quantity in the column *Registered*.

If the journal contains settings for posting pallet transports from the inbound dock to the warehouse (checkbox *Pallet transports* on the tab *Default values* in the journal header and on the tab *General* in the lines), the status is not "Registered" but "Arrived" after posting the item arrival journal. In this case, the transaction doesn't show the status "Registered" until the subsequent pallet transport has been posted.

3.5.3.4 Arrival Overview

The form *Inventory and warehouse management> Periodic> Arrival overview* provides an overview of expected item arrivals. In the upper pane of the form, choose filter criteria like the date range of expected receipts (*Days back, Days forward*), the warehouses or the vendor (*Account number*). Clicking the button *Update* applies the selected criteria. If you want to use the same filter criteria repeatedly, switch to the tab *Setup* for saving one or more filter combinations.

After selecting receipts for arrival (column *Select for arrival* in the *Receipts* or *Lines* pane), click the button *Start arrival* in the action pane strip of the *Receipts* pane. Starting the arrival creates – but does not post – an item arrival journal for the selected lines.

For posting the arrival journal, open the item arrival journals through the menu item *Inventory and warehouse management> Journals> Item arrival> Item arrival*. Alternatively, click the button *Journals/Show arrivals from receipts* in the action pane strip of the arrival overview after selecting the receipt, for which you have started arrival.

The button *Journals/Product receipt ready journals* in the arrival overview shows posted arrival journals, for which the product receipt (see section 3.5.4 below) has not been posted yet.

3.5.3.5 Reversing an Inventory Registration

In order to reverse and cancel a registration, which has been posted in an item arrival journal or in the registration form, open the registration form in the purchase order after selecting the order line concerned. In *Transactions* pane of the registration form, select the checkbox *Auto-create* in the registered transaction concerned and post the transaction like a regular inventory registration, but with a negative quantity.

3.5.3.6 Settings for Registration

The item model group of the purchased item controls whether you have to post inventory registration before posting the product receipt. You have to record inventory registration, if the checkbox *Registration requirements* on the *Setup* tab of the item model group concerned (*Inventory and warehouse management> Setup> Inventory> Item model groups*) is selected.

3.5.4 Product Receipt

Posting the product receipt (vendor packing slip / delivery note) executes the physical inventory transaction, which finally receives the item in an unchanging voucher document.

3.5.4.1 Posting Form for Product Receipts

Posting the product receipt works similar to confirming and printing the purchase order. You may open the posting form by clicking the button *Generate/Product receipt* on the action pane tab *Receive* of the purchase order form after selecting the appropriate order.

The posting form shows the familiar format. The applicable option in the lookup field *Quantity* is depending on the preceding procedure:

➢ **Registered quantity** – Select this option, if an inventory registration (item arrival) is posted before posting the product receipt. Dynamics AX applies the quantity registered (not yet received) as default for the posting lines.
➢ **Registered quantity and services** – In addition to the registered quantity of inventoried items, Dynamics AX applies the ordered quantity for order lines referring to product categories and non-inventoried items.
➢ **Ordered quantity** – Dynamics AX applies the total remaining quantity.
➢ **Receive now** – Dynamics AX applies the quantity of the order line column *Receive now*.

The posting quantity shows in the column *Quantity* on the tab *Lines* in the lower part of the posting form. If required, change the quantities there before posting.

The other parameters in the posting form are similar to the purchase order confirmation parameters described in section 3.4.8, except for following options:

➢ **Product receipt** – Column on the tab *Overview*, in which you have to enter the packing slip number of your vendor.
➢ **Print product receipt** – Checkbox in the posting form, which is usually cleared, because when receiving the vendor's packing slip you probably don't print your own document.

If there is a yellow exclamation mark (⚠) on the tab *Overview* of the posting form, it indicates a posting problem. A possible reason is that the selected quantity in the posting form is "Registered quantity", but there has not been an inventory registration before product receipt. Selecting the quantity "Ordered quantity" in the posting form usually solves this problem.

3.5.4.2 Product Receipt in the Item Arrival Journal

An alternative way for accessing the product receipt posting form is available, if an item arrival journal has been posted for the purchase order. In this case, click the button *Functions/Product receipt* in the item arrival journal (*Inventory and warehouse management> Journals> Item arrival> Item arrival*).

If a *Packing slip* number has been entered on the tab *General* in the item arrival journal before posting, it serves as default for the *Product receipt* number in the product receipt posting form.

3.5.4.3 Summary Update

As for the purchase order confirmation and the receipt lists, a posting form for summary product receipt update is available, which you may access through the menu path *Procurement and sourcing> Periodic> Purchase orders> Product receipt*. In the posting form for summary update, you have to specify a filter clicking the button *Select*.

You may then click the button *Arrange* to collect multiple purchase orders into one collective product receipt. More information on arranging orders for collective documents is available in section 4.6.2 of this book.

3.5.4.4 Canceling a Product Receipt

You may cancel a posted product receipt applying the *Cancel* feature in the product receipt inquiry form.

In order to access the product receipt inquiry, click the button *Journals/Product receipt* on the action pane tab *Receive* of the purchase order form. After selecting the appropriate receipt, click the button *Cancel* in the action pane strip of the tab *Overview*. If you just want to reduce the posted quantity, click the button *Correct* in the product receipt inquiry.

Canceling and correcting a product receipt does not change the original transaction, but posts a new transaction offsetting the original one.

3.5.4.5 Ledger Integration and Settings for Product Receipt Posting

If ledger integration is activated for the product receipt, Dynamics AX posts accrual transactions in the general ledger in parallel to the inventory transactions. These ledger transactions are reversed when posting the related invoice.

There are two relevant settings for posting product receipts to the general ledger:

➢ **Accounts payable parameters** – The checkbox *Post product receipt in ledger* on the tab *Updates* has to be selected for enabling ledger posting.
➢ **Item model group** – On the tab *Setup* in the item model group of the purchased item, the checkbox *Post physical inventory* has to be selected for ledger posting.

Apart from the setting concerning ledger integration, the item model group contains two other settings relevant for posting the product receipt:

The checkbox *Registration requirements* on the tab *Setup* of the item model group controls, if you have to post the inventory registration before posting the product receipt. The checkbox *Receiving requirement* on the tab *Setup* controls, if you have to post the product receipt before posting the vendor invoice.

3.5.4.6 New in Dynamics AX 2012

The option of cancelling a product receipt in the inquiry is new in Dynamics AX 2012, and the product receipt posting has been called "Packing slip" in former releases.

3.5.5   Receiving a Deviating Quantity

You have to post a partial delivery, if you do not receive the entire quantity of a purchase order line in one shipment, but split into several shipments. It is not possible to post partial deliveries, if the checkbox *Complete* on the tab *Line details* (sub-tab *General*) of the purchase order line is selected.

3.5.5.1   Inventory Registration of Partial Deliveries

If applying inventory registration, record applicable partial deliveries in the registration form as shown in section 3.5.3 (compare Figure 3-27). If recording the inventory registration through an item arrival journal, enter partial quantities in the journal lines there.

In the product receipt posting form, select the option "Registered quantity" in the quantity lookup field for a partial product receipt then.

3.5.5.2   Receive Now Quantity

If you do not record inventory registration, optionally enter a *Receive now* quantity in the purchase order line as preparation for posting a partial product receipt. The *Receive now* quantity shows in the right-most column on the *Purchase order lines* tab of the purchase order detail form. As an alternative to the column in the purchase order lines, enter the *Receive now* quantity in the *Line quantity* form, which shows by clicking the button *Line quantity* on the action pane tab *General* of the purchase order form.

In the quantity lookup field of the product receipt posting form, choose the option "Receive now" referring to this column then.

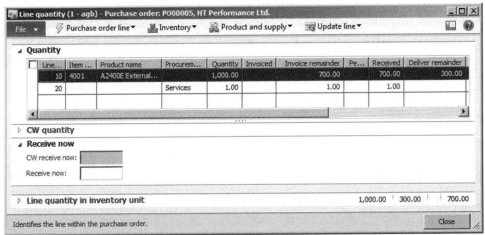

Figure 3-28:   Line quantity form for a purchase order after posting a partial delivery

3.5.5.3   Product Receipt of Partial Deliveries

Alternatively, skip the *Receive now* quantity and choose the option "Ordered quantity" in the quantity lookup field of the product receipt posting form. In this case, you have to enter received quantities in the column *Quantity* on the tab *Lines* of the posting form. After posting a partial delivery, the quantity open for future product receipts shows in the column *Deliver remainder* of the *Line quantity* form (see Figure 3-28). For accessing the line quantity form, click the button *Line quantity* on the action pane tab *General* of the purchase order. The total quantity received shows in the column *Received* there.

Once receiving further partial deliveries, post the product receipts in the same way as described for the first delivery until the total of the received quantity complies with the ordered quantity.

3.5.5.4 Settings for Over/Under Delivery

You may only post under or over deliveries, if the checkbox *Accept underdelivery* or *Accept overdelivery* on the tab *Updates* of the procurement parameters is selected.

Additional settings for over and under delivery are available on the tabs *Purchase* and *Sell* of the released product detail form (*Product information management> Common> Released products*), where you may enter the maximum percentage for over delivery and under delivery in purchase and sales orders. The percentages of the released product default to the order lines, where you may adjust them as needed in a particular order (tab *Line details*, sub-tab *Delivery*).

3.5.5.5 Under Delivery

If posting the receipt of a quantity, which is less than the ordered quantity, Dynamics AX posts a partial delivery unless you mark the receipt to be the last for the particular order line. As shown in Figure 3-29, under delivery applies by selecting the checkbox in the column *Close for receipt* on the tab *Lines* of the posting form after entering the received quantity in the *Quantity* column.

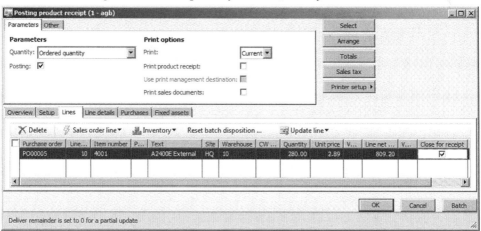

Figure 3-29: Selecting under delivery in the posting form for the product receipt

As an alternative, set the open quantity to zero by canceling the deliver remainder quantity as described in section 3.4.7. But unlike when posting an under delivery in the posting form, Dynamics AX does not control if the missing quantity is below the under delivery percentage of the order line in this case.

3.5.5.6 Over Delivery

A transaction is an over delivery, if the total received quantity exceeds the ordered quantity when posting a receipt (inventory registration or product receipt). Dynamics AX accepts over delivery, if the exceeding quantity is less than the allowed over delivery specified in the over delivery percentage of the order line.

3.5.6   Order Status and Inquiries

When posting the item receipt, Dynamics AX changes the inventory quantity and the order status.

3.5.6.1 Purchase Order Status

The purchase order list page shows the approval status (see section 3.4.6) in the column *Approval status*, and the order status in the column *Status*. The header view of the purchase order detail form additionally shows the *Document status* on the tab *General*. Whereas the order status indicates the order progress applying the lowest status of any line in the purchase order, the document status shows the highest status of a posted document.

Therefore, the order status may still be "Open order" while the document status is "Invoiced" in case of partial deliveries and invoices. Table 3-1 below shows an overview of receipt transactions and the related order status.

Table 3-1:   Order status and document status for receipt transactions

Transaction	Approval status	Order status	Document status
(Approval)	*Approved*	*Open order*	*None*
Confirmation	*Confirmed*	*Open order*	*Purchase order*
Receipts list	*Confirmed*	*Open order*	*Receipts list*
Inventory registration	*Confirmed*	*Open order*	As above, no change: *Purchase order* or *Receipts list*
Partial product receipt	*Confirmed*	*Open order*	*Product receipt*
Complete product receipt	*Confirmed*	*Received*	*Product receipt*

Clicking the button *Postings* on the action pane tab *General* of the purchase order form provides access to a form showing the last document number of posted documents for the particular order.

At line level, the status shows in the field *Line status* on the sub-tab *General* of the *Line details* tab. In addition, the *Line quantity* form indicates the status through the different quantity columns.

3.5.6.2 Inventory Transaction Status and Inquiry

Both, inventory registration and product receipt, change the quantity on hand through inventory transactions.

When entering a new purchase order line referring to an inventoried item, Dynamics AX creates an inventory transaction with the status "Ordered" in the column *Receipt*. After selecting an order line, view this transaction by clicking the button *Inventory/Transactions* in the action pane strip of the tab *Purchase order lines*.

When posting an inventory registration, the receipt status of the inventory transaction changes to "Registered". The registration date is stored in the field *Inventory date* on the tab *General* of the inventory transaction (if reversing the inventory registration, Dynamics AX clears the inventory date).

When posting a product receipt with or without a previous inventory registration, the receipt status of the inventory transaction switches to "Received". The posting date of the product receipt shows in the column *Physical date* of the inventory transaction. The *Financial date* in the inventory transaction remains empty until posting the vendor invoice. Additional detail data of the transaction like the packing slip number show on the tab *Update* of the inventory transaction.

Since reversing a product receipt is only possible by posting an offsetting transaction, the physical date of an inventory transaction never changes after posting the receipt.

In case of partial receipts, the original inventory transaction splits into two transactions with a different status according to the posted quantities. Figure 3-30 for example shows inventory transactions linked to a purchase order line after posting the product receipts of two partial deliveries.

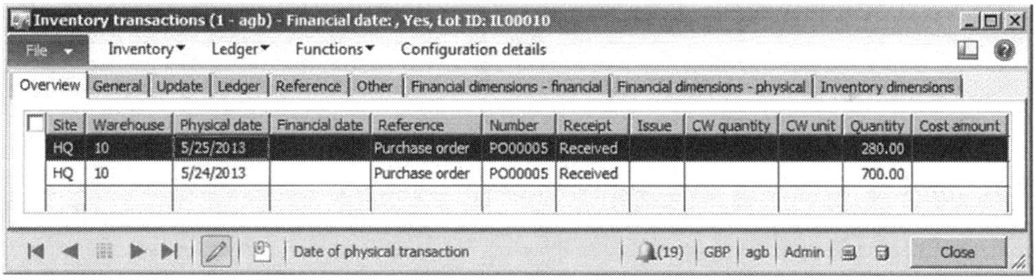

Figure 3-30: Inventory transactions after posting product receipts

3.5.6.3 Product Receipt Inquiry

In order to view posted product receipts, access the menu item *Procurement and sourcing> Inquiries> Journals> Product receipt* or click the button *Journals/Product receipt* on the action pane tab *Receive* of the purchase order form. After selecting a product receipt on the tab *Overview* of the inquiry form, switch to the tab *Lines* for displaying related receipt lines. The button *Inventory/Lot transactions* on the *Lines* tab opens the inventory transactions shown above again.

3.5.6.4 Ledger Transactions

If ledger integration is activated for the product receipt, click the button *Ledger/Physical voucher* in the inventory transaction inquiry if you want to view related general ledger transactions. For viewing the ledger transactions of the complete product receipt, access the product receipt inquiry and click the button *Vouchers* on the tab *Overview* there.

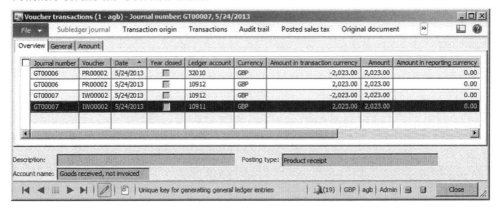

Figure 3-31:   General ledger transactions related to a product receipt

The main accounts in the ledger transactions are depending on the inventory posting setup. You may access the inventory posting setup form through the menu path *Inventory and warehouse management> Setup> Posting> Posting*.

On the tab *Purchase order* of this form, the options "Product receipt" and "Purchase, accrual" specify the main accounts applying to product receipt transactions (see section 8.4.2). In addition, the account "Purchase expenditure, un-invoiced" (account 10912 in Figure 3-32) is used as control account, generating offsetting transactions.

<u>Note</u>: For source documents like the product receipt, settings in the general ledger parameters on the tab *Batch transfer rules* determine, if transactions in subledgers are synchronously posted to the general ledger or if they are summarized in a scheduled batch. The general ledger transactions shown for a product receipt are depending on this setting.

3.5.6.5   Transaction Origin

Clicking the button *Transaction origin* in the voucher transactions opens the transaction origin form, which shows related transactions for the voucher in all modules. Depending on integration settings, the product receipt posts transactions in inventory and the general ledger. Based on the deep integration of all modules in Dynamics AX, the transaction origin form provides the option to view the effect of a document in all parts of the application.

Figure 3-32 for example shows the transaction origin of the journal line selected in Figure 3-31.

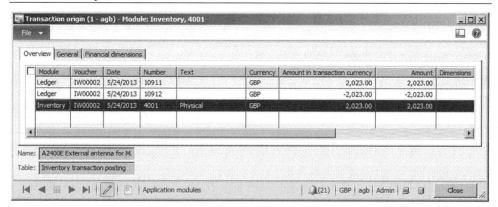

Figure 3-32: Transaction origin form showing all transactions for a product receipt

3.5.7   Case Study Exercises

Exercise 3.11 – Product Receipt

Your vendor ships the goods and services ordered in exercise 3.9 with packing slip PS311. Before posting the receipt, check following items in the purchase order:

➢ Order status and document status
➢ Inventory quantity of the ordered item (button *Inventory/On-hand*)
➢ Inventory transaction related to the order line of the product

Then post a product receipt for the complete order quantity (120 units for the first line according to exercise 3.10) referring to the vendor packing slip number mentioned above. You execute posting directly in the purchase order form.

Now review the status of the items on the list given above in this exercise again. What is different after product receipt posting?

Exercise 3.12 – Partial Delivery

You want to order your item (entered in exercise 3.5) from your vendor another time. Enter a purchase order for 80 units. You may post the product receipt of packing slip PS312 for a partial delivery of 50 units. Then post the product receipt of a second partial delivery with 10 units.

Do you know how to show the remaining quantity? Check the order status, the inventory quantity, and the inventory transactions like in exercise 3.11. What is different in comparison to exercise 3.11?

Exercise 3.13 – Product Receipt Inquiry

You want to view the product receipt of exercise 3.11. For this purpose, access the product receipt inquiry from the appropriate purchase order. In a second step, open the product receipt inquiry choosing the applicable form in the procurement and sourcing menu. Check the product receipt header and lines and try to find out, if there are related ledger transactions.

3.6   Invoice Receipt

Together with the shipment or some time later, the vendor submits an invoice. Before posting, you have to check the vendor invoice comparing it to order prices and received quantities.

Whereas the product receipt posts a preliminary inventory value, the invoice receipt posts the final value. Posting an invoice receipt therefore not only increases the open vendor balance, but also increases the financial value of inventory.

Once all lines of a purchase order are invoiced, purchase order processing in Dynamics AX is completed. Payment of vendor invoices runs through a separate process shown in section 8.3.4.

3.6.1   Different Ways for Processing Vendor Invoices

When receiving vendor invoices, we have to distinguish between following types:

➢ **Purchase order invoices** – Purchase orders and consequently related invoices always refer to products or procurements categories.
➢ **Invoices without order assignment** – Depending on whether the invoice should be directly assigned to a ledger account, there are two types:
  o **Invoices for non-stocked products or procurements categories** – These invoices are posted the same way as purchase order invoices, just without order assignment.
  o **Invoices for ledger accounts** – Usually for specific subjects like office rent or legal services.

3.6.1.1   Invoice Journals and the Vendor Invoice Form

For registering an invoice, which should directly post to a ledger account, enter a transaction in an invoice journal with or without separate approval processing (see section 8.3.3). Invoice journals are independent from purchase orders.

For invoices not entered to ledger accounts, the vendor invoice form (pending vendor invoices) applies, no matter if the invoice refers to a purchase order or not. The lines of the vendor invoice form contain products and procurement categories – instead of ledger accounts required in invoice journal lines. If the invoice entered in the vendor invoice form does not refer to a purchaser order, only procurement categories and non-inventoried items are available for selection.

3.6.1.2   Ways of Processing Purchase Order Invoices

When recording an invoice referring to a purchase order, there are two options depending on whether separate approval registration applies:

➢ **Pending vendor invoice** – Enter and post of the invoice in the vendor invoice form, with or without approval workflow.
➢ **Invoice register journal** – As a prior step to posting in the vendor invoice form, enter and post the invoice to interim accounts in the invoice register journal

first, followed by posting in the invoice approval journal or the invoice pool inquiry (see section 8.3.3).

Applying an approval workflow to pending vendor invoices enforces approval without separately posting an invoice register journal. From a financial perspective, the difference between the vendor invoice approval workflow on the one hand and invoice register posting on the other hand is, that the invoice register already posts an invoice, which is subject to tax calculation, when starting the approval process.

3.6.1.3 Approval Workflow for Pending Vendor Invoices

If approval workflows should apply to pending vendor invoices, an appropriate workflow referring to the template "Vendor invoice workflow" (*Type* "VendPro-cessInvoice") or the template "Vendor invoice line workflow" (*Type* "VendProcess InvoiceLine") has to be specified in the form *Accounts payable> Setup> Accounts payable workflows*.

The vendor portal as part of the Enterprise Portal enables authorized vendors to register pending vendor invoices through the Web for themselves. If vendor invoices are registered this way, you want to make sure applying an appropriate approval workflow before posting the invoice.

3.6.1.4 Vendor Invoice and Item Receipt

In the vendor invoice form, enter all regular purchase invoices referring to products or procurement categories. Depending on whether the invoice refers to a purchase order, the invoice lines are determined by order lines or have to be entered manually. When manually entering invoice lines, only procurement categories and non-stocked items are available.

For vendor invoices referring to a purchase order, there are two different cases – on the one hand invoices referring to a prior product receipt, and on the other hand invoices received together with the item or the service. If choosing the option "Ordered quantity" or "Receive now quantity" in the lookup field *Default quantity for lines* of the vendor invoice form, the invoiced quantity is not based on received quantities. If the quantity in an invoice line exceeds the total quantity received before for the related order line, invoice posting in parallel posts the product receipt of the exceeding quantity.

Invoice posting without a prior product receipt is useful, if you receive goods or services together with the invoice and do not post a separate item receipt in the warehouse. If you want to apply this way of invoice posting to an inventoried item, the item model group assigned to the item may not show a checkmark in the checkbox *Receiving requirement* (see section 7.2.3).

3.6.2   Posting Vendor Invoices

If you want to register regular purchase invoices referring to products or procurement categories, access the pending vendor invoice form.

3.6.2.1 Pending Vendor Invoices

Entering vendor invoices works independent from purchase orders in a separate list page and detail form – the vendor invoice form in the menu item *Pending vendor invoices* (*Accounts payable> Common> Vendor invoices> Pending vendor invoices*). This form contains all vendor invoices, which have been entered but not posted.

Clicking the button *New/Invoice* on the action pane tab *Vendor invoice* of the pending vendor invoices list page creates a new invoice. If you rather want to start entering new vendor invoices in the vendor form (*Accounts payable> Common> Vendors> All vendors*), click the button *New/Invoice/Vendor invoice* on the action pane tab *Invoice* there.

Registering an invoice not referring to a purchase order is similar to entering a purchase order in the purchase order form. After selecting a vendor number, the invoice retrieves various defaults from the vendor record, which you may view and edit in the header view. But unlike the purchase order form, new lines entered on the tab *Lines* in the lines view of the vendor invoices form may only contain non-stocked items and procurement categories.

When closing the vendor invoice detail form without posting, the invoice is stored for later posting and – if applicable – approval. Therefore it displays in the pending vendor invoices. If you want to cancel registration after starting to enter a new invoice, click the button *Maintain/Cancel* on the action pane tab *Vendor invoice* of the vendor invoice detail form. Clicking the button *Maintain/Delete* provides the option to delete a pending vendor invoice already stored.

3.6.2.2 Entering Purchase Order Invoices

For entering a purchase order invoice – a vendor invoice referring to a purchase order – you want to access the pending vendor invoice form. After clicking the button *New/Invoice* in the action pane of the invoice form, select the vendor number in the field *Invoice account*.

Then assign the purchase order number, either directly searching in the lookup *Purchase order* or clicking the button *Actions/Retrieve purchase orders* in the action pane. If entering the order number before selecting a vendor, Dynamics AX automatically retrieves the correspondent vendor.

If you are working in the purchase order form (*Accounts payable> Common> Purchase orders> All purchase orders*), alternatively register a vendor invoice directly starting there. Clicking the button *Generate/Invoice* on the action pane tab *Invoice* in the purchase order form opens the pending vendor invoice form, already referring to the appropriate order.

Although the vendor invoice form looks different to the other posting forms like the product receipt, it shares similar functionality. Like in the other posting transactions, it is depending on the preceding procedure which of the options to choose in the quantity selection (available in the lookup *Default quantity for lines*):

➢ **Product receipt quantity** – Common option, applies if a product receipt has been posted before and you want to link the invoice to the receipt.
➢ **Ordered quantity** or **Receive now quantity** – If selected, Dynamics AX does not default the received quantity to the column *Quantity* in the invoice lines. For any quantity not yet received, an item receipt will post in parallel to the invoice.

The option "Product receipt quantity" in the lookup *Default quantity for lines* defaults the quantity received not invoiced to the *Quantity* column of the *Lines* tab. For checking the product receipts included in the invoice, click the button *Actions/Match product receipts* in the action pane of the vendor invoice form.

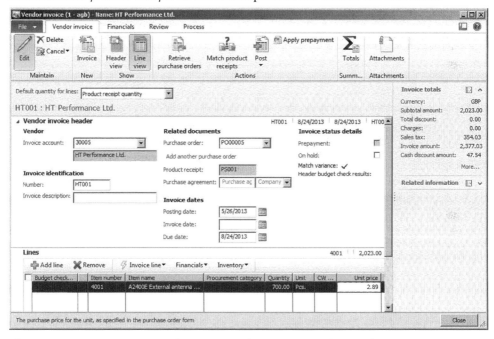

Figure 3-33:   Registering a vendor invoice referring to a purchase order

The select form shows the product receipts available for invoicing. By clearing or selecting the checkboxes in the column *Match* there you may exclude or include product receipts. After closing the select form by clicking the button *OK*, the selected product receipt displays in the column *Product receipt* on the tab *Lines* ("<multiple>", if linked to several receipts). If the vendor invoice does not include all open product receipts, adjust the quantities in the invoice lines as applicable making sure they comply with the matched product receipts then.

<u>Note</u>: After starting to register a vendor invoice, you have to cancel (button *Maintain/Cancel)* or delete it, if you do not want to save or post it. Simply closing

the invoice detail form stores the invoice, displaying it in the pending vendor invoices list page. If product receipts are assigned to this invoice, you can't assign them to a second invoice before deleting the first invoice.

3.6.2.3   Collective Vendor Invoices

If a vendor invoice refers to several purchase orders, you have to post a collective invoice. Entering collective invoices in the vendor invoice form is different to registering collective documents for other document types (e.g. collective product receipts), however.

In the vendor invoice form, click the link *Add another purchase order* below the field *Purchase order* or click the button *Actions/Retrieve purchase orders* in the action pane for accessing the select form. For selecting purchase orders in the select form, observe the lookup *Default quantity for lines* in the vendor invoice form. The selected option in this field controls which purchase orders – according to prior product receipts – are available.

In addition, accounts payable settings (*Accounts payable> Setup> Summary update parameters*) and settings at vendor level determine common settings in orders collected to a common invoice (similar to accounts receivables, see section 4.6.2).

3.6.2.4   Total Amount and Input Fields

The invoice number (mandatory field *Number* in the field group *Invoice identification*), the *Posting date*, the *Invoice date* and the *Due date* (receiving the default from payment term calculation) are available on the tab *Vendor invoice header* of the line view. More details are available in the header view, where you may also clear the checkbox *Approved* on the *Approval* tab, if you want to exclude an invoice from payment proposals.

Before finally posting an invoice, it is useful to view the FactBox *Invoice totals* or to click the button *Totals* for comparing the totals on the vendor invoice with the totals you are going to post. If necessary, adjust quantities, prices, discounts and line amounts on the tab *Lines* or *Line details* in the lines view of the invoice form.

If you want to prevent posting of an invoice (e.g. because of price differences), select the checkbox *On hold* on the tab *General* of the vendor invoice form.

3.6.2.5   Invoice Matching

If prices, discounts, charges or other items in the vendor invoice do not match the purchase order, you should not modify prices and amounts in the purchase order line, but enter the invoiced amounts in the vendor invoice form in order to keep record of price variance.

If the amounts entered in a vendor invoice do not match the assigned purchase order and product receipt, but exceed specified tolerances, the vendor invoice form shows an exclamation mark (!) in the *Match variance* field on the invoice header and – if applicable – in the column *Price match* on the tab *Lines*. In order to view details, click the button *Matching/Matching details* on the action pane tab *Review* of the vendor invoice form.

Primary settings for invoice matching are available on the tab *Invoice validation* in the accounts payable parameters. Invoice matching in Dynamics AX applies to different areas which may be activated independently and with different tolerances:

➢ **Invoice totals matching** – Compares the invoice total fields (invoice amount, sales tax, charges) with the purchase order.
➢ **Price and quantity matching**
  o **Line matching policy** – "Two-way matching" compares the invoice price and discount with the order line; "Three-way matching" in addition compares the quantity of product receipts.
  o **Match price totals** – Applies to partial deliveries and invoices, comparing the order line with the total of the current invoice line and related partial invoice lines already posted.
➢ **Charges matching** – Separate matching settings for charges.

You may access specific setup forms for these validation criteria at the level of particular vendors or items through the menu path *Accounts payable> Setup> Invoice matching*. In addition, business policies (*Accounts payable> Setup> Policies*) enable matching rules not covered by the settings mentioned above.

3.6.2.6   Invoice Posting and Ledger Integration

Once you have finished registering an invoice, optionally leave it non-posted and post it at a later time – e.g. if an approval workflow applies. If you want to finally post the pending vendor invoice, click the button *Actions/Post/Post* on the action pane tab *Vendor invoice* of the vendor invoice form. After posting, the invoice shows in the open vendor invoices list page (*Accounts payable> Common> Vendor invoices> Open vendor invoices*), which displays all invoices not yet paid.

Posting a vendor invoice posts general ledger transactions, inventory transactions, vendor transactions and transactions in other subledgers like sales tax if applicable.

As shown in section 3.2.3, the vendor posting profile specifies to which summary account in the general ledger the vendor transaction is posting. Settings for inventory transactions are available in the inventory posting setup – depending on the particular item and vendor as shown in section 8.4.2.

3.6.2.7   New in Dynamics AX 2012

In Dynamics AX 2012, you do not register vendor invoices in a regular posting form but in the new pending vendor invoice form (saving invoices before posting). The vendor invoice form also allows registering invoices not referring to purchase orders, facilitates collective invoices, and shows enhanced matching features.

3.6.3   Order Status and Inquiries

Like product receipt posting, posting the vendor invoice updates the order status.

3.6.3.1   Purchase Order Status

Depending on whether you have posted a partial or a complete invoice, the purchase order shows following status:

➢ **Partial invoice** – Order status "Received" or "Open order", document status "Invoice"
➢ **Complete invoice or last partial invoice** – Order status "Invoiced", document status "Invoice"

Posting the vendor invoice affects inventory transactions, vendor transactions and general ledger transactions.

3.6.3.2   Inventory Transactions

If you want to view the effects of the vendor invoice on inventory transactions, click the button *Inventory/Transactions* in the action pane strip on the tab *Purchase order lines* after selecting the appropriate order line in the purchase order form.

After posting the invoice, the *Receipt* status of the inventory transaction is "Purchased" and the posting date of the invoice shows in the column *Financial date*. The invoice number shows on the tab *Update* of the inventory transaction.

Site	Ware...	Physical date	Financial date	Reference	Number	Receipt	Issue	CW quantity	CW unit	Quantity	Cost amount
HQ	10	5/25/2013		Purchase order	PO00005	Received				280.00	
HQ	10	5/24/2013	5/26/2013	Purchase order	PO00005	Purchased				700.00	2,023.00

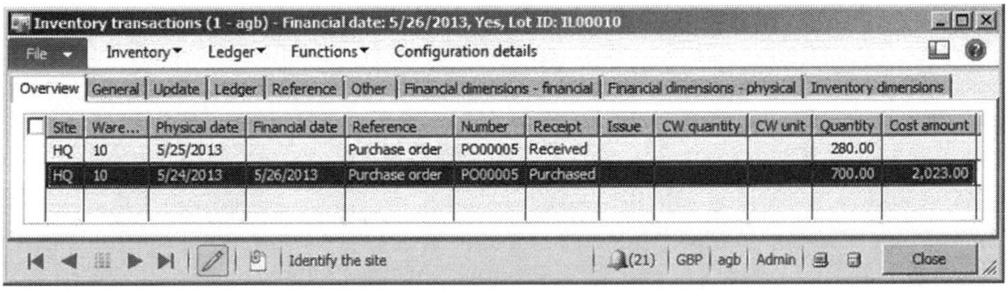

Figure 3-34:   Inventory transactions after posting the vendor invoice

The example in Figure 3-34 shows two inventory transactions referring to a purchase order line, of which only one inventory transaction has been included in invoice posting.

3.6.3.3   Invoice Inquiry

In order to access a posted invoice, access the form *Accounts payable> Inquiries> Journals> Invoice journal* or click the button *Journals/Invoice* on the action pane tab *Invoice* of in the purchase order form. After selecting the appropriate invoice on the tab *Overview* of the inquiry form, switch to the tab *Lines* for displaying related invoice lines. The button *Inventory/Lot transactions* on the *Lines* tab opens the inventory transactions as shown above already.

3.6.3.4   Ledger Transactions

For viewing the general ledger transactions related to a vendor invoice, click the button *Voucher* on the *Overview* tab of the invoice inquiry. If accessing the ledger transactions from the inventory transaction inquiry by clicking the button *Ledger/Financial voucher* there, only ledger transactions for the invoice related to the particular inventory transaction display.

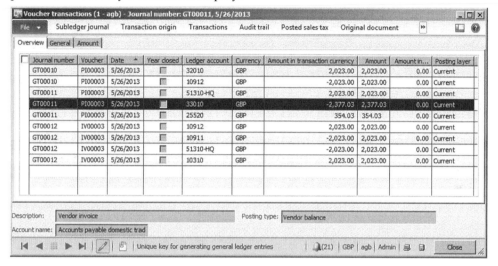

Figure 3-35:   General ledger transactions related to a posted vendor invoice

The voucher transactions form displays the general ledger transactions of all vouchers referring to the posted invoice. Figure 3-35 for example shows three ledger journals with following transactions:

➢ **Reversing the packing slip transactions** – Accounts 32010, 10911 and 10912
➢ **Vendor summary account transaction** – Posting the vendor balance (Account 33010, derived from posting profile)
➢ **Stock account transaction** – Posting inventory items (Account 10310, derived from inventory posting setup)
➢ **Input tax transaction** – Posting sales tax (Account 25520, derived from the ledger posting group of the sales tax code)

In addition, there are two transactions to the control account "Purchase expenditure for product" (account 51310) offsetting each other.

More information concerning posting profile setup is available in section 3.2.3, and concerning inventory posting setup in section 8.4.2.

Note: Like for the product receipt, settings in the general ledger parameters on the tab *Batch transfer rules* determine, if vendor invoices are summarized for posting to the general ledger. In this case, not all described transactions are available at the level of an individual invoice.

3.6.3.5 Transaction Origin

Clicking the button *Transaction origin* in the voucher transactions opens the transaction origin form, which shows related transactions for the voucher in all modules.

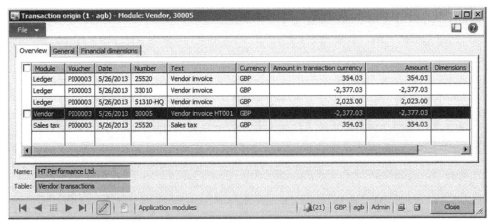

Figure 3-36:   Transaction origin form, showing all transactions for a journal

Apart from ledger transactions, the transaction origin includes vendor transactions, inventory transactions and tax transactions. Figure 3-36 for example shows the transaction origin of journal line selected in Figure 3-35.

3.6.4   Case Study Exercises

Exercise 3.14 – Purchase Order Invoice
Your vendor submits the invoice VI314, which refers to goods and services received in exercise 3.11. Before posting the invoice, check following items:

➤ Order status and document status of the purchase order
➤ Inventory transaction related to the order line of the product (button *Inventory/Transactions*)

Then register and post the vendor invoice for the received quantity. You want to register the invoice in the pending vendor invoices page, checking the invoice total before posting.

Now review the status of the items on the checklist above again. What is different after invoice posting?

Exercise 3.15 – Partial Invoice for a Purchase Order
You receive the invoice VI315, which applies to the goods received with packing slip PS312 in exercise 3.12. Post the vendor invoice starting in the purchase order form, making sure that the vendor invoice only contains the items received with packing slip PS312.

Exercise 3.16 – Vendor Invoice Not Related to a Purchase Order

Your vendor now submits the invoice VI316, showing an invoice line with one hour of the procurement category "##-assembling" (entered in exercise 3.4) for a price of GBP 105. The invoice does not refer to a purchase order.

You are accepting this invoice and want to register it in the pending vendor invoices page. Check the invoice total before posting the invoice.

Exercise 3.17 – Invoice Inquiry

You want to view the invoice of exercise 3.14. For this purpose, open the invoice inquiry for the order concerned in the purchase order form. As an alternative, choose the appropriate menu path. Check the invoice header and lines as well as the related ledger transactions.

In exercise 3.3, you were looking for the summary account for your vendor. Can you find the ledger transaction for this account? Finally, open the transaction origin form and check, to which modules your invoice has posted.

3.7   Credit Notes and Item Returns

When receiving a credit note from a supplier, you have to register and post it in purchasing. Posting a vendor credit note is similar to posting a vendor invoice, except that credit notes require a negative quantity. As with vendor invoices, you have to distinguish two different kinds of credit notes:

➢ Credit notes for inventoried items
➢ Credit notes for non-stocked items and procurement categories

Vendor credit notes referring to inventoried items have to be registered in the purchase order form. When posting a credit note for an inventoried item, Dynamics AX posts an item return (negative receipt) in parallel if no separate item return has been posted before. If the item model group does not allow physical negative inventory, posting the return is only possible if the item is still on stock.

Vendor credit notes referring to non-stocked items and procurement categories may alternatively be registered in following forms:

➢ **Purchase order form** – Like inventoried items
➢ **Pending vendor invoice form** – Entering invoice lines with negative quantity
➢ **Invoice journal** – See section 8.3.3

If posting a vendor credit note in an invoice journal, you have to respect that this kind of crediting does not affect item statistics and inventory value.

In case you have to reverse a product receipt, but not an invoice receipt, apply the functionality for canceling product receipts (see section 3.5.4).

3.7.1   Crediting Purchase Orders

For an inventoried item, you have to access the purchase order form if you want to post a credit note. In case of a credit note for a non-stocked item or a procurement category, applying a purchase order is optional.

If the parameter *Safety level of invoiced orders* in the procurement parameters (*Procurement and sourcing> Setup> Procurement and sourcing parameters*, tab *Updates*) is not set to "Locked", optionally post credit notes in the original purchase order. Otherwise, enter a new purchase order for the credit note. If invoiced orders are not locked, there are following options for a credit note with inventoried items:

➢ **Original purchase order** – Registering a new line in the original order
➢ **New purchase order** – Purchase type "Purchase order" or "Returned order"

3.7.1.1   Credit Notes in the Original Purchase Order

If you want to register a credit note in a new line of the original purchase order, you have to access the purchase order in edit mode and enter a regular order line, showing a negative sign in the column *Quantity* for the credited quantity. If you expect a replacement from your vendor, enter a second purchase order line with a positive quantity for the replacement.

Depending on change management settings, the order may be subject for approval. Posting the vendor credit note works like posting a vendor invoice – after entering the credit note number in the invoice number field you may post the credit note clicking the button *Post/Post* in the action pane of the vendor invoice form.

If the checkbox *Deductions requirement* in the item model group of the item concerned is selected, you have to post a separate product receipt (item return) before posting the credit note (negative invoice).

3.7.1.2   Returned Order

If you want to enter the credit note in a new order, register a regular purchase order (*Purchase type* "Purchase order") with lines containing a negative quantity. Alternatively, choose the *Purchase type* "Returned order" on the tab *General* in the *Create purchase order* form when creating the order. If selecting the purchase type "Returned order", pay attention to the following items:

➢ **RMA number** – The return merchandise authorization provided by the vendor has to be entered in the *Create purchase order* form.
➢ **Quantity** – Has to be negative in the order lines.
➢ **Return action** – For information purpose, available on the sub-tab *Setup* of the purchase order lines (receiving a default from the procurement parameters).

3.7.1.3   Inventory Marking

In order to avoid unintended changes of inventory value, use inventory marking for assigning the value of the returned/credited item to the corresponding receipt.

For this purpose, select the new order line in the purchase order detail form and click the button *Inventory/Marking* in the action pane strip of the purchase order lines. In the marking form, select the checkbox in the column *Set mark now* marking the original order line of the item now returned. The inventory value of the new line entered for crediting now will exactly offset the inventory value received from the original line. Without marking, Dynamics AX calculates the outgoing inventory value of the credit note according to the item model group of the item, for example applying the FIFO model.

3.7.1.4 Create Credit Note Feature

In order to facilitate entering a credit note, choose the *Create credit note* function by clicking the button *Create/Credit note* on the action pane tab *Purchase* of the purchase order form. Alternatively, click the button *Purchase order line/Credit note* in the action pane strip on the order lines.

The credit note feature is similar to the copy feature for purchase orders (see section 3.4.5). Depending on whether adding credit note lines to an existing or copying to a new order, you have to pay attention to the checkbox *Delete purchase lines* in the *Create credit note* form.

Unlike the regular copy feature, creating a credit note reverses the quantity sign, additionally reserves the original order line and applies inventory marking (exactly offsetting the inventory value received from the original line).

3.7.1.5 Transaction Settlement

Supposing the original invoice has not been paid and settled yet, optionally close the open vendor transaction of the original invoice immediately when posting the credit note.

For this purpose click the button *Settle/Open transaction* on the action pane tab *Invoice* of the crediting purchase order. In the *Settle open transaction* form, select the checkbox in the column *Mark* for the invoice concerned. After marking, simply close the form (the form does not include an *OK* button). When posting the credit note, the open vendor transaction of the invoice will be closed.

If not settling the invoice when registering the crediting purchase order, the responsible has to settle invoice and credit note later in the open transaction editing as described in section 8.2.5.

When working with settlements, take into account that there is no manual settlement if automatic settlement is selected in the applicable vendor posting profile (tab *Table restrictions*) or in the accounts payable parameters (tab *Settlement*).

3.7.1.6 New in Dynamics AX 2012

In Dynamics AX 2012, there is no option to register a credit note entering a negative *Receive now* quantity in the original purchase order line.

3.7.2   Inventory Valuation for Separate Credit Notes

If receiving a credit note from a vendor reducing the item price (e.g. refunding depreciation of damaged goods), there is no actual physical return of an item.

3.7.2.1   Crediting and Re-Invoicing

The easiest way for posting such a refund is to register and post a purchase line with negative quantity and the original price (credit note) and a new order line with positive quantity and the new price (invoice). You may register both lines in a common purchase order.

3.7.2.2   Crediting and Allocating Charges

If this is not suitable, for example if you have already shipped the credited goods, you have to post a credit note not directly referring to the item and allocate the credit amount to the item separately.

For registering this credit note, there are two options:

➢ **Vendor invoice form** – Entering an invoice line with negative quantity and an appropriate purchasing category.
➢ **Invoice journal** – Entering a journal line with negative amount and an appropriate ledger account (see section 8.3.3).

After posting the credit note, register a charges transaction for adjusting inventory valuation if applicable. For this purpose, select the original invoice in the invoice inquiry (*Accounts payable> Inquiries> Journals> Invoice journal*) and click the button *Charges/Adjustment* in the action pane strip.

In the *Allocate charges* form, enter a line for the charges transaction then. In the lookup *Charges code* of this transaction, only charges with a *Debit type* "Item" and a *Credit type* "Ledger account" are available. You may offset the balance on the credit ledger account by choosing a charges code referring to the ledger account applied in the credit note. The ledger account on the credit note is either determined by the purchasing category (if posting in the vendor invoice form) or entered as offset account in the invoice journal.

Information on the general use of charges is available in section 4.4.5 of this book, detailed information on the *Allocate charges* form in the online help of this form.

3.7.3   Case Study Exercise

Exercise 3.18 – Credit Note

The goods received in the first order line of exercise 3.11 show serious defects. You return them to your vendor and receive the credit note VC318. The vendor does not send a replacement. Which ways do you know for registering the credit note?

You decide to register the credit note in the original order. Enter the required data and post the credit note.

4 Sales and Distribution

The primary responsibility of sales and distribution is to provide customers with goods and services. In order to fulfill this task, sales and distribution needs to manage the material requirements of customers by processing sales orders from entering the order through picking and shipping to finally submitting the invoice.

4.1 Business Processes in Sales and Distribution

Before we start to go into details, the lines below give an overview of business processes in sales and distribution.

4.1.1 Basic Approach

Starting point for sales and distribution are correct master data, especially customer and product data. Instead of products, alternatively choose sales categories for selling non-stocked items.

4.1.1.1 Master Data and Transactions in Sales

In the course of sales order processing, master data are copied to transaction data. Sales quotations and orders therefore retrieve defaults from customer and product records (item records). You may modify these default data in transactions, for example if your customer requires a different delivery address in a specific order. If such a modification also applies to future orders, you should change the customer record.

Sales order processing is very similar to purchase order processing, as it mirrors the purchasing process. Figure 4-1 shows the primary steps of sales order processing.

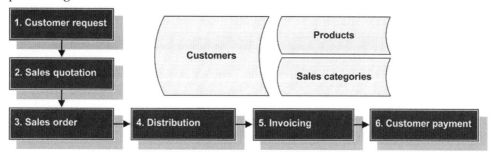

Figure 4-1:   Sales order processing in Dynamics AX

4.1.1.2 Sales Quotation

If we disregard prior marketing activities, sales order processing starts with a request from a customer or prospect. Answering this request, the sales team creates a quote and sends it to the possible or actual customer. Based on the sales quotation, Dynamics AX may generate activities to follow up on the quotation.

4.1.1.3 Sales Order

If the customer agrees to your proposal and orders your goods or services, you want to register a sales order. Like a purchase order, a sales order consists of a header, which primarily contains customer data, and one or more lines, which contain the ordered items (products and sales categories).

If required, send a sales order confirmation to the customer as hardcopy or electronic version by posting the order confirmation. Posting an order confirmation means to save it, ensuring that you may access the confirmed order data unchanged, no matter if there are modifications on the current order later.

For managing long-term contracts (blanket orders), enter sales agreements in Dynamics AX. If you want to issue a specific shipment related to the blanket order, create a release order for a partial quantity of the sales agreement. Release orders are regular sales orders referring to the agreement.

4.1.1.4 Distribution

Depending on the type and the settings of the item, master scheduling as part of operations planning covers the item supply, which is required to fulfill the sales order, through purchasing or production.

Before shipping the item, print a picking list preparing delivery if applicable. Then post the packing slip after finishing the internal shipment procedure.

The packing slip reduces both the physical quantity in inventory and the open sales order quantity. Posting a packing slip without prior posting a picking list is possible, if your company does not need picking lists.

4.1.1.5 Invoicing

After posting the packing slip, finally post the invoice. If you do not require a separate packing slip, optionally post the invoice without a prior packing slip. In this case, the invoice posts the physical and the financial transaction in parallel.

If you want to sell services or non-inventoried items, enter a sales order with order lines alternatively containing sales categories or item numbers.

Free text invoice are available, if you just need an invoice and do not require to process an order. In the lines of a free text invoice, you have to enter main accounts instead of products or sales categories.

4.1.1.6 Customer Payment

Before the due date, your customer has to pay the invoice with or without cash discount deduction. Section 8.3.4 contains a description on how to post the customer payment and to settle the invoice in the customer transactions.

If the customer does not pay in time, process payment reminders in Dynamics AX.

4.1.1.7 Ledger Integration

Because of the deep integration of Dynamics AX, all inventory and customer transactions in sales and distribution in parallel post to ledger accounts as described in section 8.4.

In order to keep record of the whole business process, Dynamics AX comprehensively applies the voucher principle to these transactions.

4.1.1.8 Comparison to Purchasing

As mentioned, sales order processing mirrors the purchasing process in many ways. Therefore Dynamics AX sales functionality is very similar to the appropriate purchasing function in various areas.

For your guidance, Figure 4-2 below shows a comparison of purchasing and sales documents in order processing.

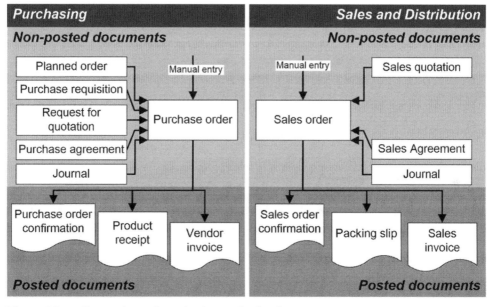

Figure 4-2:   Comparison of purchasing and sales documents

4.1.2   At a Glance: Sales Order Processing

In order to provide an overview of the main steps in sales order processing, this section shows the basics. For convenience, we create the order starting in the customer list page and post all transactions directly in the sales order form. Of course, you may alternatively enter the order in the *Sales Orders* list page and access the specific posting forms through the menu.

When creating a new sales order in the customer list page (*Sales and marketing> Common> Customers> All customers*), apply a filter for selecting the particular customer first. Clicking the button *New/Sales order* (not the big button *New/Sales quotation*) on the action pane tab *Sell* opens the line view of the sales order form in *Edit* mode, creating a new sales order header with default data like language or currency from the selected customer.

After clicking the button *Add line* on the tab *Sales order line*, or clicking on a new line there, start registering a sales order line with item number (or sales category), quantity and price. When selecting the item, Dynamics AX applies appropriate defaults for quantity, price, and other fields like site or warehouse. Clicking the button *Header view* (or *Line view*) in the action pane at the top of the form switches between the line view and the header view shown in Figure 4-3.

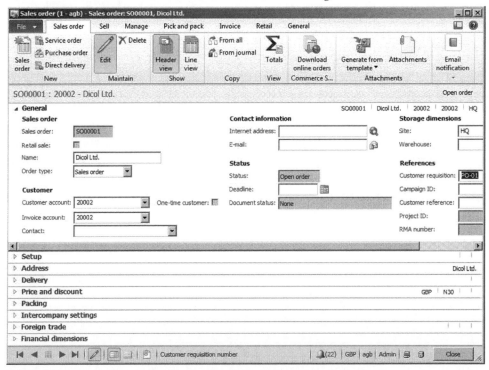

Figure 4-3:   Entering header data in the sales order header view

Note: If registering only one order line, you might need to press the *F5* key refreshing the form before you can post the order confirmation.

If you want to print the order confirmation, post it by clicking the button *Generate/Sales order confirmation* on the action pane tab *Sell*. In the posting form, make sure the checkboxes *Posting* and *Print confirmation* are selected and optionally click the button *Printer setup* for selecting a printer as described in section 2.2.1.

In order to post the packing slip in the sales order form, click the button *Generate/Packing slip* on the action pane tab *Pick and Pack* of the order form. In the posting form, choose the option "All" in the field *Quantity* in order to ship the entire quantity. Making sure the checkboxes *Posting* and *Print packing slip* are selected, click the button *OK* to post and print the packing slip. Packing slip posting in sales reduces the physical quantity in inventory and sets the order status to "Delivered".

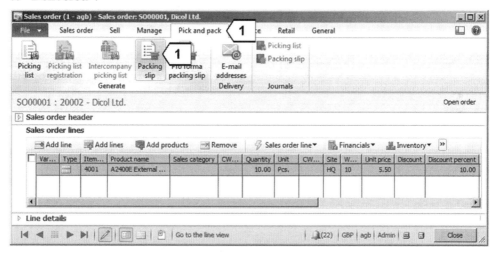

Figure 4-4: Clicking the button *Generate/Packing slip* in the action pane

Posting the sales invoice by clicking the button *Generate/Invoice* on the action pane tab *Invoice* of the order form is similar to packing slip posting. In order to invoice only shipped items, make sure to choose the option "Packing slip" in the lookup field *Quantity* of the posting form. If choosing the option "All", invoice posting in parallel ships the deliver remainder not included in prior packing slips. Invoice posting generates an open customer transaction to be paid and changes the order status to "Invoiced".

If applicable, skip transactions in the process described above. As a minimum, post the invoice immediately after entering the sales order (Selecting "All" in the *Quantity* field of the invoice posting form in this case).

4.2   Customer Management

Customer records are required for managing business partners, which receive goods or services. Whereas quotations are also available for leads and prospects, the business partner in a sales order has to be included in the customer records.

Customer records in sales mirror vendor records in purchasing not only regarding functional principles. Data management in both areas applies list pages and forms, which are very similar to each other. Example are one-time customers, payment terms, cash discounts, posting profiles, or the global address book integration, which work the same way both in customer and vendor records.

4.2.1   Basic Data and Comparison to Vendors Records

For edit existing or creating new customers, access the customer list page in the sales module (*Sales and marketing> Common> Customers> All customers*) or in the accounts receivable module (*Accounts receivable> Common> Customers> All customers*). According to the general structure of list pages, the customer page shows the list of available customers.

4.2.1.1   Create New Customer Dialog

If you want to create a new customer in the customer list page, click the button *New/Customer* in the action pane for accessing the *Create new customer* dialog. In the create dialog, which contains all core fields of the customer record, select the appropriate *Record type* ("Person" or "Organization") first. The field *Name* in the dialog is a lookup providing the option either to enter a new name or – if the customer is already a party in the global address book – to select an existing party.

Customer records are linked to the global address book in the same way vendor records refer to the global address book, which is why features like duplicate control work as described for vendors (see section 3.2.1).

Clicking the button *Save and open/Sales order* in the dialog provides the option to switch immediately to the sales order form for registering an order after entering the customer.

4.2.1.2   Customer Detail Form

If you want to view the details of a customer in the list page, double-click the line of the particular customer for accessing the related customer detail form. In the detail form, clicking the button *Edit* in the action pane switches to edit mode. Alternatively, immediately access the customer detail form in edit mode by clicking the button *Edit* in the list page after selecting the customer.

The customer form contains numerous fields, which represent default values for sales orders. Like the vendor group in vendor records, the *Customer group* in customer records is a core setting, controlling ledger integration through customer posting profiles (compare section 3.2.3). Further important fields include the *Sales tax group* (VAT group) on the tab *Invoice and delivery*, the currency on the tab *Sales demographics*, the terms of payment on the tab *Payment defaults*, and settings for blocking (lookup *Invoice and delivery on hold* on the tab *Credit and collections*).

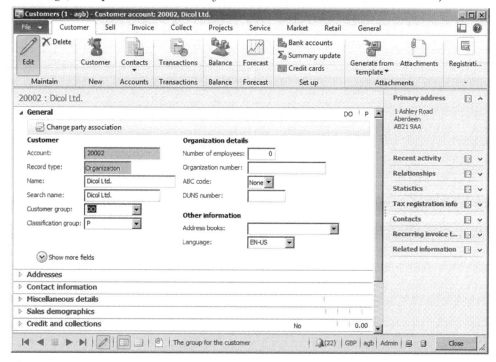

Figure 4-5:   Editing a customer in the customer detail form

Since structure and content of the fields in the customer record are very similar to the vendor record, the description below only covers deviations and elements, which primarily refer to customer records and which have not been explained for vendor records.

4.2.1.3 Invoice Account

In sales, it is sometimes required to send an invoice to a customer which is different to the order customer – e.g. if the invoice for subsidiaries of an affiliated group should be addressed to the head office. In order to comply with this situation, select the customer number of the invoice customer in the field *Invoice account* on the tab *Invoice and delivery*. A customer number registered there is the default for the field *Invoice account* in related sales order headers. If required, change the invoice account in the sales order.

Invoices of applicable orders post to the invoice customer instead of the order customer, generating an open customer transaction referring to the customer number of the invoice account. Unless chosen different in the lookup field *Invoice address* on the tab *Invoice and delivery* of the customer record, the printed invoice shows the address of the invoice account.

4.2.1.4   Alternative Address and Global Address Book Integration

Whereas the invoice account number in the customer form refers to a second customer number (assigning a separate customer record), adding addresses to a customer on the *Addresses* tab of the customer form assigns several postal addresses to a single customer number.

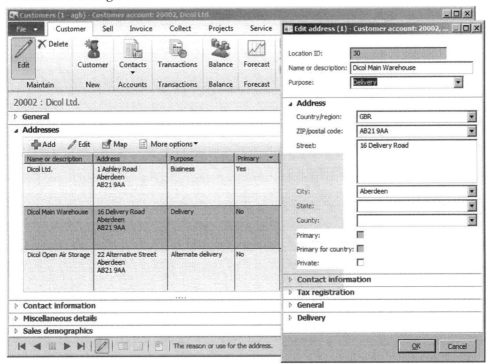

Figure 4-6:   Editing a customer delivery address in the address dialog

Like postal addresses for vendors (see section 3.2.1), customer addresses are shared with the related party in the global address book.

After clicking the button ![Add] in the action pane strip of the tab *Addresses*, the address dialog displays where you may register the name and one or several purposes. For the primary customer address, make sure the checkbox *Primary* is selected.

If entering an address with the purpose "Invoice", invoices for the customer print this address instead of the primary address. An address with the purpose "Delivery" is the default for the delivery address in sales orders. If you want to ship to an address which is different to the delivery address or the primary address (applies as default, if there is no specific delivery address), select one of the other customer addresses or enter a completely new address in the sales order then.

4.2.1.5 Print Management

Base settings for printing options like the destination (printer), the number of copies, or the footer text are available in the accounts receivable print management setup (*Accounts receivable> Setup> Forms> Form setup*, button *Print management*).

You may override these settings in the print management at customer level, accessible by clicking the button *Set up/Print management* on the action pane tab *General* of the customer form. After selecting the appropriate original or copy document in the left pane of the print management form, choose the option *Override* in the pop-up menu (which opens by right-hand clicking) before entering the individual settings. Customer print management settings are transferred to sales orders, where you may override them at order level again.

Print management settings (e.g. a specified printer) apply to documents, if the checkbox *Use print management destination* is selected in the particular posting form (see section 3.4.8).

4.2.1.6 Shipping Carrier and Mode of Delivery

If a shipping carrier interface – automatically integrating information from carrier software of selected carriers – is enabled in the form *Inventory and warehouse management> Setup> Sipping carrier> Carrier interface*, you have to select a *Mode of delivery* on the tab *Invoice and delivery* of the customer form. Modes of delivery (*Sales and marketing> Setup> Distribution> Modes of delivery*) specify the transport method, on the tab *Setup* in the mode of delivery including if and which carrier applies.

4.2.1.7 Credit Limit

Many companies want to apply credit limit control in sales operations. In order to activate credit limit control, the accounts receivable parameters (*Accounts receivable> Setup> Account receivable parameters*, tab *Credit rating*) include settings determining credit rating calculation. Depending on this setup, credit limit control includes only open invoices, or also packing slips, or additionally open orders, and shows a warning or an error message.

The tab *Credit and collections* in the customer form contains the field *Credit limit* for entering the credit limit amount of the customer. If the checkbox *Mandatory credit limit* is selected, the credit limit amount always applies. Otherwise, a credit limit amount of zero means unlimited credit.

When entering (or posting, depending on the parameter settings) a sales order, Dynamics AX checks if the customer exceeds the credit limit and either displays a warning message or prevents posting showing an error message.

4.2.1.8 New in Dynamics AX 2012

In Dynamics AX 2012, items new to customer management refer to the new user interface design, to the global address book integration, and to the carrier interface.

4.2.2   Case Study Exercises

Exercise 4.1 – Customer Record

A new domestic customer wants to order your items. Create a new record for this customer containing name (starting with our user ID), primary address, a mode of delivery without carrier and an appropriate customer and sales tax group for domestic customers. In addition, the terms of payment and the cash discount entered in exercise 3.1 apply.

The customer wants you to ship ordered goods to a separate delivery address. Therefore, enter a domestic delivery address of your choice, which should be the default for orders of this customer.

Note: If a _Balancing financial dimension_ applies, enter a default value for this dimension on the tab _Financial dimensions_ of the customer detail form.

Exercise 4.2 – Ledger Integration

You want to find out about ledger integration. To which summary account in the general ledger will an invoice for your new customer post?

4.3   Product Management for Sales

Apart from customer records (which are the main data source for sales order headers), products and sales categories (applying to order lines) are the second core area of master data for sales operations.

Product and released product records are required for inventoried items. For intangible items, alternatively apply item records (with the product type "Service" or specific item model groups) or sales categories.

The following section primarily contains an explanation of product record data necessary for sales and distribution. A more general description of product management is available in section 7.2.

4.3.1   Product Records and Categories in Sales

When entering a sales order line, alternatively enter one of the following fields in order to identify the sold item or service:

➢ **Item number** – Depending on the requirements, items may include a sales category.
➢ **Sales category** – For services and intangible products.

4.3.1.1 Sales Categories

A product category (see section 3.3.1) is a group of similar products or services, which you may access through category hierarchy administration (_Product information management> Setup> Categories> Category hierarchies_).

Product categories available in sales belong to the sales category hierarchy. An important category setting for sales is the sales tax group, which you may enter on the tab *Item sales tax groups* of the sales categories (*Sales and marketing> Setup> Categories> Sales categories*).

If creating a sales order not referring to a specific product, optionally enter the sales category in the order line and leave the item number field empty.

4.3.1.2 Product Record Structure

The product record structure in Dynamics AX shows two levels, including shared products for data common to all companies, and released products for company-specific data (see section 3.3.2 and 7.2.1).

You may access the shared product in the form *Product information management> Common> Products> All products and product masters*. Sales specific data are available in the released product form (*Product information management> Common> Released products*).

4.3.1.3 Creating a Product

In order to create a new product (item), access the shared product form and insert a record by clicking the button *New/Product* in the action pane. Apart from the basic product description in default language entered in the field *Description* of the shared product, optionally enter item descriptions in foreign languages after clicking the button *Languages/Translations* in the action pane.

Once you have finished entering shared product data, click the button *Release products* in the action pane of the shared product for creating released products. In the released product, you have to enter at least the item group, the item model group, and the dimension groups (if not specified on the shared product) then.

As an alternative to creating a shared product and releasing it, create a released product directly in the released product form by clicking the button *New/Product* on the action pane tab *Product*. In this case, the *New released product* dialog creates a shared product in parallel.

4.3.1.4 Sales Related Data

Core sales data, including the *Item sales tax group* (specifying whether regular sales tax / VAT or a reduced rate applies), are available on the tab *Sell* of the released product form.

After clicking the button *Order settings/Default order settings* on the action pane tab *Plan* of the released product form, enter settings for order quantities and lot size at company level. Site-specific settings are available after clicking the button *Site specific order settings* in the released product – in case of quantity settings selecting the checkbox *Override* in the site-specific order settings form.

The order setting forms contain data for purchasing, sales and inventory. In order to access sales-related data, switch to the tab *Sales order*. Marking the checkbox *Stopped* there blocks the product for sales transactions.

4.3.1.5   Discount Groups

Apart from the *Base sales price*, the tab *Sell* in the released product form also contains item discount groups for line discount and multiline discount. As shown below, line discount calculation is based on individual order lines whereas multiline discount calculation includes all lines of an order.

Another kind of discounts are total discounts (invoice discounts), which are specified at order header level, independent from items. But you may exclude particular products from the basis of total discount calculation by clearing the checkbox *Total discount* on the tab *Sell* in the released product form.

4.3.1.6   New in Dynamics AX 2012

In Dynamics AX 2012, shared products and sales categories are a new.

4.3.2   Sales Price and Discount

In addition to the base sales price available directly in the released product record, trade agreements provide the option to manage multiple price lists and discount agreements.

4.3.2.1   Base Sales Prices

The base sales price on the tab *Sell* of the released product form may be updated automatically based on the purchase or cost price. Settings for the automatic base price calculation are available in the field group *Price update* of the tab *Sell*, where the lookup field *Base price* provides two options:

➢ **Purchase price** – Sales price calculation refers to the base purchase price (tab *Purchase*).
➢ **Cost** – Sales price calculation refers to the base cost price (tab *Manage costs*).

The *Sales price model* specifies, if the price calculation is based on the field *Contribution ratio* or on the field *Charges percentage*. The *Sales price model* "None" means that there is no automatic calculation of the base sales price. The other options regarding base sales price (including price unit and charges) are similar to the base purchase price settings (see section 3.3.3).

In addition to the base sales price on the tab *Sell* of the released product form, base prices at site level are available in the item price form. For accessing the item price form, click the button *Set up/Item Price* on the action pane tab *Manage* costs of the released product. If applicable, run a calculation of sales prices in the item price form based on the bill of materials and the route of manufactured items.

4.3.2.2   Structure of Trade Agreements

Trade agreements in sales determine prices and discounts depending on customers and items (released products). Dynamics AX includes following types of trade agreements for this purpose:

> ➤ **Sales prices**
> ➤ **Line discounts**
> ➤ **Multiline discounts**
> ➤ **Total discounts** (Invoice discounts)

A description on managing prices in trade agreements on the example of purchase prices is available in section 3.3.3. In addition to the options available in purchasing, specify a *Generic currency* and an *Exchange rate type* in the accounts receivable parameters (*Accounts receivable> Setup> Accounts receivable parameters*, tab *Prices*) if applicable for automatically converting from price list prices in the generic currency to other currencies when registering a sales order line.

Discounts show two different levels of assignment:

> ➤ **Line and multiline discounts** – Assigned to order lines
> ➤ **Total discounts** – Assigned to order headers

In trade agreements, discounts and prices may refer to different pricing levels. A line discount agreement for example may apply to an individual customer, to a customer discount group, or to all customers. In parallel, the discount agreement may apply to an individual item, to an item discount group, or to all items.

Table 4-1 shows an overview of the different levels in two dimensions – the item and the customer dimension – available for line and multiline discounts.

Table 4-1:   Discount specification levels for line discount and multiline discount

	Item number	Item discount group	All items
Customer number	*Only line discount*	*Line and multiline*	*Line and multiline*
Customer discount group	*Only line discount*	*Line and multiline*	*Line and multiline*
All customers	*Only line discount*	*Line and multiline*	*Line and multiline*

In comparison, trade agreements for prices and trade agreements for total discounts show only one dimension. Prices are available per item, which restricts the item dimension to "Item number", whereas total discounts apply at order header level, restricting the item dimension to "All items".

4.3.2.3 Viewing Line Discount Agreements

In order to view sales line discounts, access the line discounts form from different menu items depending on the basis for the discount:

> ➤ **For an item** (including the line discount group of the item) – In the released product form, click the button *View/Line discount* on action pane tab *Sell*
> ➤ **For a customer** (including the line discount group of the customer) – In the customer form, click the button *Trade agreements/Discounts/Line discount* on action pane tab *Sell*
> ➤ **For an item discount group** – In the item discount group form (*Sales and marketing> Setup> Price/discount> Item discount groups*), click the button *Trade agreements/View line discount*

➢ **For a customer discount group** – In the customer price/discount group form (*Sales and marketing> Setup> Price/discount> Customer price/discount groups*), select the option "Line discount group" in the lookup *Show* and click the button *Trade agreements/View line discount*

If you want to view the line discounts for a customer discount group for example, open the customer price/discount groups (*Sales and marketing> Setup> Price/discount> Customer price/discount groups*) and choose the option "Line discount group" in the lookup field *Show*. After clicking the button *Trade agreements/View line discount* you may view available line discounts.

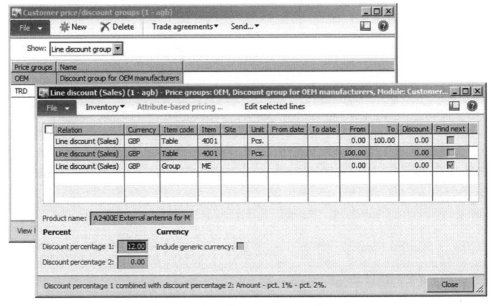

Figure 4-7:   Viewing line discounts based on a customer discount group

In the line discounts form, discount percentages display in the footer part of the form. The column *Discount* shows a discount amount.

Another important setting for discount calculation is available in the column *Find next* of the discounts form. The checkbox there should only be marked for discounts, which apply in addition to discounts entered at a different level. In Figure 4-7 for example, the discount in a sales order line would be 17 percent, if the checkbox *Find next* was marked for the 12 percent discount line and a discount of 5 percent would apply to the appropriate item discount group.

4.3.2.4   Creating, Updating and Deleting Line Discount Agreements

Like registering a new price agreement (see section 3.3.3), registering a new sales line discount agreement requires entering and posting a price/discount agreement journal (*Sales and marketing> Journals> Price/discount agreement journals*). After creating a journal by clicking the button *New* in the agreement journal header form, click the button *Lines* in order to switch to the journal lines.

When registering a sales line discount in an agreement journal line, make sure to select "Line discount (Sales)" in the column *Relation*. Similar to price agreements, line discount agreements may refer to following fields:

➢ **Period of validity** – From date and to date, depending on the accounts receivable parameters *Date type* on the tab *Prices* referring to order entry or delivery date
➢ **Quantity** – From and to quantity
➢ **Unit of measure**
➢ **Currency**
➢ **Customer dimension level** (column *Account code*) – Individual customer, customer group or all customers
➢ **Item dimension level** (column *Item code*) – Individual item, group or all

When entering line discounts you have to keep in mind, that discount percentages show in the footer part of the journal lines (compare Figure 4-7).

If you want to enter line discounts at inventory dimension level (e.g. per site or color) and the appropriate dimension column does not show, click the button *Inventory/Dimensions display* in the action pane strip and select the appropriate dimension. As a prerequisite, the dimension group of the particular item has to include the selected dimension in the price search.

After registering the line discounts in the agreement journal, click the button *Post* to activate the agreement.

If you want to update or delete an active trade agreement, access the appropriate form for viewing the trade agreement and select the agreement before clicking the button *Edit selected lines*. Like when updating purchase prices (see section 3.3.3), the update or deletion is posted through a new journal referring to the selected agreement.

4.3.2.5 Managing Multiline Discounts

Whereas line discount calculation is based on individual order lines, multiline discount calculation includes all items of the particular order, which got the same multiline discount group. You may apply multiline discounts for example if you want to give a quantity discount based on the total quantity of several items.

Viewing and managing multiline discounts is similar to managing line discounts.

4.3.2.6 Total Discounts

Unlike line discounts, total discounts (invoice discounts) are not based on items or item groups. Total discounts refer to the complete invoice and show the option to enter a discount based on the invoice total.

4.3.2.7 Settings for Discount

As a prerequisite for applying trade agreements at group level, the appropriate price and discount group has to be entered in the customer form and/or the released product form.

In the customer form, fields for assigning discount groups are available on the tab *Sales order defaults*. In the released product form, fields for assigning the line and the multiline discount group in sales are available on the tab *Sell*. The checkbox *Total discount* in the released product is available for including or excluding an item from total discount calculation.

If line discount and multiline discount in parallel apply to a particular sales order line, the lookup field *Discount* on the tab *Prices* of the accounts receivable parameters controls, how to calculate the total of line and multiline discount.

The setting, which levels ("Table", "Group", "All") are applicable in price and discount calculation, is available in the form *Sales and marketing> Setup> Price/discount> Activate price/discount*.

Within the activated elements, discount calculation searches from the specific definition to the general – first the customer and item number level, then the group level, and finally the general discount level. Depending on the setting in the checkbox *Find next* of the selected trade agreements, only one discount or the total of discounts at several levels applies to the particular order line.

4.3.2.8 Ledger Integration

Since discounts affect finance, Dynamics AX includes discount posting in ledger transactions. Concerning both, ledger transactions and revenue calculation in sales, you have to distinguish between line and multiline discounts on the one hand and total discounts on the other hand.

Line and multiline discounts are included in item revenue calculation, therefore reducing revenue and gross margin. Settings for the ledger integration of line and multiline discounts provide the option to either reduce the amount posted to revenue accounts of the sold products, or to post these discounts to separate accounts. Dynamics AX posts to separate accounts, if the inventory posting setup (see section 8.4.2) contains appropriate main accounts (*Inventory and warehouse management> Setup> Posting> Posting*, tab *Sales order*, option *Discount*).

Unlike line and multiline discounts, total discounts do not reduce the revenue at item level. As a limitation of total discounts, it is not possible to post these discounts to different main accounts. The account number for total discount transactions is available in the accounts for automatic transaction (*General ledger> Setup> Posting> Accounts for automatic transactions*), where a line for the posting type "Customer invoice discount" contains the appropriate main account.

4.3.2.9 Discounts in Sales Orders

Line discounts immediately show in an order line, if an applicable trade agreement is available. For multiline discounts and total discounts, you have to run a calculation for determining the discount amount when finishing order entry (see section 4.4.4).

If applicable in a sales order line, override the line discount default or manually enter a new discount, independently from trade agreement settings. If manually entering or changing a line discount, and later modifying data in fields of the order line which are among the basis of price calculation (e.g. the ordered quantity), Dynamics AX may overwrite the manual discount with the applicable trade agreement. Depending on the accounts receivable parameters (tab *Prices*, include the source "Manual entry" in the section *Trade agreement evaluation*), Dynamics AX shows a dialog before overwriting the manual discount.

4.3.2.10 New in Dynamics AX 2012

New items in Dynamics AX 2012 are the option of price lists in a generic currency and the requirement to post agreement journals for updating trade agreements.

4.3.3 Case Study Exercises

Exercise 4.3 – Sales Categories

Your company offers installation services to your customers. For this purpose enter a new sales category "##-installation" (## = your user ID) independent from the product categories for purchasing of exercise 3.4. When setting up the new sales category, make sure it contains the item sales tax group referring to the standard tax rate.

Exercise 4.4 – Price List

Your company requires an additional price list applicable to new sales markets. Enter a new customer price group P-## (## = your user ID) for this price list and attach it to your customer of exercise 4.1.

The new price list should show a price of GBP 90.00 starting from the current date for the item of exercise 3.5. Enter and post this price in a price/discount agreement journal. Finally you want to check if the price shows correctly on your customer.

Exercise 4.5 – Line Discount

You agree with your customer of exercise 4.1 to grant a line discount of 10 percent for all items. Enter and post a trade agreement for this discount, which only applies to your customer. Make sure to enter a percentage, not a discount amount.

Which setting is required to make use of this discount in sales order lines?

4.4 Sales Orders and Quotations

The first step of sales order processing in Dynamics AX often is a sales quote, which you may send to a prospect or customer in reply to a request for quotation.

Once the customer orders goods or services, you want to enter an appropriate sales order. With regard to the functionality and structure of forms and list pages, sales orders largely mirror purchase orders. This section therefore primarily contains the description of issues, which are different in sales compared to purchasing.

4.4.1   Basics of Sales Order Processing

Unlike purchase orders, which are primarily based on item demand available as a data source within the Dynamics AX database, sales orders in most cases originate from sources outside the database.

Apart from the manual entry of a sales order, there are only a few other options within Dynamics AX for generating a sales order. Possible preliminary steps to a sales order are as follows:

➢ **Sales quotations**
➢ **Sales agreements** – Blanket orders
➢ **Enterprise Portal** – Web shop
➢ **AIF framework** – exchanging data with other applications
➢ **Intercompany functionality** – Purchase orders of another legal entity

4.4.1.1   Sales Agreements

In Dynamics AX, blanket orders are covered by sales agreements (*Sales and marketing> Common> Sales orders> Sales agreements*), which do not only contain contracts at the level of product number and quantity, but also at the level of the sales amount for a product, or at the level of the total sales volume for a customer.

In order to ship and invoice deliveries referring to a sales agreement, you have to create release orders (regular sales orders linked to a sales agreement). The functionality of sales agreement matches the purchase agreements functionality as shown in section 3.4.9.

4.4.1.2   Sales Order Processing

Once you have finished creating a new sales order – either manually or transferring a prior document like the sales agreement – you may post and print the order confirmation. The further proceeding depends on the actual transactions in inventory and sales, and on the company settings in Dynamics AX.

As shown in Figure 4-8, there are four different options for processing a sales order in Dynamics AX:

➢ **Packing slip** – Without prior transactions in Dynamics AX
➢ **Picking list** – Posting a picking list before packing slip posting
➢ **Picking list registration** – Registration of the posted picking list before packing slip posting
➢ **Output orders and shipments** – Specific transactions in inventory (with warehouse locations and pallet transports) before packing slip posting

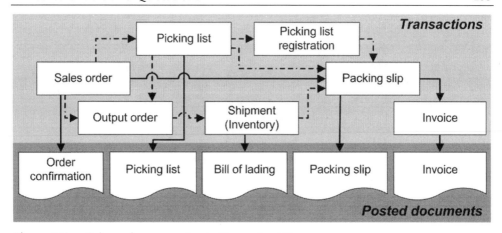

Figure 4-8:   Sales order processing in Dynamics AX

The primary difference between the available options is the way of executing picking in inventory management.

4.4.2   Sales Quotations

In Dynamics AX, the business partner in a sales quotation hasn't got to be a customer – it may be a prospect as well. But since sales orders require a customer record, you have to convert the prospect to a customer before accepting a quotation and transferring it to an order.

4.4.2.1 Managing Prospects

Prospects are parties – companies or persons – in sales, which are not customers yet. Unlike customers, which are applicable to accounts receivable transactions, prospects do not show transactions relevant to finance. But they are available for CRM activities like mailings and marketing campaigns, and for sales quotations.

If you want to register a new prospect, access the form *Sales and marketing> Common> Prospect> All prospects* and click the button *New/Prospect* in the action pane for accessing the *Create new prospect* dialog. The create prospect dialog works like the create customer dialog (see section 4.2.1), integrating prospects with the global address book.

In the detail form, check core data like the sales tax group (VAT group) and the customer group of the new prospect then. Some default data like the prospect type (*Type ID* on the tab *General*) for a new prospect derive from the tab *Prospects* in the sales and marketing parameters. A new prospect is generated automatically when entering an opportunity (*Sales and marketing> Common> Opportunities> All opportunities*) with a new party name.

If you want to convert the prospect to a customer, click the button *Convert/Convert to customer* on the action pane tab *General* of the prospect form. Depending on the setting in the type (*Sales and marketing> Setup> Prospects> Relation types*) of the prospect, the prospect is deleted automatically when converting.

4.4.2.2   Processing Sales Quotations

For creating a new sales quotation, click the button *New/Sales quotation* on the action pane tab *Quotation* of the list page *Sales and marketing> Common> Sales quotations> All quotations*. Alternatively, create a sales quotation by clicking the button *New/Sales quotation* on action pane tab *Sell* in the customer form or in the prospect form.

If creating a quotation in the sales quotation form, the *Create quotation* dialog displays where you have to select the *Account type* ("Customer" or "Prospect"). Depending on the selected type, subsequently enter a prospect or a customer in the appropriate lookup field. Dynamics AX then applies default values from the selected customer or prospect to the sales quotation, which you may override in the create dialog. Clicking the button *OK* in the dialog finally creates the quotation header and switches to the quotation detail form showing the line view.

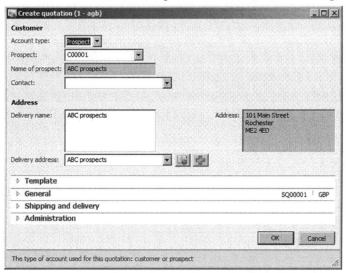

Figure 4-9:   Creating a new quotation for a prospect

In the quotation detail form, start to enter a line on the tab *Lines* by simply clicking the first line in the grid or clicking the button ![Add line] in the action pane strip. Then select an item number or a sales category and other line details as required.

Clicking the button *Generate/Send quotation* on the action pane tab *Quotation* of the quotation detail form posts and prints the quotation (similar to an order confirmation in a sales order). Depending on the answer of the prospect or customer, click the button *Confirm* on the action pane tab *Follow up* of the quotation form later for confirming the quotation and automatically generating a sales order.

If the quote refers to a prospect, you have to transfer the prospect to a customer before creating the sales order. For this purpose, the button *Convert to customer* is available on the action pane tab *Follow up* directly in the quotation form.

4.4.3 Sales Order Registration

Like in a purchase order, the order type in a sales order is a core characteristic. Sales orders may contain following order types:

➢ **Sales order** – Regular sales order
➢ **Journal** – Draft or template, not affecting inventory and finance
➢ **Subscription** – Periodic order, remains open after invoicing
➢ **Returned order** – Credit notes, see section 4.6.4

The order type "Item requirements" shown as additional option is applicable for a specific kind of sales orders generated in the Dynamics AX project module, which is beyond the scope of this book. It is not possible to manually enter orders of the type "Item requirements" in sales.

4.4.3.1 Entering a New Sales Order

If you want to enter a sales order manually, either start in the customer form (clicking the button *New/Sales order* on the action pane tab *Sell*) or in the sales order form.

If starting in the sales order form (*Sales and marketing> Common> Sales orders> All sales orders*), click the button *New/Sales order* on the action pane tab *Sales order*. In the *Create sales order* dialog, choose a customer in the lookup then (e.g. applying a *Filter by field* doing a right-hand click in the column *Name* of the lookup). Default values from the selected customer apply to the order, which you may override in the dialog. Clicking the button *OK* in the dialog finally creates the sales order header and switches to the order detail form showing the line view.

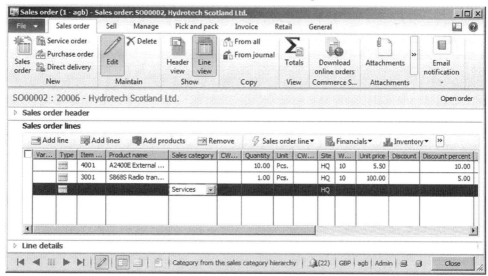

Figure 4-10: Entering a sales order line with a sales category in the order form

In the sales order detail form, start to enter a line on the tab *Lines* by simply clicking the first line in the grid or clicking the button [Add line] in the action pane strip. Then select an item number or a sales category and other line details as required.

Working in sales orders widely matches purchase orders, which is why you may refer to section 3.4.5 regarding following topics:

➢ Structure and functions in the order form
➢ Delivery address in order header and lines
➢ Sales tax / VAT (see also section 8.2.6)
➢ Copy function
➢ Using orders of the type "Journal"

In the description of purchase order processing, following subjects also apply to sales order processing:

➢ Canceling orders (Section 3.4.7)
➢ Partial delivery, over and under delivery (Section 3.5.5)
➢ Order status and inquiries (Section 0 and 3.6.3)

4.4.3.2 Deleting a Sales Order

Unlike purchase orders, sales orders do not apply change management and order approval. Among other items, there are differences between sales orders and purchase orders with regard to deleting an order. When deleting sales orders, following accounts receivable parameters (*Accounts receivable> Setup> Accounts receivable parameters*) apply:

➢ **Mark order as voided** (tab *General*) – If selected, deleted sales orders show in the form *Sales and marketing> Inquiries> History> Voided sales orders*.
➢ **Delete order line invoiced in total** and **Delete order after invoicing** (tab *Updates*) – If marked, orders or order lines are deleted when posting the invoice.

4.4.3.3 Delivery Date Calculation

An issue in sales orders, which is quite different to purchase orders, is the assignment of delivery dates. A number of aspects determine the calculation of delivery dates in sales:

➢ Order entry deadlines
➢ Sales lead time
➢ Delivery date control
➢ Availability and item requirements

Regarding delivery date, Dynamics AX distinguishes between the shipping date and the date when the customer receives the item on the one hand and between a requested and a confirmed date on the other hand. In order to manage these different dates, four different fields referring to the delivery date are available on the sub-tab *Delivery* of the tab *Line details* in the sales order lines.

4.4.3.4 Order Entry Deadlines and Sales Lead Time

Order entry deadlines (*Inventory and warehouse management> Setup> Distribution> Order entry deadlines*) determine the final time for entering same-day shipments in sales order lines. After the deadline, delivery date calculation starts with the next day.

The sales lead time is the number of days required internally until shipping an item. A general setting for the sales lead time is available on the tab *Shipments* of the accounts receivable parameters. The lead time specified there applies as a default to the ship date in the order header. Order lines accept the header ship date, if the calculated date based on the sales lead time of the item is not after the header ship date.

You may specify sales lead times for items in the default or site-specific order settings (button *Default order settings* or *Site specific order settings* on the action pane tab *Plan* of the released product form), and in trade agreements for sales prices.

4.4.3.5 Delivery Date Control

If you want to check shipping calendars and item availability for determining delivery dates when entering a sales order line, activate the delivery date control on the tab *Shipments* of the accounts receivable parameters. For this purpose, the lookup *Delivery date control* provides following options for delivery date calculation:

➤ **None** – Not applying delivery date control
➤ **Sales lead time** – Delivery date based on lead time and calendar settings
➤ **ATP** ("Available to promise") – Delivery date based on the item availability
➤ **ATP + Issue margin** – Adding the issue margin from the item coverage to the delivery date of ATP calculation
➤ **CTP** ("Capable to promise") – Immediately performing local master scheduling

Selecting the option "Sales lead time", delivery date calculation in sales order lines is only based on the applicable sales lead time and calendars.

Selecting the option "ATP", delivery date calculation is based on the item availability within the *ATP time fence*. Existing planned orders are included in the ATP calculation, if the checkbox *ATP incl. planned orders* in the accounts receivable parameters is selected. If the quantity entered in a sales order line is not available (the calculation includes the quantity on hand and transactions within the ATP time fence), the shipping date is the first day after the ATP time fence. In order to avoid unnecessary delays, the ATP time fence should consequently match the lead time.

The ATP offset time settings in the accounts receivable parameters apply to the calculation of delayed demand and supply transactions, which are scheduled for past periods.

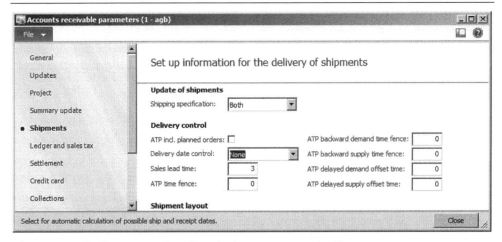

Figure 4-11: Delivery control settings in the accounts receivable parameters

Selecting the option "CTP", delivery date calculation immediately performs local master scheduling in the current dynamic master plan (see section 6.3.1), creating planned purchase and production orders as required. In case of a planned production order, the delivery date resulting from the planned order includes the delivery time for components.

Delivery date control settings on the item (default/site-specific order settings in the released product form) override the base settings in the accounts receivable parameters. If you want to activate or deactivate delivery control for a specific sales order or sales order line, optionally override the lookup *Delivery date control* on the (sub-)tab *Delivery* of the order header or line.

Delivery date calculation includes following calendar and transport time settings:

➢ *Inventory and warehouse management> Setup> Inventory breakdown> Warehouses,* tab *Master planning – Calendar* of the shipping and the receipt warehouses
➢ *Organization administration> Setup> Organization> Legal entities,* tab *Foreign trade and logistics –* General *Shipping calendar* of your company
➢ *Sales and marketing> Common> Customers> All customers –* In the detail form, *Receipt calendar* for the customer or the assigned delivery addresses
➢ *Sales and marketing> Setup> Distribution> Modes of delivery,* button *Transport calendar –* Transport calendar for delivery mode and – optionally – warehouse
➢ *Inventory and warehouse management> Setup> Distribution> Transport – Transport days* depending on delivery mode, shipping warehouse and receipt address or warehouse

In case delivery date control is activated, Dynamics AX checks if the item in the order line is available at the entered delivery date. In order to receive a proposal of possible delivery dates, click the button 🔳 near the field *Confirmed ship date* on the (sub-)tab *Delivery* in the order header or line.

If necessary, deactivate delivery date control by selecting the option "None" in the lookup *Delivery date control* on the order header or line. After deactivating delivery date control, you can enter a date which is not included in the regular dates of possible delivery.

4.4.3.6 Inquiries on Item Availability

Multiple inquiries are available in the sales order form for checking the availability of an item. If you only want to view the current inventory quantity of the item including applicable inventory dimensions (like site/warehouse), click the button *Inventory/On-hand inventory* in the action pane strip of the order line. In addition to the current quantity on hand, the form also displays data referring to reservation and transaction totals (see section 7.2.5).

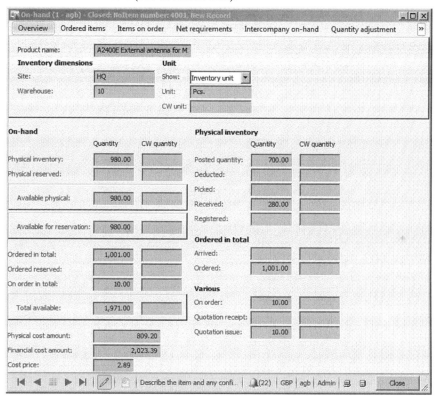

Figure 4-12: Checking inventory for an order line in the on-hand form

For viewing the distribution of the item quantity among warehouses and other inventory dimensions, click the button *Overview* in the *On-hand*-form. Clicking the button *Dimensions display* (rightmost in the action pane strip) there enables selecting displayed inventory dimensions. If clicking the button *Net requirements*, the net requirements form for starting local master scheduling displays.

For accessing the net requirements form, alternatively click the button *Product and supply/Net requirements* in the action pane strip of the sales order line. The button

Product and supply/Explosion in the action pane strip of the order line opens the explosion form, which shows the item availability at multiple BOM levels.

More details on master scheduling and BOM explosion are available in section 6.3 of this book.

4.4.3.7   Delivery Address

The delivery address for a sales order derives from the primary address or – if specified – from the delivery address of the customer. The tab *Address* in the header view of the order then provides the option to choose an alternative address:

➢ **Selecting an existing address** – An address, which is already included in the global address book, may be selected by clicking the button ▨ near the *Delivery address* lookup field.
➢ **Register a new address** – A completely new address may be entered by clicking the button ▨ near the *Delivery address* lookup field.

If a sales order requires shipping to different addresses at order line level, select appropriate addresses on the sub-tab *Address* of the order lines. In this context, a setting on the tab *Summary update* of the accounts receivable parameters specifies whether posted documents (e.g. invoices) are split based on different addresses.

4.4.3.8   Invoice Address

Unlike the delivery address, address data for the invoice address in a sales order are not directly editable. The invoice address is the address of the *Invoice account* on the tab *General* in the sales order header view. The default for the invoice account number derives from the customer record of the order customer, but you can choose a different invoice account number in an order.

If the invoice account field in the customer record is empty, Dynamics AX inserts the order customer number into the invoice account of the order. In case the customer record of the invoice account contains an address of the type "Invoice", this address prints on documents instead of the primary address of the invoice customer.

4.4.4   Sales Prices and Discounts

Based on price and discount groups in the order header, ordered products and applicable trade agreements, Dynamics AX determines prices and discounts.

4.4.4.1   Sales Price

The sales price in an order line derives from the base price in the item record, or from applicable trade agreements. Trade agreements for prices at customer number level take priority over prices at price group level.

You may assign a customer to a price group (representing a price list in Dynamics AX) by selecting the appropriate *Price group* on the tab *Sales order defaults* of the customer form. When entering a sales order, the price group of the customer defaults to the price group on the tab *Price and discount* of the sales order header view. If required, change the price group in the sales order.

In the sales order lines, override the sales price default or manually enter a new price independently from trade agreements if applicable.

If manually entering or changing a sales price, and later modifying data in fields of the order line which are among the basis of price calculation (e.g. the ordered quantity), Dynamics AX may overwrite your manual discount with the applicable trade agreement. Depending on the accounts receivable parameters, Dynamics AX shows a confirmation dialog in this case (see also section 4.3.2).

4.4.4.2 Discounts

If trade agreements include applicable total discounts, multiline discounts or line discounts, sales orders retrieve appropriate defaults. If you want to change a discount group in the order header, select the appropriate group on the tab *Price and discount* of the sales order header view.

Since the total discount is a discount at header level, the order header does not only contain the discount group for the total discount, but also the discount percentage.

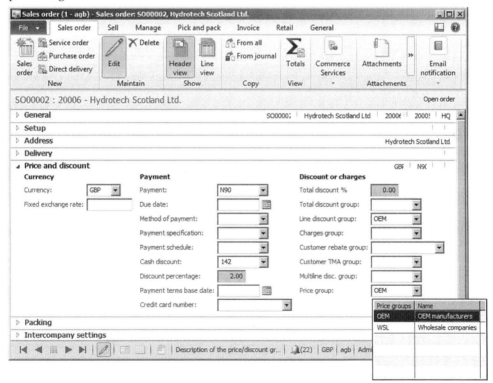

Figure 4-13:   Price and discount groups in the sales order header view

The percentage for the line discount shows in a column on the tab *Sales order lines* in the line view. Together with the multiline discount, the line discount percentage also shows on the sub-tab *Price and discount* of the tab *Line detail* in the order line. In parallel to the percentage, there are separate fields for a line discount amount and a multiline discount amount – be aware not to confuse percentage and amount fields.

Dynamics AX calculates the line discount for a sales order line whenever saving the line. Unlike line discount calculation, multiline discount and total discount calculation need to be started manually by clicking the button *Calculate/Multiline discount* or *Calculate/Total discount* on the action pane tab *Sell*.

For the total discount, optionally skip manual calculation if the checkbox *Calculate total discount on posting* on the tab *Prices* of the accounts receivable parameters is selected. In this case, Dynamics AX calculates the total discount whenever printing or posting an order.

4.4.4.3 New in Dynamics AX 2012

The option to show a dialog for retrieving prices and discounts from applicable trade agreements after changing an order line is new in Dynamics AX 2012.

4.4.5   Managing Charges

Charges (in former releases called "Miscellaneous charges") in sales and purchase orders are available to cover expenses, which are not included in the price shown in order lines – for example fees for freight and insurance.

You can enter charges manually in a sales or purchase order. In addition, default charges automatically applying when entering an order are available.

Charges are available at header level and at line level. Standard documents like the order confirmation only print the charges total amount, no matter if the applicable charges refer to the header or to specific lines.

4.4.5.1 Charges Codes

As a prerequisite for applying charges, you have to set up the required charges codes. Charges codes for sales and purchasing are independent from each other. For sales you have to access the form *Accounts receivable> Setup> Charges> Charges code*, and for purchasing the form *Accounts payable> Setup> Charges> Charges code*.

When creating a new charges code, enter the charges code ID, the description, and the item sales tax group (if applicable) before switching to the tab *Posting*, where you want to record appropriate ledger integration settings.

For sales charges posting, choose the *Debit/Type* "Customer/Vendor" if you want to calculate the charges on top of the item sales, printing them on documents (e.g. invoices) separately. The *Credit/Type* is "Ledger account" in this case, referring to an appropriate revenue account in the *Account* field.

For purchase charges shown separately on the vendor invoice, choose the option "Customer/Vendor" in the *Credit/Type*. In the *Debit/Type*, select "Ledger account" (posting to a separate ledger account) or "Item" (including the charges amount in the inventory value).

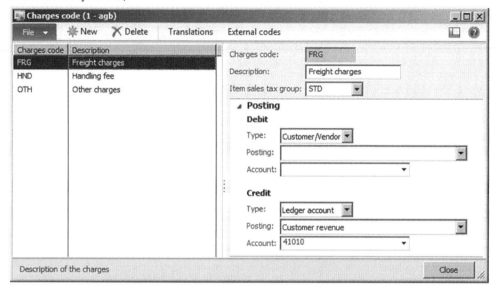

Figure 4-14: Managing charges codes for sales

In addition to the charges described above, which show separately on documents, it is also possible to set up charges codes only generating internal transactions in finance. These codes only include the types "Ledger account" or "Item" for the *Debit* and the *Credit* transaction.

4.4.5.2 Manual Charges

If you want to apply charges to a sales order or to a purchase order, access the charges transactions form.

At header level, the charges transaction form of a sales order is available by clicking the button *Charges/Charges* on the action pane tab *Sell* of the sales order form. In purchase orders, click the button *Charges/Manage charges* (or *Charges/Maintain charges*) on the action pane tab *Purchase*. For assigning line charges in the sales order or purchase order detail form, click the button *Financials/Maintain charges* in the action pane strip on the tab *Order lines* after selecting the appropriate order line.

In the charges transactions form, select the appropriate charges code first. In the column *Category* you may specify if the charge is a fixed amount or if it is calculated based on the line amount or the line quantity.

4.4.5.3 Auto Charges

If particular charges should automatically apply to sales orders, enter automatic charges in the form *Accounts receivable> Setup> Charges> Auto charges*. Auto charges default to the charges in the charges transactions of related sales orders, where you can override them if necessary.

The header of the auto-charges form contains the lookup *Level* for choosing whether to apply the charges to order headers (*Level* = "Main") or to lines (*Level* = "Line").

The right pane of the form contains the customers and items to which the charge applies. Line charges may depend on the customer (customer number, group, or all customers), the mode of delivery (mode of delivery, group, or all) and on the item (item number, group, or all). For header charges, the item selection is fixed to "All".

In order to enter the calculation formula for the charge, access the tab *Lines* then.

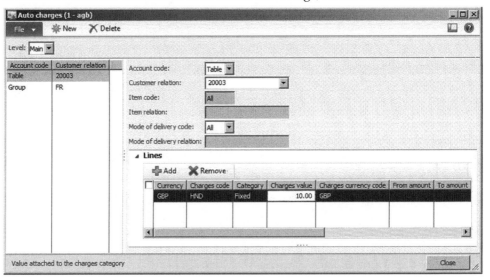

Figure 4-15:   Managing auto charges

As a prerequisite for applying auto charges in sales orders, the checkboxes *Find main charges* (for header charges) and *Find charges for line* (for line charges) on the tab *Prices* of the accounts receivable parameters have to be selected.

For purchasing, similar settings are available in the form *Procurement and sourcing> Setup> Charges> Automatic charges* and in the procurement parameters.

4.4.5.4 New in Dynamics AX 2012 R2

Compared with the initial version of Dynamics AX 2012, the R2 version contains modes of delivery as additional level for auto-charges in sales.

4.4.6   Sales Order Confirmation

Printing an order confirmation requires posting it in Dynamics AX. Like confirming a purchase order, posting a sales order confirmation does not create inventory or financial transactions.

Posting an order confirmation means to save it unchanging and separately from the current sales order. Within Dynamics AX, it is evidence of the document which has been sent to the customer.

4.4.6.1   Posting Form for Sales Order Confirmations

In order to post and print an order confirmation, click the button *Generate/Confirmation* (or *Generate/Sales order confirmation*) on the action pane tab *Sell* after selecting the appropriate order in the sales order form.

The posting form for the sales order confirmation is similar to the posting forms in purchasing (see in section 3.4.8). Like there, choose the printer by clicking the button *Printer setup* or by selecting the checkbox *Use print management destination*. Making sure the checkboxes *Posting* and *Print confirmation* are selected, click the button *OK* in the posting form for finally posting and printing the confirmation.

As an alternative to the sales order form, access the posting form for order confirmations through the appropriate menu item for summary update (*Sales and marketing> Periodic> Sales update> Sales order confirmation*). In the posting form for summary update, apply a filter by clicking the button *Select* then.

4.4.6.2   Inquiries

Once a sales order confirmation has been posted, the posted document is available for displaying and reprinting independent from modifications to the current order. For viewing posted order confirmations, access the form *Sales and marketing> Inquiries> Journals> Confirmation* or click the button *Journals/Sales order confirmation* on the action pane tab *Sell* in the sales order form.

4.4.7   Case Study Exercises

Exercise 4.6 – Sales Order
Your customer (entered in exercise 4.1) orders 20 units of the item entered in exercise 3.5. You want to register the sales order starting in the customer form. Which quantity and which price show as default, where do they come from?

Switching to the header view, you want to check the delivery address and the price group of the current order.

Exercise 4.7 – Charges
Your company wants to invoice a handling fee to customers. Enter a charges code C-## (## = your user ID) to which the standard tax rate applies, selecting the posting type "Customer revenue" and an appropriate revenue account for credit posting.

In the sales order header of exercise 4.6, make sure this new handling fee is charged to the customer by entering a charge of 10.00 pounds.

Exercise 4.8 – Order Confirmation

Post and print the order confirmation for your order of exercise 4.6, selecting to display a print preview. Can you tell which amount shows in the order line and where the confirmation prints the charges?

4.5 Distribution

On the ship date, the warehouse has to pick and to ship the ordered items. Picking, as a preparation of the shipment, is collecting required items within the warehouse.

4.5.1 Basics and Setup for Picking and Shipping

In Dynamics AX, you are not required to register picking separately. You can ship an item by immediately posting a packing slip or an invoice.

If you want to process picking in Dynamics AX, choose between following options depending on system configuration and setup:

➢ **One-step picking**
   o **Pick form** – Manual registration in the pick form
   o **Picking list** – With automatic picking list registration
➢ **Two-step picking**
   o **Order picking** – Picking list, followed by picking list registration
   o **Consolidated picking** – Output order and shipment

One-step picking applies, if you have to perform picking, but do not require confirming the picked quantity. Two-step picking requires confirming the quantity actually picked – either entering the picking list registration (order picking) or through consolidated picking, enabling combined picking of several orders.

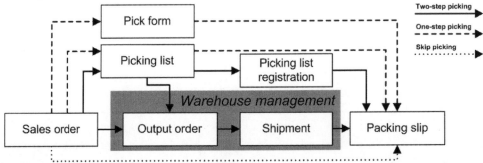

Figure 4-16: Options for sales order picking in Dynamics AX

When posting picking lists, Dynamics AX always generates output orders and shipments. Except for consolidated picking, these transactions are automatically completed and ended in the background.

4.5.1.1   Review Pending Deliveries

No matter whether you perform picking in Dynamics AX, you have to check expected deliveries continuously. In order to support in-time deliveries, there are several forms available for reviewing pending shipments:

➢ *Sales and marketing> Common> Sales orders> Backorder lines*
➢ *Sales and marketing> Inquiries> Order status> Open sales order lines*
➢ *Sales and marketing> Inquiries> Order status> Backorder lines*

In addition, pending shipments also show by filtering on the delivery date or the ship date in the posting form of picking lists and packing slips.

4.5.1.2   Release Sales Order Picking

For picking list posting, the release picking form (*Inventory and warehouse management> Periodic> Release sales order picking*) provides another option to select sales order lines for shipping.

The release picking form only shows sales order lines containing items, which are on stock currently. When opening the release picking form, an advanced filter displays for entering filter criteria on order lines. In the release picking form, modify this filter through clicking the button *Select* in the action pane strip as applicable then.

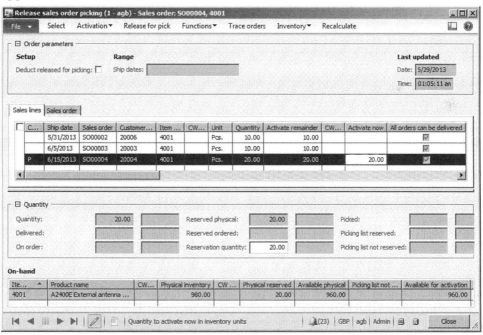

Figure 4-17:   Release sales order picking

Selecting the appropriate option of the button *Activation* in the action pane strip or manually entering quantities in the column *Activate now* activates items for picking. This activation includes reserving the item quantity.

For the quantities in the column *Activate now*, post the picking list by clicking the button *Release for pick* in the action pane strip then.

4.5.1.3 Customer Classification

You may set priorities for sales order picking by entering a *Customer classification group* on the tab *General* of the customer form. This group displays in the left-most column of the release picking form, providing the option to filter on this criterion.

4.5.1.4 Core Settings for Picking

A number of settings control the picking process. In particular, you have to check following settings:

> **Accounts receivable parameters** – One-step or two-step picking
> **Item model group** – Picking requirements, Consolidated picking

If the *Picking route status* on the tab *Updates* of the accounts receivable parameters shows the option "Completed", automatic picking list registration is enabled. Dynamics AX then immediately reduces the quantity in inventory when posting the picking list.

If the *Picking route status* is set to "Activated", two-step picking is enabled. Dynamics AX in this case does not change the quantity in inventory when posting the picking list. Depending on the item model group of the released product, you have to update subsequently either the *Picking list registration* or the *Output order*.

4.5.1.5 Settings on the Item Model Group

On the tab *General* of the released product form, each item is assigned to an item model group. For editing item model groups, open the form *Inventory and warehouse management> Setup> Inventory> Item model groups*. On the tab *Setup* of the item model group form, there are two essential checkboxes for picking:

> **Picking requirements** – If selected, picking is required before posting the packing slip.
> **Consolidated picking method** – If selected, functionality for picking multiple orders in picking routes and pallet transports applies (see section 4.5.3).

The setting for the *Consolidated picking method* is not only available in the item model group. It also shows at following levels overriding the item model group:

> **Warehouse** (*Inventory and warehouse management> Setup> Inventory breakdown> Warehouses*, tab *Warehouse management*)
> **Warehouse item** (Released product form, button *Warehouse/Warehouse items* on the action pane tab *Manage inventory*; in the warehouse item form, tab *Locations*)
> **Picking list posting form** (When posting a picking list, checkbox *Consolidated picking method* on the tab *Line details* of the posting form)

4.5.2   Pick Form and Picking List

Picking in sales mirrors inventory registration in purchasing: After picking, the related quantity shows the status "Picked" and is not available in inventory any more. Like inventory registration in purchasing, picking is a preliminary transaction not shown separately in inventory transactions.

4.5.2.1 Pick Form

The first option for picking, the pick form (manual picking of sales orders) works similar to the registration form (see section 3.5.3). In the sales order form, click the button *Update line/Pick* in the action pane strip of the order lines for accessing the pick form.

In order to record picking in the pick form, insert appropriate lines in the lower pane (*Picking list updates*) of the registration form then. Apart from manually entering records through clicking the button *Add* in the lower pane, the button *Add picking list update* in the action pane strip of the upper pane provides another option for inserting lines. After editing the quantity, the warehouse, or other inventory dimensions in the lower pane as applicable, post the picking transaction by clicking the button *Register all*.

4.5.2.2 Picking List

If you need a printed report to support picking in the warehouse, post and print a picking list instead of registering picking in the pick form. You may access the posting form for picking lists in several forms:

> **Sales order** – *Sales order* form, button *Generate/Picking list* on the action pane tab *Pick and pack*
> **Summary update** – *Sales and marketing> Periodic> Sales update> Picking list*
> **Release picking** – *Release sales order picking* form, see above

After posting and printing the picking list, hand a hardcopy of the picking list over to the warehouse personnel.

If warehouse usually picks items immediately, it is useful to enable one-step picking by setting the parameter *Picking route status* in the accounts receivable parameters to "Completed". In this case, manual picking registration is not required and the next step in Dynamics AX is posting the packing slip.

4.5.2.3 Picking List Registration

Picking list registration is required after posting a picking list, if both the parameter *Picking route status* is set to "Activated", and consolidated picking does not apply.

In this case, access the picking list registration form by clicking the button *Generate/Picking list registration* on the action pane tab *Pick and pack* of the sales order form.

Alternatively, access this form through the menu item *Sales and marketing> Journals> Sales order> Picking list registration* or the menu item *Inventory and warehouse management> Periodic> Picking list registration*. If starting in the sales order, picking list registration applies a filter on the current order. Otherwise, you have to manually enter a filter for selecting appropriate orders.

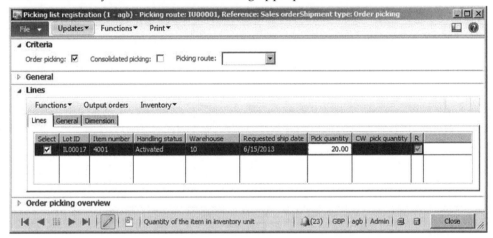

Figure 4-18:   Picking list registration accessed from a sales order (fast tab *General* collapsed)

In the *Lines* pane of the picking list registration form, choose the lines for update by selecting the checkbox in the column *Select* as shown in Figure 4-18. Before confirming the picked quantity of these lines by clicking the button *Updates/Update selected* (or *Updates/Update all* for all lines), adjust the quantity in the *Pick quantity* column as applicable.

4.5.2.4 Reverse Picking Transactions

If you want to reverse and to cancel a picking transaction, which has been posted in the pick form or through a picking list, you can use the pick form. Like when registering the original picking transaction, access the pick form in the sales order detail form by clicking the button *Update line/Pick* in the action pane strip of the order lines after selecting the order line concerned. In the upper pane of the pick form, click the button *Add picking list update* after selecting the appropriate transaction. Posting the reversing transaction by clicking the button *Register all* works similar to regular picking, but with negative quantity.

If the original picking transaction has been posted through a picking list, alternatively apply the picking list registration to reverse picking. In this case, access the picking list registration form by clicking the button *Generate/Picking list registration* on the action pane tab *Pick and pack* of the sales order form. In the picking list registration form, click the button *Functions/Unpick* in the action pane strip of the tab *Lines* in order to reverse the picking list registration. In a second step, you have to click the button *Functions/Cancel picking line* in the picking list registration form to cancel the picking list itself. Alternatively, skip the second step by selecting the checkbox *Cancel unpicked quantity* in the unpicking dialog shown in the first step.

4.5.3 Output Order and Shipment

Consolidated picking in Dynamics AX includes output orders, picking routes and pallet transports, providing the option to merge several orders into one shipment.

Dynamics AX generates output orders and shipments even if you do not apply consolidated picking. Without consolidated picking, Dynamics AX posts output orders and shipments automatically when posting and registering picking lists.

4.5.3.1 Prerequisites and Setup for Consolidated Picking

As a prerequisite for consolidated picking, locations and a location structure including outbound docks within your warehouses have to be specified in Dynamics AX. In addition, companies applying consolidated picking want to manage picking routes and pallet transports, requiring pallet management in Dynamics AX. The storage dimension group of the items therefore has to include the dimensions *Location* and *Pallet ID*.

Consolidated picking applies to items, which are assigned to an item model group with activated consolidated picking. In addition, settings on the warehouse and the released product (warehouse item) apply as described further up in this section.

Further settings required for consolidated picking include shipment templates, shipment reservation sequences and shipment reservation combinations. You may access these settings in the menu *Inventory and warehouse management> Setup> Distribution*.

A detailed description of consolidated picking is beyond the scope of this book, which is why the following lines only explain the basics of consolidated picking.

4.5.3.2 Output Order

Dynamics AX automatically generates an output order when posting a picking list. Alternatively, create an output order manually by clicking the button *Inventory/Output order* in the sales order line or in the release picking form (*Inventory and warehouse management> Periodic> Release sales order picking*).

In order to view and edit output orders, access the form *Inventory and warehouse management> Inquiries> Output orders*. As a preparation for shipments, update reservations through clicking the button *Inventory/Reservation* in the action pane strip of the output order form if applicable.

If required, delete a record in the output order form – for example if you want to stop the picking process for a sales order.

4.5.3.3 Shipment and Shipment List

Shipments in inventory are based on output orders. If you do not apply consolidated picking, Dynamics AX creates shipments of the type "Order picking" automatically in parallel to output orders when posting the picking list. In this case, you don't have to go through the steps described below (like activating the shipment).

If you do use consolidated shipping, continue with the picking process by creating a shipment in the form *Inventory and warehouse management> Common> Shipments* clicking the button *New* in the action pane strip. Depending on the options in the shipment form (button *Functions/Options*), inserting a record in the shipments starts a wizard.

Since a shipment of the type "Consolidated picking" contains one or more output orders, you have to assign output orders to the shipment. If you do not go through the wizard, assign them manually clicking the button *Add* in the shipment lines. For accessing the shipment lines form, click the button *Show lines* in the action pane strip of the shipment form.

When working with shipments and output orders, be aware that creating new shipments or adding output orders to existing shipments might happen automatically as a function of appropriate settings in the shipment templates.

If you want to print a shipment list in order to support item picking in the warehouse, click the button *Print/Shipment list* in the shipments form.

Clicking the button *Functions/Activate* in the shipment form activates the shipment. Activating generates pallet transports for lines, which may be shipped in complete pallets. For smaller quantities, picking routes are activated.

Pallet transports are available in the form *Inventory and warehouse management> Common> Pallet transports*, where you may start and complete the transport.

Picking routes are available in the form *Inventory and warehouse management> Common> Picking routes*, where you may first choose the picking route in the lookup field *Picking route*, then select – or create (button *Create picking pallet*) – a picking pallet and finally start the picking route (button *Start picking route*). Once picking is actually done, click the button *Approve details* for switching to the approve form, where you may click the button *Pick selected*. Finally, click the button *Deliver picked items* for completing the shipment in the dialog which shows next.

If using consolidated picking without pallet transports, complete an activated shipment in the picking list registration form (see section 4.5.2), which shows after clicking the button *Inquiry/Picking routes* in the shipment form.

4.5.4   Packing Slip

Posting the packing slip (delivery note) is the last transaction in the picking and shipping process.

4.5.4.1   Posting Form for Packing Slips

You may open the posting form for packing slips either by clicking the button *Generate/Packing slip* on the action pane tab *Pick and pack* of the sales order form, or through the menu item *Sales and marketing> Periodic> Sales update> Packing slip.*

The posting form shows the familiar format. The applicable option in the lookup field *Quantity* is depending on the preceding procedure:

➢ **Picked** – Select this option, if picking is executed before posting the packing slip. The picked quantity then applies to the column *Update* on the tab *Lines* of the posting form.
➢ **All** – The total remaining order quantity applies.
➢ **Deliver now** – The quantity of the column *Deliver now* in the order lines applies.

Making sure the checkboxes *Posting* and *Print packing slip* in the posting form are selected, click the button *OK* to post and print the packing slip then.

Like in purchasing, partial deliveries, over deliveries, and under deliveries (see section 3.5.5) are also available in sales. Regarding the order status and the document status update, please refer to the corresponding purchase order status described in section 0.

4.5.4.2   Ledger Integration

If ledger integration is activated for packing slip posting, Dynamics AX posts transactions to the general ledger in parallel to inventory transactions. These ledger transactions are reversed when posting the related invoice.

Following core settings control packing slip posting to the general ledger:

➢ **Post packing slip in ledger** – Checkbox in the accounts receivable parameters (tab *Updates*), which has to be selected if ledger integration applies.
➢ **Post physical inventory** – Checkbox in the item model group (tab *Setup*) of the sold item, which has to be selected if ledger integration applies.

4.5.4.3   Transaction Inquiry

If you want to view the inventory transactions in the sales order form after posting the packing slip, click the button *Inventory/Transactions* in the action pane strip of the order lines. After posting the packing slip, the issue status of the inventory transaction is "Deducted". The posting date of the packing slip shows in the column *Physical date*, the *Financial date* remains empty until posting the invoice. If you want to know the packing slip number, switch to the tab *Update*.

In order to access posted packing slips, choose the form *Sales and marketing> Inquiries> Journals> Packing slip* or click the button *Journals/Packing slip journal* on the action pane tab *Pick and pack* of the sales order form. After selecting a packing slip on the tab *Overview* of the inquiry form, switch to the tab *Lines* for viewing related packing slip lines.

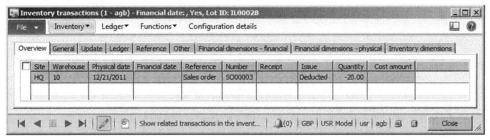

Figure 4-19:   Inventory transaction after packing slip posting

If you want to view related transactions in the general ledger, open the voucher transactions form by clicking the button *Vouchers* on the *Overview* tab of the packing slip inquiry, or the button *Ledger/Physical voucher* in the inventory transactions.

4.5.4.4   Canceling a Packing Slip

You may cancel a posted packing slip applying the *Cancel* feature in the packing slip inquiry form (*Sales and marketing> Inquiries> Journals> Packing slip*). After selecting the particular packing slip, click the button *Cancel* in the action pane strip of the tab *Overview*. If you just want to reduce the posted quantity, click the button *Correct* instead.

4.5.4.5   New in Dynamics AX 2012

The option of canceling a packing slip in the inquiry is new in Dynamics AX 2012.

4.5.5   Case Study Exercises

Exercise 4.9 – Packing Slip

You want to check which order lines are available for shipping. The inquiry should not be limited to your orders, but also include other orders available in your company. Which options do you know?

Knowing your order of exercise 4.6 is among the orders to be shipped, you want to post the packing slip. Before posting, check following items in the sales order:

➢ Order status and document status
➢ Inventory quantity of the ordered item (button *Inventory/On-hand*)
➢ Inventory transactions related to the order line (button *Inventory/Transactions*)

Post and print a packing slip for the complete order quantity directly in the sales order form, selecting a print preview as printing destination.

Now review the status of the items on the checklist above again. What is different after packing slip posting?

Exercise 4.10 – Picking List
Your customer of exercise 4.1 orders another 20 units of the item entered in exercise 3.5. Enter an appropriate sales order.

Warehouse does not want to apply consolidated picking, but requires a picking list this time. Therefore, you want to post a picking list containing 10 units of the ordered item. Can you tell which setting controls if you need to enter picking list registration? If required, update the picking list registration.

Then post the packing slip for the picked items.

Exercise 4.11 – Packing Slip Inquiry
You want to view the packing slip of exercise 4.10. Open the packing slip inquiry from the sales order form. In a second step, open the packing slip inquiry through the appropriate menu path. Check packing slip header and lines and try to find out, if there are related ledger transactions.

4.6   Invoicing

Posting the sales invoice is the last step in sales order processing. The invoice on the one hand increases the open customer balance and on the other hand reduces the financial value of inventory. After invoicing all lines of a sales order, the sales order is completed. Payment of invoices then runs through a separate process in finance (see section 8.3.4).

If you want to invoice inventoried products, you have to enter a sales order. But you are free to post the sales order invoice immediately after registering the order – without separately posting an order confirmation or a packing slip.

Free text invoices (see section 4.6.3) apply, if you want to post invoices not referring to products or sales categories. In the lines of a free text invoice, you have to enter ledger numbers instead of item numbers. Such an invoice has no connection to items and no impact on inventory and supply chain management.

4.6.1   Invoicing Sales Orders

The way of posting a sales invoice is similar to posting the packing slip.

4.6.1.1   Posting Form for Sales Order Invoices

You may open the posting form for invoices either by clicking the button *Generate/Invoice* on the action pane tab *Invoice* of the sales order form, or through the menu item *Accounts receivable> Periodic> Sales update> Invoice*.

The posting form shows the familiar format. The applicable option in the lookup field *Quantity* is depending on the preceding procedure:

➤ **Packing Slip** – Common option, since a packing slip is posted first in most cases and you want to link the invoice to the shipped quantity.
➤ **All** or **Deliver now** – If selected, Dynamics AX does not default the shipped quantity to the column *Update* in the invoice lines. For any quantity not shipped yet, a packing slip transaction is posted in parallel to the invoice.

If choosing "Packing Slip" in the lookup *Quantity*, the button *Select packing slip* in the posting form enables selecting the packing slips applicable for invoicing – similar to selecting product receipts for vendor invoices in purchasing.

Before posting, optionally click the button *Totals* in the posting form for checking the totals. Making sure the checkboxes *Posting* and *Print invoice* in the posting form are selected, click the button *OK* to finally post and print the invoice.

4.6.1.2 Transaction Inquiry

Posting the invoice generates transactions in the general ledger, inventory transactions, customer transactions, and transactions in other subledgers like sales tax, if applicable. Once all lines of an order are completely invoiced, the order status changes to "Invoiced".

If you want to view the inventory transactions in the sales order form after posting the invoice, click the button *Inventory/Transactions* in the action pane strip of the order lines. After posting the invoice, the issue status of the inventory transaction is "Sold" and the posting date of the invoice shows in the column *Financial date*.

In order to access posted sales invoices, choose the form *Accounts receivable> Inquiries> Journals> Invoice journal* or click the button *Journals/Invoice* on the action pane tab *Invoice* of the sales order form. After selecting an invoice on the tab *Overview* of the inquiry form, switch to the tab *Lines* for displaying related lines.

If you want to view corresponding transactions in the general ledger, open the voucher transactions form by clicking the button *Voucher* on the *Overview* tab of the invoice inquiry, or the button *Ledger/Financial voucher* in the inventory transactions.

4.6.1.3 Transaction Origin

Clicking the button *Transaction origin* in the voucher transactions form opens the transaction origin form, which shows related transactions for the voucher in all modules. Figure 4-20 for example shows a domestic invoice for an item, which has been shipped with a separate packing slip.

When classifying the transactions of the invoice shown in Figure 4-20, distinguish following kinds of transaction:

Table 4-2:   Transactions of the sales invoice in Figure 4-20

Transaction	General ledger		Subledger	
Packing slip reversing	Account 10921 offsetting account 10922	[1]		
Inventory	Account 51310 for COGS offsetting stock account 10310	[2a]	Financial inventory transaction for item 4001	[2b]
Customer	Summary account 20010 offsetting tax account 35210 and revenue account 40210	[3a] [4a] [5]	Customer transaction and sales tax transaction	[3b] [4b]

Invoice posting only generates reversing packing slip transactions, if a prior packing slip has been posted to the general ledger.

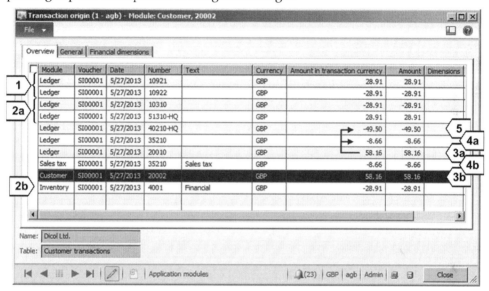

Figure 4-20:   Transactions of a sales invoice in the transaction origin form

The particular ledger accounts in all transactions are depending on the actual operation and on the applicable setup. Therefore, you may notice additional or missing transactions if comparing the transactions of Figure 4-20 to other invoices. For example, sales tax transactions are missing for invoices to foreign countries.

The customer summary account related to the customer transaction is specified in the applicable customer posting profile, which works similar to the vendor posting profile (see section 3.2.3). Apart from the sales tax transaction, settings for the other transactions are available in the inventory posting setup (see section 8.4.2).

4.6.2   Collective Invoice

If you want to post an invoice referring to several sales orders (e.g. a monthly invoice), you have to post a collective invoice in a summary update. Collective documents are available for all document types. Therefore, apart from collective invoices you may also post collective packing slips for example.

The way to post collective documents is not different from posting an individual document. Settings at company and customer level control, whether to generate a collective document.

4.6.2.1 Setup for Summary Update

Basic configuration settings for collective documents in sales are available on the tab *Summary update* of the accounts receivable parameters. The first setting there is the lookup field *Default values for summary update*, where you choose if settings for collective document posting are available at order level. In most cases the choice is "Automatic summary", which allows deselecting specific orders from a collective document in the order form. If selecting the option "Invoice account", excluding a particular order is only possible by removing it in the posting form.

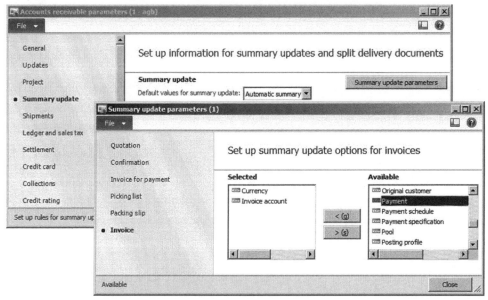

Figure 4-21:   Summary update parameters for sales

Clicking the button *Summary update parameters* in the accounts receivable parameters form, displays the summary update parameters form. This form contains a separate tab per document type, where you may select the fields which must be equal in sales orders to join a collective document.

If "Automatic summary" is selected in the *Default values for summary update*, automatic summary has to be enabled on the particular customers in addition (button *Setup/Summary update* on the action pane tab *Customer* in the customer form). The setting on the customer defaults to sales orders, where you may change it after clicking the button *Setup/Summary* on the action pane tab *General* of the sales order form.

4.6.2.2 Posting Collective Invoices

In order to post a collective invoice, open the summary update form *Accounts receivable> Periodic> Sales update> Invoice*. In most cases you want to select "Packing slip" in the lookup field *Quantity* of the posting form, making sure invoice posting only refers to shipped quantities.

As shown in Figure 4-22, click the button *Select* [1] in order to select appropriate sales orders in the advanced filter form next. After closing the filter form, the selected orders show on the tab *Overview* of the posting form.

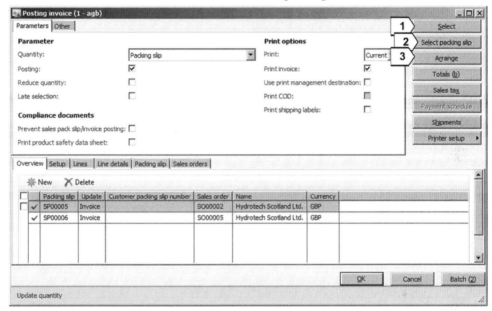

Figure 4-22:   Posting a collective invoice receipt

If there are orders which you do not want to invoice, delete the appropriate lines. Deleting a line in the posting form only removes the selection. It does not delete the order or the packing slip, which is why the order will show again, whenever you want to post an appropriate invoice the next time.

If you want to exclude particular packing slips from invoice posting, click the button *Select packing slip* [2].

Once you have finished selecting sales orders and packing slips, click the button *Arrange* [3]. The *Arrange* feature combines the orders into a common invoice according to the summary update parameters. If the setting in the accounts receivable parameters is not suitable for posting a particular invoice, choose a different option on the tab *Other* of the posting form before arranging.

In the example shown in Figure 4-22, the *Arrange* feature will merge the two orders into one common line. Clicking the button *OK* in the posting form afterwards posts the collective invoice.

4.6.3   Free Text Invoices

Free text invoices apply to sales invoices, which do not refer to order processing and do not include product numbers or sales category.

The structure of free text invoices is similar to sales orders: Every free text invoice consists of a header and one or more lines. But instead of product numbers and sales categories, the lines of a free text invoice contain main accounts.

Once you have finished registering the free text invoice, post and print it. The only posted document available in free text invoices is the invoice – it is not possible to post an order confirmation for example.

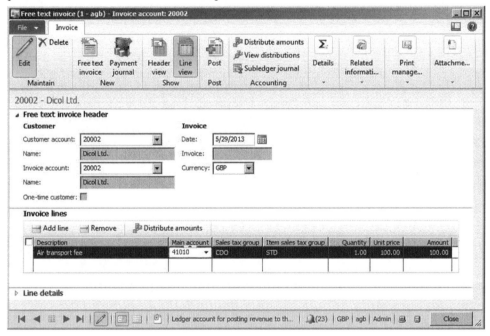

Figure 4-23:   Registering an invoice line of a free text invoice

Entering a negative invoice amount in the free text invoice form creates a credit note. But free text invoices and credit notes do not affect item statistics and inventory valuation.

4.6.3.1 Registering Free Text Invoices

In order to enter a free text invoice, access the form *Accounts receivable> Common> Free text invoices> All free text invoices* and click the button *New/Free text invoice* in the action pane. Alternatively, access the customer form and create a free text invoice by clicking the button *New/Free text invoice* on action pane tab *Invoice* there.

The free text invoice consists of a header, where you have to select the customer account number, and invoice lines. Unlike the sales order form, the free text invoice does not show a separate *Create new* dialog when creating a new invoice starting in the free text invoice list page. But the free text invoice provides the option to select the customer in the line view, showing a field for the *Customer account* and the *Invoice account* on the tab *Free text invoice header*.

On the tab *Invoice lines* of the free text invoice form, enter the lines with *Description*, *Main account* and *Amount* (or *Quantity* and *Unit price*) then. If a line requires a longer description, enter it in the invoice text field on the sub-tab *General* of the *Line details* tab. If sales tax (VAT) applies, make sure to choose a correct *Sales tax group* and *Item sales tax group*.

If you want to check financial dimensions like department or cost center, switch to the sub-tab *Financial dimensions line* of the tab *Line details* and enter applicable dimension values. Alternatively, choose a financial dimension default template in the lookup *Template ID*.

For selling fixed assets, enter the *Fixed asset number* on the sub-tab *General* of the *Line details* tab.

4.6.3.2 Posting and Inquiry

In order to post the free text invoice, click the button *Post/Post* in the action pane of the free text invoice form. After posting, you can view the posted invoice by clicking the button *Related information/Invoice journal* in the action pane.

In the invoice inquiry *Accounts receivable> Inquiries> Journals> Invoice journal*, free text invoices display in parallel to sales order invoices. You may recognize free text invoices in this inquiry by the missing order number and by different invoice numbers (if a separate number sequence applies).

4.6.3.3 Recurring Free Text Invoices

If you want to post and to print a particular free text invoice periodically, apply recurring free text invoices. As a prerequisite for this kind of invoices, set up a free text invoice template (*Accounts receivable> Setup> Free text invoice templates*) first. Next you may assign customers to one or more templates by clicking the button *Set up/Recurring invoices* on the action pane tab *Invoice* of the customer form.

For generating a periodical free text invoice then, access the menu item *Accounts receivable> Periodic> Recurring invoices> Generate recurring invoices*. The periodic activity generates regular free text invoices, which you may access in the free text invoice form before posting.

4.6.3.4 New in Dynamics AX 2012

In Dynamics AX 2012, new features for free text invoices include recurring free text invoices and the option to enter quantities and unit prices.

4.6.4   Credit Notes and Item Returns

If a customer returns an item to your company and receives a replacement or a financial compensation, you want to post a credit note. Other types of crediting apply, if the customer does not actually return defective items or if you have to credit a price variance.

In order to manage customer returns, apply the return order management in Dynamics AX. In case of a simple return process, alternatively use regular sales orders instead of return orders.

If crediting does not refer to the delivery of items, use a free text invoice.

4.6.4.1 Setup of Disposition Codes

As a prerequisite for return orders, you have to configure disposition codes (*Sales and marketing> Setup> Sales order> Returns> Disposition codes*). The core setting in a disposition code is the field *Action*, which controls handling of a defective item:

➢ **Credit only** – Credit without item return
➢ **Credit** or **Scrap** – Return items and credit
➢ **Replace and credit** or **Replace and scrap** – Return items and replace
➢ **Return to customer** – Do not credit

If scrap applies, an item receipt has to be posted (similar to an item receipt for products returned to stock). But in parallel to the packing slip of the return order, Dynamics AX posts an inventory transaction for scrapping.

4.6.4.2 Return Order Registration

In order to process item returns, open the list page *Sales and marketing> Common> Return Orders> All return orders*. Return orders are sales orders of the type "Returned order", showing the sales order number in the return order header.

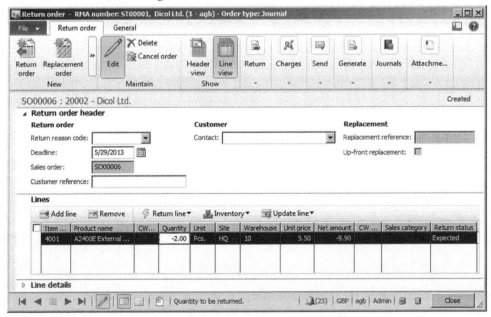

Figure 4-24: Registering an item in the return order form

But except for return orders referring to a disposition code "Credit only", return orders do not show in the regular sales order form until posting the item arrival.

When creating a return order by clicking the button *New/Return order* in the action pane of the return order form, optionally select a *Return reason code* in the header for statistical purposes and – if applicable – for automatically assigning charges.

Clicking the button *Return/Find sales order* on the action pane tab *Return order* enables copying existing sales invoice lines into the return order. Alternatively, enter return order lines with a negative quantity manually. The *Disposition code* for a line is available on the sub-tab *General* of the *Line details* tab. But don't enter the disposition code before item arrival (except for disposition codes "Credit only", crediting without item return).

Optionally, click the button *Send/Return order* for printing a RMA document, which you may send to your customer then.

If you want to send a replacement for returned items to the customer in advance, create an appropriate sales order clicking the button *New/Replacement order* in the return order form.

4.6.4.3 Return Orders without Physical Returns

If you do not want your customer to return the item, choose a disposition code without item return ("Credit only") on the sub-tab *General* of the *Line details* tab in the return order. In this case, you can immediately post the credit note in the sales order form (*Sales and marketing> Common> Sales Orders> All sales orders*) or in the summary update *Accounts receivable> Periodic> Sales update> Invoice*.

4.6.4.4 Return Orders – Item Arrival and Crediting

Once receiving the items of a return order, you have to enter inventory registration. Like the inventory registration in purchasing (see section 3.5.3), the registration for return orders may be done either in the registration form (button *Update line/Registration* in the return order lines) or in the item arrival journal.

If applying an item arrival journal (*Inventory and warehouse management> Journals> Item arrival> Item arrival*, see section 7.4.2), select the return order in the journal header and/or lines. For this purpose, switch to the journal header tab *Default values* after creating a new journal, select the option "Sales order" in the lookup *Reference*, and enter the return order number in the lookup *RMA number*. Since a *Disposition code* is required for posting the item return, optionally enter it in the header as a default for the journal lines. In order to create the journal lines, either click the button *Functions/Create lines* in the journal header, or enter them manually after switching to the lines by clicking the button *Lines*. After posting the item arrival journal by clicking the button *Post*, the status of the return order line updates to "Registered".

Then optionally print an acknowledgement of the receipt by clicking the button *Send/Acknowledgement* in the action pane of the return order form.

For completing the item receipt, post the packing slip either in the return order form (button *Generate/Packing slip*) or in the sales order form (button *Generate/Packing slip* on the action pane tab *Pick and pack*).

In order to credit the item return finally, access the sales order form and click the button *Generate/Invoice* on the action pane tab *Invoice*, or choose the summary update *Accounts receivable> Periodic> Sales update> Invoice*.

4.6.4.5 Crediting through Sales Orders

As an alternative to return orders, credit a customer in the regular sales order form. Since the order type "Returned order" is not available for manual selection, the order header looks like the header of a regular sales order providing following options for crediting:

➢ Credit note registered in the original order line
➢ Credit note in a new order line
➢ Credit note in a new sales order

The options for registering a new order or a new line are similar to purchasing (see section 3.4.5). If you want to register a credit note in the original order line, enter a negative quantity in the column *Deliver now* of the appropriate sales order line. When posting the credit note, choose the option "Deliver now" – which refers to the *Deliver now* column – in the quantity lookup field of the invoice posting form.

4.6.4.6 Inventory Valuation for Returned Items

If registering a credit note in a new order or order line, you should enter the original invoice number in the lookup *Return lot ID* (sub-tab *Setup* of the *Line details* tab) in the order line before posting. This link ensures that the inventory value of the crediting line exactly matches the inventory value of the original delivery.

Dynamics AX automatically applies the return lot ID, if you either click the button *Return/Find sales order* in the action pane of the return order form, or the button *Create/Credit note* on the action pane tab *Sell* of the sales order form.

If you do not select a return lot ID, Dynamics AX applies the *Return cost price* on the sub-tab *Setup* of the crediting order line for inventory valuation.

4.6.4.7 Scrapping Items

If you do not ask the customer to return a defective item, select the checkbox *Scrap* on the sub-tab *Setup* of the *Line details* tab in in the crediting order line. When posting the invoice (credit note) then, Dynamics AX posts the item receipt and a related inventory loss at the same time.

In return orders, the checkbox *Scrap* is controlled by the disposition code.

4.6.4.8 Refunds not Referring to Returns

The free text invoice form (see section 4.6.3) is an option for registering and posting customer refunds. But if a refund refers to an item, you should not use a free text invoice, since this kind of invoicing does not affect item statistics and inventory valuation.

In case of crediting a price variance, rather enter a new sales order containing a line with a negative quantity and the old price and a second line with a positive quantity and the right price. Applying *Inventory/Marking* as shown in section 3.7.1 enables linking the two transactions for offsetting inventory value.

4.6.5   Case Study Exercises

Exercise 4.12 – Invoice
You want to invoice the items shipped in exercise 4.9. Before posting the invoice, check following items:

➤ Order status and document status of the sales order
➤ Inventory transaction related to the order line (button *Inventory/Transactions*)

Post and print the invoice directly in the sales order form, checking the invoice total in the posting form before posting.

Now review the status of the items on the checklist above again. What is different after invoice posting?

Exercise 4.13 – Partial Invoice
You want to invoice the items picked and shipped in exercise 4.10. Post and print the invoice directly in the sales order form, making sure to invoice only shipped items.

Exercise 4.14 – Shipping with Invoice
Your customer of exercise 4.1 orders another unit of the product entered in exercise 3.5. In addition, he wants to order one hour of the installation service entered in exercise 4.3 for a price of GBP 110. This time you do not post a packing slip, you want to ship the items with the invoice.

Enter an appropriate sales order and immediately post the invoice. After posting the invoice, review the order status, the document status and the inventory transaction of the product.

Exercise 4.15 – Invoice Inquiry
You want to view the invoice posted in exercise 4.12. Open the invoice inquiry and check the invoice header and lines as well as the related ledger transactions.

In exercise 4.2, you were looking for the summary account for your customer. Can you find the ledger transaction for this account? Finally, open the transaction origin form and check, to which modules your invoice has been posting.

Exercise 4.16 – Free Text Invoice

You want to invoice specific services, for which no product or sales category is available, to your customer of exercise 4.1. Enter a free text invoice choosing an appropriate revenue account and post the invoice. What is the difference between a free text invoice and an invoice related to a sales order?

Exercise 4.17 – Credit Note

Your customer complains defects on the items invoiced in exercise 4.12. You agree to an item return before crediting the invoice. Enter an appropriate return order and post the item receipt applying a suitable disposition code. After posting the packing slip return, you want to post and print the credit note.

4.7   Direct Delivery

Direct delivery means shipping goods from a vendor directly to a customer. Avoiding a warehouse in between saves time and expenses for transportation and stocking.

4.7.1   Processing Direct Deliveries

In order to process direct deliveries, there are two different options in the sales order form:

➢ Create purchase order
➢ Create direct delivery

Both options start by entering a sales order for the customer receiving the items.

4.7.1.1   Registering the Sales Order

When registering an order for direct delivery, there is no difference to registering a regular order. However, selecting a specific warehouse for direct deliveries avoids mixing direct deliveries and regular inventory transactions in the warehouse.

When you have finished registering the sales order, create a related purchase order by clicking the button *New/Purchase order* or *New/Direct delivery* on the action pane tab *Sales order* of the sales order form.

4.7.1.2   Using the Create Purchase Order Option

The button *New/Purchase order* in the sales order provides the option to generate a regular purchase order, which refers to the sales order. You may choose this option, if you want to process the purchase order separately from other purchases, but nevertheless receive and ship it through a warehouse of your company.

When generating the purchase order, you have to select the vendor in the *Create purchase order* form in case no main vendor is specified for the item. Processing of purchase and sales order works like processing regular orders, including change management for the purchase order.

In the purchase order, the delivery address for the vendor is the warehouse or company address (like in any regular purchase order). You may post the product receipt in your warehouse and then perform picking and shipping to the customer.

4.7.1.3 Using the Create Direct Delivery Option

The button *New/Direct delivery* generates a purchase order like the create purchase order option, but links it closer to the sales order. The delivery address of the purchase order is the customer address, modifications of the address and other data in the sales order relevant to purchasing – like quantity or delivery date – synchronize to the purchase order. In case of changes you have to respect the purchase order change management, at least requiring confirmation of the modified purchase order.

When posting the product receipt for a direct delivery in purchasing, Dynamics AX automatically posts the related sales packing slip. If you are required to print a packing slip for the customer, select the checkbox *Print sales documents* in the posting form for the product receipt (see Figure 4-25).

Invoice posting in sales is independent from the purchase invoice then.

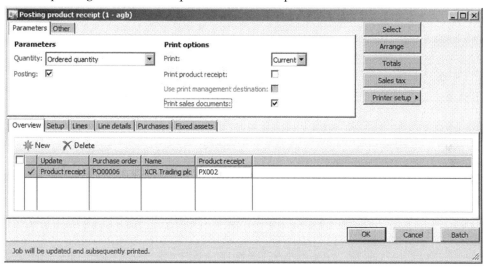

Figure 4-25: Printing a sales packing slip when posting the product receipt

4.7.1.4 Links between Purchase and Sales Order

If you want to know the sales order line linked to a purchase order line or the other way around, check the item reference on the sub-tab *Product* (tab *Line details*) of the purchase or sales order line.

In the header of purchase or sales orders, the reference is available by clicking the button *Related information/References* on the action pane tab *General*. In the sales order form, click the button *Related information/Purchase order* on the action pane tab *General* if you want to directly access the assigned purchase order.

4.7.2   Case Study Exercise

Exercise 4.18 – Direct Delivery

Your customer of exercise 4.1 orders 100 units of the item entered in exercise 3.5. In order to avoid stocking that large quantity in your warehouse, you want to process a direct delivery. Enter an appropriate sales order and choose the option *Direct delivery* for generating a purchase order from your vendor of exercise 3.2.

Your vendor confirms shipping the item with packing slip PS418. You want to post this product receipt in the purchase order. In the next step, check the status of the sales order, then post and print the sales invoice. After receiving the purchase invoice VI418, post the invoice receipt.

5   Production Control

The primary responsibility of production control is to manufacture finished goods. In order to meet this task, items and resource capacity (men and machinery) are consumed. The manufacturing process may include semi-finished items, which are included in the bill of materials of finished items.

5.1   Business Processes in Manufacturing

Depending on the requirements of your company, apply following manufacturing concepts in Dynamics AX:

➤ **Discrete manufacturing** – Core production functionality including bills of materials (BOM), resources, routes and production orders.
➤ **Process manufacturing** – Supporting additional requirements of batch-producing industries like formulas and co-products.
➤ **Lean manufacturing** – Supporting production flows and Kanbans (working independently from routes and production orders).

You can use these concepts in mixed mode, for example choosing process manufacturing for components, and lean manufacturing for finished products.

The explanations in this book are limited to the core production functionality, covered by discrete manufacturing. Before we start to go into details, the lines below give an overall picture of discrete manufacturing.

5.1.1   Basic Approach

Like in purchasing and sales, correct master data are an essential prerequisite for successfully executing production control.

5.1.1.1 Master Data and Transactions in Production Control

The released product form contains the main characteristics of an item. The bill of materials (BOM) then describes the structure of a finished or semi-finished item, consisting of components (raw materials, parts or semi-finished products).

Resources (e.g. machines or human resources) are another basic element, providing capacity for manufacturing. Required resources are then included in routes and operations, which describe the necessary activities for producing an item.

In the course of production order processing, master data are copied to transaction data. You may modify these default data in transactions, for example choosing a non-standard bill of materials in a specific production order.

Figure 5-1 below shows the required steps in production order processing.

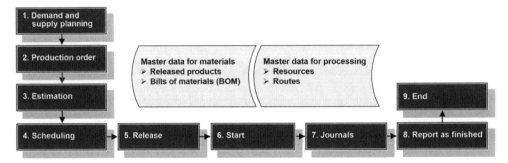

Figure 5-1:   Production order processing in Dynamics AX

5.1.1.2 Demand and Supply Planning

The first step in the manufacturing process is to identify material supply, which is required for covering item demand, in operations planning (master planning, see section 6.3). Depending on item coverage settings, the item demand derives from different sources: Master planning may include forecasts, current sales quotations, sales orders, quantity in inventory and coverage settings for minimum stock.

5.1.1.3 Creating a Production Order

As a preliminary step for creating production orders, master scheduling in operations planning generates planned production orders, which you may transfer to actual production orders. Apart from transferring planned orders, following options are available for creating a production order:

- ➢ **Manually** – Entering an order in the production order form
- ➢ **Sales order** – Creating a production order in a sales order line
- ➢ **Pegged supply** – Automatically creating a production order for a semi-finished item (sub-production) in the production order of a finished item

A production order consists of an order header, which refers to the produced item, and order lines. Unlike purchase and sales orders, which only contain lines for items, production orders contain two different types of lines: BOM item lines and route operation lines. These line types show in separate forms.

After creating a production order, you have to execute all subsequent steps – from estimating to ending – one after the other. But depending on parameter settings, optionally skip steps which you do not require in a particular order.

5.1.1.4 Estimating and Scheduling

Estimation is the first step in order processing after creating a production order. Estimation determines the quantity and cost of all items and resources, which are required for manufacturing the product.

Whereas estimation only calculates item quantity and resource capacity demand without timing it, scheduling as the next step calculates exact dates for production.

5.1.1.5 Releasing and Starting

Releasing a production order means to hand it over from the front office to the shop floor. When releasing the order, print the production papers if required.

Once manufacturing of a production order should actually start, set the order status to "Started". This status enables posting item and working time consumption. When starting an order, optionally print the picking list and post automatic consumption of items and resource capacity.

5.1.1.6 Production Journals

In the course of the manufacturing process, the shop floor consumes material and resource capacity. Reporting this consumption requires posting production journals. Depending on production settings, post these journal either manually or automatically (applying estimated data). Alternatively, use shop floor terminals in the *Manufacturing execution* module in order to report consumption.

5.1.1.7 Reporting as Finished and Ending the Production Order

Once manufacturing is completed for the entire or a partial quantity of the finished product, post a reporting as finished transaction. After posting, the reported quantity of the finished product is available in inventory. Ending the production order is the last step in production order processing, calculating actual costs of production and finally posting to the general ledger.

5.1.1.8 Ledger Integration and Voucher Principle

Yet before ending an order, production journals for material and resource consumption on the one hand and finished product receipts on the other hand are posting to ledger accounts (see section 8.4.3).

According to the general principle for processing transactions in Dynamics AX, the voucher principle also applies to transactions in manufacturing. You have to register a transaction in a journal before you can post it.

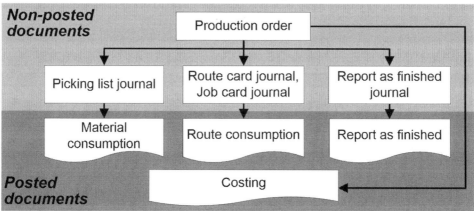

Figure 5-2: Posted and non-posted documents in production control

5.1.2   At a Glance: Production Order Processing

In order to provide an overview of the main steps in production order processing, this section shows the basics. For convenience, we post all transactions directly in the production order form.

If you want to create a new production order manually, access the form *Production control> Common> Production Orders> All Production Orders* and click the button *New/Production order* on the action pane tab *Production order*. Dynamics AX then shows the *Create production order* form, where you want to choose the *Item number* of the manufactured item. The selected item provides default data like quantity, BOM number and route number to the production order. Clicking the button *Create* in the create order form finally creates the new production order.

The action pane tab *Production order* of the production order form provides access to the form showing material components (button *Production details/BOM*) and route operations (button *Production details/Route*).

Note: Pressing the *F5* key refreshes the form for displaying the new order.

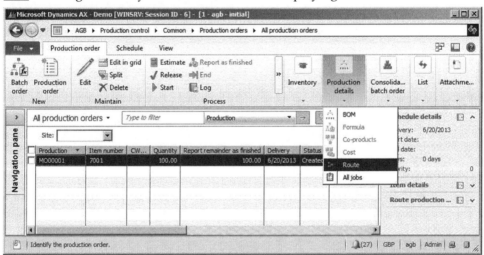

Figure 5-3:   Managing a production order in the production order form

For processing the production order, change the order status by clicking following buttons one after the other:

➢ *Process/Estimate* (action pane tab *Production order*)
➢ *Production order/Schedule operations* or *Schedule jobs* (action pane tab *Schedule*)
➢ *Process/Release* (action pane tab *Production order*)

When changing the status, select applicable parameters – e.g. setting the scheduling direction – on the tab *General* of the update dialog of each step. When releasing the order, optionally select to print production papers (job card, route card) in the update dialog. When starting the order, print the picking list if necessary.

Once the production order should be processed in the shop floor, click the button *Process/Start* for starting the order and posting automatic material and route consumption as applicable. If you start an order without separately performing the preceding steps, they are executed automatically when starting.

In order to register consumption of items configured for manual posting, click the button *Journals/Picking list* on the action pane tab *View* of the production order. In the production journal, click the button *Picking list/Create lines* for generating a proposal with picking list lines. Selecting "Remaining quantity" in the lookup field *Proposal* of the *Create lines* dialog provides a default for open quantities to the journal lines. If required, edit the consumption quantity, the warehouse, or other data in the journal lines before posting the picking list by clicking the button *Post*.

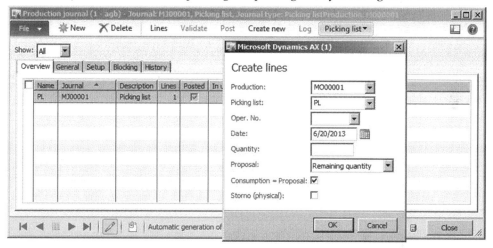

Figure 5-4: Creating a proposal for the picking list lines

Depending on the scheduling type (*Operations scheduling* or *Job scheduling*) executed for scheduling the production order, register the actual working time consumption either at route level or at job level (button *Journals/Route card* or *Journals/Job card* on the action pane tab *View* of the production order).

Unlike picking lists, route card and job card journals do not contain proposals for manual working time consumption. Click the button *Create new* in the route card or job card journal header for creating a new journal, and enter operation/job number, resource, hours and good quantity in the lines before clicking the button *Post*.

Clicking the button *Process/Report as finished* on the action pane tab *Production order* of the production order form increases the quantity on stock of the finished item. If you want to ignore missing consumption postings, select the checkbox *Accept error* on the tab *General* in the update dialog.

Once posting of all transactions for the production order is finished, cost and close the order by clicking the button *Process/End*.

5.2   Product Data and Bills of Materials

All material components required for production control are included in the product and released product records (item records). Apart from inventoried items like finished products, semi-finished products and raw material or parts, product records are also necessary for phantom items or purchased services.

A bill of materials (BOM) controls, which material components are included in a finished product. You may assign an individual bill of materials to only one item, to multiple items, or multiple bills of material to one individual item. Multiple bills of material for one item are required, if the applicable bill of materials for example is depending on the lot size or on the production date.

If you want to manage a product with variants, choose the product subtype "Product master" when creating a shared product (see section 7.2.1). A multi-model production is available through the use of product configuration models or configuration groups and rules. A detailed description of the options for product configuration is beyond the scope of this book, however.

5.2.1   Product Master Data for Manufacturing

The item records of all finished products and raw materials or parts are available in the shared product form (*Product information management> Common> Products> All products and product masters*) and in the released product form (*Product information management> Common> Released products*).

Details on general product data are included in section 7.2 of this book. The lines below therefore only cover product data specifically applying to production control. Except for the product type, which is specified in the product form, these data are included in the released product form.

5.2.1.1 Item Model Group, Production Type and Default Order Type

The first essential setting in the released product is the *Item model group* shown on the tab *General* of the released product form. All items in production control – including finished products, semi-finished products and raw materials or parts – have to be linked to an item model group for stocked products (see section 7.2.1). Since this setting is also required for non-inventoried BOM-components like subcontractor work, choose the *Product type* "Service" for non-inventoried products in order to avoid inventory control for these items.

In the item record of finished or semi-finished products, select the option "BOM" in the lookup field *Production type* on the tab *Engineer*. The production type "None" – an option for purchased raw materials or parts – prevents assigning a BOM to the item. The production types "Formula" and "Co-product" enable assigning a formula instead of a BOM, which is applicable to process manufacturing.

Controlling item sourcing, the default order type is another important setting. The lookup field *Default order type* is available on tab *General* in the default order settings form, which you may access clicking the button *Default order settings* on the action pane tab *Plan* of the released product form. Following options are available for the default order type:

➢ **Purchase order** – Supply through planned or actual purchase orders
➢ **Production** – Supply through planned or actual production orders
➢ **Kanban** – Supply through planned or actual Kanbans (lean manufacturing)

If you need to override the default order type for a specific site, warehouse or other inventory dimension, open the item coverage form (button *Item coverage* on the action pane tab *Plan* of the released product form). On the tab *General* there, the lookup field *Planned order type* enables overriding the default order type.

5.2.1.2 Settings for Quantity and Price

Apart from the default order type, the default order settings contain additional default data for production orders including lot size (field *Multiple*) and order quantity on the tab *Inventory*. Site-specific order settings, accessible through the button *Site specific order settings* on the action pane tab *Plan* of the released product form, may override the default order settings at site level.

On the tab *Manage costs* in the released product form, the field *Price* specifies the general cost price for the item. Site-specific cost prices are available in the item price form, accessible by clicking the button *Set up/Item Price* on the action pane tab *Manage costs* of the released product form (see section 7.2.4).

If the item model group of the released product applies the valuation model "Standard cost", you have to activate a cost price with a costing version referring to the costing type "Standard cost" in the item price form.

5.2.1.3 Phantom Item

The checkbox *Phantom* on the tab *Engineer* in the released product form determines a default, which applies to the *Line type* when inserting the item as a component in a BOM line. Phantom items are semi-finished products with a bill of materials and optionally a route. When estimating a production order, Dynamics AX explodes BOM lines of the type "Phantom". As a result, the production order contains BOM lines with the components of the phantom item (instead of a line with the phantom item itself).

5.2.1.4 Flushing Principle

The *Flushing principle* on the tab *Engineer* of the released product form controls, if production orders should post automatic consumption of the particular item in BOM lines. It contains three different options:

➢ **Start** – Automatic consumption when starting the production order
➢ **Finish** – Automatic consumption when reporting as finished
➢ **Manual** – No automatic consumption

In the BOM line, override the flushing principle specified in the released product record if necessary.

As a prerequisite for automatic consumption based on the released product or BOM line setting, you have to select the option "Flushing principle" in the lookup *Automatic BOM consumption* on the tab *General* of the update dialog when starting – or reporting as finished – a production order (see section 5.4.3).

5.2.1.5 Calculation Group

Another setting available on the tab *Engineer* in the released product form is the *Calculation group*. If you select a calculation group in a released product, this group overrides the general calculation group in the inventory management parameters (*Inventory and warehouse management> Setup> Inventory and warehouse management parameters*, tab *Bills of materials*) when calculating costs for the item.

You may access calculation groups in the form *Inventory and warehouse management> Setup> Costing> Calculation groups*. Calculation groups control the basis for calculating the cost price and sales price of items.

5.2.1.6 New in Dynamics AX 2012 and in AX 2012 R2

Referring to product master data relevant for manufacturing, Dynamics AX 2012 replaces the item type "BOM" by the default order type "Production".

Compared with the initial version of Dynamics AX 2012, the R2 version contains the additional field *Production type*.

5.2.2   Bills of Materials (BOM)

A bill of materials (BOM) primarily is a list of products and quantities. The main purpose of a bill of materials is to determine the components (raw material or parts) of a finished item.

5.2.2.1   Bill of Materials Structure

Items, which are part of a BOM, may themselves consist of other items and therefore refer to a secondary BOM. Such items are semi-finished goods, generating a multi-level product structure.

As shown in Figure 5-5, bills of materials in Dynamics AX are independent from items. You may assign only one or multiple bills of materials to an individual item.

In order to make use of a bill of materials in production control, it has to be approved. In addition, the bill of materials has to be activated if it should apply as a default in production orders and in master planning. An active BOM has to be unique per period, quantity and site.

If a single bill of materials is assigned to multiple finished items, approve and activate the BOM for the different items independently. As an example referring to Figure 5-5, you might approve and activate BOM 1 and BOM 2 for other finished items, no matter if they are approved or activated for the first finished item.

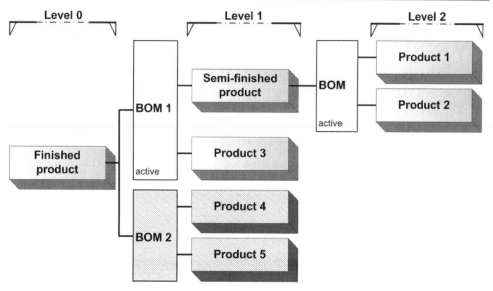

Figure 5-5:   Example of a multi-level product structure

5.2.2.2 Managing Bills of Materials

You may access bills of materials in two ways:

➢ **From the released product** (*Product information management> Common> Released products*, button *BOM/Lines* on the action pane tab *Engineer*)
➢ **From the menu** (*Inventory and warehouse management> Common> Bills of materials*)

Although both forms show the same BOM records with a common data structure, the functionality and structure of these forms is different.

Since understanding the data structure is easier starting in the menu, choose the BOM form accessed from the menu first. The upper part of the BOM form in this case shows a list of available bills of materials, and the lower part the finished items assigned to the BOM selected in the upper part (see Figure 5-6).

In order to enter a new bill of materials, click the button *New* in the action pane strip of the BOM form (inserting a record in the upper pane). Depending on the settings of the applicable number sequence, the BOM number is assigned automatically or has to be entered manually.

If the bill of materials is site-specific, enter the site in the column *Site*. Leaving the site empty creates a general bill of material for all sites.

In the next step, enter a record in the lower part of the form in order to assign the BOM to a finished product. Dynamics AX applies the expression "Versions" for the assignment of bills of materials to items. This expression is another name for the BOM assignment.

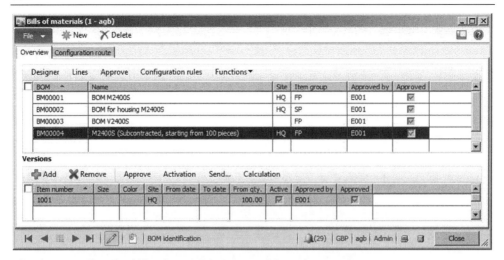

Figure 5-6:   Viewing bills of materials (accessed from the menu)

In the assignment line, enter the *Item number* of the finished product. If the BOM is only valid for a particular period, enter the *From date* and the *To date*. If the BOM assignment depends on the lot size, enter a *From qty*. And if the BOM assignment depends on the site, enter the *Site* in the assignment line.

If you want to assign the BOM to another finished item, enter a second assignment line.

5.2.2.3   BOM Lines

Clicking the button *Lines* in the upper pane of the BOM form opens the BOM lines form, which contains the components of the finished product. BOM lines include raw materials and parts required for producing the finished item.

When inserting a new BOM line, enter at least the *Item number* and the *Quantity*. The column *Per series* determines the quantity of finished items produced with the component quantity entered in the column *Quantity*.

If a bill of materials is site-specific, you can enter a picking warehouse in the column *Warehouse* of the BOM lines. For bills of materials not referring to a particular site, the picking warehouse in the BOM lines is not available. In both cases, the checkbox *Resource consumption* is available for applying the picking warehouse of the resource group or production unit.

Two other important fields are available on the tab *General* of the BOM lines form:

➢ Operation number (*Oper.No.*)
➢ Line type

Production order scheduling as well as master planning calculates item demand in a way that all components have to be available at the start date of the production order. If this does not apply to some components because they are required at a later date, enter the operation number of the route operation, for which the component is required, in the BOM line. Available operation numbers are depending on the route assigned to the finished item. Therefore, the lookup for the operation number only works if accessing the BOM lines – or the BOM designer, see below – from the released product form.

The *Line type* controls the explosion of a BOM line providing following options:

➢ **Item** – Semi-finished or purchased item, considered as demand in inventory
➢ **Phantom** – Semi-finished item, replaced by its components when estimating a production order
➢ **Pegged supply** – Semi-finished or purchased item, creating a linked sub-production order, Kanban, or purchase order for the item in the BOM-line when estimating the production order of the finished item
➢ **Vendor** – Service item for subcontracting

BOM lines of the line type "Item" generate a demand in inventory. For generating production or purchase orders, master planning pools different demands (orders and warehouse replenishing proposals) according to item coverage settings. The default order type (or the order type in the item coverage) controls, if master planning creates a planned purchase order, production order, or Kanban. There is no direct link between the order for the semi-finished item and the original production order of the finished product.

On the tab *Setup* of the BOM lines, optionally select a *Flushing principle* (see section 5.2.1 above) for automatic consumption. If the flushing principle in the BOM line is empty, the setting in the released product record of the BOM line item applies.

If you want to enter a new bill of materials, which is similar to an existing one, use the copy-function by clicking the button *Functions/Copy* in the action pane strip of the BOM lines.

5.2.2.4 Approving and Activating

Only approved bills of materials are available when creating a production order. In order to approve the bill of materials itself and the assignment of the BOM to a finished product (*Version*), click the button *Approve* in the upper and in the lower pane of the BOM form. If approving the BOM version in the lower pane before approving the BOM itself in the upper pane, a checkbox in the approval dialog provides the option to approve the BOM in parallel to the BOM version.

If you want to default the bill of materials in production orders and in master planning, activate the BOM assignment by clicking the button *Activation*. Activated BOM assignments show a checkmark in the column *Active*.

5.2.2.5 Bills of Materials in the Released Product

As an alternative to the menu item, access bills of materials from the released product (*Product information management> Common> Released products*).

Clicking the button *BOM/Lines* on the action pane tab *Engineer* in the released product form after selecting a finished item opens the BOM lines form, displaying the bills of materials assigned to that item. If a bill of materials is assigned to several items, you have to keep in mind that modifying the bill of materials in this form applies to all other items concerned in parallel.

Unlike the BOM form accessed from the menu, the BOM lines form accessed from the released product form shows the BOM lines of the selected bill of materials directly in the lower pane (see Figure 5-7).

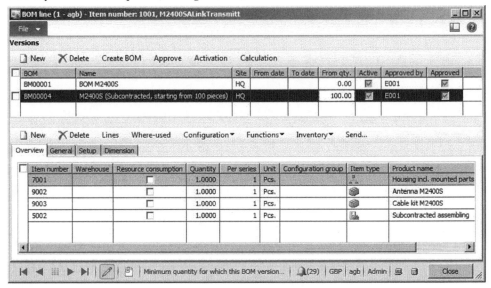

Figure 5-7:   Working in the BOM line form accessed from the released product form

If you want to enter a new bill of materials in this form, click the button *Create BOM* in the action pane strip of the upper pane. Clicking the button *New* in the upper pane for inserting a line is only applicable, if you want to assign the item to an existing bill of materials.

Note: If the *Production type* of the finished item is not "BOM", but "Formula" or "Co-product", the item refers to process manufacturing. In this case, you can assign a formula to the item instead of a BOM. Formulas, which you may access by clicking the button *Formula/Lines* on the action pane tab *Engineer* in the released product form of these items or through the menu item *Inventory and warehouse management> Common> Formula*, work similar to BOMs, but offer additional options required for process industries.

5.2.2.6 BOM Designer

The BOM designer is an alternative option for viewing and editing bills of materials. You may access the BOM designer by clicking the button *BOM/Designer* on the action pane tab *Engineer* of the released product form, or the button *Designer* in the action pane strip of the BOM form.

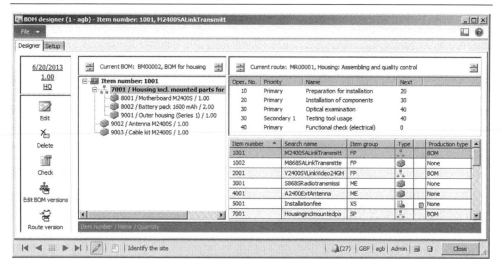

Figure 5-8: Working in the BOM designer accessed from the released product form

The BOM designer shows a multi-level structure of the bill of materials with the option to insert items into the selected BOM by simply dragging and dropping them from the right pane into the left pane.

If accessing the BOM designer from the released product form, it does not only show the bill of materials but also the route of the selected item. Dragging and dropping a BOM line to a route operation there specifies the operation number (*Oper.No.*, see above) of the route operation, for which the component is required.

If you want to change display settings in the BOM designer, switch to the tab *Setup*. On this tab, for example choose the *Display principle* "Selected/Active" (or "Selected") for viewing another BOM version instead of the active BOM. Unlike other settings, choosing the display principle "Selected" then requires clicking the button *Edit BOM versions* on the tab *Designer*. In the *BOM versions* form, select the appropriate BOM and click the button *Select* in the action pane strip before closing the form.

5.2.2.7   Where-Used

The bill of materials shows the components of an item. If you need to know for a component, in which products it is included, open the where-used form. The where-used form, which shows all bills of materials and assigned finished items, is available by clicking the button *BOM/Where-used* on the action pane tab *Engineer* of the released product form after selecting the particular component item.

5.2.3   Case Study Exercises

Exercise 5.1 – Components

Your company wants to produce a new finished item, which consists of two components. Enter these components in Dynamics AX, registering an item with the product number I-##-C1 and the name "##-Component 1" (## = your user ID) and an item with the number I-##-C2 and the name "##-Component 2" in the released product form. Variants, serial or batch numbers do not apply and inventory control is at the level of site and warehouse.

For both items, choose applicable settings for product type, product subtype, dimension groups, item group (raw material/parts), and production type. The item model group should refer to the inventory model "FIFO". The unit of measure is "Pieces", and the items are subject to the standard tax rate. Approved vendors are not required.

The base purchase price and the base cost price of both items is 100 pounds. In addition, choose your vendor of exercise 3.2 as main vendor for the items. The flushing principle should be "Manual". For purchasing and inventory, enter the main site in the *Default order settings* and the main warehouse of the main site in the *Site specific order settings*.

Notes: If a *Balancing financial dimension* applies, enter a default value for this dimension on the tab *Financial dimensions* of the released products. If the number sequence for product numbers is set up for automatic numbering, don't enter a product number.

Exercise 5.2 – Finished Item
For the finished item, enter an item with the product number I-##-F (if no automatic number sequence applies) and the name "##-Finished product" in the released product form. Variants, serial or batch numbers do not apply and inventory control is per site and warehouse.

Choose applicable settings for product type, product subtype, dimension groups, item group (finished product), and production type. The item model group should refer to the inventory model "FIFO". The unit of measure is "Pieces", and the item is subject to the standard tax rate.

The base cost price is 500 pounds and the base sales price 1,000 pounds. In the *Default order settings*, make sure the appropriate *Default order type* is selected and enter the main site in the settings for inventory and sales. Finally register the main warehouse as default for inventory and sales in the *Site specific order settings*.

Note: If a *Balancing financial dimension* applies, enter a default value for this dimension on the tab *Financial dimensions* of the released product.

Exercise 5.3 – Bill of Materials
After registering item records for the finished item and its components in the exercises above, enter a bill of materials for the finished item of exercise 5.2 starting in the released product form.

The BOM applies to the main site and contains two units of the first and one unit of the second item entered in exercise 5.1. The warehouse for picking the components should be the main warehouse. Once you have finished entering the components, approve and activate the BOM.

5.3   Resources and Routes

Resources are entities in a company executing the operations in manufacturing. They include working places and personnel as well as machines, tools and vendors (subcontractors). Resources provide the available capacity, which master planning compares with capacity requirements.

Routes are the basis for calculating the capacity requirement, specifying necessary resources and working time for producing a particular item.

Along with items and bills of materials, resources and routes therefore are the second area of master data required for production control.

5.3.1   Production Units and Resource Groups

Production units represent plants for capacity management. Within a production unit, resource groups collect resources according to the physical organization in the shop floor. Resources within a resource group may show different capabilities and do not need to be interchangeable.

5.3.1.1   Production Units

Production units, which refer to capacity management, are controlled separately from the storage dimension "Site", which refers to material management. Multiple production units may be linked to one common site.

Setting up production units is optional. If you want to create a production unit, access the form *Production control> Setup> Production> Production units* and enter identification, name and site of the new production unit. On the tab *General*, optionally enter a picking warehouse applying to BOM lines with a checkmark in the checkbox *Resource consumption*.

For linking resource groups to the production unit, access the resource groups form (*Organization administration> Common> Resources> Resource groups*). Production units are not included in inventory transactions, but they are available for filtering/sorting in applicable production control forms (e.g. *Production control> Common> Current operations*).

5.3.1.2   Resource Groups and Resource Assignment

Resource groups in Dynamics AX reflect the physical organization of resources and serve following purposes:

➤ **Resource structure** – Linking resources to production units, sites and warehouses
➤ **Operations scheduling** – Capacity planning at resource group level

Assigning resources to resource groups is date effective, providing the option to manage organizational and seasonal changes. At a given date, a resource may not be member of more than one resource group.

When creating a new resource or when detaching a resource from the resource group (setting an expiry date), the resource is not member of any group. Because of required settings like the site specified on the group, resource scheduling includes only resources which are assigned to a resource group.

5.3.1.3 Managing Resource Groups

For editing resource groups, access the form *Organization administration> Common> Resources> Resource groups*. If you want to insert a new resource group there, click the button *New/Resource group* in the action pane and enter the applicable identification, name and site.

On the tab *General* of the resource group form, optionally assign a production unit. The *Input warehouse* specifies the warehouse for consuming BOM lines, which show a checkmark in the checkbox *Resource consumption* (overriding the default of an applicable production unit). Other parameters like scheduling and operation settings correspond to equivalent settings on resources in the resource form (see section 5.3.2 below).

The tab *Resources* of the resource group on the one hand shows the resources which are already member of the group, and on the other hand enables assigning additional resources by clicking the button *Add* in the action pane strip of this tab. For viewing past resource assignments, click the button *View/All*. As an alternative to assigning resources to resource groups in the resource group form, start in the resource form and select the resource group of a resource there.

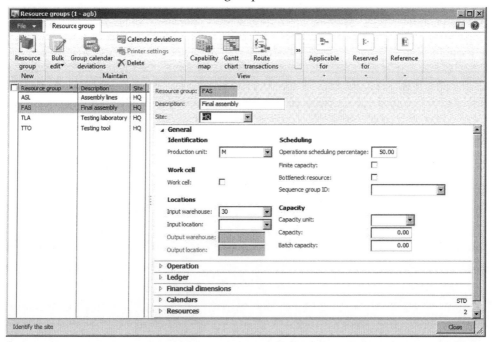

Figure 5-9:   Managing resource groups

By selecting the checkbox *Work cell* on the tab *General* in the resource group form, the resource group refers to lean manufacturing and is not available for operations and production orders in discrete manufacturing. In addition, the tab *Work cell capacity* specifying capacity for lean manufacturing is editable in this case.

5.3.1.4 Working Time Calendars and Templates

The working time calendar assigned determines the operating hours of a resource or resource group. Accordingly, the available capacity is the result of working time calendar and efficiency percentage.

The calendar assignment for resource groups is available directly on the resource group record. For resources, the calendar assignment is specified on the resource assignment line (assignment of the resource to the resource group) and not directly on the resource record.

If you want to assign a calendar to a resource group, access the tab *Calendars* of the resource group form. Calendar assignment is date effective, providing the option to record a future change of the calendar – for example changing the working time of a particular resource group from regular business hours to a 24 hour operation.

Before you may assign a calendar to a resource group, the calendar has to be set up in the form *Organization management> Common> Calendars> Calendars*. If you need to enter a new calendar (for example if a resource group has working times different to all existing calendars), insert a new record in the calendar form by clicking the button *New* or copy an existing calendar by clicking the button *Copy calendar*.

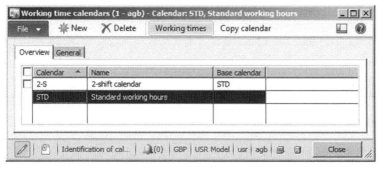

Figure 5-10:   Managing calendars in the calendar form

In order to assign working days and working hours, click the button *Working times* in the calendar form. In the working times form, insert individual dates in the upper pane and enter the working hours for the particular day in the lower pane. Alternatively, create working days and hours automatically by clicking the button *Compose working times* in the working times form.

As a prerequisite for composing working times automatically, you need to set up working time templates. Working time templates are available in the form *Organization management> Common> Calendars> Working time templates*, where you may specify the weekly working hours on the tabs *Monday* to *Sunday* after selecting the appropriate template on the tab *Overview*.

When executing the activity *Compose working times* in the working times form, select a working time template for defaulting daily working times.

5.3.1.5 New in Dynamics AX 2012

Dynamics AX 2012 introduces the new operations resource model, also shown by terminology changes (replacing "Work center" by "Resource"). The new model includes a flexible and date effective assignment of resources to resource groups. Since the assignment of route operations to resources is provided by resource requirements and not by a direct link, the resource group does not refer to a resource type and resources of a resource group do not need to be interchangeable.

5.3.2   Resources and Capabilities

Resources are the lowest level for capacity management in Dynamics AX, and therefore constitute the entities used for job scheduling.

5.3.2.1 Managing Resources

For editing resources, access the form *Organization administration> Common> Resources> Resources*. If you want to insert a new resource, take into account that the resource identification needs to be unique – not only within the resources, but also within resource groups.

When entering a resource, you have to select one of the following resource types distinguishing between different kinds of resources:

➢ **Machine** – General default, for production machines
➢ **Human resources** – Linking workers from the human resources module
➢ **Tool** – Device, often subject to wear through usage
➢ **Location** – Represents physical space (independent from warehouse locations)
➢ **Vendor** – External resource, for subcontracting

In many cases, you do not require separate resources for a machine and its operating staff. You may manage them in a common resource of the type "Machine". If you want to manage tools, enter tool usage as a secondary operation in routes (see section 5.3.3 below).

On the tab *Resource groups* you may view and change the resource group and the calendar assignment of the resource. In order to change the group assignment, click the button *Maintain/Add to resource group* in the action pane. The default for the calendar in the assignment line is the resource group calendar.

5.3.2.2 Resource Capabilities

Resource capabilities determine the kind of activities, which a resource may execute – for example welding or cutting. You may assign one or more capabilities to an individual resource temporarily or permanently.

In the resource requirements of each route, assign resources to operations by specifying required capabilities in addition or instead of assigning resource groups (see section 5.3.3 below).

For setting up capabilities (shared across companies), access the form *Organization administration> Common> Resources> Resource capabilities* and enter the identification and description of the capability. On the tab *Resources* of the capabilities form, assign resources to the particular capability.

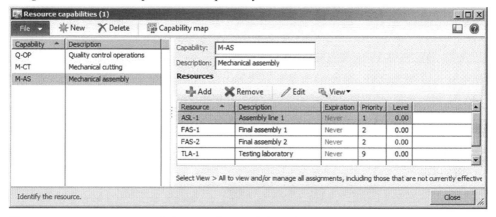

Figure 5-11: Managing capabilities in the capabilities form

As an alternative for assigning capabilities to resources in the capability form, start in the resource form and select the capabilities of each resource by clicking the button *Maintain/Add capability* in the action pane – or the button *Add* on the tab *Capabilities* – there.

Capability assignment is date effective, providing the option to record future changes of resource abilities. In addition, a *Priority* is available in the assignment line. When executing job scheduling, Dynamics AX searches for the applicable resource with the lowest priority number (priority "1" is selected first).

5.3.2.3 Resource Scheduling

There are two types of resource scheduling in production orders, which may run alternatively or successively (see also section 5.4.3):

➢ Operations scheduling
➢ Job scheduling

Operations scheduling is a rough scheduling, calculating the production time per day. It reserves capacity on the resource group allocated through resource requirements in routes. Resource requirements may include capabilities, resource types, and resource groups. If resource requirements for operations scheduling directly refer to a resource number, capacity reservation is on the particular resource instead of the group.

Operations scheduling simultaneously respects the overall capacity of the resource group, the capacity per resource type, and the capacity per capability. The available capacity of a resource group is the total capacity of its resources.

Job scheduling at a later stage of production order processing calculates the capacity at individual resource level, reserving capacity with exact start and end times. Depending on scheduling parameters, the selected resource is the available resource with the shortest duration (throughput time) or with the lowest priority number.

5.3.2.4 Capacity Settings on the Resource

On the tab *General* of the resource form, enter the *Efficiency percentage* of the resource for reducing or increasing the scheduled time of a route. The default for the efficiency percentage is 100. If creating a resource, which – for example – is 25 percent faster than the other resources, enter 125 in the efficiency percentage. Scheduling of an operation usually lasting 10 hours for this resource results in a scheduled time of only 8 hours (= 10 * 100/125).

The checkbox *Finite capacity* controls, if scheduling for the selected resource is based on limited capacity utilization. If this checkbox is selected, Dynamics AX does not schedule operations of multiple orders to run at the same time on that resource. Otherwise, scheduling calculates every production order separately without consideration of other orders on the same resource. In most cases, finite capacity only applies to selected resources and resource groups with limited capacity not available for increasing (e.g. by overtime hours).

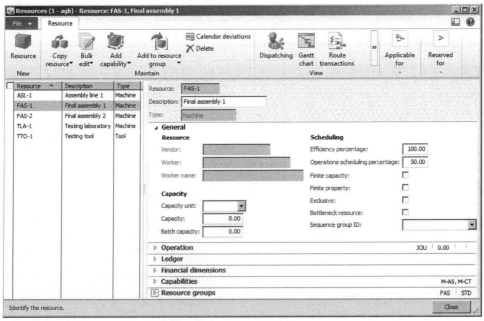

Figure 5-12:   Managing capacity settings of a resource

If you want to apply finite capacity, make sure that the master plan for master scheduling on the one hand and the update dialog for operations and job scheduling on the other hand select to include finite capacity.

The unit of time for scheduling a resource is hours. If you need a different unit of time for a resource, enter a conversion factor in the field *Hours/time* on the resource form (field group *Times* on the tab *Operation*). If the time entered in routes for example is in minutes, insert $1/60 = 0.0167$ in the field *Hours/time*.

If a particular resource does not apply a unit of time for the unit of measure, optionally select an alternative *Capacity unit* on the tab *General* of the resource form. The field *Capacity* then contains the conversion factor to hours. In related route operations, choose the option "Capacity" in the field *Formula* on the tab *Setup* then.

Further fields on the tab *Operation* in the resource form contain defaults for route operations. These defaults apply when selecting the resource or resource group as costing resource in a route operation.

5.3.2.5 Settings for Ledger Integration

The tab *Ledger* in the resource form contains the main accounts applying to route consumption. When posting a route card or job card journal in production, Dynamics AX in parallel posts the cost amount of the consumed working time to the main accounts specified in the field group *Accounts-WIP* of the resource form. When costing and ending a production order, ledger transactions are posted to the accounts in the field group *Accounts-Costing*.

The ledger settings in the resource only apply, if the option "Item and resource" is selected in the lookup field *Ledger posting* of the production order (see section 8.4.3). If the option "Item and category" is selected, the cost categories in the route operation determine applicable main accounts.

5.3.2.6 New in Dynamics AX 2012

As part of the new operations resource model, shared capabilities replace and significantly extend the task group functionality of previous versions.

5.3.3 Routes and Operations

Routes determine the required operations for producing an item. They are a supplement to the bill of materials, which contains the required material.

Like bills of materials, routes contain planned figures providing targets for production. In the course of manufacturing, your workshop reports actual figures in production journal transactions. Comparing and analyzing target and actual figures is a basis for possible improvements.

In order to sufficiently describe the operations in manufacturing, a route has to contain at least following data:

➤ **Manufacturing activity** – *Operation*

➤ **Provider of capacity** – *Resource requirements*

➤ **Sequence of operations** – Next operation (*Next*)

➤ **Time consumption** – *Setup time, Run time*

➤ **Finished item** – *Item number* in route assignment (route version)

➤ **Required material** – Assigned operations in BOM lines

If the workshop does not require all components of the bill of materials to be available when starting the first operation, link items in the bill of materials to the applicable operation of the route as shown in section 5.2.2.

5.3.3.1 Managing Operations

Operations, available in the form *Production control> Setup> Routes> Operations*, are a prerequisite for setting up routes in Dynamics AX. After creating an operation, select it in as many routes as required.

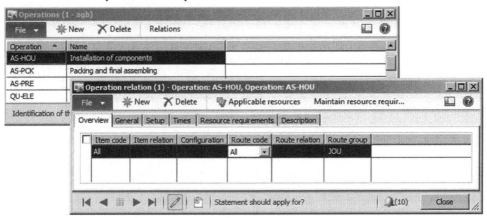

Figure 5-13: Managing general operation relations for an operation

Operations are independent from routes, containing only a unique identification and a name to describe the performed activity. Other details required to execute an operation – like the allowed time or the resource assignment – are not available in the operation record itself, but in the operation relations.

In order to view and edit operation details (operation relations), click the button *Relations* in the operations form. Depending on your requirements, set up operation relations at a general level, or specific to only one route:

➤ **General** – For entering operation details at a general level, select the option "All" in the columns *Item code* and *Route code* on the tab *Overview* of the operation relations form (see Figure 5-13).

➤ **Route-specific** – Route-specific operation details show the option "Route" in the *Route code* and the route number in the *Route relation* column.

After switching to the other tabs of the operation relations form, enter details of the particular operation relation including applicable resources and times. More information on this subject is available in the description of route operations further below in this section.

5.3.3.2 Operation Sequence

The sequence of operations is not specified in the operation record, but in the route. You may distinguish two types of operation sequences:

➢ Simple sequence
➢ Complex sequence

If the checkbox *Route network* on the tab *General* of the production control parameters is cleared, simple operation sequences apply. Routes in this case only contain operations executed one after the other.

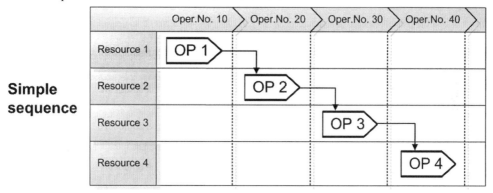

Figure 5-14:   Example of a simple operation sequence

If the checkbox *Route network* is selected, you have to enter the next operation in each operation of a route. This setting enables complex operation sequences, where you may connect a particular operation to several independent prior operations.

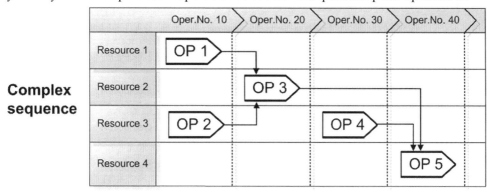

Figure 5-15:   Example of a complex operation sequence

Irrespective of simple or complex operation sequences, operations to be performed on multiple resources in parallel are available by entering a secondary operation in routes (selecting the *Priority* "Secondary" for the particular route operation).

If the available options in the route do not meet your specific requirements, set up an intermediate level of a virtual semi-finished item in the structure of the finished product. The line type of the BOM line, which contains the virtual item, should be "Pegged supply" for connecting the production order for the virtual semi-finished item directly to the production order of the finished item.

5.3.3.3 Managing Routes

Managing routes in Dynamics AX is similar to managing bills of materials, including the way for accessing the particular Dynamics AX form:

> **From the released product** (*Product information management> Common> Released products*, button *View/Route* on the action pane tab *Engineer*)
> **From the menu** (*Production control> Common> Routes> All routes*)

Although both forms show the same route records with a common data structure, the functionality and structure of the forms is different. Like the assignment of bills of materials, the assignment of routes to finished items is called "Version" optionally containing validity dates and a from-quantity. Unlike bills of materials, a route version always refers to a site.

If accessing routes from the menu item, Dynamics AX displays the routes in a list page. Clicking the button *Maintain/Route versions* in the action pane of the list page opens the route detail form of the specific route, showing the route header and one or more assigned finished items ("Versions").

In order to access the route operations from the routes list page, click the button *Maintain/Edit* in the action pane or double-click a route record in the list page. If you are in the route detail form (showing the route versions), clicking the button *Maintain/Route* in the action pane opens the route operations – the button *Edit* there switches between view mode and edit mode.

The route form shows the list of operations for the selected route in the upper pane. In the lower pane of the route form, you can edit the operation relations (operation details) of the operation selected in the upper pane. Depending on the requirements, route-specific operation relations or a general operation relation – applicable to all routes and items for an operation – may apply.

5.3.3.4 Creating a Route

In the routes list page, create a new route by clicking the button *New/Route* in the action pane. In the route detail form, the route number derives from the appropriate number sequence or has to be entered manually. After entering a *Name* for the new route in the upper pane, assign one or more finished items together with the applicable site in the lower pane.

Clicking the button *Maintain/Route* in the action pane of the route detail form opens the route operations, where you may insert the particular route operations.

Like bills of materials, routes and route assignments (*Versions*) have to be approved before they are available for production orders. You may approve a route clicking the button *Approve* in the action pane of the route list page or detail form. In order to approve a route version, click the button *Approve* in the action pane strip of the tab *Versions* in the route detail form. If approving the route version before approving the route, a checkbox in the approval dialog provides the option to approve the route in parallel.

If you want to default the route in production orders and in master scheduling, activate the route version by clicking the button *Activation*.

5.3.3.5 Route Operations

If accessing the route from the routes list page, the sequence of route operations shows in the upper pane of the form. Making sure the upper pane is selected, insert a new route operation by pushing the shortcut key *Ctrl+N* or choosing the command *File/New* in the jewel menu.

After selecting the operation number in the column *Oper.No.*, choose the applicable operation in the column *Operation*. Operation details (operation relations) are available in the lower pane of the form.

If a general operation relation – indicated by the option "All" in the column *Route code* – exists for the selected operation, it shows in the lower pane of the route form after saving the record in the upper pane. If you change data of a general operation relation in the route form, keep in mind that these changes apply to all routes referring to the particular general operation relation.

If you want to register route-specific operation details, insert a line for a new operation relation in the lower pane of the route from. When inserting this operation relation, select the option "Route" in the column *Route code* and enter required data on the other tabs of the lower pane.

In the upper pane of the route form, you have to enter the number of the next route operation (except for the last operation) in the column *Next*, if the production control parameters (checkbox *Route network*) specify complex operation sequences.

If the shop floor should execute operations in parallel, enter two operations with the same operation number, but a different *Priority*. In the example of Figure 5-16, the operation number 30 shows two parallel operations – one with priority "Primary" and the other with priority "Secondary 1".

5.3.3.6 Routes in the Released Product

As an alternative to the appropriate menu item, access the routes from the released product form (*Product information management> Common> Released products*). Clicking the button *View/Route* on the action pane tab *Engineer* in the released product form after selecting a finished item opens the routes form, displaying the routes assigned to this item.

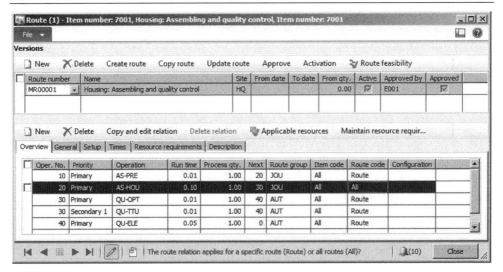

Figure 5-16:   Managing routes in the route form, accessed from the released product

The route form accessed from the menu looks different to the route form accessed from the released product – it shows the route version (or versions) in the upper pane and the operations with operation number and operation relation details in the lower pane. If you want to enter a completely new route in this from, click the button *Create route* in the upper pane. Clicking the button *New* in the upper pane is applicable, if you want to create a version assigning the item to an existing route.

If a general operation relation – indicated by the option "All" in the column *Route code* – exists for an operation, detail data from this relation apply to the route operation. Unlike the route form accessed from the menu, overriding data from the general operation relation in this form automatically creates a route-specific operation relation – indicated by the option "Route" in the column *Route code*.

In order to create a route-specific operation relation based on an applicable general operation relation, optionally click the button *Copy and edit relation* in the action pane strip of the lower pane (in order to view the new route-specific operation relation, it might be required to refresh the form pushing the *F5* key afterwards). If you want to delete a route-specific operation relation for applying the general operation relation again, click the button *Delete relation* in the action pane strip.

If no general operation relation exists for a route operation, enter a new operation relation with all required data in the lower pane manually.

5.3.3.7   Route Groups

An essential setting for posting working time consumption related to an operation is the *Route group* on the tab *Overview* (also available on the tab *General*) of the operation relation in the route form. If you want to apply automatic posting of time consumption (actual = estimate), you have to select a route group with appropriate settings for automatic route consumption.

In order to access route group settings, choose the form *Production control> Setup> Routes> Route groups*. In route groups for automatic posting, the checkboxes for *Setup time, Run time* and *Quantity* in the field group *Automatic route consumption* on the tab *General* have to be selected. In addition, clear the checkboxes in the column *Job management* on the tab *Setup* for these route groups (automatic consumption is posted through route cards).

The checkboxes in the field group *Estimation and costing* control, if to include assigned operations in estimation and cost calculation. For regular operations, you want to select the checkboxes for time based cost calculation or the checkbox for quantity based cost calculation.

5.3.3.8 Costing Resource and Cost Categories

The tab *Setup* of the operation relations in the route form contains the *Costing resource* specifying the resource applicable for the cost estimation of production orders. When selecting a costing resource in a route operation, data from the resource default to the *Cost categories* and the fields on the tab *Times* as applicable.

Cost categories are a second setting in addition to the route group for controlling cost estimation and cost calculation. You can assign different cost categories for setup time, run time and quantity. When assigning cost categories, make sure the appropriate checkbox in the route group is selected for including time or quantity in the cost calculation.

Before creating a new cost category, you have to enter a shared category in the form *Production control> Setup> Routes> Shared categories* (alternatively accessible through the table reference – *View details* – on the field *Category ID* of the cost categories form). Shared categories ensure common category definitions across companies. For categories applicable to production, the checkbox *Can be used in Production* in the shared category has to be selected.

In production control, required cost categories are available in the form *Production control> Setup> Routes> Cost categories*. These categories contain three important settings:

➢ **Cost price** – Determining the hourly rate of capacity
➢ **Cost group** – Classifying cost types in cost calculation (see section 5.4.1)
➢ **Ledger-Resources** – Determining main accounts similar to ledger integration settings of resources (see section 5.3.2 above), if the production order applies the option "Item and category" in the lookup field *Ledger posting*

In order to specify a cost price for a category, click the button *Price* in the cost categories form for accessing the cost category price form. In the item price form, enter a cost price for the category per site or – if leaving the field *Site* empty – company-wide with a start date, assigned to a costing version (for costing versions, please refer to section 7.2.4). In order to apply the price, activate it by clicking the button *Activate*.

5.3.3.9 Route Operation Times

The tab *Times* of the operations relations contains the allowed time for the operation, split into setup time, run time, queue times and transit time. The field *Run time* contains the time, in which the workshop should process the quantity of the product entered in the field *Process qty*.

If the *Process qty*. is 1.00, the run time is the time in hours to produce one unit. You may apply other units of time, entering a conversion factor *Hours/time* in the route operation or selecting a capacity unit in the resource (see section 5.3.2).

The processing time of an operation calculates according to following formula:

$$PROCESSING \ \ TIME = \frac{Setup \ time + (Run \ time \times Quantity \,)}{Efficiency \ \ percentage \ \ of \ the \ resource}$$

In order to calculate the total lead time, add queue and transit times.

5.3.3.10 Resource Requirements

On the tab *Resource requirements* of the operation relations, specify which resources are applicable for the operation (independent from the costing resource). If there are several requirement lines, applicable resource must meet all requirements.

You may specify requirements for *Operations scheduling* independent from the requirements for *Job scheduling*, selecting the checkbox in the appropriate column as applicable. In the column *Requirement type*, choose if a requirement is based on a resource group, resource, resource type or capability. The options "Skill", "Courses", "Certificate" and "Title" apply to job scheduling for resources of the resource type "Human resource", referring to worker data in human resource management.

Clicking the button *Applicable resources* at the top of the lower pane in the route form helps checking which resources meet the requirements entered for a route operation. Since the assignment of resources to resource groups and capabilities is date effective, you have to choose a date for displaying applicable resources.

5.3.3.11 New in Dynamics AX 2012

Items new in Dynamics AX 2012 related to routes include the resource requirements on route operations (replacing direct work center and work center group assignment in previous releases) and shared categories for cost categories.

5.3.4   Case Study Exercises

Exercise 5.4 – Route Setup
In order to better understand the function of capabilities, route groups and cost categories, you want to set up an example.

As a start, create a capability C-## (## = your user ID) with the name "##-specific". Then you want to enter a route group R-## for manual posting of working time consumption. Estimation and costing should be based on setup time and run time.

Next you want to set up a new cost category G-## (together with a shared category applying to production). Assign the cost category to an appropriate cost group of your choice and enter main accounts similar to the settings in existing cost categories. For the hourly rate, enter a cost price of 100 pounds specific for a costing version of the costing type "Planned cost" and the main site. Then activate the cost price.

Exercise 5.5 – Resources and Resource Group

In order to produce the finished product of exercise 5.2, new resources are required. Enter a new resource group W-## with the name "##-assembly", referring to the main site and an appropriate production unit. The cost categories are the ones entered in exercise 5.4. For the resource group calendar, select a regular calendar of your choice.

Then create two new resources, W-##-1 and W-##-2, of the type "Machine". For both resources, the route group and – for setup and for run time – the cost category of exercise 5.4 applies. The main accounts for the resources may be similar to existing resources. Assign both resources to the new resource group W-##, but only the resource W-##-2 to the capability entered in exercise 5.4. The resources use the same calendar as the resource group.

Note: If a *Balancing financial dimension* applies, enter a default value for this dimension on the tab *Financial dimensions* of the resources and the resource group.

Exercise 5.6 – Operation

In order to produce your product, you need a new operation. Register this operation O-## (## = your user ID) with the name "##-processing".

Generally, the setup time for the operation is one hour and the run time two hours per unit. Select the resource W-##-1 of exercise 5.5 as costing resource, providing defaults for route group and cost categories. Resources applicable to the operation belong to the resource group W-## and show the capability C-## of exercise 5.4.

Exercise 5.7 – Route

Manufacturing your product also requires a new route, which you want to enter based on the elements set up in the previous exercises.

After selecting your item I-##-F of exercise 5.2 in the released product form, open the route form by clicking the appropriate button. Insert a new route, which contains the operation O-## of exercise 5.6 as the only route operation. There is no setup time, and the run time for the operation is one hour per unit. The other settings of route operation – including costing resource, route group, cost categories and resource requirements – are the same as the applicable general operation relation entered in exercise 5.6.

Once you are finished entering the route details, approve and activate the route. Can you check applicable resources for executing the route operations? Finally, check all operation relations referring to the operation of exercise 5.6.

5.4   Production Orders

A production order is a request to manufacture a particular product. Apart from the item number and quantity of the finished or semi-finished item, production orders contain data regarding required materials and resources.

The production status displays the progress of a production order. Therefore, the status is updated with every step in the sequential flow of order processing.

5.4.1   Basics of Production Order Processing

You may create a production order either manually or automatically. For automatic creation, following options are available:

➤ **Master scheduling** – Within the firming time fence immediately generating a production order (see section 6.3.3)
➤ **Planned production order** – Transfer to a production order by firming (see section 6.3.4)
➤ **Pegged supply** – Automatic generation from the BOM line of another production order (sub-production, see section 5.4.3)
➤ **Sales order** – Creating a production order by clicking the button *Product and supply/New/Production order* in the action pane strip of a sales order line

5.4.1.1   Production Order Status

If you create a production order manually, the first status is "Created". The status "Created" is the only status, which allows deleting a production order. If you need to delete a production order in a later status, you have to reset the status first.

After creating a production order, it runs through the manufacturing cycle updating the order to following status:

➤ Created
➤ Estimated
➤ Scheduled
➤ Released
➤ Started
➤ Reported as finished
➤ Ended

The order status changes every time when you update the production order, either by clicking an appropriate button on the action pane tab *Production order* or *Schedule* of the production order form, or by running a periodic activity in the menu *Production control> Periodic> Production orders* or *Production control> Periodic> Scheduling*. Depending on production control parameters, you can skip particular steps. In this case, Dynamics AX automatically executes the omitted steps when starting a subsequent step, applying standard parameter settings in this case.

If you want to reset the status of an order, click the button *Process/Reset status* on the action pane tab *Production order* of the production order form. When resetting the status, keep in mind that Dynamics AX reverses all posted transactions referring to the reversed status.

5.4.1.2 Default Values in Update Dialogs

When updating the status of a production order, an update dialog displays. In the update dialog, click the button *Default values* if you need default values different to the standard defaults. Clicking the button *User default* in the default values form applies customized default values to all users.

5.4.1.3 Production Control Parameters and Scheduling Parameters

Unlike parameter settings in other areas, production control parameters are not only available at company level, but also per site. The lookup field *Parameter usage* in the production control parameters at company level (*Production control> Setup> Production control parameters*) controls in this context, if site-specific parameters apply to your company. Site-specific parameters in this case are available in the form *Production control> Setup> Production control parameters by site*.

On the tab *Status* of the production control parameters (general or site-specific) you may specify from which status to which status production orders may be updated. These settings on the one hand apply to skipping steps in regular production order processing and to resetting the production order status on the other hand.

Scheduling parameters, providing defaults to the update dialogs for scheduling production orders, are available in the form *Organization administration> Setup> Scheduling> Scheduling parameters* separate from the production control parameters. Like the production control parameters, they are available at company level and per site. Key scheduling parameters include the *Primary resource selection*, specifying if capability-based scheduling is to be based on the shortest duration (latest start date when scheduling backwards) or on the lowest priority number.

5.4.1.4 Production Journals

As a prerequisite for posting transactions in manufacturing, you have to set up the required journals in the form *Production control> Setup> Production journal names*. Picking lists, route cards, job cards and report as finished journals refer to different journal names, which you have to set up selecting the appropriate *Journal type*.

5.4.1.5 Cost Groups

Cost calculation requires two basic settings:

➢ Cost groups
➢ Costing sheets

Cost groups classify and group different types of costs in cost calculation on the one hand and specify different margins for sales price calculation on the other hand. You may access cost groups in the form *Inventory and warehouse management> Setup> Costing> Cost groups* or in the form *Production control> Setup> Routes> Cost groups*. The *Cost group type*, which provides the basic costing structure, contains following options:

> ➢ **Direct materials** – Material consumption
> ➢ **Direct manufacturing** – Resource operations
> ➢ **Direct outsourcing** – Purchased subcontracting services
> ➢ **Indirect** – Overhead margins
> ➢ **Undefined** – Unspecific cost classification

In one cost group per *Cost group type* you should select the checkbox *Default* to specify appropriate default groups.

In order to specify margins applying to sales price calculation, access the tab *Profit* of the cost group form. You may register up to four lines with a different *Profit-setting* on this tab, entering an appropriate *Profit percentage* per profit-setting level. When executing cost calculation or estimating production orders later, choose an appropriate *Profit-setting* in the calculation dialog – e.g. if you want to apply a lower margin in a competitive situation.

In the released product form, there is the field *Cost group* on the tab *Manage costs* for assigning a cost group to the particular item. For items not assigned to a specific cost group, the default cost group for the cost group type "Direct materials" applies to BOM lines.

Route operations are not directly assigned to a cost group. As shown in section 5.3.3, route operations are linked to cost categories, and cost categories refer to cost groups.

5.4.1.6 Costing Sheet

In order to establish a clear structure of costs for estimation and costing, there is the costing sheet in the form *Inventory and warehouse management> Setup> Costing> Costing sheets*. The costing sheet has got two different purposes:

> ➢ **Classify costs** – Classification by cost groups
> ➢ **Overhead costs** – Specifying rules for calculating overhead costs of manufactured and purchased items

For classification purposes, the costing sheet constitutes a multi-level structure of the different costs. Apart from the cost groups, which are the bottom level in the structure, the costing sheet may contain nodes for totals at multiple levels.

Directly below the *Root* node, the costing sheet may show two primary nodes with the *Node type* "Price", characterized by a different *Type* in the field group *Setup* for distinguishing following items:

➢ **Manufactured items** – Applying the node with the *Type* "Cost of goods manufactured"

➢ **Purchased items** – Applying the node with the *Type* "Costs of purchase" (optional structure, if you want to apply indirect costs from the costing sheet instead of indirect costs through charges in purchase orders)

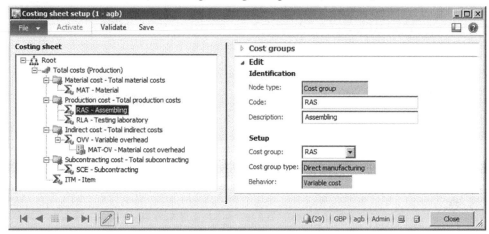

Figure 5-17:   Setting up a simple costing sheet

If you want to enter a new node in the costing sheet, do a right-hand click on the higher-level node and choose the option *Create* in the pop-up menu.

In case you want to create a node for a cost group, choose the option "Cost group" in the lookup field *Select node type* of the dialog shown next. Then select the appropriate *Cost group* on the tab *Edit* in the new node.

If you want to specify calculation rules for overhead costs, choose (or create) a node in the costing sheet with a *Cost group* referring to the *Cost group type* "Indirect". The nodes specifying calculation rules for overhead costs are sub-nodes of such a node. When creating a sub-node for overhead cost calculation, choose the option "Surcharge" or "Rate" for the *Node type* in the sub-node. On the tab *Calculation* of the sub-node, select a *Code* specifying the basis for the calculation. Then you may enter a percentage or rate referring to a costing version (see section 7.2.4) in the lower pane of the form and activate it clicking the button *Activate*. Main accounts for posting indirect costs to the general ledger have to be entered on the tab *Posting*.

Before closing the costing sheet setup, save your changes clicking the button *Save*.

5.4.1.7   New in Dynamics AX 2012

Items new in Dynamics AX 2012 include the scheduling parameters. In the costing sheet, the additional node type "Output unit based" for indirect costs and the option to specify indirect costs for purchasing are available.

5.4.2   Production Order Registration

Like all documents, production orders contain a header with data common for the whole order – including the order number, the item number of the finished product, the order quantity and the delivery date. But unlike sales or purchase orders, production orders include two different types of lines:

➢ **BOM lines** – Containing required material
➢ **Route lines** – Containing required operations

The production order detail form, which you may access double-clicking an order in the production order list page (*Production control> Common> Production Orders> All Production Orders*) only includes the production order header.

In order to access the BOM lines of a specific production order, click the button *Production details/BOM* on the action pane tab *Production order* of the production order form. Clicking the button *Production details/Route* in the action pane of the production order shows the production route (containing resource operations).

Note: In parallel to orders for producing BOM items, the production order list page contains orders for formula items (with the *Production type* "Formula" or "Co-product") referring to process manufacturing. The button *New/Batch order* in the production order form creates a new order for a formula item. For accessing the formula lines of a batch order (working similar to a production order), click the button *Production details/Formula*.

5.4.2.1   Defaults for Production Orders

Production orders contain a copy of the bill of materials and the route, which you may modify within the particular order.

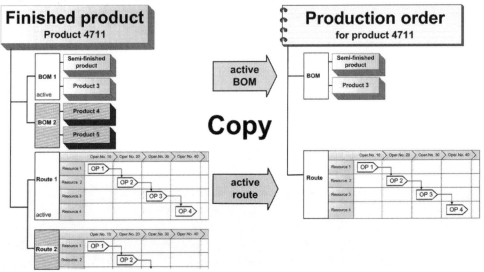

Figure 5-18:   Deriving BOM and route when creating a production order

When creating a production order, Dynamics AX copies the active BOM and route of the finished item into the production order. If several BOMs and routes are active for a finished item, the applicable version is determined based on site, validity date, order quantity, and item configuration. For the validity date, the field *BOM date* – receiving its default from the delivery date – in the *Create production order* dialog determines the date applied for BOM selection.

If you do not want to apply the active BOM or route in a particular production order, select another approved BOM or route version – e.g. an alternative BOM and route for subcontracting – in the create order dialog.

5.4.2.2   Entering a New Production Order

In order to manually enter a new production order, access the form *Production control> Common> Production Orders> All production orders* and click the button *New/Production order* on the action pane tab *Production order* or push the keyboard shortcut *Ctrl+N*. Dynamics AX then shows the *Create production order* dialog, where you have to choose the item number of the finished product. Depending on the selected item, Dynamics AX applies several defaults. If required, override these default values in the create dialog, for example selecting a different BOM.

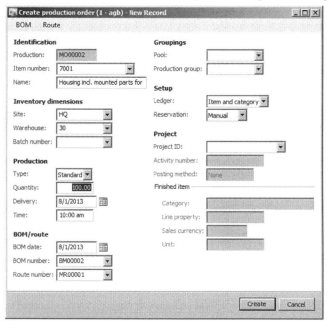

Figure 5-19:   Creating a production order

You may also change settings in a production order later, for example modifying the BOM or route lines in the order. If estimation or scheduling has been executed, you should update estimation and/or scheduling after changing the production order to ensure correct production data. If production papers have been printed already, you might need to reprint them with updated data.

Clicking the button *Create* in the create order dialog then, Dynamics AX inserts the production order. After creating, the order shows the status "Created" and switches to a subsequent status when updating the order. A summary of executed status updates is available on the tab *Update* of the production order detail form, which you may access by double-clicking an order in the list page.

5.4.2.3 References to the Origin

Production orders, which are not created manually, show a reference to their origin on the tab *References* of the production order detail form. If the production order refers to another order, this original order displays in the item reference type and number.

If you have created the production order in a sales order line, the item reference type is "Sales order". In production orders generated as sub-production for the BOM line of another production order, the item reference type is "Production line".

5.4.3   Processing Production Orders

After creating a production order, you want to update the status in order to prepare production order processing.

5.4.3.1 Estimation

Estimation is the first step after creating a production order. The primary task of estimation is to calculate the material and of resource capacity requirements for executing a production order. The basis for this calculation is the bill of materials and the route of the order.

In order to run estimation, click the button *Process/Estimate* on the action pane tab *Production order* of the production order form. The tab *General* in the estimation dialog contains a lookup field for the profit setting in the sales price calculation.

In parallel to calculating required quantities and times, estimation determines estimated costs based on the cost price of material components and route operations. The markup of the calculated sales price derives from the cost groups of the items and route operations.

After estimation, the cost estimation is available by clicking the button *Related information/Price calculation* of the action pane tab *View* of the production order form. The tab *Overview estimation* of the price calculation form contains the list of individual estimation lines. For viewing a summary according to the costing sheet setup, switch to the tab *Costing sheet* in the price calculation form.

The BOM lines of the production order create inventory transactions, which look similar to the inventory transactions of open sales and purchase order lines, when estimating. For accessing them, click the button *Inventory/Transactions* in the BOM lines of the production order.

The inventory transaction for the finished item, accessible by clicking the button *Inventory/Transactions* on the action pane tab *Production order* of the production order form, is generated when creating the production order (independently from estimation).

For BOM lines of the *Line type* "Pegged supply", estimation creates a referenced order:

> ➢ **Sub-production order** – For BOM lines containing an item with the default order type "Production", estimation creates and estimates a sub-production order (regular production order linked to the main production order).
> ➢ **Purchase order** – For BOM lines containing an item with the default order type "Purchase order", estimation creates a referenced purchase order.

For BOM lines of the line type "Phantom", estimation replaces the BOM line by the components of the phantom item (BOM and route).

5.4.3.2 Scheduling

Scheduling of a production order is necessary to calculate exact dates for material and resource requirements. There are two types of order scheduling: Operations scheduling and job scheduling. Whereas operations scheduling is the first step, determining dates at an aggregate level of capacity planning, job scheduling itemizes planned data:

> ➢ **Split resource groups** – Reserving capacity on individual resources
> ➢ **Split operations** – Reserving capacity for jobs with start and end time

Depending on the requirements, execute either only operations scheduling, or only job scheduling, or both (first operations scheduling, then job scheduling).

Operations scheduling calculates and reserves required capacity per day at the level of resource groups (for operations in the route not directly assigned to a particular resource). The applicable resource group is determined based on the resource requirements of the operation (capabilities, resource groups, resource types).

Job scheduling calculates exact start and end times and generates jobs, splitting the route operations of a production order to individual tasks. These individual tasks show different job types, corresponding to the different time fields – including *Setup time* and *Run time* – on the tab *Times* of the route operation. Available job types for a particular operation are determined by the *Route group* of the operation (settings on the tab *Setup* in the route group form).

Job transactions (referring to job scheduling) are independent from route transactions (referring to operations scheduling). Therefore you have to decide whether to schedule capacity and post actual time consumption at operations level or at detailed job level. Jobs are recorded in a separate table, which you may access by clicking the button *Production details/All jobs* on the action pane tab *Production order* of the production order or *Inquiries/Jobs* in the production route form (*Production details/Route* in the action pane of the production order).

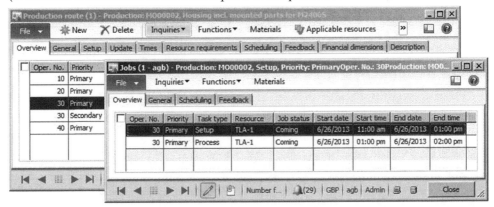

Figure 5-20: Jobs form, accessed from the production route

Jobs are not available for a production order, if you skip job scheduling.

In order to run scheduling, click the button *Production order/Schedule operations* or *Production order/Schedule jobs* on the action pane tab *Schedule* of the production order form. If you want to schedule multiple orders, access the corresponding periodic activity in the menu item *Production control> Periodic> Scheduling*.

On the tab *General* of the update dialog for scheduling, following parameters are available:

➢ **Scheduling direction** – Choose an option of forward or backward scheduling
➢ **Schedule references** – Select for scheduling sub-productions in parallel
➢ **Finite capacity** and **Finite material** – Select for considering resource or item availability
➢ **Keep warehouse from resource** – Prevents selecting a resource assigned to a different input warehouse when re-scheduling a production order (applicable if the checkbox *Resource consumption* in BOM lines is selected)
➢ **Primary resource selection** – For job scheduling, specifying whether capability based resource selection should primarily search for the shortest duration (latest start date when scheduling backwards) or for the lowest priority number

In addition, choose to skip job types on the tab *Cancellation* if applicable. This is useful if it is for example possible to skip queue time for a particular production order of high importance.

If you do not execute operations or job scheduling as a separate task, scheduling runs automatically when updating to a later status like *Release*. In this case, the *Scheduling method* on the tab *Automatic update* of the production control parameters specifies, whether Dynamics AX runs operations scheduling or job scheduling.

5.4.3.3 Releasing

At the time you want to transfer the production order to the shop floor, you have to release the order clicking the button *Process/Release* on the action pane tab *Production order* of the production order form.

On the tab *General* of the update dialog for releasing, optionally choose to print production papers like job cards or route cards. Selecting the checkbox *References* releases referenced sub-production orders in parallel.

5.4.3.4 Starting

Starting a production order (button *Process/Start* on the action pane tab *Production order*) enables posting inventory and resource transactions referring to this order. If you do not want to start the entire production quantity, enter a partial quantity on the tab *General* of the update dialog for starting. Entering a *From Oper.No.* and a *To Oper.No.* only starts the selected operations.

The automatic posting of route consumption (working time consumption) is controlled by the field group *Route card journal* on the tab *General* of the update dialog. The field *Route card* there specifies the journal name for posting, showing a default from the production control parameters. In order to control posting of *Automatic route consumption*, the following options are available:

➢ **Route group dependent** – Automatic consumption, depending on the route group of the operation (see section 5.3.3)
➢ **Always** – Automatic consumption of the whole route
➢ **Never** – No automatic consumption

The checkbox *Post route card now* controls whether to post the consumption journal immediately. If automatic route consumption is selected but not posted, Dynamics AX generates a non-posted journal for manual editing.

Controlling automatic BOM consumption in the field group *Picking list journal* of the update dialog works similar to the automatic route consumption. If you want to post automatic consumption depending on settings in the BOM lines, choose the option "Flushing principle" (see section 5.2.1) in the lookup field *Automatic BOM consumption*. This option refers to the corresponding field on the tab *Setup* of the BOM in the production order.

Selecting the checkbox *Print picking list* in the update dialog prints the picking list in parallel to starting the order. For a complete picking list, select the checkbox *Complete picking list journal*. Otherwise, the picking list only contains items, which are included in the picking list journal generated for automatic consumption.

5.4.4   Case Study Exercises

Exercise 5.8 – Production Order

Your company has a demand for five pieces of the finished item entered in exercise 5.2. Enter an appropriate production order and check the bill of materials and the route in the order.

Exercise 5.9 – Change Status

Run the estimation for your production order of exercise 5.8. Once the estimation is finished, check the price calculation. Then you want to update the order – first operations scheduling, then job scheduling, and finally releasing the order.

When starting the order, make sure to print a complete picking list as a print preview. You do not want to post the picking list. Is it possible to apply these settings as a default for all users?

5.5   Production Journal Transactions

In order to update scheduling and to analyze production performance, reporting of actual material and working time consumption is required.

Reporting of actual consumption is done through production journals, which may be registered and posted in one of three ways:

> **Manually** – Entering and posting journals as described below (if applicable, usually done in the office based on manual reports of the shop floor).
> **Automatically** – Creating journals based on route group and flushing principle.
> **Through terminals** – Applying the shop floor control module (*Manufacturing execution*) in Dynamics AX, consumption may be reported on touch-screen terminals in the shop floor.

5.5.1   Journal Transactions and Ledger Integration

Production journals for posting consumption include following types:

> **Picking list** – Posting item consumption
> **Route card** – Posting time consumption referring to operations
> **Job card** – Posting time consumption referring to jobs

Another journal type available – *Report as finished* – does not refer to item consumption, but to finishing production receiving the product in inventory.

For automatic route and item consumption, Dynamics AX creates production journals automatically when starting a production order or when reporting as finished. Production journals are also generated automatically, if registrations are transferred from the shop floor control module (*Manufacturing execution*).

If BOM lines or route operations require manual entries in the production control module, you have to create production journals. Manual journals apply to the following lines:

> ➤ **Operations** – If assigned to a route group, in which the checkboxes for automatic route consumption are cleared
> ➤ **Items** – If showing a flushing principle "Manual"

The setting for automatic consumption in the operation (route group) or BOM line (flushing principle) applies, if you refer to these settings in the dialog when starting a production order or reporting as finished. Usually, this is the default setting. If choosing the option "Never" for automatic consumption in the dialog for both order status updates, you have to post manual journals for all BOM lines and operations.

When ending and costing a production order, item and resource consumption are posted to the general ledger. When posting production journal transactions, the consumption may post to clearing accounts for WIP (work in progress).

As a prerequisite for posting item consumption to WIP accounts, the checkbox *Post picking list in ledger* on tab *General* of the production control parameters has to be selected. In addition, the checkbox *Post physical inventory* on the tab *Setup* in the item model group of the picked item has to be selected.

Like ledger transactions referring to packing slips in purchasing and sales, general ledger transactions for route/job consumption journals and picking lists are reversed when ending and costing the production order.

5.5.2   Picking List

Picking list journals are there for posting item consumption. In order to access the picking list journals, click the button *Journals/Picking list* on the action pane tab *View* of the production order form or select the menu item *Production control> Journals> Picking list*.

Journals are non-posted vouchers, consisting of a header and a lines part. When accessing the picking list journals, the form shows a list of registered journals. The lookup field *Show* at the top of the journal header form controls whether posted or open journals are displayed.

If you want to enter a new journal, insert a new line by clicking the button *New* in the action pane strip of the journal header form. After selecting an appropriate journal name, switch to the journal lines by clicking the button *Lines*. The button *Create new* in the journal header, creating a header and immediately switching to the lines, provides an alternative way for creating a journal.

5.5.2.1 Consumption Proposal

In order to facilitate picking list registration, click the button *Picking list/Create lines* in the journal header form instead of the button *Create new*.

In the *Create lines* dialog box, choose the item selection for the proposal then. Selecting "Remaining quantity" in the field *Proposal* defaults the open BOM line quantity of the order estimation to the column *Proposal* of the picking list lines. If selecting the checkbox *Consumption=Proposal*, the column *Consumption* in the journal lines also receives the proposal quantity. In this case, you can immediately post the journal without manually entering quantities.

5.5.2.2 Journal Lines

When registering regular picking list lines manually in the journal, you have to select a *Lot ID* linking the consumption to a BOM line before entering the *Consumption* quantity. Selecting the checkbox in the column *End* of the journal line sets the BOM line to finished, no matter if consuming the total estimated quantity or less.

If you want to record the consumption of an item not included in the BOM lines of the production order, insert a picking list line entering the item number and leaving the lot ID empty. Dynamics AX in this case automatically creates a corresponding BOM line on the order and applies the lot ID to the picking list line.

Figure 5-21 shows an example of lines in a picking list journal, which are generated by a consumption proposal. The checkbox *Consumption=Proposal* has been selected in the consumption proposal dialog, which is why the column *Consumption* in the journal lines contains defaults for the actual quantity. The last line in Figure 5-21 shows a manual entry for an item not included in the BOM. Therefore, the columns *Proposal* and – only before saving the line – *Lot ID* are empty in this line.

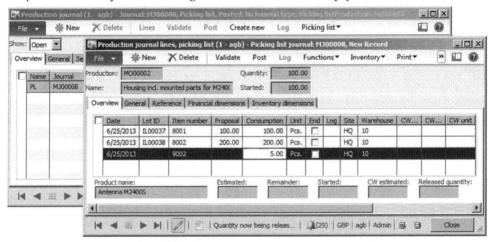

Figure 5-21: Registering picking list lines

Once you have finished picking list registration, post the journal clicking the button *Post* in the journal header or lines. The posted transactions are similar to the packing slip transactions of sales orders, reducing the quantity in inventory of the picked items.

In inventory valuation, the journal posting applies a preliminary valuation. Financial valuation is posted later when ending and costing the production order. Costing a production order is the corresponding action to invoicing a sales order.

5.5.2.3 Inquiries and Reversal

For viewing a posted journal, access the picking list journal form and select the option "All" or "Posted" in the lookup field *Show*. The posted journal shows a checkmark in the column *Posted* and does not allow modifications.

Alternatively, view the posted transactions in the production posting form. For accessing this form, click the button *Related information/Production posting* on the action pane tab *View* of the production order form or choose the menu item *Production control> Inquiries> Production> Production posting*.

If you want to reverse a posted picking list journal, register and post a picking list journal with negative quantities. In order to facilitate registration, create an appropriate picking list proposal by clicking the button *Picking list/Create lines* and selecting the option "Full reversal" in the field *Proposal* of the proposal dialog.

5.5.3 Working Time Registration

Depending on route group settings and on the way of scheduling the production order, choose route cards or job cards for recording working time consumption.

5.5.3.1 Route Card and Job Card

If not executing job scheduling for a production order, there are no records in the job table for this order. Therefore, report resource consumption in route cards.

If job scheduling has been executed, register resource consumption in job cards. This is required for operations with a route group with activated job management (checkmarks in the column *Job management* on the tab *Setup* of the route group).

5.5.3.2 Journal Registration

You may access route card journals clicking the button *Journals/Route card* on the action pane tab *View* of the production order form or through the menu item *Production control> Journals> Route card*. For job cards, click the button *Journals/Job card* in the production order or access the menu item *Production control> Journals> Job card*.

Entering of journal headers and lines for resource consumption works like entering picking list journals. But except for automatic consumption, you do not have the option to create a consumption proposal for route cards or job cards.

When inserting a journal line for resource consumption, select the operation number or the job identification first. Then you may enter the resource, the number of hours, the produced quantity (*Good quantity*), and other data like the worker or – if applicable – the defective quantity (*Error quantity*) of the finished product. In a job card, in addition register the start time and the end time usually.

Once you have finished entering journal lines, post the journal clicking the button *Post* in the journal header or lines.

5.5.3.3 Reporting as Finished

When registering the last operation or job in a journal line, selecting the checkbox in the column *Production report as finished* enables posting a report as finished journal for the good quantity of the finished item in parallel to the route card or job card. A default for the report as finished setting in journal lines is available in the production control parameters (tab *Journals*, checkbox *Automatic report as finished*).

5.5.3.4 Inquiries

After posting the route card or job card, the posted journals show in the particular journal form. In addition, the posted transactions are also available in the inquiry after clicking the button *Related information/Route transactions* or *Related information/ Production posting* on the action pane tab *View* of the production order form.

5.5.4   Case Study Exercises

Exercise 5.10 – Purchasing Components

In order to process the production order of exercise 5.8, the required components have to be available in inventory.

Enter a purchase order, purchasing nine units of the first and five units of the second item of exercise 5.1 from your vendor of exercise 3.2. Once you have finished entering and confirming the purchase order, post the product receipt and the vendor invoice.

Exercise 5.11 – Picking List

You may now pick the components required for the production order of exercise 5.8. Enter and post a picking list journal, picking nine units of the first and five units of the second item. Picking should be done from the warehouse to which you have posted the items in exercise 5.10.

Exercise 5.12 – Job Card

Choosing a job card, you want to record the working time required to execute the manufacturing operations. Enter and post a job card referring to the production order of exercise 5.8, producing five units in the time between 8:00 AM and 2:00 PM (6 hours). You do not want to post reporting as finished in parallel.

5.6   Reporting as Finished and Ending Production

In the cycle of production order processing, reporting as finished and ending are the last steps. Since reporting as finished posts physical transactions, it increases the inventory quantity of the finished product. Ending the order is the final step of order processing, in parallel costing the order and posting financial transactions.

5.6.1   Reporting as Finished

Reporting as finished physically receives the finished item in inventory. In Dynamics AX, there are three options to report a production order as finished:

➢ **Order status update** – Updating the status of the production order
➢ **Production journal** – Posting a report as finished journal
➢ **Time registration** – Reporting as finished when posting the route card or job card for the last operation

Section 5.5.3 shows the option of reporting as finished together with the time registration of the last operation – the description below shows the other options.

5.6.1.1 Order Status Update

In order to report as finished by updating the order status, click the button *Process/ Report as finished* on the action pane tab *Production order* of the production order form or select the periodic activity *Production control> Periodic> Production order> Report as finished*. If you want to report only a part of the entire order quantity, adjust the *Good quantity* on the tab *Overview* or *General* of the update dialog.

If you do not expect additional receipts for the current order to be reported as finished, select the checkbox *End job* to clear any remaining open quantity.

If the actual consumption of items and working time has been posted, select the checkbox *Accept error* on the tab *General* if you want to enable the report as finished update in spite of missing consumption.

5.6.1.2 Automatic Consumption

Like the appropriate option when starting the production order (see section 5.4.3), reporting as finished posts automatic item and route consumption.

In the BOM line, select the flushing principle "Start" for consumption when starting the production order, and "Finish" for consumption when reporting as finished. This setting allows consuming some items at the start, and other items at the end of a production order.

Route operations do not show this option. For all operations with automatic posting, you have to decide in common for the production order, whether automatic posting should apply when starting or when reporting as finished. In order to avoid duplicate posting, select the option "Route group dependent" in the lookup field *Automatic route consumption* only in the dialog for starting, or for reporting as finished – not in both dialogues.

5.6.1.3 Production Journal

Apart from the status update, reporting as finished is also possible by posting a production journal. In order to access this journal, click the button *Journals/Report as finished* on the action pane tab *View* of the production order form, or choose the menu item *Production control> Journals> Report as finished*.

Posting a report as finished journal in a production order works similar to posting a product receipt in a purchase order. Inventory physically receives the item with a preliminary value and the quantity in inventory then includes the received quantity.

5.6.1.4 Ledger Integration

If you want to post the items to clearing accounts in the general ledger when reporting as finished, ledger integration has to be activated for reporting as finished. For this purpose, select the checkbox *Post report as finished in ledger* on tab *General* of the production control parameters. In addition, the checkbox *Post physical inventory* on the tab *Setup* in the item model group of the finished item has to be selected.

General ledger transactions for reporting as finished are reversed when ending and costing the production order.

5.6.2 Ending and Costing

Ending a production order is required for cost-accounting and closing the order. In parallel, WIP ledger transactions for production journals are reversed. BOM-item and route consumption as well as finished item receipts post to the final ledger accounts.

You should end a production order in time. Otherwise, the finished item is still included in the WIP account balance instead of the stock account balance.

5.6.2.1 Ending

Ending a production order closes the order. Since it is not possible to post any transaction for a closed production order, you should not end the order until you are sure all transactions have been posted.

In order to end the production order, click the button *Process/End* on the action pane tab *Production order* of the production order form. If you want to end multiple orders, access the corresponding periodic activity in the menu item *Production control> Periodic> Production orders> End*.

After ending, the ending date of the production order shows in the field *Financial date* of the inventory transactions. The receipt status in inventory transactions of items reported as finished is "Purchased". For consumed items (BOM lines), the issue status is "Sold".

5.6.2.2 Costing

When costing the order in the course of the ending routine, Dynamics AX calculates the actual costs for all item and route consumption transactions. Based on these actual costs of the production order, the cost price of the finished item is calculated. If standard cost valuation applies to the finished item, costing posts cost price differences to deviation accounts.

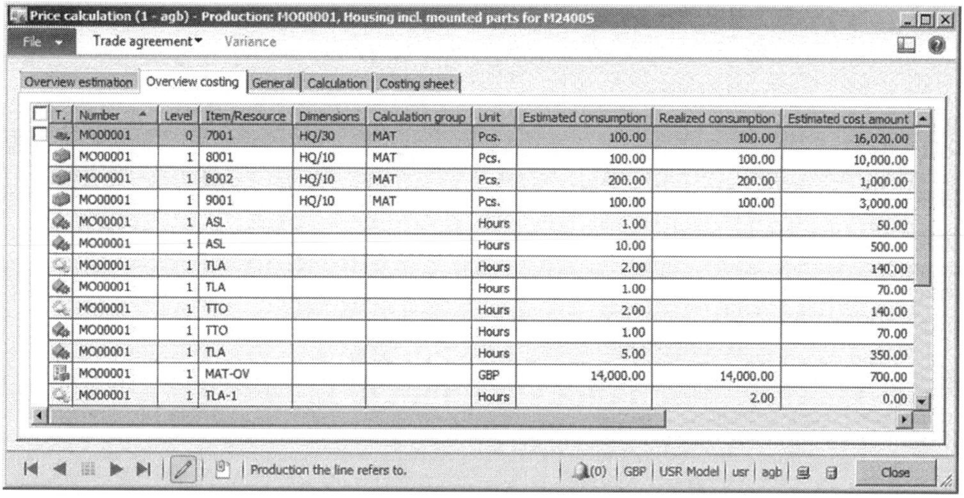

Figure 5-22:   Comparing estimation and costing in the calculation form

For comparing the actual and the estimated consumption, click the button *Related information/Price calculation* on the action pane tab *View* of the production order form. The tab *Overview Costing* of the price calculation form then shows – at item and operation line level – a comparison of estimated and realized quantity consumption, and of estimated and realized costs. The tab *Costing sheet* contains a summary of estimation or costing according to the costing sheet setup.

5.6.2.3   Ledger Integration and Inquiries

Like when posting invoices in purchasing or sales, costing a production order posts financial transactions for the items consumed and reported as finished.

In the first step of ledger posting, costing reverses the WIP ledger transactions posted through picking list journals, route card journals, job card journals and report as finished journals. In the second step, costing posts following ledger transactions for closing the order in finance:

> **Consumption of components** – To the stock accounts of the BOM line items
> **Consumption of working time** – To the costing accounts of the resources
> **Receiving the finished item** – To the stock account of the finished item

Main accounts applying to the item transactions are specified in the inventory posting setup (*Inventory and warehouse management> Setup> Posting> Posting*). Main accounts for resource consumption may derive from settings in the resource form or in cost categories. As an alternative, choose production groups for specifying applicable main accounts.

Receiving a default from production control parameters, the lookup *Ledger* on the tab *Setup* of the production order detail form determines which setting actually applies to retrieve appropriate main accounts (see section 8.4.3).

In order to view the transactions generated when ending and costing the order, click the button *Related information/Production posting* on the action pane tab *View* of the production order form. Alternatively, access the menu item *Production control> Inquiries> Production> Production posting*.

In the production posting form, the transactions posted when ending and costing the production order show the type "Costing". In order to view related ledger transactions, click the button *Ledger/Voucher*.

5.6.3 Case Study Exercise

Exercise 5.13 – Ending Production
By clicking the button *Process/Report as finished* in the production order form, report the entire quantity of the production order in exercise 5.8 as finished. On the tab *General* of the update dialog, select the checkboxes *End job* and *Accept error*. Finally, end the production order locking it for further postings. After ending, view the price calculation inquiry to compare estimation and costing.

5.7 Subcontracting

If a company cannot process a specific operation internally for technological reasons or because of the current capacity utilization, this operation is usually subcontracted to an external vendor. BOM and/or route of the finished item then have to include the subcontracted service.

In addition, there are situations where a finished product is produced internally or at a subcontractor alternatively. In this case, there are two (or more) approved route and/or BOM versions for the item.

In Dynamics AX, there are two basic options for subcontracting:

➢ **Outsourced operation** – Resource of the type "Vendor" in an operation
➢ **Purchased service** – Service item in a BOM line with the line type "Vendor"

Since a purchase order requires purchasing a (service) item, only the second option includes creating a purchase order.

5.7.1 Outsourced Operation

An outsourced operation not linked to a BOM line with a service item applies, if you do not need to generate a corresponding purchase order – for example if it is based on a contract with fixed capacity reservation and a fixed monthly payment.

In this case, create a separate resource group and resource per subcontractor. The resource is similar to a regular internal resource (see section 5.3.2), but applies the *Type* "Vendor" enabling to enter the vendor number in the field *Vendor* on the tab *General* of the resource form. In addition, make sure to apply appropriate settings for the cost categories (depending on the contract, maybe only a *Quantity category*) and main accounts for posting right amounts to the right accounts in finance. The selected calendar and finite capacity settings are depending on the contract.

In the related route operation, select the *Route type* "Vendor" on the tab *General* and enter the vendor resource as *Costing resource* together with appropriate resource requirements. Processing the outsourced operation in a production order works similar to a regular internal operation.

5.7.2   Purchased Service

If you need a purchase order for the outsourced operation, create a service item and include it in the BOM of the finished product. Optionally, the BOM line for the service item may be linked to an outsourced operation for scheduling purposes.

5.7.2.1   Master Data for Purchasing Subcontracting Services

The required service item is a product of the *Product type* "Service" with an *Item model group* generating inventory transactions ("Stocked product"). In the *Cost group* on the tab *Manage costs* of the released product, select a cost group of the type "Direct outsourcing". The flushing principle should be "Finish". Other relevant settings in the released product include the item group, the cost price, dimension groups, units of measure, the purchase price, the main vendor, the default order settings, and the site-specific order settings.

In the BOM of the finished product, insert a BOM line with the service item and the *Line type* "Vendor", optionally including a *Vendor account* overriding the main vendor from the released product.

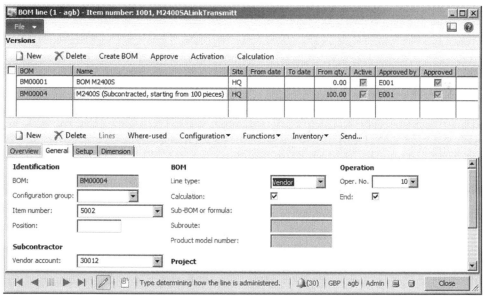

Figure 5-23:   Settings in a BOM line for a subcontracted service

If you need an outsourced operation for scheduling purposes, you can set it up as described in the previous section. But unlike the settings for an outsourced operation not linked to a BOM line service item, the operation should contain a route group with settings for automatic consumption and – if all subcontracting costs are included in the service item – deactivated cost calculation (cleared checkboxes in the field group *Estimation and costing* of the route group). In order to link the BOM line with the service item for the subcontracted activity to the route operation for the same activity, select the appropriate operation number in the field *Oper. No.* on the tab *General* of the BOM line and make sure the checkbox *End* there is selected (the service item is not required before the operation is finished).

If material is supplied to the subcontractor, link the BOM lines of the appropriate components to the outsourced operation the same way as for an internal operation.

5.7.2.2   Production Order Processing with Purchased Services

Production orders including subcontracted service items are created manually or automatically the same way as regular production orders (see section 5.4.2). When estimating the production order, a purchase order is created for a BOM line with the *Line type* "Vendor". The purchase order number shows on the tab *Reference* in the production BOM, which you may access by clicking the button *Production details/BOM* on the action pane tab *Production order* of the production order. Like any other purchase order, the order has to be confirmed before you can receive the service item.

Scheduling and releasing the production order is similar to other production orders. For starting the order, alternatively access the list page *Production control> Common> Subcontracted work* and click the button *Start* in the action pane after selecting the order there. On the tab *General* in the *Start* dialog, make sure to apply appropriate settings for automatic consumption (not consuming BOM items which are consumed when receiving the purchase order). In the *Print options* for the picking list accessible from the dialog, you can select the checkbox *Use delivery note layout* for the picking list if supplying BOM items as components to the subcontractor.

When posting the product receipt for the purchase order afterwards, settings in the field group *Receive purchase order* on the tab *Automatic update* of the production control parameters determine if BOM and route consumption is posted in parallel to the product receipt. Choosing the option "Flushing principle" for the *Automatic BOM consumption* there ensures posting the consumption of appropriate BOM lines including the service item.

Reporting the production order as finished and ending the order works the regular way.

6 Operations Planning

The primary responsibility of operations planning is to make sure that items are available when needed while meeting the target of high economic efficiency at the same time. Accordingly, operations planning has to solve the conflicting priorities of high supply readiness on the one hand and low inventory on the other.

6.1 Business Processes in Operations Planning

In Dynamics AX, long-term forecasting and short-term master planning are covered by the operations planning module ("Master planning").

6.1.1 Basic Approach

Operations planning includes forecasting in order to identify the item demand on a long-term basis. On the other hand it includes master planning used for calculating requirements and planned orders on a daily basis.

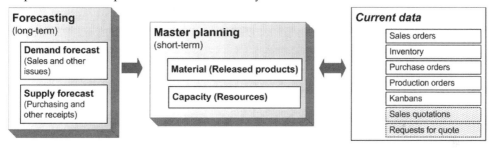

Figure 6-1: Operations planning in Dynamics AX (Forecasts and master planning)

6.1.1.1 Forecasting

Forecasting is a long-term prognosis for planning and budgeting purposes. It includes demand forecasts (sales and other issues) as well as supply forecasts (purchasing and other receipts). Different versions of forecasts provide the option of running multiple scenarios for the total forecast in parallel.

6.1.1.2 Master Planning

Master planning covers short-term planning for daily business. Based on current orders and on-hand inventory, master scheduling calculates demand and supply for scheduling actual and planned purchase and production orders. Like in forecasting, different scenarios of master planning are possible in parallel. Dynamics AX distinguishes a static master plan for current master scheduling and a separate dynamic plan for simulation.

6.1.2   At a Glance: Master Planning

Before we start to go through the details of master planning, this section shows the basics on the example of the net requirements for a finished item.

As a basis for analyzing net requirements, enter a sales order to be delivered today with a line containing a finished item (default order type "Production") which is out of stock. Clicking the button *Product and supply/Net requirements* in the action pane strip of the sales order line provides access to the net requirements of the item. If existing production orders and the quantity in inventory do not cover the item requirements, click the button *Update/Master scheduling* in the action pane strip of the lower pane to run local master scheduling for the item.

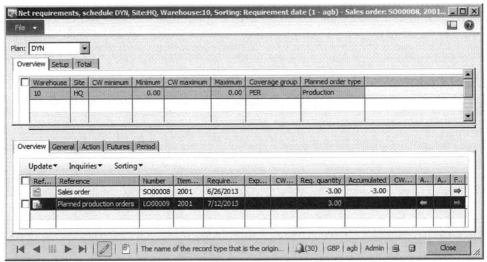

Figure 6-2:   The net requirements form after running local master scheduling

Master scheduling then generates a planned production order for producing the finished item. If the requested delivery date in the sales order line is not feasible, the planned production order shows the earliest possible delivery date. The arrows in the columns on the right side show proposals in order to avoid missing the delivery date. Details are available on the tab *Action* and *Futures*.

Master scheduling is available in multiple scenarios, distinguishing between a static and a dynamic plan. The static plan is the operations plan used in purchasing and production. If applying a dynamic plan for simulation purposes, this is the default for master scheduling in the net requirements form. In order to switch between the different plans, choose the appropriate option in the lookup field *Plan* at the top of the net requirements form.

6.2   Forecasting

Forecasting is a long-term prognosis, required to estimate and adjust future capacities of resources and material supply. In parallel, forecasting is also a basis for budgeting in finance. In order to support planning of alternative scenarios for business development, multiple forecasts are available in parallel.

Forecasting in Dynamics AX does not only include sales forecasts. Demand forecasts also include other sources of item issue. In addition, supply forecasts are available, which for example may be a basis for long-term contracts with vendors.

6.2.1   Basics of Forecasting

When entering forecast figures in Dynamics AX, you have to select a forecast model in inventory. Forecast models represent the different planning scenarios.

Forecast models are then assigned to forecast plans, which are the basis for calculating forecasts in forecast scheduling. You may also include forecast plans in master scheduling.

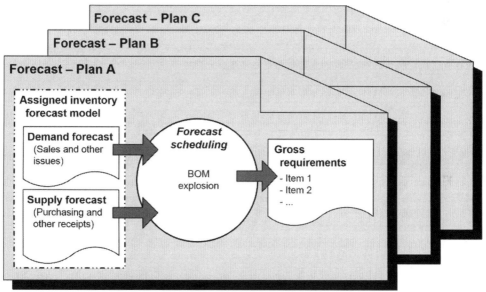

Figure 6-3:   Forecasting in Dynamics AX

6.2.1.1   Demand/Sales Forecast

Forecasting demand with estimated sales figures is the starting point of the forecasting process. You may enter a sales forecast at item or at item group level. Apart from direct sales, a demand forecast also may contain other demand – e.g. the demand for semi-finished items (instead of finished items) if it is not possible to determine reliable forecast figures at the detail level of finished products.

Since forecast scheduling and master scheduling are based on item numbers, you have to enter an item allocation key if you do not enter forecasts per item number.

Item allocation keys are groups, containing a percentage for each item included in the key.

6.2.1.2 Supply Forecasts

In parallel or after finishing demand forecasting, optionally enter a separate supply forecast which includes purchasing and other receipts. In the next step, the inventory forecast enables aligning demand and supply forecasts.

6.2.1.3 Forecast Scheduling

Once you have finished registering forecast figures, forecast scheduling is available for calculating the gross requirements of finished items, based on corresponding bills of materials. Depending on settings of the selected forecast plan, Dynamics AX creates planned purchase and production orders covering the gross requirements of forecasting as a result of forecast scheduling. These planned orders refer to the selected forecast plan.

If entered, the supply forecast provides the minimum figures for generating planned purchase or production orders, no matter if they exceed the direct and indirect demand from the demand forecast.

Since forecast scheduling refers to a long-term prognosis, the calculation does not include the current inventory and current orders.

6.2.1.4 Forecasts in Master Scheduling

You may include forecasts in master scheduling. For this purpose, settings in master planning determine if and how to include forecasts.

The *Reduction principle* in master plans and the *Reduction key* in coverage groups are there to avoid duplicate consideration of future demand. Without reduction, a duplicate consideration results from a forecasted demand for periods in the near future already including actual sales orders – supposing these sales orders are part of the forecasted quantity and not in addition to the forecast.

6.2.2 Forecast Settings

Before starting to register forecasts, you have to finish the required setup in Dynamics AX.

6.2.2.1 Forecast Models

Forecast models represent the different scenarios for forecasting. In order to register forecasts, you have to set up at least one forecast model in the form *Inventory and warehouse management> Setup> Forecast> Forecast models*.

If you want to apply a structure to forecasts (e.g. grouping forecasts by region), you can set up two-stage forecasts by assigning submodels to a main model. If applying submodels, first set up the submodels in the forecasts model form like regular forecast models. Then enter the main model and assign submodels on the tab *Submodel* of the forecast model form.

If you want to protect forecasts from changes, select the checkbox *Stopped* in the forecast model. Blocking applies for example, if an annual forecast should not change once it is finished – use a separate forecast model for the next year then.

6.2.2.2 Forecast Plan

Whereas forecast models are used for entering forecasts, forecast plans are the grouping element of separate forecast scenarios in master planning. For assigning forecast models to forecast plans, access the form *Master planning> Setup> Plans> Forecast plans*. Selecting a main model in the lookup field *Inventory forecast model* on the tab *General* of the forecast plans includes related submodels. In addition, the forecast plan contains settings for including supply or demand forecasts.

On the tab *Time fences* of the forecast plan, enter the period in days (starting from the day of calculation) which should be covered by forecast scheduling.

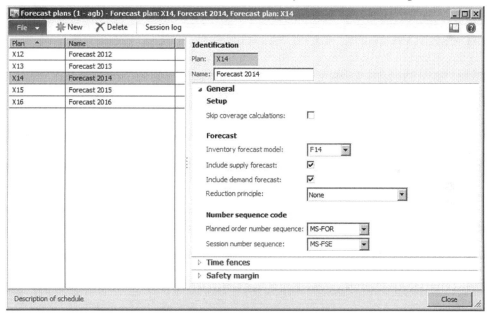

Figure 6-4: Editing a forecast plan in the forecast plans form

6.2.2.3 Parameters and Item Allocation Keys

The forecast plan in the field *Current forecast plan* of the master planning parameters (*Master planning> Setup> Master planning parameters*) is the default forecast plan for displaying forecast scheduling results. Another important setting for item forecasts is the coverage group, which specifies how to summarize net requirements. More information on coverage groups is available in section 6.3.3 later in this chapter.

If you do not want to enter forecasts for individual items, use item allocation keys entering a forecast total for a group of items. For setting up item allocation keys, access the form *Inventory and warehouse management> Setup> Forecast> Item allocation keys*. After selecting or inserting an item allocation key there, click the button *Lines* in the action pane strip for accessing the item allocation lines containing items with their percentage of the group total.

6.2.3   Forecasts and Forecast Scheduling

For entering forecasts, access the appropriate form in the menu tree node *Inventory and warehouse management> Periodic> Forecast> Entry*. An alternative access is available by clicking the button *Forecasting* or *Forecast* in the particular master table form, for example in the released product form or in the customer form.

Forms referring to items and item groups allow registering both, demand forecasts and supply forecasts. Demand forecasts are also available in the customer and customer group form, supply forecasts in the vendor and vendor group.

6.2.3.1   Entering Demand/Sales Forecast

This section contains a description for entering a demand forecast based on an item group. But registering forecasts based on other elements – e.g. a customer – works the same way.

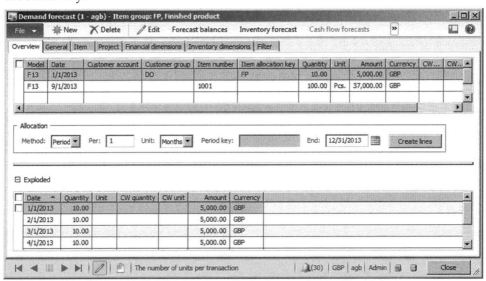

Figure 6-5:   Registering a sales forecast line in the demand forecast form

In order to access the demand forecast for an item group, click the button *Demand* in the form *Inventory and warehouse management> Periodic> Forecast> Entry> Item groups*. In the demand forecast form, insert records selecting the appropriate (forecast) model then. If you want to record different scenarios, enter different models in separate lines.

In the date column, enter the start date of the individual forecast period – for example the first day of a month if entering a line per month. If choosing an allocation method in pane *Allocation* the middle of the form, enter one line for the whole period and distribute it by clicking the button *Create lines*.

In order to enable gross requirement calculation, enter either an item number or an item allocation key. Depending on the dimension groups of the item (checkbox *Coverage plan by dimension* in the tracking and the storage dimension group) you have to enter inventory dimensions in the forecast line.

6.2.3.2 Supply Forecast and Inventory Forecast

If you want to register a supply forecast independent from the demand forecast, enter it – similar to the demand forecast – after clicking the button *Forecast/Supply forecast* in the action pane of the appropriate master table form. Forecast scheduling then may include the supply forecast in parallel to the demand forecast.

In addition to demand and supply forecasts, inventory forecasts are available for showing the result of supply and demand forecasts at the level of item numbers and individual periods. You may access inventory forecasts in appropriate master table forms by clicking the button *Inventory forecast*.

6.2.3.3 Forecast Scheduling

The results of forecasting are a valuable basis for preparing future production and purchase of merchandise, finished items, raw materials, parts, and components.

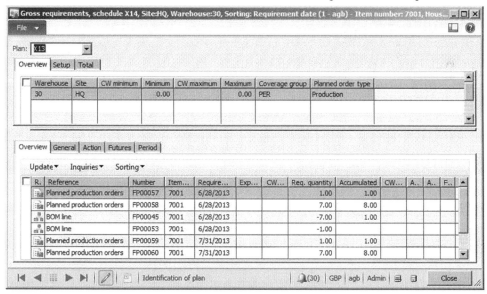

Figure 6-6:   Forecasting results for a semi-finished item in the gross requirements

In order to determine these multi-level forecast figures, execute forecast scheduling (*Master planning> Periodic> Forecast scheduling*) which includes the explosion of bills of materials. The update form for forecast scheduling includes the lookup field *Forecast plan* for selecting the forecast plan to be calculated.

The results of forecast scheduling are available in the gross requirements form, which you may access clicking the button *Requirements/Gross requirement* on the action pane tab *Plan* of the released product form. By default, the form shows the forecast plan set up as current forecast plan in the master planning parameters. You may select a different scenario in the lookup *Plan* at the top of the net requirements form.

Forecast scheduling results are not only available in the gross requirements form. The list page *Master planning> Common> Planned orders* also shows planned orders generated by forecast scheduling after selecting the appropriate forecast plan in lookup field *Plan*.

6.2.3.4   Budget Transfer

If you want to apply demand and supply forecasts for budgeting in finance, transfer them to ledger budgets. Transferring requires running the corresponding periodic activity for sales and/or purchase in the menu *Inventory and warehouse management> Periodic> Forecast> Update* for the ledger budget model, which should receive forecast figures.

6.2.3.5   New in Dynamics AX 2012

In Dynamics AX 2012, the terminology for sales and purchase forecasts has changed to demand and supply forecasts reflecting flexible forecasting options.

6.2.4   Case Study Exercises

Exercise 6.1 – Forecast Settings
You need a sales forecast for items, which you have set up in previous exercises – the merchandise item of exercise 3.5 and the finished item of exercise 5.2. Your forecast should be in a scenario separate from other forecasting scenarios.

In order to meet this requirement, create a new forecast model F-## (## = your user ID) without applying submodels. In a second step, insert a new forecast plan Y-##. Assign your forecast model to this forecast plan and make sure demand forecasts are included in this plan. The number sequences required may be similar to settings in existing forecast plans.

Exercise 6.2 – Demand Forecast
For the next quarter, you expect your customer of exercise 4.1 to order 200 units of your merchandise item and 100 units of your finished item on the last day of each month.

You want to record these figures in a sales forecast, applying your forecast model of exercise 6.1. Once you have finished, run forecast scheduling for your forecast plan and check the results afterwards.

6.3   Master Planning

Master planning in Dynamics AX covers the short-term calculation of material and capacity requirements. It is the basis for the daily work in purchasing and production management.

For this purpose, the calculation in master planning includes relevant information of setup, master and transaction data for items and resources in all areas of Dynamics AX. Depending on the setup, these data contain the current quantity in inventory, purchase orders, production orders, sales orders, forecast plans as well as master data in released product and resource records.

As a result, master planning generates planned orders for purchasing, production, Kanbans and inventory transfer on the one hand, and action and futures messages for adjusting existing orders on the other hand.

6.3.1   Basics of Master Planning

Data regarding item transactions – including orders – and quantity in inventory are an essential basis for master planning. In addition, master planning may cover sales quotations, requests for quotation, approved purchase requisitions, and forecasts. You may reduce the demand from forecasts and sales quotations by applying a probability percentage or a reduction principle.

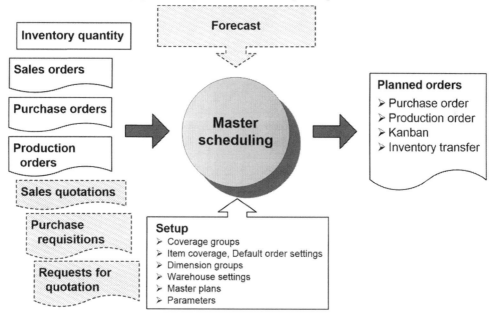

Figure 6-7:   Elements of master planning

Like forecasting, master planning optionally includes multiple scenarios. A scenario is represented by a master plan, which contains the particular settings for the scenario. These settings include on the one hand the elements covered by scheduling, and on the other hand the calculation principles for planned orders.

6.3.1.1   Master Planning Strategies

Master scheduling usually is a batch job, which runs every night for calculating net requirements for all items. The result of this calculation is available in a scenario called *"Static master plan"*. The static plan is the master plan to be used in purchasing and production control for scheduling orders. It is the default plan when accessing planned order forms.

On the other hand, the sales department needs a plan to run simulations for determining possible delivery dates in sales orders and quotations. This requires executing a master scheduling simulation locally, only for a particular item. The result of this simulation is available in a scenario called *"Dynamics master plan"*.

Based on both requirements, the master planning parameters enable two different strategies:

➤ **One plan strategy**
➤ **Two plan strategy**

If applying the same master plan for the static and the dynamic master plan in the master planning parameters, you run a one master plan strategy. Planned orders of current master scheduling simulations in the sales department are updating the static plan, which is used in purchasing and production control. Depending on the requirements of your company, this strategy may fit to your business.

For applying a two master plan strategy, enter a different master plan for the static and the dynamic plan. When running the batch job for static master scheduling in the night, you probably want to copy the static plan into the dynamic plan in order to base simulations on the current static plan.

In this case, simulation in sales starts with the same data basis as purchasing and production control in the morning. Simulation throughout the day does not change planned orders in the static plan, thereby avoiding problems in purchasing and production control caused by planned orders changing every moment.

6.3.1.2   Customer Order Decoupling Point

Depending on the structure of your products, there are two key supply policies in production control for fulfilling demand from customer orders:

➤ **Make-to-Stock** – Produce based on sales forecasts and historical demand
➤ **Make-to-Order** – Produce based on confirmed sales orders

In addition, there are hybrid supply strategies applying a make-to-stock strategy for purchased or semi-finished items with a long lead time and a make-to-order strategy for finished products. If applying a hybrid strategy, the customer order decoupling point (push/pull point) determines the level in the product structure, to which the items are built to stock.

Dynamics AX supports all of these strategies by choosing appropriate coverage groups (see section 6.3.3). In case of a hybrid supply strategy, you can enter forecasts at semi-finished product level – which is the customer order decoupling point for these items. As mentioned in section 6.2.1, reduction settings in master plans determine how master scheduling offsets forecasted demand with actual sales orders. Since forecasts on semi-finished products are not offset by sales orders, you should choose to include all inventory transactions – including demand from selling finished products derived through bills of materials – in the coverage groups of applicable semi-finished items in order to comply with this situation. In the coverage group form, the lookup field *Reduce forecast by* contains the required option for this purpose.

6.3.1.3 Master Scheduling and Planned Orders

Master scheduling generates planned purchase orders, planned production orders, planned Kanbans, and planned inventory transfer orders based on item demand and settings for master planning.

Once master scheduling is finished, check and edit the planned orders. In the planned orders form, you can transfer planned orders to actual purchase orders, production orders, Kanbans and inventory transfer orders.

6.3.1.4 New in Dynamics AX 2012 and in AX 2012 R2

Dynamics AX 2012 supports flexibly specifying the customer order decoupling point – entering forecasts and calculating offsetting current demand at any level of the product structure.

Compared with the initial version of Dynamics AX 2012, the R2 version enables to include approved purchase requisitions in master planning.

6.3.2 Master Planning Setup

Before running master scheduling, you have to finish the setup for requirements calculation in Dynamics AX.

6.3.2.1 Master Plans

A master plan is a scenario, which contains requirement calculations independent from other scheduling scenarios. Depending on the planning strategy, one or two master plans apply. If you need more simulation scenarios, set up additional master plans.

For accessing master plans, choose the menu item *Master planning> Setup> Plans> Master plans*. Selecting the appropriate checkboxes on the tab *General* determines whether to include following items in the particular master plan:

> **Current inventory**
> **Inventory transactions** (open orders)
> **Sales quotations** (reduced by an optional probability percentage)
> **Approved purchase requisitions** (only for requisitions with the requisition purpose "Replenishment", which has to be enabled in the purchasing policy)
> **Requests for quotation** (entered in purchasing)
> **Forecasts** (supply and demand forecasts)

If you want to include forecasts and forecast scheduling, select the appropriate forecast plan in the lookup *Inventory forecast model* of the master plan. If forecasts are included in master planning, offset forecast figures by sales orders and other demand in order to avoid excessive demand resulting from adding forecasts to current orders.

The lookup field *Reduction principle* in this case determines the way of reducing forecast figures. If the selected principle refers to a *Reduction key*, you have to enter reduction keys in the applicable coverage groups (tab *Other* in the coverage group form, see section 6.3.3).

The *Scheduling method* on the master plans form controls whether to run operations scheduling or job scheduling (see section 5.4.3) for planned production orders. Among other settings for scheduling planned production orders, there is the option to apply finite capacity.

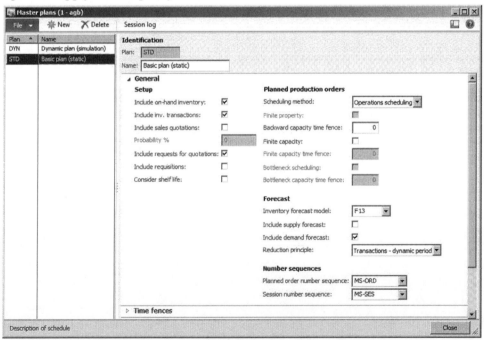

Figure 6-8:   Editing a master plan in the master plans form

The tab *Time fences* on the master plans form contains settings for overriding the time fences specified in the coverage group or in the item coverage.

On the tab *Futures message,* choose whether master scheduling may set the requirement date in planned orders to a date, which is after the actual requirement date, if it is not possible to meet the actual requirement date because of applicable lead times. This setting prevents impossible dates like a delivery date before today.

On the tab *Action message,* select whether to postpone planned purchase orders to a later date, if it is not necessary to receive the item as early as specified in the planned order date.

6.3.2.2 Master Planning Parameters

General parameters for master planning are available on the form *Master planning> Setup> Master planning parameters.* A core setting controls the planning strategy: If applying a one master plan strategy, enter the same master plan in the field for the *Current static master plan* and the *Current dynamic master plan.*

If applying a two master plan strategy, select two different master plans. In addition, optionally select the checkbox *Automatic copy* for resetting the dynamic plan to the status of the static plan when running master scheduling.

Master planning parameters also contain the *General coverage group.* This group applies to items, which do not include a coverage group in the released product.

6.3.2.3 Warehouse Settings

If master scheduling should not include the quantity in inventory of specific warehouses – e.g. a consignment stock managed by the customer – select the checkbox *Manual* on the tab *Master planning* of the warehouse form (*Inventory and warehouse management> Setup> Inventory breakdown> Warehouses*).

The warehouse form also contains settings, if the warehouse should be refilled from another warehouse (main warehouse). If selected, master scheduling generates item transfer proposals. As a prerequisite, the item has to contain a storage dimension group in which the checkbox *Coverage plan by dimension* is selected for the dimension "Warehouse".

6.3.3   Item Coverage and Item Settings

Coverage groups and settings on the released product control the calculation of lot sizes and dates of planned orders generated by master scheduling.

6.3.3.1 Managing Coverage Groups

The coverage group is a core setting for item coverage, specifying the coverage principle and further settings for lot size and delivery date calculation. In order to access coverage group form, choose the menu item *Master planning> Setup> Coverage> Coverage groups.*

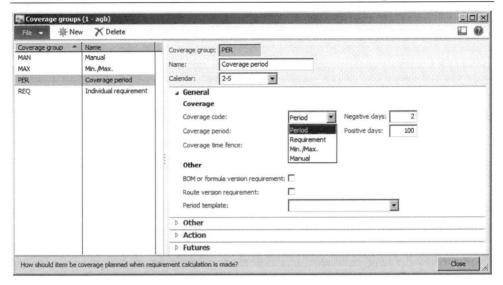

Figure 6-9:   Selecting the coverage code in a coverage group

The main setting in a coverage group is the *Coverage code*, which specifies the coverage principle. The coverage principle controls, how requirements summarize into a planned order.

6.3.3.2   Coverage Principle and Period Settings

In Dynamics AX, the following options are available for the coverage principle as shown in Figure 6-10:

➢ **Period** – Summarizing requirements within the coverage period
➢ **Requirement** – Planned order per requirement ("Make-to-Order")
➢ **Min./Max.** – Replenishing to the maximum quantity when inventory drops below the minimum quantity
➢ **Manual** – Planned orders are not generated in master scheduling

Master scheduling generates a planned order, if the calculated inventory at a date is below the minimum quantity (or below zero, if a minimum quantity is not entered in the item coverage of the released product).

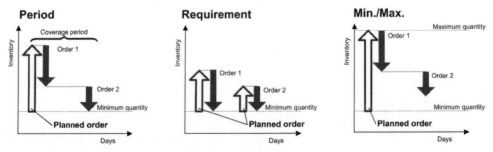

Figure 6-10:   Coverage principles in Dynamics AX

The *Coverage time fence* and the time fence fields on the tab *Other* of the coverage group form determine the periods included in master scheduling. Depending on the planning strategy and the lead time of the items, the number of days entered in the time fence fields should cover an applicable number of weeks or months.

The *Positive days* on the tab *General* sets the time fence to include the current quantity in inventory for covering requirements and should correspond to the lead time or the coverage time fence (depending on the order history).

On the tab *Other*, the *Firming time fence* determines the period, for which master scheduling does not create a planned order but an actual purchase or a production order. If no main supplier is entered in the item record or in the applicable trade agreement for a purchased item (supposing the checkbox *Find trade agreement* in the master planning parameters is selected), master scheduling generates a planned purchase order instead of an actual order also within the firming time fence.

6.3.3.3 Forecast Plan Calculation and Reduction Keys

On tab *Other* of the coverage groups, the time fence for forecasts and forecast reduction settings control the calculation of forecast in master scheduling.

Reduction keys (*Master planning> Setup> Coverage> Reduction keys*) control the periods and percentages applied for reducing forecast figures in the course of time. As a prerequisite for applying the reduction key selected in the coverage group, the reduction principle in the master plan has to refer to reduction keys.

The reduction principle in the master plan controls the way forecasted figures are reduced for considering them as demand. If entering forecasts for semi-finished items (hybrid supply strategy with customer order decoupling point, see section 6.3.1), reduction should not only include direct sales order demand for the semi-finished product, but also demand derived from the finished product. Choosing the option "All transactions" in the lookup *Reduce forecast by* of the coverage group offsets forecasts not only by sales orders, but also by all issue transactions.

6.3.3.4 Settings for Action and Futures Messages

Action messages, which are activated on the tab *Action* of the coverage group form, are messages from master scheduling to adjust actual or planned purchase and production orders. The aim of action messages is to support adjustments, which may not be done automatically (like postponing a purchase order, which is too early). They show proposals for optimizing quantities and dates of item receipt. Item availability is granted, no matter if you disregard action messages.

Unlike action messages, futures messages show actual problems of item availability. A futures message is created, if the lead time of items required at all BOM levels results in a necessary supply before today, therefore causing delays in order fulfillment.

If activating both futures and action messages, select the option "Futures date" in the lookup field *Basis date* on the tab *Action*. In this case, action messages are based on the earliest possible date and not the original – impossible – requirement date.

6.3.3.5   Coverage Group Assignment

The assignment of a *Coverage group* to an item is available at three different levels. Master scheduling identifies the applicable coverage group in following order:

➤ **Item coverage** – Button *Coverage/Item coverage* on the action pane tab *Plan* of the released product form
➤ **Released product** – Tab *Plan* on the released product detail form
➤ **Master planning parameters** – *General coverage group* on the tab *General*

The coverage group specifies the method for calculating lot sizes. If there is a big difference in the lead time or in the cost price of your items, you want to control lot sizes accordingly and group the items by entering different coverage groups in the released products based on the inventory value and the lead time.

6.3.3.6   Dimension Group Settings

Settings in the storage and tracking dimension groups control the inventory dimensions covered separately in coverage calculation. The dimension groups of an item therefore determine the available dimensions in the item coverage and the dimensions calculated separately in master scheduling (e.g. calculating supply and demand per warehouse).

For accessing dimension groups, choose the menu path *Product information management> Setup> Dimension groups* (see section 7.2.2). In the dimension groups, select the checkbox *Coverage plan by dimension* for storage and tracking dimensions to be calculated separately in master scheduling. This checkbox is always selected for the dimension *Site* and for product dimensions.

The assignment of dimension groups to an item shows after clicking the button *Set up/Dimension groups* on the action pane tab *Product* in the shared or released product.

6.3.3.7   Item Coverage

Apart from the coverage group and the dimension groups, the item coverage is another important setting for master scheduling in the released product.

Clicking the button *Coverage/Item coverage* on the action pane tab *Plan* of the released product displays the item coverage form, where you may enter a minimum and – if applicable – a maximum quantity for the item. Depending on the dimension groups of the item and applicable dimension group settings (see above) you may register item coverage settings per site, warehouse or other dimensions like color or configuration.

The item coverage form contains specific settings for the item at dimension level – e.g. for a particular warehouse by selecting a coverage group on the tab *General*, which is different to the coverage group in the released product form. This also enables specifying to create planned transfer orders to a production warehouse per requirement (per production order) and at the same time summarizing requirements for the item on sales warehouses per period.

In addition, choose a specific main vendor and a different planned order type if applicable, for example purchasing the item from an external vendor for one specific warehouse but producing it internally for other warehouses.

If entering a minimum quantity, the lookup field *Minimum key* on the tab *General* enables recording a seasonal trend for the minimum quantity. The results of the selected minimum key show on the tab *Min./Max.* of the item coverage form.

In order to set up minimum keys, access the form *Master planning> Setup> Coverage> Minimum/Maximum keys* and enter a factor per period.

6.3.4   Master Scheduling and Planned Orders

Master scheduling generates planned orders for purchasing, production and inventory transfer, based on item requirements and coverage settings. You may run master scheduling on two different occasions:

➢ **Local master scheduling** – Availability check, e.g. in a sales order line
➢ **Global master scheduling** – Regular master scheduling for all items

6.3.4.1   Global Master Scheduling

In daily business, global master scheduling is the basis for releasing orders in purchasing and production. For starting global master scheduling access the menu item *Master planning> Periodic> Master scheduling*. Depending on the company size and the item structure, master scheduling involves extensive calculations causing a heavy server load. Usually it runs as a batch job in the nighttime.

In the update form for master scheduling, select the applicable *Master plan* – for global master scheduling usually the current static master plan. It is not required to run the current dynamic master plan separately, if the checkbox *Automatic copy* in the master planning parameters is selected.

The lookup field *Principle* in the master scheduling update form determines the calculation principle with following options:

➢ **Regeneration** – Complete calculation, deleting all not approved planned orders
➢ **Net change** – Generating action and futures messages for all requirements, but planned orders only for new requirements
➢ **Net change minimized** – Like net change, limiting new messages to new requirements

If selecting the static plan, only the principle "Regeneration" is available. In order to apply current data to scheduling, you should also choose "Regeneration" for dynamic plans if there are changes of coverage settings like the minimum quantity in items.

The tab *Scheduling helper* in the update form contains settings for distributed master scheduling on several servers.

6.3.4.2 Local Master Scheduling

Unlike global master scheduling, local master scheduling aims to check item availability and possible delivery dates limited to a particular item. You may execute local master scheduling in the net requirements form, which is accessible by clicking the button *Requirements/Net requirements* on the action pane tab *Plan* of the released product form or clicking the button *Product and supply/Net requirements* in the action pane strip of order lines.

The net requirements form shows the result of the last master scheduling calculation for the dynamic master plan. If a one master plan strategy is in place, the lines in the net requirements are identical to those used in purchasing and production control. If the master planning parameter *Automatic copy* is selected, this also applies to a two master plan strategy as long as no local master scheduling has been executed and the static plan has not been edited.

Clicking the button *Update/Master scheduling* in the action pane strip of the lower pane in the net requirements form starts local master scheduling. Local master scheduling updates the current dynamic master plan for the selected item and its components. When viewing the results, you have to take into account that not all dependencies of other items are covered by the calculation, in particular regarding resource capacity requirements.

6.3.4.3 Working with Futures and Action Messages

If futures messages (showing availability problems) and action messages (for optimization requiring manual decisions) are activated in the applicable coverage groups, master planning generates corresponding messages. They show on the corresponding tabs in the net requirements form.

In addition, the list page *Master planning> Common> Requirements> Futures messages* contains an overview of all futures messages. Clicking the button *Reference* in the action pane of the futures message form opens the related order, which you may adjust as applicable.

An overview of all action messages is available in the list page *Master planning> Common> Actions> Actions*. Apart from the button *Reference* for accessing related orders, the action pane in the actions form also contains the button *Apply action* for immediately executing the action message of the particular line – e.g. deleting a purchase order. The button *Action graph* in the actions form provides access to a chart showing dependencies between action messages.

6.3.4.4 Planned Orders

Planned orders generated by master scheduling display in the list page *Master planning> Common> Planned orders*. When accessing the planned orders list page, the default plan is the current static master plan. The lookup field *Plan* then provides the option to select the current dynamic or any other master plan.

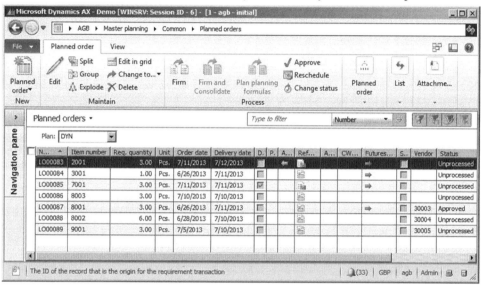

Figure 6-11:   Planned orders in the planned orders list page (preview pane hidden)

The planned order form in the master planning menu shows planned orders for purchasing, for production and for inventory transfers. The icon in the column *Reference* and the field *Reference* in the preview pane or in the detail form shows if a line contains a planned order for purchasing, production or inventory transfer.

In procurement, the menu item for planned orders (*Procurement and sourcing> Common> Purchase orders> Planned purchase orders*) refers to planned purchase orders, in production control (*Production control> Common> Production orders> Planned production orders*) to planned production orders.

Apart from the delivery date and the requirement quantity, the planned orders list page displays corresponding action and futures messages in separate columns. The planned order detail form, which opens by double-clicking a planned order in the list page, shows action and futures message details on the tabs *Action* and *Futures*. The tab *Pegging* in the detail form shows the requirements covered by the particular planned order – e.g. sales orders, BOM lines of production orders, demand forecasts, or safety stock.

6.3.4.5   Firming an Order

You may edit the delivery date and the quantity on the tab *Planned supply* of the planned orders detail form. For planned purchase orders, to make sure that a vendor number is entered in the lookup field *Vendor*.

If your company applies status management for planned orders, change the status to "Approved" (or to the status "Completed" if the planned order should not be firmed) by clicking the button *Process/Change status* or *Process/ Approve* on the action pane tab *Planned order*.

After selecting one or several planned orders in the planned orders list page, clicking the button *Process/Firm* on the action pane tab *Planned order* generates corresponding purchase orders, production orders and transfer orders. If you want to create a request for quotation (see section 3.4.4) instead of a purchase order, click the button *Maintain/Change to/Request for quotation*.

6.3.4.6   Net Requirements and Explosion

In order to get an overview of the net requirements related to a planned order, click the button *Requirements/Requirement profile* on the action pane tab *View* of the planned order form. The requirement profile shows the net requirements, which is the common form also available in the released product form or in order lines.

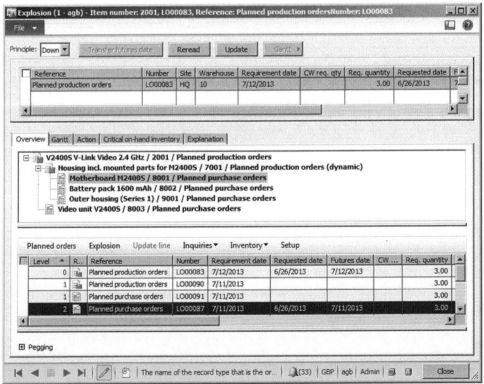

Figure 6-12:   The explosion form for analyzing the availability within the BOM structure

The button *Requirements/Explosion* on the action pane tab *View* of the planned order form provides access to another inquiry form, the explosion form. This form, which you may also access from the released product or from order lines in parallel to the net requirements, shows the item availability including components at all BOM levels. Clicking the button *Setup* in the lower pane of the explosion form provides the option to change display settings.

The lookup field *Principle* at the top of the explosion form determines the direction for the explosion: If selecting "Down", the form shows semi-finished items and raw materials or parts of the selected item at all BOM levels. If selecting "Up", the form shows a where-used analysis.

When updating the calculation by clicking the button *Update* in the explosion form, a dialog displays where you can select the checkbox *Enable trace*. With this setting, Dynamics AX creates a log of the impacts and results of master planning, which you can view on the tab *Explanation* in the explosion form afterwards.

6.3.4.7   New in Dynamics AX 2012 R2

Compared with the initial version of Dynamics AX 2012, the R2 version in addition contains the features *Apply action* and *Action graph* in the actions form and the master scheduling explanations in the explosion. A full log of explanations for master scheduling may be enabled through the Performance Monitor on the server.

6.3.5   Case Study Exercises

Exercise 6.3 – Min./Max. Principle
You want to apply a Min./Max. coverage principle to your finished item of exercise 5.2. Select an appropriate coverage group in the released product form and enter a minimum quantity of 500 units and a maximum quantity of 1000 units in the item coverage of the item.

Once you have finished, run local master scheduling in the net requirements form and check the result. In a second step, change the minimum quantity to one unit. After executing local master scheduling a second time, can you explain the result?

Exercise 6.4 – Period Principle
You want to apply a coverage principle summarizing requirements per period for your finished item of exercise 5.2 now. Choose an appropriate coverage group in the item record and delete the Min./Max. record in the item coverage.

Your customer of exercise 4.1 orders 100 units of the finished item. Enter a sales order for this requirement without posting a packing slip or invoice. Execute local master scheduling in the net requirements form then. After checking the results, enter a second order of your customer containing 150 units of the finished item for the same delivery date as the first order.

Start local master scheduling a second time and check the result again.

7   Inventory Management

The primary responsibility of inventory and warehouse management is to control the item stock by quantity and value. In order to meet this task, changes of the inventory quantity in Dynamics AX require posting inventory transactions, which have to be registered in vouchers before posting.

The current quantity in inventory therefore always is the total of item issue and receipt transactions. Most of the transactions are not a result of business processes within the inventory management module, but created automatically in other modules. Dynamics AX for example posts a receipt transaction in inventory when posting a product receipt in the procurement module.

7.1   Principles of Inventory Transactions

Before we start to go into details, the lines below show the principles of transactions in inventory management.

7.1.1   Basic Approach

Core master data in inventory management are the product records of inventoried items. Inventory management then controls the inventory per product (item number). Depending on the dimension groups assigned to the specific product, item quantity and value are available at the level of specific inventory dimensions. These dimensions include storage dimensions (e.g. warehouse or location), tracking dimensions (e.g. serial numbers), and product dimensions (e.g. configurations).

7.1.1.1   Types of Transactions

In order to change the quantity on hand, you need to post an item transaction. Depending on the direction of this transaction, it belongs to one of the three available types:

➢ **Item receipts** – Inward transactions
➢ **Item issues** – Outward transactions
➢ **Inventory transfers**

Item receipts increase the quantity on hand. They include product receipts in purchasing, customer returns in sales, reporting as finished in production as well as positive inventory counting adjustments and manual journals in inventory.

Item issues on the other hand include vendor returns in purchasing, packing slips in sales, picking lists in production as well as negative inventory counting adjustments and manual journals in inventory.

Inventory transfers include transfer orders and transfer journals. Transfer orders support the transfer of items form one warehouse to another, providing the option to post and print picking lists. Transfer journals on the other hand are not only available for transfers from one warehouse to another, but also for changing other dimension values (e.g. adjusting a serial number).

Although registering a transfer in a transfer journal only requires entering a single line, the posted transactions shows two lines. A transfer between warehouses for example creates one transaction line for the item issue from the output warehouse and one for the item receipt at the input warehouse.

7.1.1.2 Transactions from Other Areas

As mentioned, most of the inventory transactions do not originate in the inventory and warehouse management module, but derive from other areas of Dynamics AX. Therefore, the transaction origin in the other module – e.g. in the purchase order line – has to contain all data required for the inventory transaction (including warehouse, quantity and cost price).

When viewing a posted inventory transaction then, it shows the reference to the transaction origin including voucher number and date.

7.1.1.3 Inventory Quantity and Value

In order to grant an accurate inventory valuation, Dynamics AX distinguishes between the physical transaction (affecting quantity) and the financial transaction (affecting valuation).

For illustration purposes, Figure 7-1 shows the physical and the financial part of an inventory transaction related to a purchase order line.

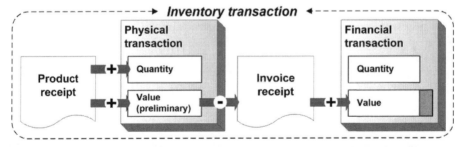

Figure 7-1: Physical and financial transaction in inventory for a purchase order line

The physical transaction in Dynamics AX causes a change of the quantity on hand in inventory. An example for posting a physical transaction is the product receipt in purchasing.

In terms of inventory quantity, the transaction is already finished when posting the product receipt. But inventory valuation only receives a preliminary cost price. The value of the product receipt shows in the field *Physical cost amount* separately from the field *Cost amount*, which contains the inventory value in finance.

The second part of the inventory transaction is the financial transaction, which contains the cost amount referring to the invoiced quantity. An example for posting a financial transaction is the purchase order invoice.

Posting the vendor invoice reverses the related preliminary posting of the product receipt (physical amount) and posts the cost amount of the invoice. Quantity and amount of the invoice are included in the financial inventory value then.

7.1.1.4 Posting Inventory Transactions

The differentiation between the physical and the financial transaction applies to every inventory transaction, no matter in which module it is generated. The way of posting depends on the origin, however.

For receipt transactions in purchase orders, posting the product receipt generates the physical transaction, and posting the vendor invoice the financial transaction. In production, reporting as finished of finished items posts the physical transaction. The financial transaction is posted by ending the production order.

For issue transactions in sales orders, the packing slip posts the physical and the invoice the financial transaction (similar to purchasing). In production, posting the picking list of BOM components posts the physical transaction. As with receiving finished items, the financial transaction of BOM components is posted by ending and costing the production order.

Unlike the other transactions, journals in inventory management do not post physical and financial transaction in two separate steps, but in parallel.

7.1.1.5 Inventory Closing

Receipt transaction got their final financial value when posting the invoice (except for later manual adjustments). But for issue transactions, the financial value often is not known and therefore not final when posting the invoice. You may for example receive a purchase invoice after posting the related sales invoice. If the purchase invoice shows a higher price than the preliminary amount posted with the product receipt, the contribution margin of the sales transaction will change.

Except for items referring to a standard cost price or moving average valuation, you need to reevaluate issue transactions through inventory closing. The main purpose of inventory closing, usually a month-end procedure, is to recalculate the financial value of issue transactions based on the value of receipt transactions.

7.1.1.6 Ledger Integration

Inventory journals post to ledger accounts depending on applicable settings (see section 8.4) in the same way as inventory transactions generated in other modules.

7.1.2   At a Glance: Inventory Journal Transactions

Inventory journals are used for manual changes of the quantity on hand, independent from orders in purchasing, sales or production. For convenience, the example below shows a manual item receipt in an inventory adjustment journal. In regular business, such transactions are an exception, since problems or missing end-to-end business processes are the reason for receiving an item without a purchase, production or customer return order in most cases.

For accessing the inventory journals for manual adjustments, choose the form *Inventory and warehouse management> Journals> Item transactions> Inventory adjustment*. Inventory journals are vouchers and therefore consist of a header and a lines part. Unlike purchase or sales orders, inventory journals do not show header and lines in one common, but in two separate forms.

In order to register a transaction, insert a record in the journal header form by clicking the button *New* in the action pane strip (or by pushing the shortcut key *Ctrl+N*) and select a journal name in the column *Name*. The journal number in the column *Journal* then defaults from the number sequence.

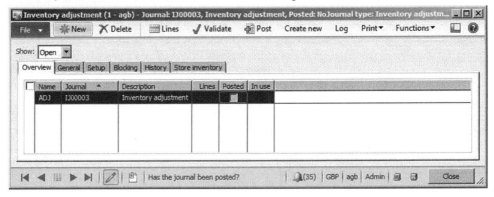

Figure 7-2:   Entering a journal header in the inventory adjustment journal form

If you want to support later analysis, enter a short text explaining the transaction in the column *Description*. The column *Lines* shows the number of lines in the journal.

If somebody works in a particular journal currently, the journal shows a red "X" in the column *In use*. You may view the user blocking the journal on the tab *Blocking*. It is not possible to access the lines of the journal until the other user leaves the journal.

The checkbox *Posted* contains a checkmark, if a journal has been posted already. You may view posted journals by selecting the option "All" or "Posted" in the lookup field *Show* in the upper pane of the form.

An alternative way for creating a journal is to click the button *Create new* in the action pane strip, inserting a header record and immediately switching to the lines.

If you do not want to apply the *Create new* feature, click the button *Lines* in order to access the journal lines.

In the journal lines form, select the item number before registering site, warehouse and other dimensions like batch number or location depending on the settings of applicable dimension groups. In order to control the dimension columns displayed in the lines, click the button *Inventory/Dimensions display*.

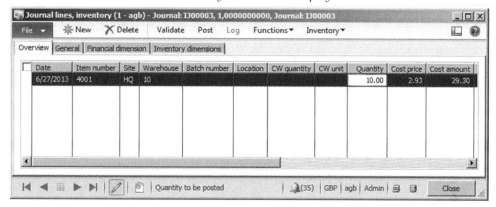

Figure 7-3:   Registering a journal line

Defaults for warehouse, quantity and cost price derive from the released product. The default for the quantity is 1.00, if the released product (default or site-specific order settings) does not contain a default inventory quantity. You may override all defaults in the journal line except for the cost price of a standard cost item.

If entering a positive quantity, the transaction is an item receipt. A negative quantity creates an item issue.

Inventory journals post the physical and the financial transaction at the same time. Unlike transactions in purchasing, inventory journal transactions do not receive a corresponding financial transaction from an invoice. Therefore, make sure that the journal line contains a correct cost price when posting the inventory journal – especially in item receipts.

In order to post the journal after entering the last journal line, click the button *Post* in the journal header or lines.

Before posting, optionally click the button *Validation* for checking potential problems. Validation does not check all possible problems, however, which is why you might sometimes receive an error message when posting a journal, even if the validation does not show a problem.

7.2   Product Information Management

Since all business processes related to inventory require inventoried products, product data are the core element of master data in supply chain management.

The data structure of products in Dynamics AX includes two levels – shared products holding basic item data common to all companies, and released products holding company-specific item data.

Product records contain all physical items including raw materials, parts, semi-finished products and finished products. In addition, product records also include non-inventoried items like service or phantom items, which do not exist physically, but are required in order management or in bills of materials.

In some areas of the application, the label "Item" refers to released products.

7.2.1   Product Master Data

Product master data have already been discussed in section 3.3, 4.3, 5.2.1 and 6.3.3 in connection with purchasing, sales, production, and master planning. Therefore, this section does not include the topics covered there. Apart from general features of the product and released product form, the focus in this section is on item data in inventory and on inventory valuation.

7.2.1.1   Structure of Product Data

In order to view shared products, access the form *Product information management> Common> Products> All products and product masters* showing a list of all products. The list pages *Products* (for items without configurations and variants) and *Product masters* (for configurable items) show a filtered view of all shared products.

Shared products are not available in the current company or any other company of your enterprise until the product has been released to the particular company.

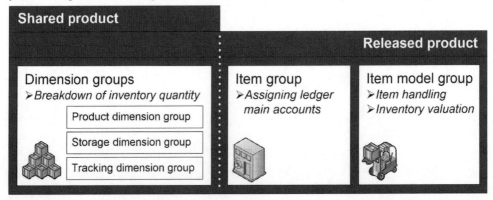

Figure 7-4:   Main control groups of a product

Core data – common to all companies to which a product has been released – in the shared products include product number, product type and subtype (non-inventoried, inventoried or configurable item) and dimension groups. If applicable, skip the dimension groups in the shared product and enter them at company level in the released products. Depending on number sequence settings, you might also use independent item numbers at company level.

Most product details are specified at company level – in the released product form (*Product information management> Common> Released products*). Required fields there include the dimension groups (if not shared), the item model group, and the item group.

7.2.1.2 Creating a Product

Depending on the requirements in your company, there are two ways for creating a new product (see section 3.3.2):

> ➢ **Start with the shared product** – Create a shared product and release it.
> ➢ **Start with the released product** – Create a product in the released product form, automatically generating a shared product in the background.

In order to create an item in the shared product form, click the button *New/Product* in the action pane. If you want to release this product to one or more companies then, click the button *Release products* in the action pane and select applicable companies on the tab *Select companies* of the release product dialog. Releasing the shared product to additional companies later can be done the same way.

The released product form is available through the appropriate menu item. Alternatively, access a released product directly from the shared product by clicking the link *More* in the FactBox *Authorized by company* and then applying the table reference (*View details*) on the column *Item number* in the dialog. You might need to refresh the shared product form (pushing the *F5* key) for viewing new released products in the FactBox.

Instead of creating a new product in the shared product form, alternatively create a product in the released product form clicking the button *New/Product* in the action pane there. The *New released product* dialog then contains data for the shared and for the corresponding released product in parallel. After clicking the option *Show more fields* at the bottom of the dialog, it shows all mandatory fields of the released product. If there are templates for released products, the additional field *Apply template* for choosing an appropriate template shows in the dialog.

You may also apply templates (see section 2.3.2) for released products at a later date. For this purpose, click the button *Maintain/Apply template* on the action pane tab *Product* overriding data of the released product with data from the template. For creating a template for released products, click the button *New/Template* in the released product detail form.

7.2.1.3 Product Number and Name

The *Product number* identifying shared products has to be unique across companies. It is assigned automatically to new products, if the settings of the number sequence for product numbers (*Product information management> Setup> Product information management parameters*, tab *Number sequences*) do not specify a manual assignment.

The *Item number* identifying items at released product level is identical to the shared product number, if there is no other setting in the number sequence for item numbers (*Inventory and warehouse management> Setup> Inventory and warehouse management parameters*, tab *Number sequences*) of the particular company.

The *Product name* and *Description* is only editable at shared product level, but the *Search name* is editable at released product level.

When creating a shared product, the default for the product name and the search name derives from the product number. You may override this default and enter a longer product description is the field *Description*. If there are different product names and descriptions in foreign languages, enter them after clicking the button *Translations* in the action pane of the shared product form.

7.2.1.4   Product Type and Subtype

The *Product type* controls, if a product is an inventoried item. Whereas the product type "Item" refers to regular items, the product type "Service" specifies an item without inventory control in any company.

The *Product subtype* refers to the item configuration. Whereas the product subtype "Product" applies to a regular standard item, the product subtype "Product master" characterizes a base item for assigned product variants.

7.2.1.5   Product Master

If a product refers to the product subtype "Product master", the product number alone does not uniquely identify the item in inventory. Transactions in addition require entering the product variant in this case, distinguishing different sizes, colors, styles or configurations of a product.

When creating a product master, the *Product dimension group* – one of the three dimension groups discussed in section 7.2.2 below – is available in the *Create product* dialog. The product dimension group is selected at shared product level, determining which of the dimensions *Configuration*, *Size*, *Color* and/or *Style* apply.

The *Configuration technology*, which is the second mandatory field when creating a product master, determines the way of creating product variants.

If selecting the configuration technology "Predefined variant", click the button *Product master/Product dimensions* in the shared product for entering dimension values for product variants. The left pane of the product dimensions form then shows the dimensions, which are applicable to the product according to the selected product dimension group.

After entering product dimension values for applicable dimensions in the product dimensions form, you have to specify available variants (dimension value combinations) by clicking the button *Product master/Product variants* in the shared product. The button *Variant suggestions* in the product variants form facilitates creating new variants. Managing variants in the product variants form is applicable, if the particular product is – for example – not available in all colors for each size. If a product only includes one active product dimension or if all dimension combinations are available, select the checkbox *Generate variants automatically* in the shared product detail form before starting to enter product dimension values.

Before choosing a product variant in a transaction, you have to release it by clicking the button *Release products* in the action pane of the shared product. In the release product dialog, select applicable variants for releasing in the right pane. Apart from releasing product variants in parallel to releasing the product master, releasing variants is also possible at a later date.

7.2.1.6 Non Inventoried Items and Services

Apart from regular products, which you want to track in inventory through transactions and the quantity on hand, there are items – e.g. services or office supplies – which you do not want to track in inventory.

Dynamics AX provides two separate options specifying whether inventory control applies to a product:

➢ **Product type** – Option "Item" or "Service"
➢ **Item model group** – Checkbox *Stocked product*

Depending on the combination of both settings, inventory control works different (see Table 7-1).

Table 7-1:   Options for inventory control of products

| Product type | Item | Service |
Item model group		
Stocked product	Inventory transactions, inventory quantity	Inventory transactions, no quantity
Non-stocked product	No transactions	No transactions

The product type "Service" applies to products, which do not show inventory quantity in any company. But if assigned to an item model group for stocked products, products of this type show inventory transactions. This setting is required for intangible items and services which are used as part of a BOM.

When setting up items of the product type "Service", you have to assign a specific item group and item model group for granting correct inventory valuation and ledger postings.

Linking a released product to an item model group, which shows a cleared checkbox *Stocked product*, does not only avoid showing inventory quantity but also prevents inventory transactions. Since the item model group is assigned to the released product, this setting enables deactivating inventory control for an item at company level.

7.2.1.7   Core Settings in Released Products

Whereas the shared product form only contains a limited number of fields, the released product form includes a wide range of detail data for characterizing a particular item.

Only a few fields in the released product are mandatory, including the *Item model group*, the *Item group* and – either at shared product or at released product level – the dimension groups. The button *Maintain/Validate* on the action pane tab *Product* of the released product form supports checking if a released product contains all mandatory data.

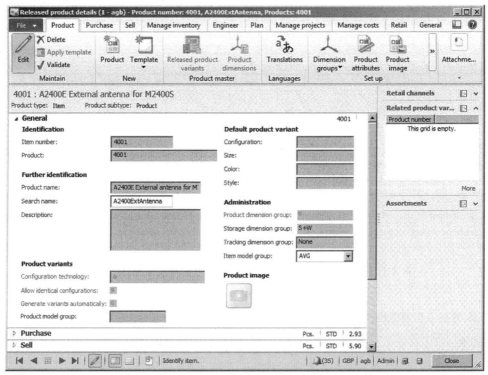

Figure 7-5:   Managing an item in the released product form

Other data in the released product like the item sales tax groups, the units of measure and the cost price are not mandatory, but nevertheless crucial depending on the specific requirements.

7.2.1.8   Item Group

The main purpose of item groups is to pool products, which post to a common main account in the general ledger. Therefore you need at least as many item groups, as there are different stock and revenue accounts for inventory items in finance. You may find more details on the inventory posting setup in section 8.4.2.

When releasing a product, you have to keep in mind that you should not change the item group after registering the first transaction of the released product. Dynamics AX displays a warning, saying that are possible issues in finance regarding inventory reconciliation if you do not carefully check the consequences of changing the group. But the warning does not prevent you from changing the item group, if necessary.

Item groups do not only control ledger integration, they also are a filtering and sorting criteria in many reports.

7.2.1.9   Units of Measure

The unit of measure has to be entered in the released product before you can register an inventory transaction. When releasing a new product, Dynamics AX applies the default unit specified in the inventory management parameters (field *Unit* on the tab *General*). As long as no inventory transaction is recorded for the item, it is possible to change the inventory unit of a released product.

If an item requires different units of measure in purchasing, sales, and inventory, assign the applicable units on the tabs *Purchase, Sell* and *Manage inventory* of the released product form. The unit in the released product defaults to transactions entered for the item, e.g. in a sales order line. If necessary, select a different unit in a particular transaction then. When choosing a different unit, the selected unit requires a unit conversion to the inventory unit.

Units of measure are shared across companies. If you require a new unit of measure, you have to set it up in the units form (*Organization administration> Setup> Units> Units*) before assigning it to a released product. The *Unit class* (e.g. "Quantity" or "Weight") determines the area to which a unit of measure applies. For one unit within each unit class, optionally select the checkbox *System unit* in order to apply this unit to fields not associated to a specific unit of measure (e.g. the net weight field in the released products).

Clicking the button *Unit conversions* in the action pane strip of the units form provides access to the unit conversion calculation. Conversion factors between units entered on the tab *Standard conversion* apply to all products. The tab *Intra-class conversions* enables entering conversions per item number within a *Unit class*.

7.2.1.10 Number Groups

When entering a batch or serial number in a transaction, the batches or serial numbers table (*Inventory and warehouse management> Inquiries> Dimensions*) has to include this number.

If you want Dynamics AX to generate batch or serial numbers automatically, set up appropriate groups in the number groups form (*Inventory and warehouse management> Setup> Dimensions> Number groups*). On the tab *General* of the number groups form, specify the structure of related numbers and assign a number sequence if the structure includes a *Number sequence No.* Settings on the tab *Activation* determine which transactions are generating numbers.

In the released product form, the *Tracking dimension group* (see section 7.2.2 below) controls, if batch or serial numbers apply to an item. If tracking dimensions apply, optionally select a batch or serial number group on the tab *Manage inventory* of the released product for automatically generating batch or serial numbers for the item.

7.2.1.11 Catch Weight Products

A catch weight product (*CW product*) in Dynamics AX 2012 R2 is an item with weight as primary unit of measure, and a secondary unit (catch weight unit) showing the number of pieces in parallel. The weight per unit varies, and as a result there is no fixed unit conversion between the weight unit and the catch weight unit. In the order lines of purchase or sales orders, only the catch weight quantity (the number of pieces) is entered. When registering inventory transactions, both weight and catch weight quantity have to be entered in parallel.

The catch weight functionality originates from process industries. Typical examples of catch weight products are animals (or parts of animals) requiring to show the counted number and the weight in parallel. Usually, catch weight only applies to items with batch and/or serial number control.

In Dynamics AX, the catch weight functionality is generally available in inventory, purchasing and sales, where all applicable forms contain additional fields for the catch weight. Usage in production is limited to batch production orders, since only formulas – not regular bills of materials – may include catch weight items. Because of its complexity, you should only use catch weight if you actually need to track weight and catch weight quantity independently from each other.

For setting up a catch weight item, select the checkbox *CW product* when creating the shared product. Then click the button *Unit conversions* in the action pane of the shared product form and enter an *Inter-class conversion* between the inventory unit (weight) and the catch weight unit (pieces). The catch weight unit has to be a unit without decimals (*Decimal precision* zero in the unit).

When releasing the product, the inventory unit of the item has to be a weight unit (the default unit in the inventory parameters usually is a weight unit in applicable companies). On the tab *Manage inventory* in the released product form, select the catch weight unit in the field *CW unit* and enter the *Minimum quantity* and the *Maximum quantity* below, determining a range for the allowed conversion factor (weight per unit). Like for other products, enter further required data including item model group, item group and dimension groups as applicable then.

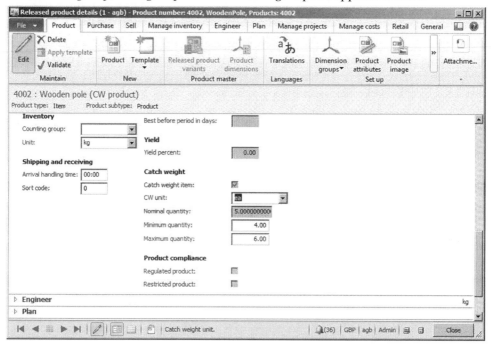

Figure 7-6:   Entering catch weight settings in the released product

When registering a purchase order line, enter the catch weight quantity (number of pieces) in the column *CW quantity*. The column *Quantity*, which is not editable for a catch weight item, shows the quantity according to the regular unit conversion. The item receipt through inventory registration or an item arrival journal (see section 3.5.3) then requires independently entering the CW quantity and the inventory quantity in parallel, providing a default for the inventory quantity derived from the unit conversion.

The requirement of independently entering the CW quantity and the quantity in inventory unit applies to all inventory transactions, including sales order picking and inventory journals. Inquiries of the current inventory then show both weight and catch weight quantity in parallel.

7.2.1.12 New in Dynamics AX 2012 and in AX 2012 R2

In Dynamics AX 2012, product master data show in a separate module, applying the concept of shared products and released products (former "Items"). Compared with the initial version of Dynamics AX 2012, the R2 version in addition contains the catch weight functionality.

7.2.2   Inventory Dimension Groups

Inventory dimensions control the breakdown of inventory quantity within released products. Applying dimensions splits inventory quantity and transactions to a more detailed level than the item number.

Inventory dimensions in Dynamics AX therefore are a prerequisite for showing the quantity of an item for a particular warehouse location or a particular batch.

7.2.2.1   Available Dimensions

Inventory dimensions in Dynamics AX belong to one of the following groups:

➢ **Product dimensions** – Configuration, size, color and style provide the option to subdivide an item based on these characteristics (only for product masters).
➢ **Storage dimensions** – Site, warehouse, location and pallet apply to inventory structures.
➢ **Tracking dimensions** – Batch and serial number control tracking options.

If required, rename the product dimensions *Size, Color* and *Style* by clicking the button *Rename* in the product dimension groups form. In the tracking dimension groups, the dimensions *Inventory profile, Owner* and *GTD number* refer to functionality required in Eastern European countries.

The dimension groups of an item determine which inventory dimensions have to be entered when registering an inventory transaction. If the batch number dimension is active in the tracking dimension group of the item for example, you have to enter batch numbers.

7.2.2.2   Dimension Groups and Settings

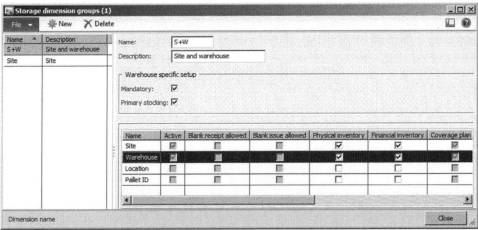

Figure 7-7:   Managing storage dimension groups

In order to access dimension group management, choose the menu path *Product information management> Setup> Dimension groups* and select the option *Product dimension groups, Storage dimension groups* or *Tracking dimension groups* there. The forms for these three types of dimension groups look similar, except for the applicable dimensions which are specific to the particular group type.

As shown in Figure 7-7 on the example of the storage dimension group form, the dimension group form shows the list of dimension groups in the left pane. The right pane of the form provides access to the inventory dimension settings for the dimension group selected on the left pane.

If you need an additional dimension group, insert a new record by clicking the button *New* in the action pane strip. Then enter the inventory dimension settings of the new dimension group selecting the checkboxes as explained in Table 7-2.

Table 7-2:   Available settings for inventory dimensions in a dimension group

Parameter	Explanation
Active	Dimension available for transactions of the item
Primary stocking	Mandatory dimension for reservation; in addition displays in the on-hand inquiry as default dimension
Blank receipt allowed	Dimension value not required for receipt transactions
Blank issue allowed	Dimension value not required for issue transactions
Physical inventory	Item availability per dimension value (depending on the item model group, no negative inventory e.g. per batch number)
Financial inventory	Inventory value per dimension value (necessary for calculating value and cost price, e.g. per batch number)
Coverage plan by dimension	Separate item coverage in master planning per dimension value (see section 6.3.3)
For purchase prices	Dimension available for purchase price agreements (see section 3.3.3)
For sales prices	Dimension available for sales price agreements

In storage dimension groups, the dimension *Site* (see section 9.1.7) is always active, which is why a site has to be entered in every inventory transaction. For the dimension *Warehouse*, selecting the additional parameter *Mandatory* requires registering a warehouse already when entering a transaction (if not selected, the warehouse may remain empty until posting).

In product dimension groups, only the parameters *Active*, *For purchase prices* and *For sales prices* are available.

When setting up dimension groups, you should only activate dimensions actually required in your business processes. In addition, you should apply a limited number of dimension groups. System load, complexity and time for registration increase with the number of dimensions in use.

On the other hand, you have to activate all dimensions required. For example, the quantity on hand is only available per location, if the dimension *Location* is active for the particular item. If you need a particular dimension for some, but not all transactions of an item, the best way is to apply a pseudo-value for transactions where the dimension is not applicable. If warehouse locations are not applicable to all of your warehouses for example, insert a pseudo-location providing a default for warehouses without locations.

7.2.2.3 Dimension Groups in the Released Product

For assigning applicable inventory dimensions to a released product, click the button *Set up/Dimension groups* on the action pane tab *Product* of the released product form. If a dimension group is already specified on the corresponding shared product, it is shown in the released product and can't be changed there.

In order to avoid invalid dimension values in posted transactions, it is not possible to change inventory-related settings of a dimension group once a transaction refers to the dimension group. For the same reason, it is not possible to change the dimension group of an item, if there is an open transaction or an on-hand quantity in inventory.

If you need to change dimension settings for an item, post transactions issuing the complete stock physically and financially. After inventory closing, assign the new group and then post transactions according to the actual stock on hand in the warehouse.

7.2.2.4 Dimension Display

The default for displaying dimension columns in detail forms is available on the tab *Inventory dimensions* in the parameters form of all relevant modules. For example, the inventory dimensions in the sales order lines are controlled in the accounts receivable parameters (*Accounts receivable> Setup> Accounts receivable parameters*, tab *Inventory dimensions*).

Forms containing inventory dimension columns allow changing the display of dimension columns by clicking the appropriate button in the action pane strip – e.g. *Sales order line/Display/Dimensions* in the action pane strip of the sales order lines or *Inventory/Dimensions display* in inventory journal lines.

When selecting inventory dimensions for displaying reports and inquiries of inventory quantity and inventory value, you have to take into account that only these queries show a reliable result, which comply with the dimension setup. It is not useful for example to report inventory value and cost price per warehouse, if the checkbox *Financial inventory* is not selected in the applicable storage dimension group. The reason is, that inventory valuation according to this setting does not link item issue transactions with item receipt transactions per warehouse separately, causing a result which is different to your expectation.

7.2.2.5 New in Dynamics AX 2012 and in AX 2012 R2

In Dynamics AX 2012, inventory dimension groups are split to three different groups according to their purpose – product, storage and tracking dimensions.

Compared with the initial version of Dynamics AX 2012, the R2 version contains the additional dimension *Style* and – for Eastern Europe – *Inventory profile*, *Owner* and *GTD number*.

7.2.3   Item Model Groups

Item model groups include settings for the valuation method on the one hand and for item handling on the other hand. They are a core setting for inventory valuation and ledger integration.

For editing the item model groups, choose the menu item *Inventory and warehouse management> Setup> Inventory> Item model groups*. The left pane of the item model group form displays a list of available groups. The right pane of the form then provides access to the settings for the group selected on the left pane.

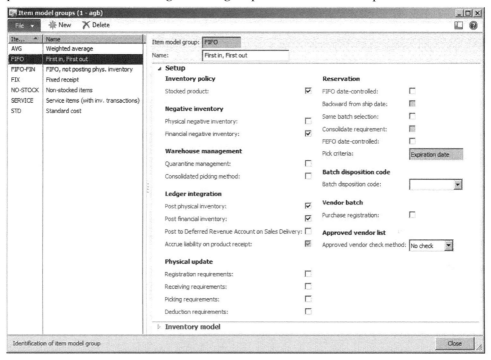

Figure 7-8:   Available settings in the item model group

7.2.3.1   Item Handling

In item model groups for inventoried items, the checkbox *Stocked product* needs to be selected. If this checkbox is cleared, products assigned to the group do not generate inventory transactions. This is the right choice for non-inventoried products like service items (except subcontracted production services).

The parameters *Quarantine management* and *Consolidated picking method* control the automatic generation of internal orders. If selecting the checkbox *Quarantine management*, Dynamics AX automatically creates a quarantine order (see section

7.4.4) when posting an item receipt. If selecting the checkbox *Consolidated picking method*, output orders for shipping assigned items show the type "Consolidated picking" (see section 4.5.3).

The checkbox *Registration requirements* controls, if you have to post an inventory registration in an item arrival journal or in the registration form, before you may post the product receipt in purchasing (see section 3.5.3). The checkbox *Picking requirements* in a similar way applies to picking list posting before packing slip posting in sales.

The checkboxes *Receiving requirements* and *Deduction requirements* control, if you have to post a packing slip in sales or a product receipt in purchasing before posting the invoice.

7.2.3.2 Negative Inventory

In most cases you do not allow a negative physical inventory for inventoried items, but you do accept a negative financial inventory. A negative financial inventory results from posting a sales invoice before posting the corresponding purchase invoice (supposing no other stock is available for the item).

With regard to the settings for negative inventory in the item model group, respect the dimension groups: Dynamics AX controls negative physical (or financial) inventory at the level of the inventory dimensions, for which the checkbox *Physical inventory* (or *Financial inventory*) is selected.

7.2.3.3 Inventory Model

Selecting an inventory model (FIFO, LIFO, average or standard cost) on the tab *Inventory model* determines the inventory valuation method. The valuation method is the way Dynamics AX links issue transactions to receipt transactions in terms of valuation.

Details on inventory valuation methods are available in section 7.3, details on ledger integration in section 8.4.2.

7.2.3.4 Setting Up Item Model Groups

If you change the *Inventory model* or *Ledger integration* settings of an item model group after posting corresponding item transactions, reconciliation of inventory and finance may become difficult. Before changing any of these settings, you should carefully plan the consequences.

The number of required item model groups depends on the requirements of your company for processing items. In a regular Dynamics AX installation, you have to apply at least two groups – one for inventoried items and one for service items. The item model group for service items should allow physical and financial negative quantity and deactivate ledger integration.

7.2.3.5 New in Dynamics AX 2012 and in AX 2012 R2

In Dynamics AX 2012, the new checkbox *Stocked product* enables products without inventory transactions. Compared with the initial version of Dynamics AX 2012, the R2 version contains additional settings for reservation and approved vendors.

7.2.4   Cost Price Settings

Core settings regarding the inventory valuation of an item are available on the tab *Inventory model* of the item model group: The lookup field *Inventory model* controls, if the valuation method is FIFO, LIFO, weighted average, moving average or standard cost. For the methods FIFO, LIFO and weighted average, select the checkbox *Fixed receipt price* if you want to apply a standard cost price only for item receipts.

7.2.4.1 Item Cost Price

The tab *Manage costs* of the released product form includes a base cost price in the field *Price*. This base cost price does not apply to the valuation method "Standard cost", however.

All other valuation methods apply the base price in the item record as a default for the cost amount of item receipts in inventory journals and counting journals, if no site-specific cost price applies. Therefore you should ensure a correct base price.

7.2.4.2 Costing Versions and Item Price Form

The cost price per site – and the site-specific standard purchase or sales price – is available in the item price form, accessible by clicking the button *Set up/Item Price* on the action pane tab *Manage costs* of the released product form.

Before entering a record in the item price form, the appropriate costing version (*Inventory and warehouse management> Setup> Costing> Costing versions*) has to be available. Costing versions contain separate versions of prices, which may differ in calculation. The *Costing type* "Standard cost" is required for versions, which apply to standard cost prices in the item price form.

In order to register a new cost price in the item price form, switch to the tab *Pending prices* there. For a cost price, choose the *Price type* "Cost" and select the costing version in the column *Version*. If no default value for *Site* and *From date* applies from the costing version, enter these fields manually. Apart from the *Price* itself, the item price form contains additional price details like the *Price unit* or price charges in (similar to corresponding settings in the released product form, see section 3.3.3). For finished or semi-finished items referring to a bill of materials, the button *Calculation* provides the option to run a cost calculation.

Once you have finished entering the pending price, activate it by clicking the button *Activate* in the action pane strip of the item price form. Active prices then show on the tab *Active prices* of the form.

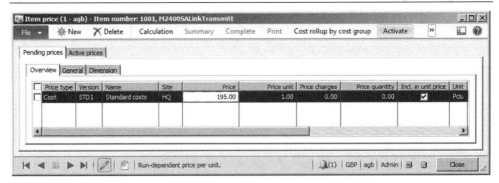

Figure 7-9:   Entering a pending price in the item price form

For product master records, cost prices are available with applicable product dimensions at product variant level, if the checkbox *Use cost price by variant* (on the tab *Manage costs* in the released product) of the product master is selected.

7.2.5   Transaction and Inventory Inquiry

The transactions and the inventory quantity of an item are directly accessible from the released product form. Both inquiries, the transaction inquiry and the on-hand inquiry, are also available by clicking the button *Inventory* in the action pane strip of various forms for registering transactions (e.g. the sales order lines).

The list page *Inventory and warehouse management> Common> On-hand inventory* and the form *Inventory and warehouse management> Inquiries> On-hand* show overview of the quantity on hand for multiple items. A complete inquiry of inventory transactions is available in the form *Inventory and warehouse management> Inquiries> Transactions> Transactions*.

7.2.5.1   Transactions Form

If you want to access inventory transactions from the released product form, click the button *View/Transactions* on the action pane tab *Manage inventory* of the released product. When accessing the inventory transactions from the released product, the transactions form shows all transactions of the particular item. The columns *Reference* and *Number* display the original voucher.

In addition to posted transactions, the transactions form also shows future transactions not posted yet. These transactions include order lines in sales, purchasing and production, for which no packing slip/product receipt or invoice has been posted. You may recognize these lines by the empty physical and financial date. In addition, the transactions show a receipt status "Ordered" or an issue status "On order".

Inventory transactions (1 - agb) · Financial date: 5/27/2013, Yes, Lot ID: IL00013Item number: 4001

File ▼   Inventory▼   Ledger▼   Functions▼   Configuration details

Overview | General | Update | Ledger | Reference | Other | Financial dimensions - financial | Financial dimensions - physical | Inventory dimensions

Site	Warehouse	Physical date	Financial date	Reference	Number	Receipt	Issue	CW quantity	CW...	Quantity	Cost amount
HQ	10			Purchase order	PO00003	Ordered				1.00	
HQ	10			Purchase order	PO00004	Ordered				1,000.00	
HQ	10			Quotation	SQ00001		Quotation...			-10.00	
HQ	10			Sales order	SO00003		On order			-10.00	
HQ	10	5/22/2013	5/22/2013	Purchase order	PO00001	Purchased				10.00	29.30
HQ	10	5/24/2013	5/26/2013	Purchase order	PO00005	Purchased				700.00	2,023.00
HQ	10	5/25/2013		Purchase order	PO00005	Received				280.00	
HQ	10	5/27/2013	5/27/2013	Sales order	SO00001		Sold			-8.00	-23.13
HQ	10	5/27/2013	5/27/2013	Sales order	SO00001		Sold			-2.00	-5.78

◄ ◄ ▦ ► ►| | | Date of physical transaction   (1) | GBP | agb | Admin | Close

Figure 7-10:   Inventory transactions of an item in the transactions form

7.2.5.2   Physical and Financial Transaction

When posting a product receipt in purchasing, a packing slip in sales, a picking list in production, or a report as finished journal, Dynamics AX applies the posting date to the *Physical date* in the inventory transaction. In parallel, the status of the transaction changes to "Received" or "Deducted". The field *Physical cost amount* on the tab *Update* shows the preliminary inventory value of the transaction.

The *Financial date* in an inventory transaction is updated when posting the invoice in purchasing or sales, or when ending the production order. In parallel, the status of the transaction changes to "Purchased" or "Sold" and the inventory value of the transaction displays in the column *Cost amount*.

Dynamics AX does not change the posted financial cost amount any more. If posting an adjustment of the inventory value in the course of inventory closing or through a manual adjustment, the posted difference shows separately in the field *Adjustment* on the tab *Update* of the transaction.

7.2.5.3   Inventory Picking and Registration

Inventory picking in sales (see section 4.5.2) and registration in purchasing (see section 3.5.3) are peculiar steps of an inventory transaction. When posting a picking or registration transaction, the quantity on hand of the item and the status of the inventory transaction are updated. Unlike product receipt and packing slip transactions, picking and registration do not generate an unchanging voucher.

After posting the packing slip in sales (or the product receipt in purchasing), the date of picking (or registration) shows in the field *Inventory date* on the tab *General* of the inventory transaction. If you do not proceed the regular way – posting a packing slip after picking, or posting a product receipt after registration – but cancel the registration, it is not possible to view the original picking or registration transaction in the inventory transactions any more.

7.2.5.4 Arrived Status

If your company uses the warehouse module with pallet transports and inventory locations, an additional receipt status "Arrived" applies. This is the status after posting an item arrival journal with activated pallet transports.

In this status, transactions are not included in the physical quantity. After posting the corresponding pallet transport, the posted quantity adds to the physical inventory and the transaction status changes to "Registered".

7.2.5.5 Voucher Data

Apart from data showing on the tab *Overview*, data on the tab *Update* contain valuable information on inventory transactions. The fields on this tab are grouped by the columns *Physical*, *Financial* and *Settlement*.

The field group *Physical* contains the date, number and preliminary value of the product receipt or packing slip. Invoice data are available in the field group *Financial*.

If the value of a transaction changes (according to the valuation method through inventory closing, or through manual adjustments), the value difference shows in the field *Adjustment*. The original financial *Cost amount* does not change any more, all later adjustments add in the field *Adjustment*.

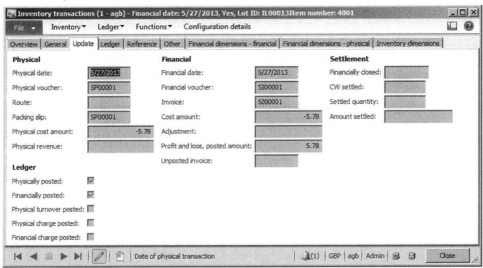

Figure 7-11: Voucher data in an inventory transaction

The field group *Settlement* shows if an inventory transaction is settled by inventory closing already. If the quantity of a transaction completely settles matching item issues or receipts, inventory closing records the closing date in the field *Financially closed* and closes the transaction (the lookup *Value open* on the tab *General* then shows "No"). But registering a manual adjustment to a closed transaction reopens it again.

7.2.5.6 Ledger Integration

The checkbox *Physically posted* on the tab *Update* of an inventory transaction shows if the product receipt or packing slip has been posted to the general ledger. As a prerequisite, ledger integration for physical transactions has to be activated in the item model group of the particular item.

Assuming ledger integration for financial transactions is activated, a checkmark in the checkbox *Financially posted* indicates that the invoice has been posted. For purchase invoices, the checkbox is selected after invoice posting even if ledger integration is not active for an item, though. The reason is that a purchase invoice for items always posts a ledger transaction: To a stock account for the receipt transaction if ledger integration is active or to an expense account for immediate consumption otherwise.

7.2.5.7 Quantity on Hand

In order to view the current inventory quantity of an item, click the button *View/ On-hand inventory* on the action pane tab *Manage inventory* of the released product form. The tab *Overview* of the on-hand form then displays a list of inventory quantities, grouped by the inventory dimensions selected as primary stocking dimensions for the item.

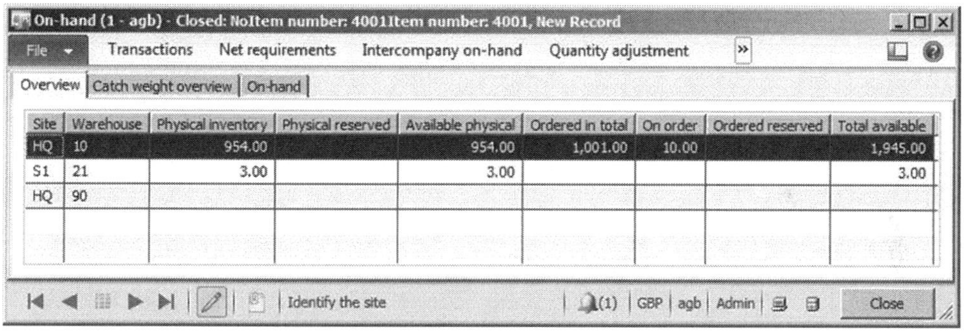

Figure 7-12: On-hand overview of an item

7.2.5.8 Dimensions Display

The button *Dimensions display* in the action pane of the on-hand inquiry opens a dialog box, where you may select which dimension columns display in the inquiry. This dialog box is also available in many other forms after clicking the appropriate button in the action pane strip – e.g. *Sales order line/Display/Dimensions* in the sales order lines.

If choosing to show an additional column for example containing the batch number, the lines in the form display the quantity per batch number. In order to view the total quantity of an item, clear all dimension checkboxes in the display dialog.

7.2.5.9 On Hand Details

In order to view the details of a line in the on-hand inquiry, switch to the tab *On-hand*. Apart from the *Physical inventory*, which is the current quantity in inventory, the form shows availability data and the current cost price (average cost price, except for standard cost and fixed receipt price items).

The physical inventory is the total of the transactions with following status:

> **Posted quantity** – Invoiced quantity of purchasing deducting sales
> **Received** – Product receipt in purchasing, added to the posted quantity
> **Deducted** – Packing slip in sales, deducted from the posted quantity
> **Registered** – Registration and item arrival, added to the posted quantity
> **Picked** – Picking in sales, deducted from the posted quantity

Apart from purchasing and sales, the same status and calculation applies to transactions in production.

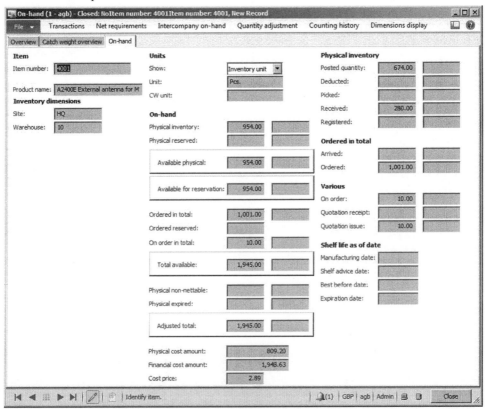

Figure 7-13: On-hand details

All data shown in the on-hand form refer to the selected dimensions. The dimensions for example selected in Figure 7-13 are the site "HQ" and the warehouse "10". According to this selection, Dynamics AX applies a filter showing the quantity and cost amount for this site and warehouse. When viewing the cost price and cost amount, you have to take into account that cost figures are only reliable for dimensions with separate financial inventory according to the dimension group settings.

7.2.5.10 On Hand Inventory in the Past

For viewing the physical inventory on a date in the past, choose the report *Inventory and warehouse management> Reports> Status> Physical inventory> Physical inventory by inventory dimension*.

7.2.5.11 New in Dynamics AX 2012 R2

Compared with the initial version of Dynamics AX 2012, the R2 version in inventory inquiries contains additional fields showing catch weight quantity.

7.2.6   Case Study Exercises

Exercise 7.1 – Dimension Groups
In order to investigate the functionality of dimension groups, create a new storage dimension group D-## and a tracking dimension group D-## (## = your user ID). Set up the dimension groups in a way that the dimensions *Site*, *Warehouse* and *Batch number* are required in every transaction. For the warehouse dimension, separate financial inventory valuation should apply.

Exercise 7.2 – Item Model Group
In order to prepare the next exercise, create a new item model group T-## (## = your user ID) with FIFO valuation, assigning the inventory model "FIFO". The ledger integration for physical and financial inventory should be active. The item model group applies to stocked products and a negative financial inventory is allowed. All other checkboxes remain cleared, approved vendors are not required.

Then you want to set up a second item model group S-## for standard cost valuation, which got the same settings as the first group, except that the inventory model is "Standard cost" and a negative physical inventory is possible.

Exercise 7.3 – Product Record
Entering two new items in the released product form you want to examine the consequences of the settings in the dimension groups and the item model group:

➢ Item I-##-S applying standard cost valuation (item model group S-##)
➢ Item I-##-T applying FIFO valuation (item model group T-##)

For both items, the product subtype is "'Product" and the storage and the tracking dimension group are the groups you have set up in exercise 7.1. In addition, select an appropriate item group for merchandise and the unit of measure "Pieces". The item sales tax groups for purchasing and sales should refer to the standard tax rate. The base purchase price and the base cost price are 50 pounds, the base sales price is 100 pounds. For purchasing, inventory and sales, you should enter the main site in the *Default order settings* and the main warehouse of the main site in the *Site specific order settings*.

For the item I-##-S you need to register and activate a standard cost price. Enter a standard cost price of 50 pounds for the main site in the item price form.

Note: If a *Balancing financial dimension* applies, enter a default value for this dimension on the tab *Financial dimensions* of the released products.

Exercise 7.4 – Inventory Value of Transactions

Enter a purchase order referring to your vendor of exercise 3.2, which contains a line of 100 units of the first and 100 units of the second item entered in exercise 7.3. Enter 60 pounds in the purchase price of both order lines and confirm the purchase order.

Try to find out, if you may post a product receipt without inserting a batch number. Choosing the option *View details* in the batch number column, create the batch number B001 for both items in the batch table then. In the purchase order lines, insert this batch number afterwards.

Then post the product receipt and the invoice receipt for the complete quantity. If you look at the item transactions and the quantity on hand, can you explain the difference of the cost amount and the cost price of the two items?

Note: If required, show the column for the dimension *Batch number* in the order lines by clicking the button *Inventory/Dimensions display*.

7.3   Inventory Valuation

Based on the deep integration of the entire application, Dynamics AX provides a very accurate calculation of inventory values. Apart from the valuation methods for average costs or standard costs, an end-to-end FIFO or LIFO valuation is available as well.

The basis of inventory valuation is a simple principle:

➢ **Receipt costs** – Cost amounts are provided by the receipt transaction
➢ **Issue costs** – Cost amounts are calculated according to the valuation model

The cost amount of the issue transaction derives from the receipt transactions, which are linked to the issue according to the valuation model (FIFO, LIFO, average). It is not possible to enter the cost price and cost amount in an issue transaction.

Exceptions to this principle are the moving average valuation (for issue transactions keeping the average cost price shown at the time of posting) and the standard cost valuation. For the standard cost price, two different options are available:

➢ Fixed receipt price
➢ Standard cost

The option "Fixed receipt price" is available in combination with the valuation methods FIFO, LIFO and average cost. Applying this option fixes the receipt cost price in advance, preventing to change it when recording a transaction.

Unlike the fixed receipt price, the inventory model "Standard cost" provides true standard costs, immediately applying the standard cost price of an item for all issue and receipt transactions.

The difference between the methods "Standard cost" and "Fixed receipt price" shows, when changing the standard cost price of an item. Whereas the standard cost method immediately posts an adjustment of inventory value, the fixed receipt price method does not adjust the value of stock on hand. For this method, the new price only applies to new receipts – existing inventory will issue to the old price until it is consumed completely.

7.3.1   Valuation Method

Dynamics AX provides the following valuation methods – available in the field *Inventory model* of the item model group – for calculating the cost amount of issue transactions:

➢ FIFO
➢ LIFO
➢ LIFO date
➢ Weighted average
➢ Weighted average date
➢ Standard cost
➢ Moving average

7.3.1.1 Valuation of Item Receipts

Receipt transactions receive their financial value when posting the related financial transaction (invoice). Except for the standard cost method, the different transaction types therefore provide the receipt cost price and amount as follows:

➢ **Purchase order receipt** – Amount of the invoice line including related item charges, adding indirect costs from the costing sheet as applicable
➢ **Production receipt** – Actual cost amount of the production order (total cost of consumed BOM line items and resource time, including applicable indirect costs)
➢ **Sales return** – Original value of the returned item if assigned to an original sales order; otherwise return cost price entered in the return order
➢ **Other receipt** – Cost amount entered in the journal line

7.3.1.2 Valuation of Item Issues

The cost price and amount of item issues always complies with the average cost price when posting the transaction. The valuation method applies when closing inventory, determining the assignment of item receipts to item issues according to the inventory model (FIFO, LIFO or average).

Inventory closing calculates the cost price and amount of an issue transaction based on assigned receipts. The issue price and amount therefore is not final until you have posted the financial transaction (invoice) of all assigned receipts and inventory closing is finished.

As an exception, individual assignment of issue transactions to receipt transactions does not apply to following valuation methods:

➢ **Standard cost price** – The standard cost price ("Standard cost" or "Fixed receipt price") immediately applies to issue and receipt transactions.
➢ **Moving average** – Keeps the posted cost price of issue transactions and does not require inventory closing.

7.3.1.3 Standard Cost Price

For items of the inventory model "Standard cost", inventory closing is not required because all receipts and issues immediately post the standard cost price specified in the item price form (see section 7.2.4).

When activating a new standard cost price, Dynamics AX immediately applies an adjustment of inventory value for the current stock, which posts in inventory and in the general ledger. The new standard cost price therefore applies to issues of existing stock right away.

7.3.1.4 Fixed Receipt Price

The checkbox "Fixed receipt price" in the item model group applies in combination with the valuation methods FIFO, LIFO or average cost. When selecting this option, the cost price entered in the released product form or in the item price form specifies a fixed cost price for receipt transactions.

The cost price and cost amount are calculated according to the valuation method and – as long as you do not change the item cost price – always comply with the standard cost price of the item.

When changing the item cost price, consumption transactions immediately apply the new cost price. Since there is no posting of revaluation when changing a fixed receipt price, the financial value of existing stock however still complies with the old price. As a result, inventory closing is required for the option "Fixed receipt price" in order to adjust the cost amount of issue transactions to the old price according to the valuation method (until all inventory received with the old price has been consumed).

7.3.1.5 Moving Average Price

For items of the inventory model "Moving average", receipt transactions are posted with the price provided by the transaction (e.g. through a vendor invoice).

When posting an issue transaction, the average cost price at the time of posting applies. This cost price does not change through inventory closing.

If a vendor invoice refers to a purchase receipt, which is not completely on stock any more, for the quantity not on stock a difference between the physical cost amount and the financial cost amount of the purchase transaction is posted as an adjustment to a price difference account. For the quantity still on stock, posting the purchase invoice posts the total amount – including possible differences – to the financial cost amount.

7.3.1.6 Calculating Inventory Value

Following table shows an overview of the different valuation methods available in Dynamics AX:

Table 7-3:   Inventory models controlling the valuation methods in Dynamics AX

Inventory model	Explanation
FIFO *First In First Out*	Item issues refer to the oldest item receipt still on stock
LIFO *Last In First Out*	Item issues refer to the newest item receipt on stock available when closing inventory
LIFO date	Like LIFO, limiting the assignment of issues to receipts before the particular issue
Weighted average	The cost price of item issues in a period is the average cost price of all receipts (including the beginning balance) in this period (inventory closing period)
Weighted average date	The cost price of item issues is the average cost price calculated separately for each day
Standard cost	The cost price of item issues and receipts is equal to the active standard cost price of the item
Moving average	The cost price of item issues is the average cost price of the inventory quantity at the time of posting the issue

Table 7-4 shows a short example of the cost price calculation for the different valuation methods. Basis of the example are three receipt transactions with different cost prices and an issue transaction in between:

Table 7-4:   Posted transactions for comparing valuation methods

Date	Transaction	Quantity	Cost amount
July 1	Receipt	10	100
July 2	Receipt	10	200
July 3	Issue	10	(to be calculated)
July 4	Receipt	10	300

After inventory closing, the cost amount of the issue shows following figure depending on the valuation method:

Table 7-5:   Valuation of the item issue in Table 7-4

Inventory Model	Amount	Explanation
FIFO	100	From the receipt on July 1
LIFO	300	From the receipt on July 4
LIFO date	200	From the receipt on July 2
Weighted average	200	Average of all receipts
Weighted average date	150	From the receipts on July 1 and July 2
Moving average	150	Current average when posting the issue

In addition to the inventory model, the inventory dimension settings have got an impact on calculating the cost amount of an item issue. An assigning of issues and receipts is not possible across dimensions with a separate financial inventory according to the dimension group settings.

If separate financial inventory is activated for the dimension *Warehouse* for example, issues of a warehouse "20" only assign receipts to the warehouse "20" (including transfers). If separate financial inventory is not active for the dimension *Warehouse*, assignments comply with the date sequence independent from the warehouse in the transactions.

7.3.1.7   Inventory Marking

Marking is another option, influencing the automatic assignment according to the inventory model. Markings work like lots for inventory valuation, assigning the cost amount of a specific receipt to a specific issue – e.g. applicable to vendor returns (see section 3.7.1). If you want to mark a transaction, click the button *Inventory/Marking* in transactions inquiries, order lines or journal lines.

7.3.1.8   New in Dynamics AX 2012 R2

Compared with the initial version of Dynamics AX 2012, the R2 version contains the new valuation model "Moving average".

7.3.2   Inventory Closing and Adjustment

When posting an issue transaction, Dynamics AX always applies the average cost price (except for the standard cost model). In order to calculate the correct cost price and amount according to the valuation method (*Inventor model*) of the item, you have to close inventory. Only items assigned to the inventory model "Standard cost" or "Moving average" do not apply inventory closing.

You need to close inventory periodically – usually as part of the month closing procedure in finance – in order to show correct item costs in finance and to close inventory transactions. After closing inventory, it is not possible to post inventory transactions in the closed period any more. If you have to post a transaction in a closed period, cancel inventory closing.

7.3.2.1 Inventory Closing

For inventory closing, access the form *Inventory and warehouse management> Periodic> Closing and adjustment* which shows a list of previous closings. If you want to close a period there, click the button *Close procedure*.

The first and second option in the close procedure, checking open quantities and cost prices, generate reports to assess inventory transactions. You may run these reports to take corrective actions – e.g. in case of missing or wrong transactions – before actually closing a period. But it is not required to perform these steps.

In order to finally close an inventory period, click the button *Close procedure/3.Close* in the inventory closing form. Depending on the number of transactions, it might be useful to run closing as a batch job not within regular business hours.

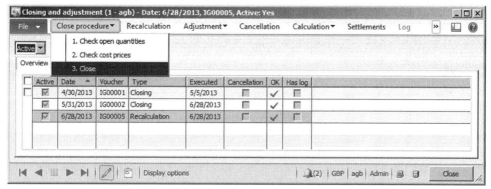

Figure 7-14:   The inventory closing and adjustment form

As a prerequisite for closing a period in inventory, the accounting period in the ledger calendar has to be open. As far as possible, you should post vendor invoices for all item receipts in purchasing, and end all production orders which are reported as finished. The corresponding product receipts in purchasing and production then show the financial cost amount (instead of the physical cost amount which shows before invoicing), minimizing the number of open transactions as far as possible.

After closing inventory, the posted adjustment transactions are available by clicking the button *Settlements* in the inventory closing form. If you have to cancel inventory closing, click the button *Cancellation*. The button *Recalculation* calculates and posts adjustment transactions like closing, but does not actually close a period.

7.3.2.2 Manual Adjustment of Inventory Value

If you want to adjust the inventory value of an item manually, click the button *Adjustment* in the inventory closing form. Choose the option *Adjustment/On-hand* for adjusting the cost price and cost amount of the current inventory quantity at the level of inventory dimensions. The other choice, the button *Adjustment/*

Transactions, provides the option to adjust the cost amount of individual receipt transactions.

In the adjustment form, click the button *Select* for choosing applicable items or transactions. In the selected records, enter a positive or negative adjustment amount. Alternatively, retrieve a proposal for the adjustment through the applicable option in the button *Adjustment*. Clicking the button *Post* in the adjustment form finally posts the adjustment.

7.3.3   Case Study Exercises

Exercise 7.5 – Valuation of Purchase Orders
You want to order 100 units of the first and 100 units of the second item of exercise 7.3 from your vendor of exercise 3.2. Enter an appropriate purchase order choosing the batch number B001 and a purchase price of GBP 80.00 in both order lines.

Once you have finished entering the order, confirm it and post the product receipt and the vendor invoice for the entire quantity. In the *Product receipt date* (on the tab *Setup* of the product receipt posting form) and in the *Posting date* (in the vendor invoice), enter the day after the posting date of exercise 7.4 (e.g. July 2, if exercise 7.4 has been on July 1).

After posting the invoice, check the inventory transactions as well as the inventory quantity and value (cost amount) of the two items.

Exercise 7.6 – Valuation of Sales Order
Your customer of exercise 4.1 orders 150 units of the first and 150 units of the second item of exercise 7.3. Enter an appropriate sales order choosing the batch number B001 in both order lines. Then post the sales invoice for the entire order quantity. In the *Invoice date* on the tab *Setup* of the posting form, enter the day after the posting date of exercise 7.5 (e.g. July 3, if exercise 7.5 has been on July 2).

After posting the invoice, check the inventory transactions as well as the inventory quantity and cost amount of the two items again.

Exercise 7.7 – Closing Inventory
Run a *Recalculation* in the inventory closing form in order to calculate the correct inventory value of your items according to the valuation method. In the recalculation form, select an appropriate filter restricting calculation to your items and set the recalculation date to the posting date of exercise 7.6 (e.g. July 3).

Then check the cost price and amount of the inventory transactions and the inventory quantity for the two items. Which changes are a caused by recalculation, can you explain the result?

7.4   Business Processes in Inventory

The only way for changing the inventory quantity of an item is to post an inventory transaction. Yet most business processes changing inventory quantity do not origin in inventory management, but refer to procedures in other functional areas like purchasing, sales or production. These procedures generate inventory transactions automatically in the background.

Descriptions of processes in these areas are available in the corresponding chapter of this book. The lines below therefore only cover business processes within inventory management itself.

7.4.1   Inventory Structures and Parameters

As a prerequisite for entering inventory transactions, the setup of inventory management has to be finished and required product records have to be available.

7.4.1.1 Warehouse and Location Structure

In order to represent the physical structure of inventory, Dynamics AX provides three storage dimensions for grouping inventory within a company: *Site*, *Warehouse* and *Location*. Depending on the applicable dimension group, you need to record these dimensions in an inventory transaction.

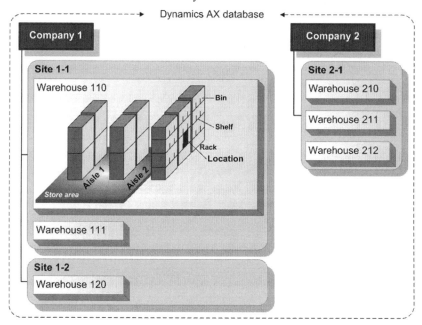

Figure 7-15:   Warehouse and location structure in Dynamics AX

Within one site, warehouses are the upper grouping level of inventory. Within one warehouse, the structure of locations may include the following elements (compare Figure 7-15):

➤ Aisle
➤ Rack
➤ Shelf
➤ Bin

In addition, group locations by store areas and store zones if applicable. An example for the use of store zones is the assignment of frozen products to chilled locations by entering the applicable store zone on the tab *Locations* of the warehouse items form (accessible by clicking the button *Warehouse/Warehouse items* on the action pane tab *Manage inventory* of the released product form).

7.4.1.2 Warehouse Management

For setting up a new warehouse, access the form *Inventory and warehouse management> Setup> Inventory breakdown> Warehouses*. When inserting a new warehouse by clicking the button *New*, enter the warehouse ID and the name. Then enter a *Site* in order to link the warehouse to a site.

In the lookup field *Type*, specify if the warehouse is a regular warehouse ("Default"), a quarantine warehouse, or a transit warehouse. Quarantine warehouses are used for quarantine orders (see section 7.4.4), and transit warehouses for transfer orders (see section 7.4.5).

The tab *Master planning* contains specific settings for the warehouse referring to master planning. The tabs *Warehouse management* and *Location names* control warehouse locations.

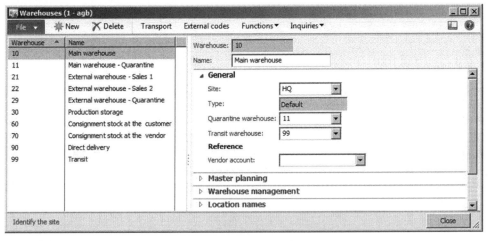

Figure 7-16:   Managing warehouses in the warehouse form

7.4.1.3 Locations

The further organization of warehouses including aisles and locations as well as the setup and assignment of store areas and store zones is available in the items of the menu path *Inventory and warehouse management> Setup> Inventory breakdown*. A detailed description of location and pallet management in inventory is beyond the scope of this book, however.

7.4.1.4 Storage Dimensions

When setting up warehouse structures, be aware that the storage dimension group of the individual released product controls, which inventory dimensions apply to a particular inventory transaction. If you need locations for a particular warehouse, the storage dimension groups of all involved items have to contain an active dimension *Location*. Since this setting activates locations for all warehouses, you need to set up at least one (pseudo-)location for each warehouse in this case.

7.4.1.5 Inventory Parameters and Journal Setup

If you want to enter a manual transaction in inventory, you have to register it in a journal. Apart from warehouse structures, inventory journals therefore are another required setup. They consist of two different groups:

➢ Inventory journals
➢ Warehouse management journals

Inventory journals apply to registering general transactions like item receipt, item issue, item transfer, and inventory counting. In order to configure inventory journals, access the form *Inventory and warehouse management> Setup> Journals> Journal names, inventory*. You have to set up at least one journal name for the *Journal type* "Movement", "Inventory adjustment", "Transfer", "BOM" and "Counting", before you can enter and post corresponding transactions. Assigning an appropriate number sequence in the lookup *Voucher series* enables separate number sequences for different journals.

Warehouse management journals as the other group of journals apply to registering item receipts from vendors and – for item returns – customers in item arrival journals, and item receipts of finished goods in production. For configuring warehouse management journals, access the form *Inventory and warehouse management> Setup> Journals> Journal names, warehouse management*.

Inventory parameters are available in the form *Inventory and warehouse management> Setup> Inventory and warehouse management parameters*. Among others, they contain settings for number sequences, the default unit of measure, the default calculation group, and defaults for journal names. On the tab *Inventory dimensions*, choose the dimensions which display as default per journal.

7.4.2 Journal Transactions

You have to use an inventory journal, if you want to record a transaction independent from other functional areas like purchasing, sales or production.

7.4.2.1 Journal Structure

Since inventory transactions affect financial values, the voucher principle applies: In a first step, the journal has to be entered, before it is possible to post it in a second step. Every journal consists of a journal header and at least one line.

Inventory journals in Dynamics AX show a common structure with following journal types for the different kinds of transactions:

➢ Movement
➢ Inventory adjustment
➢ Transfer
➢ Bills of materials
➢ Item arrival
➢ Production input
➢ Counting
➢ Tag counting

7.4.2.2 Movement Journals and Inventory Adjustment Journals

If you want to record manual item issues or receipts in inventory, either use a journal of the type "Movement" or a journal of the type "Inventory adjustment".

The difference between movement journals and inventory adjustment journals is that movement journals show the field *Offset account*. The offset account contains the expense or revenue account for the item receipt or consumption.

In inventory adjustment journals, the offset account derives from the inventory posting setup and does not show in the journal lines. Therefore, choose a movement journal for example if you want to post an item consumption of a department referring to a specific main account.

Section 7.1.2 at the beginning of this chapter explains how to register and to post an inventory adjustment journal.

For registering a movement journal, insert a new record in the form *Inventory and warehouse management> Journals> Item transactions> Movement*. In the field *Offset account* on the tab *General* of the journal header, optionally enter a default for the offset account in the journal lines. After switching to the lines, enter one or more lines with posting date, item number, appropriate inventory dimension values, and quantity (negative for item issues) as applicable. For item receipts, the cost price is editable (receiving its default from the item). Finally post the movement after making sure to apply the right main accounts in the column *Offset account*, and appropriate financial dimension values on the tab *Financial dimensions*.

7.4.2.3 Transfer Journals

Unlike movement journals and inventory adjustment journals, which record issues and receipts, transfer journals are used for registering the transfer of product inventory from one dimension combination to another. In most cases, this is the transfer from one warehouse or location to another. But you may also post a transfer to change the batch or serial number.

For registering an item transfer, open the form *Inventory and warehouse management> Journals> Item transactions> Transfer*. In addition to the data entered in inventory adjustment journal lines, enter the applicable inventory dimensions to which the item should be transferred.

Entering the *Quantity* with a negative sign issues the item from the "from-dimensions" and receives it at the "to-dimensions".

7.4.2.4 BOM Journals

Bill of materials journals, accessible through the menu item *Inventory and warehouse management> Journals> Item transactions> Bills of materials*, provide the option to post a receipt of a finished items while consuming the components at the same time. Entering a negative quantity enables posting the disassembly of a finished item.

Unlike the proceeding for other journals, you do not need to enter journal lines manually in a bill of materials journal. In order to create journal lines, click the button *BOM/Report as finished* in action pan strip of the BOM journal lines.

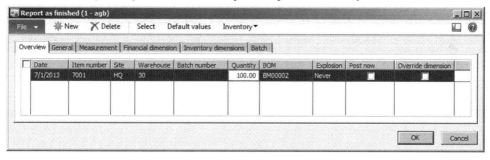

Figure 7-17:   Report as finished form, opened from the bill of materials journal

In the report as finished form, create a line – e.g. pushing the shortcut key *Ctrl+N* – and select the finished item which you want to receive in inventory. If you put a checkmark in the column *Post now*, the bill of materials journal will immediately post once you close the report as finished form by clicking the button *OK*. If the checkbox *Post now* is cleared, the finished item and its component lines show in the bill of materials journal lines, where you may edit them before posting.

7.4.2.5 Item Arrival Journals

Item arrival journals, accessible through the menu item *Inventory and warehouse management> Journals> Item arrival> Item arrival*, provide the option to post item receipts related to purchase orders (see section 3.5.3) or customer returns (see section 4.6.4). Production input journals, which are similar to item arrival journals, apply to production order receipts.

Entering an item arrival journal works similar to entering an inventory journal. For registering the reference to the purchase order, switch to the tab *Default values* in the journal header, and select the order number in the field *Number* after choosing the option "Purchase order" in the lookup field *Reference*. For customer returns, enter the *Reference* "Sales order" and the *RMA number*. Clicking the button

Functions/Create lines in the journal header then provides the option to default items and open quantity from the order lines to the journal lines.

For posting the arrival journal, click the button *Post* after entering all lines. Unlike inventory journals, which immediately post physical and financial transactions, arrival journals require posting the product receipt and the vendor invoice of the corresponding purchase order to generate physical and financial transactions.

If you want to apply warehouse transactions with locations and pallets, select appropriate checkboxes in the arrival journal header (tab *Default values*, field group *Mode of handling*).

7.4.3   Inventory Counting

In order to determine the actual quantity in inventory, you have to physically execute inventory counting (stocktaking) in the warehouse. Depending on legal and other requirements, periodical item counting might be required for making sure that the posted quantity complies with the actually counted quantity.

In Dynamics AX, item counting is done in inventory journals for item counting. When posting the item counting journal, the difference between the counted quantity and the quantity in Dynamics AX posts as an item issue or receipt – similar to the transactions in an inventory adjustment journal.

Since the counting difference is calculated as of the date entered in the counting journal line, you do not need to stop other transactions in inventory while counting. But if required because of organizational issues, lock inventory while counting (*Lock items during count* on the tab *General* of the inventory parameters).

7.4.3.1   Counting Journal

For registering a new counting journal, insert a journal header in the form *Inventory and warehouse management> Journals> Item counting> Counting*. When creating the journal header, you have to choose the inventory dimensions which are the basis for the counting journal. In the lines, there are two options for registering inventory counting:

➢ Manual registration
➢ Automatically creating counting lines

If you want to enter a counting journal line manually, insert a line with counting date, item number, warehouse and applicable dimensions like in any other inventory journal. The counted quantity has to be entered in the column *Counted*. The column *On-hand* then shows the corresponding current inventory quantity in Dynamics AX as of the counting date. The difference between the counted and the on-hand quantity shows in the column *Quantity*, which also is the quantity of the issue or receipt transaction posted when posting the inventory journal.

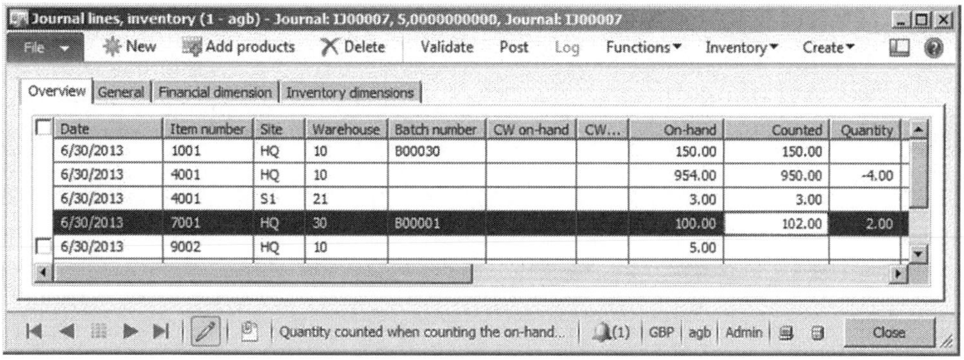

Figure 7-18:   Entering the counted quantity in a counting journal line

If you want to create counting lines automatically instead of manually entering them, click the button *Create/On-hand* in the action pane strip of the counting journal lines. In the *Create on-hand counting journal* dialog, select a filter for the lines – e.g. for counting on a particular warehouse. Additional parameters in the dialog enable to restrict counting for example on items and inventory dimensions, which show an inventory transaction after the last inventory counting.

Once you have finished creating counting journal lines manually or automatically, print a counting list by clicking the button *Print/Counting list* in the counting journal header if required (before or after entering the counted quantity).

7.4.3.2 Counting Groups

In order to support the selection of items when automatically creating counting lines, you can filter on counting groups in the *Create counting journal* dialog. Counting groups contain settings like the *Counting code*, which controls when to execute counting (periodically, when equal or below minimum stock, or when reaching zero stock). You may set up counting groups in the form *Inventory and warehouse management> Setup> Inventory> Counting groups* and assign items in the released product form (tab *Manage inventory*) or in the warehouse items form (button *Warehouse/Warehouse items* on the action pane tab *Manage inventory* of the released product form).

In order to apply counting code settings when automatically creating counting lines, select the checkbox *Activate counting code* in the *Create counting journal* dialog.

7.4.3.3 Tag Counting

Tag counting (*Inventory and warehouse management> Journals> Item counting> Tag counting*) is an option to pre-register counting lines. The principle of tag counting is to attach numbered tags to the warehouse locations. When counting physically, write the item number, the quantity, and applicable dimensions like warehouse and serial number on each tag. Then collect the tags and register them in the tag-counting journal. When posting the tag-counting journal, there is no posting of inventory transactions, but a transfer of the lines to a regular counting journal.

7.4.4   Quarantine and Inventory Blocking

If you want to exclude a particular quantity of an item from available stock – for example because of the test results in quality control – you can alternatively use following functionality in Dynamics AX:

➢ Quarantine Management
➢ Inventory Blocking

Inventory blocking manually or automatically generates a temporary transaction, usually for quality inspection.

Quarantine management is based on quarantine orders, which post a transfer to a quarantine warehouse. For this purpose, quarantine orders are generated automatically with every item receipt, or manually when required. When working with quarantine warehouses you have to take into account, that quarantine locks items only by posting a quarantine order, and not by simply posting an inventory transfer to the quarantine warehouse.

7.4.4.1 Setup for Quarantine Management

As a prerequisite for working with quarantine in Dynamics AX, you have to set up at least one warehouse of the type "Quarantine". In the warehouse form (*Inventory and warehouse management> Setup> Inventory breakdown> Warehouses*), additionally assign a quarantine warehouse to each regular warehouse with quarantine if you want to use automatic quarantine for item receipts.

Automatic quarantine applies to released products, for which the checkbox *Quarantine management* is selected in the corresponding item model group.

7.4.4.2 Manual Quarantine

For manually locking a particular quantity in inventory, open the form *Inventory and warehouse management> Periodic> Quality management> Quarantine orders*. The quarantine order form shows a list of open quarantine orders, selecting the checkbox *View ended* you may also view ended quarantine.

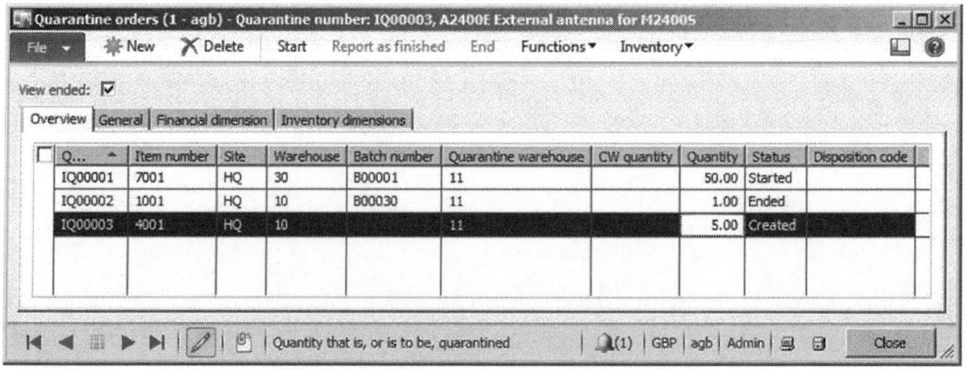

Figure 7-19:   Managing quarantine in the quarantine order form

For creating a quarantine order, insert a record with item number, quantity, warehouse and applicable dimensions. The default for the quarantine warehouse in the line derives from the quarantine warehouse of the initial warehouse in the quarantine order. All other inventory dimensions for quarantine by default are equal to the initial dimension values of the quarantine order. If you want to change quarantine dimensions, display appropriate storage dimension columns by clicking the button *Inventory/Dimensions display*, or switch to the tab *Inventory dimensions*.

Clicking the button *Start* in the quarantine order form transfers the quantity to quarantine. Transfer to quarantine includes moving the item to the quarantine warehouse and reserving it for quarantine in order to block issue transactions. In parallel to the quarantine transaction, Dynamics AX generates a second inventory transaction without date for the future re-transfer to the original warehouse.

If you want to partly or completely scrap an item in quarantine later, click the button *Functions/Scrap*.

In order to end quarantine with or without prior scrapping of a partial quantity, click the button *End* in the quarantine order form. Ending quarantine posts the re-transfer to the original warehouse and makes the quantity available again.

Clicking the button *Report as finished* in the quarantine order posts the completion of inspections as an intermediate step. The item is not available in inventory before ending the quarantine order, which is why you want to apply this step only if you separately post pallet transports in warehouse management.

7.4.4.3 Automatic Quarantine

When posting item arrival journals, production input journals or product receipts, Dynamics AX automatically creates and starts quarantine orders for items, which are assigned to an item model group with *Quarantine management* selected. The further proceeding of quarantine works similar to manual quarantine.

7.4.4.4 Inventory Blocking

Inventory blocking usually applies in combination with quality orders in Dynamics AX quality management. But you can also execute manual inventory blocking without applying the quality management functionality.

In order to manually block an item, access the form *Inventory and warehouse management> Periodic> Inventory blocking* and insert a record registering item number, quantity and – on the tab *Inventory dimensions* – applicable dimensions. If you expect the item to become available again (like a quarantine order), select the checkbox *Expected receipts*. Depending on the expected receipt, Dynamics AX generates one or two inventory transactions showing "Inventory blocking" in the column *Reference*. In order to end inventory blocking, simply delete the particular line in the inventory blocking form.

7.4.4.5   New in Dynamics AX 2012

Inventory blocking is a new feature in Dynamics AX 2012.

7.4.5   Transfer Orders

Whereas inventory transfer journals are there for transferring items immediately without shipping documents, transfer orders provide the option to consider transport time and to print shipping documents.

7.4.5.1   Setup for Transfer Orders

As a prerequisite for working with transfer orders, you have to set up at least one warehouse of the type "Transit". This transit warehouse receives the items during the transport time. In the warehouse form, additionally assign a transit warehouse to each regular warehouse as a default for transits. If items apply the storage dimension *Location*, you should specify a *Default receipt location* and a *Default issue location* for the transit warehouse in the warehouse form.

Optionally, delivery date control applies to transfer orders (similar to sales orders, see section 4.4.3).

7.4.5.2   Processing Transfer Orders

In order to enter a transfer order, access the form *Inventory and warehouse management> Periodic> Transfer orders* and click the button *New* in the action pane strip. The transfer order consists of a header, where you have to enter the *From warehouse* and the *To warehouse*, and transfer order lines.

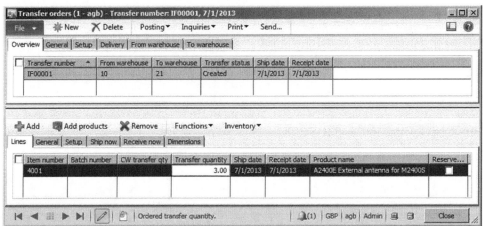

Figure 7-20:   Registering a line in a transfer order

After selecting the *From warehouse* in the header, the transfer order retrieves the related transit warehouse. In the transfer order lines, enter one or more lines with item number, transfer quantity and inventory dimensions as applicable then. Similar to sales order processing, alternatively execute picking (see section 4.5.2) or immediately post the shipment.

If you want to post the shipment, click the button *Posting/Ship transfer order*. In the upper pane of the *Shipment* posting form, choose the option "All" in the column *Update* for shipping the complete quantity (or, depending on the previous steps, choose the picked or the ship-now quantity) and then select the checkbox in the column *Edit lines*. The checkbox *Print transfer shipment* enables printing a shipping document. Clicking the button *OK* in the posting form posts a transfer to the transit warehouse.

When receiving the item at the destination warehouse, process the receipt – optionally posting separate inventory registration or item arrival before – similar to a purchase order receipt.

For posting the transfer receipt, click the button *Posting/Receive* in the transfer order form (similar to the product receipt in purchasing). In the *Receive* posting form, choose the option "All" in the column *Update* (or, depending on previous steps, choose the registered or the receive-now quantity) and select the checkbox *Edit lines*. Clicking the button *OK* in the posting form then posts a transfer from the transit warehouse to the final warehouse.

7.4.6 Case Study Exercises

Exercise 7.8 – Journal Transaction
In the main warehouse, you find 100 units of the item I-##, which you have set up in exercise 3.5. Post an appropriate transaction in an inventory adjustment journal.

Exercise 7.9 – Transfer Journal
You want to transfer the quantity received in exercise 7.8 to another warehouse. Register an appropriate inventory transfer journal and post it. After posting, check the transactions and the quantity of your item on the selected warehouse.

Exercise 7.10 – Inventory Counting
You want to execute inventory counting on the main warehouse for the item I-##, which you have set up in exercise 3.5. The counted quantity is 51 units. You may create a counting journal line either registering it manually or automatically generating it, filtering on your item and the main warehouse. After entering the counted quantity, post the journal and check the quantity on hand.

Exercise 7.11 – Manual Quarantine
Because of reported quality issues, you want to execute a quality check of the quantity you have transferred in exercise 7.9. Enter a manual quarantine order, choosing an appropriate quarantine warehouse. Check the quantity on hand of your item and start the quarantine order. After performing quality inspection, end quarantine and check the inventory quantity before and after ending.

Exercise 7.12 – Transfer Order

You want to transfer 60 units of the item relocated in exercise 7.9 back to the main warehouse by processing a transfer order. Before entering the transfer order, make sure a transit warehouse is assigned to the warehouse from where the item ships. Then register an appropriate transfer order and post the shipment. After posting, check the inventory transactions as well as the inventory quantity of your item on all warehouses. Finally, receive the item transfer at the main warehouse.

8 Finance Administration

The primary responsibility of finance administration is to control and to analyze all value-based transactions of an enterprise. These transactions occur in business processes all over the organization, including both transactions only within the enterprise and transactions with external parties.

Finance management therefore is the core area of business management solutions. In Dynamics AX, a deep integration of the application supporting business processes in all departments grants accurate financial figures, available immediately.

8.1 Principles of Ledger Transactions

Before we start to go into details, the lines below show the principles of ledger transactions.

8.1.1 Basic Approach

The core task of finance is to manage accounts in the general ledger, constituting the basis for balance sheet and income statement (profit and loss statement). In addition to the general ledger, accounting keeps subledgers like accounts receivables, accounts payables, fixed assets, projects and inventory. These subledgers contain detailed data supporting particular parts of the general ledger. In inventory as example of a subledger, inventory transactions show details of changes in stock account balances.

When posting to subledgers, every value-based transaction in Dynamics AX – an invoice in sales as well as a counting difference in inventory – also generates a transaction in the general ledger. Posting a sales order invoice for example affects following areas:

➢ **Inventory** – Item transaction
➢ **Accounts receivable** – Customer debt
➢ **General ledger** – Stock account, revenue account, account for COGS, customer summary account

Ledger integration, which is a core characteristic of Dynamics AX, provides traceability of all financial vouchers back to the origin in other modules. Depending on settings for transfer, subledger transactions are immediately posted to the general ledger, keeping the general ledger always up-to-date.

As a basis for ledger integration, Dynamics AX comprehensively applies the voucher principle to transactions: Throughout the whole application, you have to register a voucher before you can post it. After posting, it is not possible to modify the voucher any more.

8.1.2   At a glance: Ledger Journal Transactions

In order to record manual ledger transactions in Dynamics AX, you have to register a journal. The lines below show how to post a single-line transaction, similar to processing an inventory journal (see section 7.1.2).

After accessing the form *General ledger> Journals> General journal*, you have to register a voucher header before you may enter journal lines. For this purpose, insert a new record by clicking the button *New* or pushing the shortcut key *Ctrl+N* in the journal header and select a journal name in the column *Name*. In the column *Description*, optionally enter a text explaining the transaction. If sales tax (VAT) applies, the corresponding checkbox on the tab *Setup* of the journal header controls whether the amount in the debit or credit column of journal lines includes tax.

Then click the button *Lines* in the journal header in order to switch to the journal lines. For registering a simple ledger transaction in the journal lines, leave the default option "Ledger" in the column *Account type* and select the account number – according to segmented entry control including applicable financial dimensions – in the column *Account*. If you want to post to a subledger, choose the appropriate account type and corresponding account number – e.g. "Vendor" in the *Account type* and the vendor number in the *Account* for accounts payable.

In a single-line transaction, enter the offset account (including applicable financial dimensions) directly in the journal line.

Once you have finished registering the line, post the journal by clicking the button *Post/Post* in the journal header or lines.

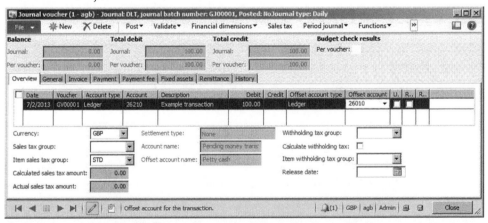

Figure 8-1:   Registering a general journal line (referring to an account structure without dimensions)

8.2   Setting up Finance

Since finance in Dynamics AX contains core settings of the application, you have to complete the basic finance configuration before setting up other modules and before posting a transaction in any part of the application.

This basic configuration includes the following elements:

➢ Fiscal and ledger calendar
➢ Currencies and exchange rates
➢ Chart of accounts

In Dynamics AX 2012, charts of accounts (including applicable main accounts), fiscal calendars, and currencies/exchange rates can be shared across multiple companies.

For this purpose, assign the appropriate shared chart of accounts, fiscal calendar, and accounting currency to your company in the ledger form. But if applicable, you can keep a separate chart of accounts or fiscal calendar at company level by choosing a different assignment per company.

8.2.1   Fiscal and Ledger Calendars

The primary purpose of fiscal calendars is to determine the fiscal year, providing the start date and the end date for financial periods. The ledger calendar – based on the fiscal calendar – then controls at company level which financial periods are open for transactions.

8.2.1.1   Fiscal Calendar

Fiscal calendars are shared across all companies within a common Dynamics AX database and partition. For assigning the applicable fiscal calendar to the current company, enter it in the field *Fiscal calendar* of the ledger form (*General ledger> Setup> Ledger*) in the course of the initial setup of the company.

Accounting periods within the fiscal years of a fiscal calendar are limited by their start date and end date. When setting up a period, you are free to choose any period length according to your specific requirements.

For editing fiscal calendars, access the form *General ledger> Setup> Fiscal calendars*. In order to create a new fiscal calendar there, click the button *New fiscal calendar* and enter a calendar identification as well as applicable settings for the first fiscal year. If you want to add a fiscal year to an existing fiscal calendar, select the particular calendar and click the button *New fiscal year*. A dialog box then provides the option to enter start date, end date, period length, and unit – be sure to select the unit "Months" if you want to create monthly periods. Clicking the button *OK* in the dialog box then creates the accounting periods.

8.2.1.2 Closing and Opening Periods

Apart from regular operating periods showing the *Type* "Operating", there are two specific period types not available for posting regular transactions: *Closing periods* and *Opening periods*. Dynamics AX 2012 provides the option to attach multiple closing periods to each regular operating period if required.

Closing periods contain period-end or year-end transactions. Registration and posting of these transactions is only possible in closing sheets (*General ledger> Periodic> Fiscal year close> Closing sheet*).

Opening periods contain the opening transactions for a fiscal year, which are transferred in the form *General ledger> Periodic> Fiscal year close> Opening transactions* after closing a year.

8.2.1.3 Ledger Calendar

As a prerequisite for posting a transaction in Dynamics AX, the posting date of the transaction has to be included in an applicable ledger period with the period status "Open". The required period status is controlled at company level in the ledger calendar, not in the shared fiscal calendar.

The ledger calendar itself is based on the accounting periods of the fiscal calendar, which is assigned to your company in the ledger form. In order to access the ledger calendar, open the ledger form (*General ledger> Setup> Ledger*) and click the button *Ledger calendar* in the action pane there.

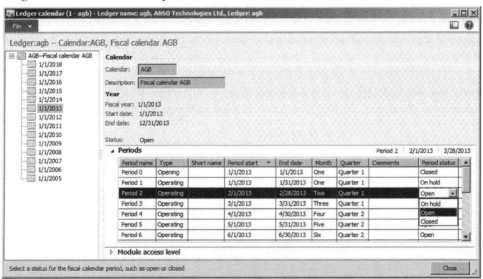

Figure 8-2:   Managing the period status in the ledger calendar

After selecting a fiscal year in the left pane of the ledger calendar form, open or close corresponding periods in the column *Period status* as applicable (scroll to the rightmost column on the tab *Periods*).

The period status "Open" enables posting of transactions in the period, whereas the period status "On hold" blocks posting. The status "Closed" also blocks posting – but unlike periods on hold, closed periods are not available for reopening. Therefore, the status "Closed" should only apply if a period is definitely closed in accounting after reporting to the authorities.

The tab *Module access level* provides the option to set blocking per module and to except user groups from blocking.

8.2.1.4 New in Dynamics AX 2012

Items new in Dynamics AX 2012 referring to ledger periods include shared fiscal calendars and the option of multiple closing periods.

8.2.2   Currencies and Exchange Rates

Every value-based transaction refers to currencies – general ledger transactions just the same as subledger transactions like inventory or customer transactions. A transaction is always recorded in the accounting currency of your company, and sometimes additionally in a foreign currency. Currencies therefore are a main requirement before you can post any transaction in Dynamics AX.

8.2.2.1 Currencies

In order to facilitate currency management in multi-company organizations, the currency table is shared across all companies within a common Dynamics AX database and partition. In addition, Dynamics AX by default contains present major currencies.

For accessing the currencies form, choose the menu item *General ledger> Setup> Currency> Currencies*. Apart from currency code and name, major settings for a currency include the definition of the rounding precision on the tab *Rounding rules*.

The tab *Currency converter* contains the setting for including the particular currency in the online currency conversion tool (see below).

8.2.2.2 Exchange Rates

Exchange rate types (*General ledger> Setup> Currency> Exchange rate types*) in Dynamics AX 2012 provide the option to manage multiple exchange rates per currency in parallel. Different exchange rates are for example required, if you want to use other rates for budget entries than for current transactions.

For accessing the *Currency exchange rates* form, choose the menu item *General ledger> Setup> Currency> Currency exchange rates* or click the button *Exchange rates* in the *Exchange rate types* form.

After selecting an *Exchange rate type* at the top of the currency exchange rates form (see Figure 8-3), view or add appropriate currency relations in the left pane. The *Quotation unit* specifies the applicable factor for exchange rate calculation.

After selecting a currency relation in the left pane, the right pane shows the exchange rates in chronological order. The filter *From date* and *To date* determines the date range for displaying exchange rates. The bottom line of the right pane shows the conversion result, providing the option to check if exchange rates are entered the right way.

In daily business, you have to continuously enter or import new exchange rates in order to ensure correct currency conversion. Usually, the exchange rates include a line without a start date applicable for currency conversion of transactions before the start date of data entry for currency conversion.

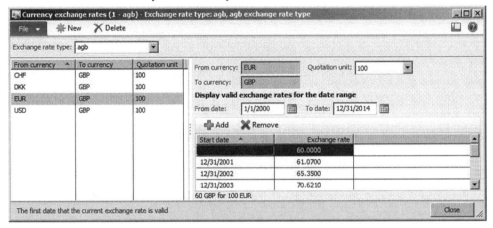

Figure 8-3:   Managing exchange rates in the currency exchange rates form

Currency exchange rates and exchange rate types are shared across all companies. But if required, you can keep exchange rates at company level by choosing a different exchange rate type per company in the ledger form.

8.2.2.3   Currency Settings in the Ledger Form

The ledger form (*General ledger> Setup> Ledger*) determines the *Accounting currency* of your company. All financial transactions are posted in this currency, which may not be modified once transactions are registered in the particular company. If you need to change the local currency later (e.g. converting to a new currency in your country), specific conversion tools are required.

Concerning exchange rate conversion, the ledger form contains the *Default exchange rate type* determining the exchange rate type for regular transactions. In addition, a separate default for budget transactions is available.

The lower part of the ledger form contains the main accounts for posting exchange rate gains and losses in your company.

8.2.2.4   Currency Converter

Transaction forms in Dynamics AX, which may contain transactions in foreign currencies (e.g. purchase orders or bank transactions), apart from fields for the transaction amount always contain a corresponding field for entering the currency code of the transaction.

Fields for entering or viewing amounts in the accounting currency do not show a corresponding currency code field. For these fields, the currency converter enables viewing the amount in a different currency (e.g. in the currency of a parent company).

The currency converter dialog is accessible by double-clicking the currency field in the status bar. In the dialog, select the applicable currency with a second double-click. Figure 8-4 for example shows the *Credit limit* in the preview pane at the bottom in US-dollars after selecting "USD" in the currency converter.

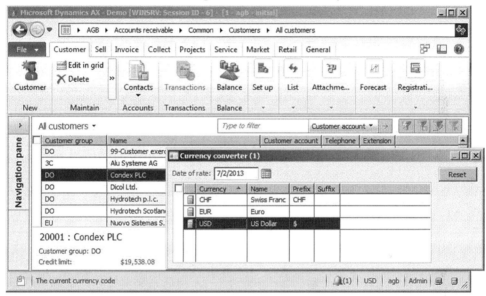

Figure 8-4:   Applying the online currency conversion feature

The currency field in the status bar shows, which currency presently applies to displaying amounts. The currency converter is limited to displaying amounts – if selecting a particular field with a mouse-click for editing, the amount in this field shows in accounting currency. Therefore, all amounts entered in applicable fields are in accounting currency.

In order to reset currency conversion, open the currency converter dialog again and click the button *Reset*. The currency converter only shows currencies, for which the currency converter has been enabled in the currencies form (see above).

8.2.2.5   New in Dynamics AX 2012

In Dynamics AX 2012, currencies are shared across legal entities. Exchange rate types enable maintaining different exchange rates in parallel.

8.2.3 Financial Dimensions

In addition to the main accounts specified in the chart of accounts, financial dimensions provide further levels for structuring financial transactions. Depending on the account structures assigned to your company, you are required to enter dimension values for financial dimensions – e.g. recording the cost center – when posting transactions.

Based on the posted dimension values, financial analysis and reports are not only available at company level, but also at the level of financial dimensions. This is also important for the multisite functionality: Assigning a financial dimension to the inventory dimension "Site" (see section 9.1.7) for example enables reporting the income statement for subsidiaries within a legal entity.

8.2.3.1 Managing Financial Dimensions

In Dynamics AX 2012, financial dimensions and dimension values are shared across all companies within a common Dynamics AX database and partition.

Financial dimensions are not limited to standard dimensions like department, cost center and purpose. You may easily set up as many financial dimensions as required. Taking into account practical consequences like structural clearness, probability of wrong entries and effort for registration, you should not set up and apply more dimensions as needed, however.

For setting up a new financial dimension, access the menu item *General ledger> Setup> Financial dimensions> Financial dimensions* and insert a record by clicking the button *New*. The lookup field *Use values from* then specifies the origin of related financial dimension values:

➢ **<Custom dimension>** – Creating a dimension not referring to other areas of the application.
➢ **One of the other options** – Linking the dimension to other entities of the application like customers, item groups or operating units.

If selecting the option "Departments" in the lookup field *Use values from* for example, the financial dimension is linked to operating units of the type "Department". In this case, all departments entered in the organization management (*Organization administration> Setup> Organization> Operating units*) are automatically financial dimension values for the dimension.

If selecting the option "<Custom dimension>" in the lookup field *Use values from*, the financial dimension values have to be entered manually after clicking the button *Financial dimension values*.

8.2.3.2 Financial Dimension Values

For custom dimensions, new records with dimension value and description are entered in the financial dimension values form. The lookup field *Select level of dimension value to display* determines whether data on the other tabs apply to all

companies ("Shared value"). If selecting the option "Companies", click the button
[+ ▾] near the field *Companies* for applying a particular company.

If you want to prevent future transactions referring to a particular dimension value
at the selected level, select the checkbox *Suspended* or enter an appropriate *Active
from* or *Active to* date.

In the financial dimension values form, it is not possible to create records for
financial dimensions which are not custom dimensions. But for all dimensions, it is
possible to edit dimension value settings like suspending a value at shared or at
company level.

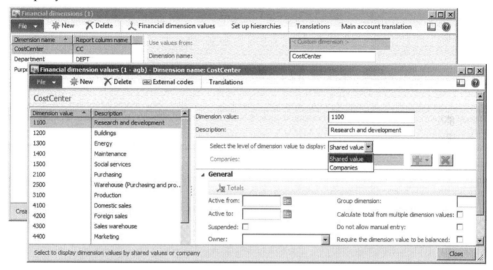

Figure 8-5:   Managing financial dimension values for a custom dimension

8.2.3.3 Applying Financial Dimensions

Once a financial dimension is created, it has to be included in account structures or
advanced rule structures applying to your company before you can use it in
transactions and inquiries. In addition, the account structures and applicable
advanced rule structures specify if and which dimension value is optional or
required when posting to a particular account.

On forms for editing master data like main accounts, customers or items (released
products), the tab *Financial dimensions* shows all financial dimensions included in
account structures and advanced rule structures applying to your company.
Dimension values entered there apply as default dimension value when registering
an order or a journal line.

When registering a transaction in a ledger journal line or any other form containing
a ledger account field, financial dimensions are not available as separate fields.
According to segmented entry control (see section 8.3.2), you have to enter
financial dimensions together with the main account in one – segmented – field.

8.2.3.4   Balancing Financial Dimension and Interunit Accounting

Interunit accounting, an optional feature in Dynamics AX 2012 R2, ensures a balanced balance sheet for a selected financial dimension – the balancing dimension. If you want to use interunit accounting, provide following settings:

➤ **Accounts for automatic transactions** – Enter appropriate main accounts for the *Posting type* "Interunit-debit" and "Interunit-credit" in the accounts for automatic transactions (see section 8.2.4 below).
➤ **Balancing financial dimension** – Select the balancing dimension in the ledger form.

If the field *Balancing financial dimension* in the ledger form is not empty, you have to provide a dimension value for this dimension when posting any transaction. If the from-value and the to-value for the balancing dimension are different in a transaction, Dynamics AX posts additional balancing transactions to the main accounts "Interunit-debit" and "Interunit-credit". This applies for example in a transaction from one department to another, if departments are the balancing dimension.

8.2.3.5   New in Dynamics AX 2012 and in AX 2012 R2

In Dynamics AX 2012, financial dimensions are shared across legal entities and provide the option to easily add dimensions as well as to populate dimension values from other tables. Account structures specify which financial dimensions apply and segmented entry control changes the way to enter dimension values.

Compared with the initial version of Dynamics AX 2012, the R2 version additionally contains the balancing financial dimension for interunit accounting.

8.2.4   Account Structures and Charts of Accounts

Account structures and charts of accounts are basic master data for structuring financial transactions in Dynamics AX.

In Dynamics AX 2012, charts of accounts and main accounts are shared across companies. Choosing a specific chart of accounts in the ledger form determines applicable main accounts for the current company. The assignment of account structures controls applicable financial dimensions.

8.2.4.1   Ledger Account and Main Account

When entering a financial transaction, the ledger account is composed of the main account and financial dimensions. The applicable account structure controls which financial dimensions are included in the ledger account.

8.2.4.2   Charts of Accounts

For accessing all charts of accounts in your enterprise, choose the menu item *General ledger> Setup> Chart of Accounts> Chart of Accounts*. Depending on the structure of your organization and the number of legal entities, the left pane of the carts of accounts form shows one or more charts of accounts. The right pane of the form contains the main accounts of the chart of accounts selected in the left pane.

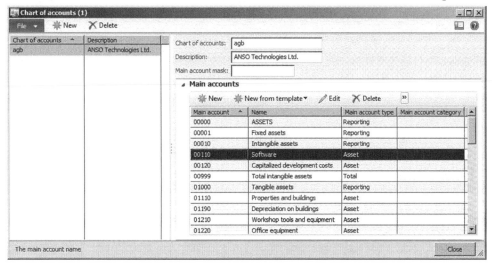

Figure 8-6:   Managing charts of accounts in the chart of accounts form

Clicking the button *New* or *Edit* on the tab *Main accounts* of the chart of accounts form opens the main accounts form, where you can insert or modify the main accounts of the selected chart of accounts as described further below.

<u>Note</u>: The charts of accounts form in the original release of Dynamics AX 2012 also contains a tab for assigning account structures. In Dynamics AX 2012 R2, this assignment is replaced by the assignment at company level in the ledger form.

8.2.4.3   Settings in the Ledger Form

Settings in the ledger form (*General ledger> Setup> Ledger*) determine the chart of accounts and the account structures applicable to your company. These settings are required before registering the first transaction.

You may share a chart of accounts, assigning several companies to one common chart of accounts. After posting the first transaction in a company, it is not possible to change the chart of accounts assignment any more.

The *Account structures* pane of the ledger form in Dynamics AX 2012 R2 contains the account structures for the current company. In order to add an account structure, click the button ⊞Add▾ in the action pane of this pane. Since account structures determine the available financial dimensions when posting to a main account, each main account included in the chart of accounts has to be assigned to exactly one account structure without overlapping or missing assignments.

If applying interunit accounting in a company, the balancing financials dimension has to be included in all account structures of this company.

8.2.4.4   Account Structures

For accessing the account structure configuration form, choose the menu item *General ledger> Setup> Chart of Accounts> Configure account structures* or click the button *Configure account structures* in the *Account structures* pane of the ledger form.

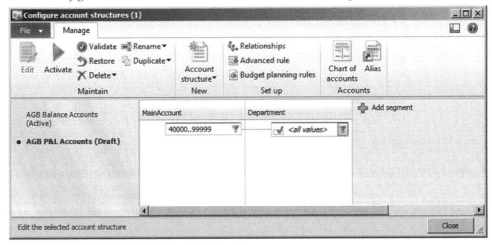

Figure 8-7:   Configuring an account structure

If you want to create a new account structure in order to specify a new segment combination of main account and applicable financial dimensions, click the button *New/Account structure* in the account structures configuration form.

In the create dialog, the checkbox *Add main account* usually remains selected for including the main account as the first segment. You may clear this option in case you want to use a financial dimension, and not the main account, as first segment – e.g. if divisions apply and should be the first segment when entering transactions.

When creating a new account structure or editing an existing structure, it shows in *Draft* mode. You may add dimensions to the account structure by clicking the button *Add segment*. The filter button ▥ in the segment fields provides the option to restrict available dimension values. When selecting the checkbox *Allow blanks* for financial dimensions in the filter dialog, entering a dimension value is optional and you are not required to select a dimension value when registering a transaction for a main account referring to the account structure.

The example in Figure 8-7 shows a simple account structure applying to main accounts starting with account 40000, containing the financial dimension "Department" without restricting available dimension values on this dimension.

If applicable to your account structure, you can add one or more lines (nodes) for a segment – with appropriate filters in the specific nodes – in order to specify multiple applicable dimension value combinations.

Once you have finished the setup of account structure segments, click the button *Activate* to make the account structure available. If you want to edit an existing account structure later, click the button *Edit* in the action pane. The account structure then is in draft mode, which also allows deleting it.

8.2.4.5 Advanced Rule Structures

In addition to the account structures, advanced rules and advanced rule structures provide the option to add dimension segments only applying to a limited number of specific accounts. A typical example is tracking marketing campaigns applying a financial dimension "Campaigns" only for a particular marketing main account.

For setting up a new advanced rule structure, create it in the form *General ledger> Setup> Chart of Accounts> Advanced rule structures* and enter applicable financial dimensions (similar to setting up account structures as described above).

In order to apply the advanced rule structure, access the account structures form and click the button *Advanced rule* when editing the appropriate account structure. In the advanced rules form, click the button *New* and enter an advanced rule ID and name in the create dialog. In order to specify the main accounts applicable to the new advanced rule, click the button ✚ Add filter in the middle of the right pane of the advanced rules form.

Clicking the button 🗗Add▾ on the tab *Advanced rule structures* links advanced rule structures to the advanced rule as applicable. Activating the account structure, to which the advanced rule applies, activates the advanced rule in parallel.

8.2.4.6 Main Accounts

The structure and the format of the main accounts in the chart of accounts are depending only on the internal requirements of your company. In order to comply with the different reporting structures for balance sheet, income statement and other reports in finance, apply financial statements with a structure which is independent from the chart of accounts.

If you want to edit the main accounts, open the list page *General ledger> Common> Main accounts* and click the button *Edit* there. Alternatively, access the chart of accounts form (*General ledger> Setup> Chart of Accounts> Chart of Accounts*) and edit the main accounts by clicking the button *Edit* on the tab *Main accounts* after selecting the appropriate chart of accounts there.

The main accounts list page – and the main accounts form accessed from the list page – contains the chart of accounts applying to the current company. In the main accounts form, the form header shows the name of the applicable chart of accounts. If other companies are also assigned to this chart of accounts, you have to keep in mind that changes on main accounts also affect the other companies.

If you want to enter a new account, click the button *New* in the action pane strip for inserting a record including a unique account number, an account name and an account type. Clicking the button *Translations* in the action pane strip provides access to the translation form for entering the account name in multiple languages.

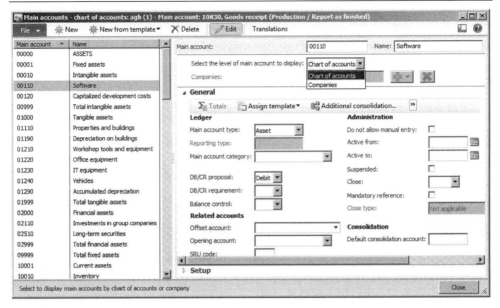

Figure 8-8:   Editing a main account

In the lookup field *Select level of main account to display* of the main accounts form, choose the option "Chart of accounts" for editing data (e.g. active dates) applying to all companies assigned to the current chart of account. If selecting the option "Companies" for editing data specific to a particular company, you have to click the button ➕▾ near the field *Companies* to select the applicable company.

In the structure of the main accounts, you have to distinguish between transaction accounts and auxiliary accounts. The *Main account type,* a lookup field in the main accounts form, groups main accounts as shown in to table 8-1 below.

Table 8-1:   Structure of main accounts

Type		Main account type in Dynamics AX
Transaction accounts	Balance accounts	➢ Balance sheet ➢ Asset ➢ Liability ➢ Equity
	Nominal accounts	➢ Profit and loss ➢ Expense ➢ Revenue
Auxiliary accounts		➢ Reporting (Choose *Reporting type* "Header", "Empty header" or "Page header") ➢ Total ➢ Common (only required in China)

The core difference between transaction accounts and auxiliary accounts is that financial transactions only include transaction accounts. Auxiliary accounts support a clear structure of the chart of accounts. They are not necessarily required.

Transaction accounts include balance accounts on the one hand and nominal accounts (income statement accounts) on the other hand. In Dynamics AX, these two types are different when closing a fiscal year: Whereas the balance of nominal accounts is zero in the opening transactions of the next year, balance accounts transfer their balance.

Distinguishing between asset accounts and liability accounts supports grouping and selecting balance accounts in reports. But if you do not want to apply this grouping, only use the account type "Balance sheet".

As with balance accounts, you are free to split nominal accounts (type "Profit and loss") into cost accounts and revenue accounts.

In addition to the *Main account type*, the lookup field *Main account category* on the tab *General* of the main account form provides another classification of main accounts. For setting up the main account types – which are a basis for calculating performance indicators (KPIs) included in some cubes and role centers – access the form *General ledger> Setup> Chart of accounts> Main accounts categories*.

In main accounts receiving transactions from other modules based on ledger integration settings (e.g. summary accounts for vendor liabilities), you should select the checkbox *Do not allow manual entry* blocking manual transactions.

On the tabs *General, Setup* and – at company level – *Financial statement* and *Financial dimensions* of the main account form, optionally enter default data and settings for allowed transactions.

In the main accounts list page, the FactBox *Balance* shows the account balance of the period select through clicking the button *Balances/Parameters* in the action pane. Clicking the button *Journal entries/Posted* in the main accounts list page provides direct access to the ledger transactions of the selected main account. The transaction form itself contains following buttons in the action pane strip for accessing further information:

➢ **Voucher** – Shows all transactions of the voucher in the general ledger
➢ **Transaction origin** – Shows related transactions in all modules
➢ **Original document** – Provides the option of reprinting the document

Note: For initializing and updating balances, click the appropriate buttons in the financial dimension sets (*General ledger> Setup> Financial dimensions> Financial dimension sets*).

8.2.4.7 Financial Statements

In order to comply with different regulations for various internal and external reports, alternative groupings of ledger accounts for showing business data – independent from the account structure in the chart of accounts – are required frequently.

For this purpose, you can set up multiple different financial statements. These financial statements for example may include a revenue report and different versions of balance sheet and income statement.

For running a financial statement, choose the menu item *General ledger> Reports> Transactions> Financial statement* and export it to different file types like XBRL and Excel. Before starting a financial statement, you need to complete the setup of the particular financial statement in following menu items:

> *General ledger> Setup> Financial dimensions> Financial dimension sets*
> *General ledger> Setup> Financial statement> Row definition*
> *General ledger> Setup> Financial statement> Financial statement* (setting up columns)

8.2.4.8   Accounts for Automatic Transactions

Settings in the *Accounts for automatic transactions* apply to ledger transactions, which are posted automatically through ledger integration and for which other settings are missing or – as with invoice discounts – are not available.

If you want to enter a new setting for automatic transactions, access the form *General ledger> Setup> Posting> Accounts for automatic transactions* and insert a record selecting the posting type and the assigned main account. Clicking the button *Create default types* generates a basic set of posting types for which you may enter default accounts.

Essential settings in the accounts for automatic transactions are as follows:

> **Error account** – Applying in case of missing account settings
> **Penny difference in accounting currency** – For small payment differences
> **Year-end result** – Account for profit/loss when closing the fiscal year
> **Sales tax rounding**
> **Order invoice rounding** – Sales invoice rounding
> **Purchase invoice rounding-off** – Purchase invoice rounding
> **Vendor invoice discount**
> **Customer invoice discount**

If the checkbox *Interrupt in case or error account* in the general ledger parameters is selected, Dynamics AX displays an error message instead of posting to the error account when trying to post a transaction for which no main account is specified in the integration settings.

8.2.4.9   New in Dynamics AX 2012 and in AX 2012 R2

In Dynamics AX 2012, set up charts of accounts with corresponding main accounts independent from companies – sharing them across legal entities as required. Account structures specify combinations of main accounts and financial dimensions required for registering transactions.

Compared with the initial version of Dynamics AX 2012, the R2 version assigns account structures in the ledger form (and not in the chart of accounts), which means that companies may use a common chart of accounts while applying different financial dimensions. In addition, main account translations are available.

8.2.5   Customer, Vendor and Bank Accounts

When entering a ledger journal line, there is the option to select customers, vendors, bank accounts or fixed assets instead of ledger accounts.

8.2.5.1 Bank Accounts

Before selecting a particular bank account, you have to set it up in the menu item *Cash and Bank management> Common> Bank accounts*. When creating a new bank account by clicking the button *New/Bank account*, enter the bank account ID, the *Routing number* identifying the bank, your *Bank account number* as specified by the bank, and a *Name* for the bank account.

On the tab *Currency management* of the bank account form, enter the main account referring to the particular bank account in the *Main account* field. The *Currency* field specifies the currency of the bank account. If you want to enable transactions in other currencies additionally, select the checkbox *More currencies*.

If your company has got multiple bank accounts at a particular bank, optionally enter a bank group (*Cash and Bank management> Setup> Bank groups*) containing default values for data like address, routing number and contact data, which are common to these bank accounts.

8.2.5.2 Vendors

As shown in section 3.2.1, vendor records are available in the list page *Accounts payable> Common> Vendors> All vendors*. If you want to view vendor transactions (invoices and payments) there, click the button *Transactions* on the action pane tab *Vendor* after selecting the particular vendor. Apart from the invoice or payment amount, the vendor transaction form shows the open, not yet settled amount in the column *Balance*.

8.2.5.3 Settlement of Vendor Transactions

In order to apply a payment to an invoice, access the open vendor transactions by clicking the button *Settle/Settle open transaction* on the action pane tab *Invoice* of the vendor form. In the open transactions form, select the checkbox *Mark* in the transaction lines which you want to settle – only one or multiple invoices on the one hand and only one or multiple payments or credit notes on the other. For transactions in foreign currencies, choose the settlement date (for calculating exchange rate gains or losses) in the lookup field *Settlement posting date* on the upper part of the form.

The lookup field *Date used for calculating discounts* determines the date for cash discount calculation. It includes following options:

➢ **Transaction date** – Select the transaction line containing the date for discount calculation and click the button *Mark payment* in the action pane strip.
➢ **Selected date** – Manually enter the discount calculation date.

You may check the balance of marked transactions in the field *Marked total* in the upper pane of the form. Clicking the button *Update* posts the settlement.

If you do not want to post settlements separately from the original transaction, you can register the settlement already when entering a payment (see section 8.3.4).

If you want to cancel a posted settlement, access the closed transaction form by clicking the button *Settle/Closed transaction editing* on the action pane tab *Invoice* of the vendor form and reverse the settlement there.

8.2.5.4 Customers

Explanations on the customer record (*Accounts receivable> Common> Customers> All Customers*) are available in section 4.2.1. The way to execute transaction inquiries and to settle transactions (on the action pane tab *Collect*) is similar to the procedures in vendor management.

8.2.6   VAT / Sales Tax Settings

The sales tax/VAT functionality in Dynamics AX supports different tax regulations – e.g. the sales tax in the United States or the value added tax in Europe.

Sales tax codes, determining the tax rate, are the basis for sales tax calculation. In an invoice line, the applicable sales tax code is depending on both, the item sales tax group of the item and the sales tax group of the customer or vendor.

A primary setting for tax calculation is whether US sales tax applies: If it does, select the checkbox *Apply U.S. taxation rules* on the tab *Sales tax* of the general ledger parameters. With this setting, sales tax jurisdictions are an additional grouping in tax calculation. More information on the specific requirements of US sales tax is available in the Dynamics AX online help.

Apart from common settings in the general ledger parameters, the setup of sales tax / VAT calculation includes following items:

➢ Sales tax authorities
➢ Sales tax settlement periods
➢ Ledger posting groups
➢ Sales tax codes
➢ Item sales tax groups
➢ Sales tax groups

8.2.6.1 Sales Tax Authorities

The first step when setting up sales tax calculation is to enter the competent authorities in the form *General ledger> Setup> Sales tax> Sales tax authorities* with their authority ID, name and report layout for tax reporting.

8.2.6.2 Sales Tax Settlement Periods

Applicable periods for tax reporting – usually monthly periods – are specified in the form *General ledger> Setup> Sales tax> Sales tax settlement periods*.

When creating a new settlement period definition with ID and description, you have to assign the applicable *Authority* and – through *Period interval* and *Number of units* – the period length on the tab *General*. After specifying the period length, switch to the tab *Periods* in order to enter the first period manually (e.g. Jan 1 – Jan 31). In order to create further periods automatically, click the button *New period* in the action pane strip at the top of the form.

8.2.6.3 Ledger Posting Groups

Sales tax ledger posting groups control the main accounts in sales tax transactions (depending on the sales tax code of the original invoice transaction).

For setting up a sales tax ledger posting group, access the form *General ledger> Setup> Sales tax> Ledger posting groups*. After entering the group ID and description, select the main account for sales tax payable (input tax), for sales tax receivable, and – if applicable – for use tax. The *Settlement account* field contains the balance account for the amount to be paid to the tax authorities.

8.2.6.4 Sales Tax Codes

Sales tax codes control the tax rate and the calculation base.

For setting up a sales tax code, access the form *General ledger> Setup> Sales tax> Sales tax codes* and insert a record with code and name. On the tab *General*, assign the settlement period and the ledger posting group.

Detailed calculation parameters are available on the tab *Calculation*. For specifying the tax rate, click the button *Values* in the action pane strip of the sales tax codes form and enter the applicable rate in the column *Value* of the values form.

After creating a sales tax code, assign it to applicable sales tax groups and item sales tax groups. Dynamics AX determines the sales tax code of an invoice line from the sales tax code, which is included in the settings of both – the item sales tax group of the item, and the sales tax group of the customer (or vendor).

In order to apply a tax code "V175" in a sales invoice line for example, the line has to comply with both of the following conditions:

> **Item sales tax group** – The item sales tax group (e.g. "STD" for a standard rate) of the item contains the sales tax code "V175"
> **Sales tax group** – The sales tax group of the customer (e.g. "CDO" for domestic customers) contains the sales tax code "V175"

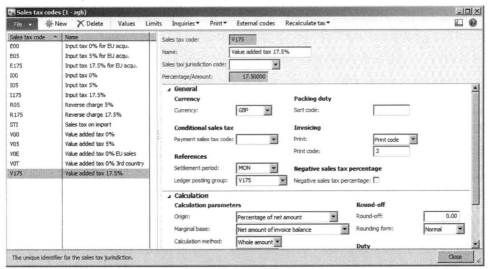

Figure 8-9:   Managing sales tax codes

8.2.6.5   Item Sales Tax Groups

For setting up an item sales tax group, access the form *General ledger> Setup> Sales tax> Item sales tax groups*. After entering the tax group identification and description on the tab *Overview*, switch to the tab *Setup* and register applicable sales tax codes for the items belonging to the group.

In order to assign item sales tax groups to items, access the released product form (*Product information management> Common> Released products*). In the corresponding detail form, select the *Item sales tax group* for sales (on the tab *Sell*) and for purchasing (on the tab *Purchase*) – usually when creating an item.

For assigning item sales tax groups to product categories, access the procurement categories form (*Procurement and sourcing> Setup> Categories> Procurement categories*) and the sales categories form (*Sales and marketing> Setup> Categories> Sales categories*) and select the *Item sales tax group* on the appropriate tab.

8.2.6.6   Sales Tax Groups

The menu item *General ledger> Setup> Sales tax> Sales tax groups* provides access to the sales tax groups, which apply to customers and vendors. Setting up sales tax groups is similar to setting up item sales tax groups.

In order to assign the sales tax groups to customers and vendors, access the customer or vendor form and switch to the tab *Invoice and delivery* there.

8.2.6.7 Sales Tax Transactions

When registering a transaction in a journal or order line, Dynamics AX defaults the sales tax code according to the combination of item and customer/vendor. For viewing the calculated tax before posting, click the button *Sales tax* on the appropriate tab of the action pane (or action pane strip) in journal lines, sales and purchase order headers or lines, or in the posting form when posting a transaction (e.g. a sales invoice).

If necessary, change the sales tax groups or the sales tax code in a journal or order line before posting. When posting an invoice, Dynamics AX generates a transaction for sales tax in the general ledger (according to the ledger posting group assigned to the sales tax code) as well as a sales tax transaction in the appropriate subledger.

8.2.6.8 Sales Tax Payment

In order to calculate the sales tax, which is payable to the authorities for a particular period, execute the periodic activity *General ledger> Periodic> Sales tax payments> Sales tax payments*. As a prerequisite, the reporting codes for the report layout assigned to the sales tax authority have to be set up in the form *General ledger> Setup> Sales tax> External> Sales tax reporting codes*.

8.2.7   Case Study Exercises

Exercise 8.1 – Financial Dimensions
Your organization introduces business areas for reporting purposes. In order to support this requirement, create a new financial dimension "##Areas" (custom dimension) with the shared values "Area ## 1" and "Area ## 2" (## = your user ID).

Note: Numbers are not allowed in the dimension name.

Exercise 8.2 – Main Accounts
Following new main accounts are required in your company (## = your user ID):

➢ Main account "111C-##", Name "Petty cash", account type "Balance Sheet"
➢ Main account "111B-##", Name "##-Bank", account type "Balance Sheet"
➢ Main account "6060##", Name "## - Consulting", account type "Expense"
➢ Main account "ZZ##", Name "## account structure test", account type "Balance Sheet"

Create these accounts making sure to apply the right chart of accounts.

Exercise 8.3 – Account structures
Unlike the other main accounts created in exercise 8.2, your main account "ZZ##" is not included in an account number range referring to existing account structures. For this reason, set up a new account structure only applying to this main account.

Create and activate a new account structure "ZS##", with the main accounts and the financial dimension "##Areas" (and additionally the balancing dimension, if interunit accounting applies) as segments. Your main account "ZZ##" is the only applicable main account in this account structure. Then assign the account structure to your test company.

Note: If you are sharing the Dynamics AX training database, remove your account structure once you have finished all exercises in order to avoid confusing other people with too many applicable financial dimensions.

Exercise 8.4 – Bank Accounts
Your company opens a new bank account at you preferred bank. Create an appropriate bank account "B-##" with any routing number and bank account number. On the tab *Currency management*, select the main account "111B-##".

8.3   Business Processes in Finance

Every business process related to monetary amounts in Dynamics AX generates financial transactions for ledger accounts. Most of the transactions do not origin in accounting, but refer to transactions in other areas like purchasing, sales, or production. Transactions in these areas automatically generate ledger transactions in the background.

Some ledger transactions directly derive from activities in accounting. In order to record these transactions, register and post a journal in the general ledger module.

8.3.1   Basics Setup for Journal Transactions

In addition to the basic setup of finance described in the previous section, you have to configure journal names before registering a journal transaction in the general ledger.

8.3.1.1   Journal Names

Journal names in Dynamics AX classify transactions by subject matters. For setting up journal names, access the form *General ledger> Setup> Journals> Journal names*. In the journal names, the lookup field *Journal type* of a journal name controls, to which journals is applies. The most common journal types are:

➢ **Daily** – General journal
➢ **Periodic** – Periodic journal
➢ **Post fixed assets** – Fixed asset transactions
➢ **Vendor invoice recording** – Invoice journal in accounts payable
➢ **Vendor disbursement** – Vendor payment
➢ **Customer payment** – Payment of customers

If your company applies invoice register and invoice approval journals in purchasing, the journal types "Invoice register" and "Approval" are required in addition.

Ledger journals show a common structure independent from the journal type. As a difference between different journal types, different fields show in the particular journal registration forms. In addition, some journals show additional functionality – e.g. the payment proposal feature in the vendor payment journal.

Selecting different number sequences in the *Voucher series* field of journal names, supports distinguishing the voucher numbers of different journals.

The default for the offset account in journal lines is available in the fields *Account type* and *Offset account* of the journal names form. The example in Figure 8-10 shows the bank account "E001" provided as default for the offset account in journal lines applying the journal name "GEB".

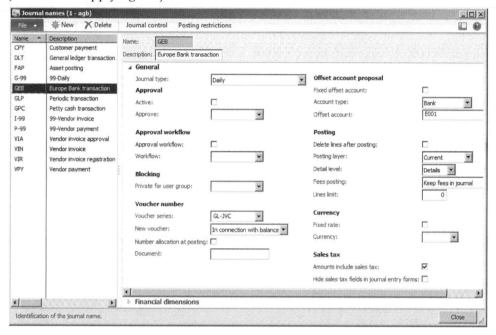

Figure 8-10:   Managing journal names

Another important setting on journal names is the checkbox *Amount include sales tax*. If this checkbox is selected, an amount entered in the journal lines includes sales tax (or input tax) if applicable. Otherwise, the line amount entered is a net amount, to which sales tax is added.

8.3.1.2   Journal Approval

There are two options for ensuring that a registered journal is approved before posting:

➢ **Journal approval system** – Enabled in the field group *Approval*
➢ **Approval workflow** – Enabled in the field group *Approval workflow*

If you want to activate the journal approval system for a journal name, select the checkbox *Active* in the field group *Approval*. Then choose the user group being responsible for approval in the corresponding lookup field *Approve*.

If you want to apply the approval workflow, an appropriate general ledger workflow has to be specified in the form *General ledger> Setup> General ledger workflows*. The template "Ledger daily journal workflow" (*Type* "LedgerDaily

Template") for example applies to approval workflows linked to daily journals. More information on workflows is available in section 9.4.

8.3.1.3 Posting Layer

The *Posting layer* on journal names usually is "Current". If you need to cut off particular ledger transaction (for example because of local tax regulations), there is the option to create separate journal names for the posting layers "Operations" and "Tax". Selecting the appropriate posting layer – through the journal name when posting a journal transaction or in the closing sheet when executing the fiscal year closing – enables printing of different finance statements based on postings in these layers.

8.3.1.4 General Ledger Parameters

The general ledger parameters form (*General ledger> Setup> General ledger parameters*) contains further basic settings for journal transactions. As an example, you should reject duplicate vouchers in order to avoid confusion when looking at posted documents.

8.3.2   General Journals

For posting a manual ledger transaction, register a general journal in the form *General ledger> Journals> General journal*. Depending on the particular transaction, alternatively choose a specific journal like a fixed assets journal in the fixed assets menu, or an invoice journal in the accounts payable menu, or a payment journal in the accounts payable and the accounts receivable menu.

If you do not need the advanced functionality – like payment proposals – available in the specific journals, it does not matter if you register a transaction in the specific journal or in the general journal.

8.3.2.1 Journal Header

Journals are vouchers and therefore consist of a header and at least one line. The header contains common settings and defaults for the corresponding lines.

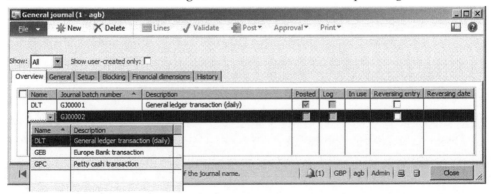

Figure 8-11:   Selecting a journal name when inserting a general journal header

You can override the header defaults in each line, for example choosing other posting dates. Before you can post a journal, the balance of the individual vouchers (lines with the same voucher number) and the balance of the complete journal (shown in the header pane of the lines form) have to be zero.

The option selected in the lookup field *Show* at the top of the general journal form determines whether open or posted journals display. In order to register a new journal, click the button *New* and choose a journal name. In a general journal, journal names of the journal type "Daily" are available.

On the tab *Setup* of the journal header, optionally change defaults like the offset account and the currency deriving from the journal name. If somebody works in the lines of a particular journal while you are viewing the journal header, the journal shows a red "X" in the column *In use*. The user ID of the user, who blocks the journal, shows on the tab *Blocking*.

8.3.2.2 Journal Lines

For accessing the journal lines, click the button *Lines* in the journal header. The default for the posting date when entering a new line is the current session date. Dynamics AX retrieves the voucher number from the number sequence of the journal name which you have selected in the header. Depending on the option selected in the column *Account type* of the lines, you have to enter a ledger account, vendor, customer, bank account or fixed asset number in the column *Account*.

Figure 8-12:   Registering a voucher with multiple offsetting lines

If entering a ledger account in the *Account* field, segmented entry control applies (see below). The main account usually has to be entered in the first segment of the ledger account field in this case. If and which financial dimension segments are available and need to be entered depends on the applicable account structure for the selected main account. Depending on the currently active segment in the ledger account field, the value lookup shows available values for that segment.

Depending on the transaction, enter the applicable amount in the column *Debit* or *Credit*. In a single-line transaction, which shows the same amount for the debit and the credit account, enter the offset account type and the offset account (including segments for financial dimensions as applicable) in the appropriate columns of the journal line.

If a transaction splits to more than one offsetting account, register the voucher in multiple lines. In this case, do not enter an offset account in the first line, but in one or more separate offsetting journal lines. As long as the balance of the voucher is not zero, Dynamics AX retrieves the same voucher number as in the previous line.

Once the voucher balance is zero, the next line shows a new voucher number (supposing the selection for *New voucher* in the journal name settings is "In connection with balance").

In order to support data entry, a separate pane at the top of the lines form shows the balance of the voucher of the selected line and the balance of the complete journal.

8.3.2.3 Segmented Entry Control

Segmented entry control supports entering the ledger account in account fields across all areas of the application. Since Microsoft Dynamics AX 2012 merges the main account and all applicable financial dimensions (like department and cost center) into one single ledger account field, entering this field – by selecting main account and financial dimension values one after the other – provides the complete posting information according to the account structure.

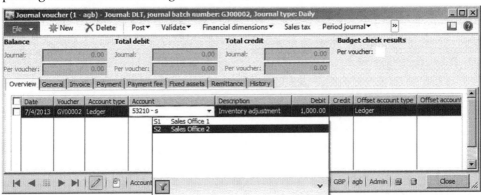

Figure 8-13: Segmented entry for main account and financial dimensions

When entering the ledger account, the value lookup refers to the currently active segment of the account field. In order to search a segment value, directly enter the search content – the first characters of the identification or name – in the appropriate segment of the account field before or after opening the value lookup by clicking the lookup button ⯆ or by pushing the shortcut key *Alt + Down Arrow*.

Unlike the value lookup in other fields, the value lookup related to segmented entry control does not offer the option to open a filter/search form for searching within the lookup. At the bottom of the value lookup for segments, the buttons 🔲 and 🔽 provide additional filtering options.

The example in Figure 8-13 shows the segment value lookup after entering an "S" in the second segment of the ledger account field. The lookup in this case shows the departments list filtered on departments beginning with "S" in the ID or the name.

The order and the number of segments are depending on the account structure applicable to the selected main account (see section 8.2.4). If the account structure does not apply financial dimensions or allows blanks for a particular segment, it is not required to enter a corresponding segment value.

8.3.2.4 Posting Financial Journals

Once you have finished entering voucher lines, post the journal by clicking the button *Post/Post* in the action pane strip of the journal header or lines. In case of incorrect data, Dynamics AX shows an error message and does not post the transaction.

Alternatively clicking the button *Post/Post and transfer* in the journal also posts correct vouchers, but transfers incorrect vouchers to a new journal.

8.3.2.5 Applying the Journal Approval System

If journal approval – applying either the journal approval system or the approval workflow – is activated for the applicable journal name, you can't post the journal before receiving the required approval.

In case of the journal approval system, request approval by clicking the button *Approval/Report as ready* in the journal header. The person responsible for approval then clicks the button *Approval/Approve* for releasing the journal to be posted.

8.3.2.6 Periodic Journals

If a particular transaction has to be registered and posted repeatedly, optionally apply one of the two options supporting recurrent registration:

➢ Periodic journals
➢ Voucher templates

Periodic journals support registering transactions like office rent or monthly installments, which recur periodically. For creating a periodic journal, access the form *General ledger> Periodic> Journals> Periodic journals* and enter a journal header and journal lines (similar to registering a general journal). An alternative way for creating a periodic journal is to copy a general journal to a periodic journal by clicking the button *Period journal/Save journal* in the lines of a general journal.

The column *Date* in the periodic journal lines specifies the start date for the periodic transactions. In the columns *Units* and *Number of units*, which are also available on the tab *Periodic*, enter the frequency of the transaction (e.g. once a month).

In order to post the periodic journal, you have to register a corresponding general journal in each period. In the lines of this general journal, retrieve the periodic journal by clicking the button *Period journal/Retrieve journal*. Once the journal has received the periodic journal lines, edit and post the general journal lines as required.

The option of retrieving a periodic journal is not only available in general journals, but also in invoice journals in the accounts payable.

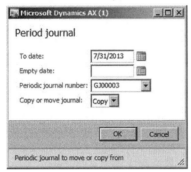

Figure 8-14:   Retrieving a periodic journal for posting

The column *Date* in the lines of a periodic journal then shows the next date for posting the journal, which is calculated by adding the frequency period to the date shown before retrieving the periodic journal. The date, when the periodic journal has been retrieved the last time, shows in the column *Last date*.

8.3.2.7 Voucher Templates

Unlike periodic journals, voucher templates are templates for copying journals without managing a periodic interval.

For creating a voucher template, click the button *Functions/Save voucher template* in the journal lines of a general journal (or an invoice journal). The option "Percent" for the *Template type* in the dialog when saving the template then applies a proportional distribution of line amounts.

If selecting such a template later in a journal after clicking the button *Functions/Select voucher template*, a separate dialog pops up for entering the amount which should be distributed to the lines according to the proportion in the template.

8.3.2.8 New in Dynamics AX 2012

In Dynamics AX 2012, items new to general journal functionality are related to account structures and the segmented entry control.

8.3.3   Invoice Journals

Depending on the particular invoice, there are different ways for registering and posting an invoice. Dynamics AX provides following options for this purpose:

> ➢ **Sales order invoice** – for items shipped to customers (see section 4.6.1)
> ➢ **Free text invoice** – for sales invoices not related to items (see section 4.6.3)
> ➢ **Vendor invoice** – for items and procurement categories received from vendors (with or without reference to a purchase order, see section 3.6.2)
> ➢ **General journal** – for manual purchase or sales invoices (not to be printed)
> ➢ **Invoice journal** – for purchase invoices not referring to items and procurement categories

8.3.3.1   Registering Invoices in the General Journal

For registering a vendor invoice directly related to a ledger account, the usual option is the vendor invoice journal. For corresponding customer invoices, a free text invoice applies in most cases.

Alternatively, it is possible to register an invoice in the general journal (*General ledger> Journals> General journal*). This might for example be useful, if you want to record sales invoices which are not printed in Dynamics AX (e.g. invoices written manually or printed in a separate upstream application like a POS solution).

When entering a sales invoice in a general journal, select the *Account type* "Customer" and enter the customer number in the column *Account* of the journal lines. In the column *Offset account*, enter an appropriate revenue account. On the tab *Invoice*, you have to enter the invoice number and the terms of payment or the applicable cash discount. Before posting, you should check whether correct sales tax groups apply on the tab *Overview* (or *General*). Optionally check the sales tax calculation by clicking the button *Sales tax* in the action pane strip.

Registering a vendor invoice in a general journal works similar to the sales invoice (for a vendor invoice, choose the *Account type* "Vendor").

8.3.3.2   Accounts Payable Invoices

Whereas sales and accounts receivables have got a specific form – the free text invoice – for registering an invoice directly referring to ledger accounts, there is no such form in purchasing or accounts payables.

You may register a vendor invoice – with or without reference to a purchase order – in the vendor invoice form (*Accounts payable> Common> Vendor invoices> Pending vendor invoices*, see section 3.6.2), but this form requires entering item numbers or procurement categories and does not contain a field for entering ledger accounts.

In order to register a vendor invoice not referring to an item number or a procurement category, but directly to a ledger account (usually for subjects like office rent), you have to enter a journal transaction. In accounts payable, following journals are available for registering and approving invoices:

> **Invoice register** – in conjunction with the *Invoice approval journal*
> **Vendor invoice pool excluding posting details** – in conjunction with the *Invoice journal*
> **Invoice journal** – alternatively without pre-registration in the vendor invoice pool
> **General journal** – as described in the section above

If you want to apply an approval workflow to invoice journals, set up an appropriate workflow with a template referring to the particular journal type in the form *Accounts payable> Setup> Accounts payable workflows* and assign it to the particular journal name.

The list page *Accounts payable> Common> Vendor invoices> Open vendor invoices* shows all invoices not yet paid, irrespective of the way of posting the invoice. The button *New/Invoice* in the action pane of this list page provides an alternative access to the different vendor invoice journals and the vendor invoice form. Similar options are available on the action pane tab *Invoice* of the vendor form.

8.3.3.3 Invoice Journal

The invoice journal, accessible through the menu item *Accounts payable> Journals> Invoices> Invoice journal*, is the main journal form for registering invoices. In the invoice journal, alternatively enter a new invoice or retrieve an invoice from the *Vendor invoice pool excluding posting details*.

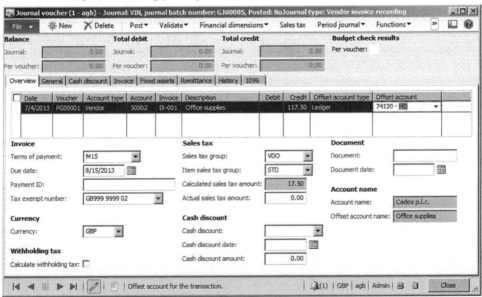

Figure 8-15:   Registering invoice journal lines

As with every voucher, you have to insert a header record in the invoice journal before switching to the lines. Once you have finished registering the invoice lines – manually entering or transferring from the *Vendor invoice pool excluding posting details* – including vendor number (*Account*), vendor invoice number (*Invoice*), transaction text, amount, offset account, terms of payment, approver (*Approved by* on the tab *Invoice*) and other data like sales tax and cash discount as applicable, post the invoice by clicking the button *Post/Post* in the action pane strip of the header or lines.

8.3.3.4   Vendor Invoice Pool Excluding Posting Details

The form *Accounts payable> Journals> Invoices> Vendor invoice pool excluding posting details* provides an option for pre-registering purchase invoices. It is a way for storing a vendor invoice without posting any financial transaction. The vendor invoice pool does not apply the regular journal structure (header and lines).

In order to register an invoice in the vendor invoice pool, simply create a new record by pushing the shortcut *Ctrl+N* or choosing the command *File/New* in the jewel menu. Once you have finished entering the invoice pool lines including posting date, vendor number, amount, vendor invoice number and other data as applicable, close the form.

In the *Invoice journal*, start the transfer of the invoice from the vendor invoice pool by clicking the button *Functions/Invoice pool excl. posting* in the journal lines. After selecting the appropriate invoice in the invoice pool selection dialog, click the button *Accept* there to transfer it to the invoice journal lines.

8.3.3.5   Invoice Register

Apart from the vendor invoice pool, the invoice register (*Accounts payable> Journals> Invoices> Invoice register*) provides another option for pre-registering vendor invoices. Unlike the vendor invoice pool, the invoice register functionality includes actually posting a vendor transaction, applicable sales tax transactions, and ledger transactions (to interim accounts). Depending on your requirements, assign a purchase order to the particular invoices in the invoice register.

The structure of the invoice register with journal header and lines is similar to the structure of the general journal, restricting the account type to "Vendor". In the journal lines, you have to enter the employee responsible for approval (*Approved by* on the lower pane of the tab *Overview*) as well as terms of payment, cash discount and sales tax groups.

If the invoice refers to a purchase order, select the purchase order number in the appropriate field on the tab *Overview* or *General* of the journal in order to facilitate later approval. In order to post a journal in the invoice register, click the button *Post/ Post* in the action pane strip of the header or lines.

Posting a journal in the invoice register creates a regular vendor transaction, accessible from the vendor list page (*Accounts payable> Common> Vendors> All vendors*) by clicking the button *Transactions* after selecting the particular vendor.

The checkbox *Approved* on the tab *General* of this transaction is not selected, which is why the invoice is not included in payment proposals.

The ledger transactions of the invoice register are posted to interim accounts. These interim accounts are specified in the posting profile (columns *Arrival* and *Offset account* on the tab *Setup* of the form *Accounts payable> Setup> Vendor posting profiles*).

Sales tax posting of invoice register transactions is controlled by the accounts payable parameters, where the lookup field *Time of sales tax posting* on the tab *Ledger and sales tax* determines if sales tax is already posted with the invoice register or later with the invoice approval.

8.3.3.6 Invoice Approval Journal

After posting a journal in the invoice register, the employee responsible for approval may approve it in the invoice approval journal.

Invoice approval starts with inserting a new header in the invoice approval journal (*Accounts payable> Journals> Invoices> Invoice approval journal*). After switching to the approval journal lines, click the button *Find vouchers* in order to retrieve the posted invoice register.

The find vouchers form shows available invoice registers in the upper pane. The button *Select* there provides the option to choose one or more invoices for approval. Closing the find vouchers form then by clicking the button *OK* transfers the selected invoice or invoices to the approval journal lines.

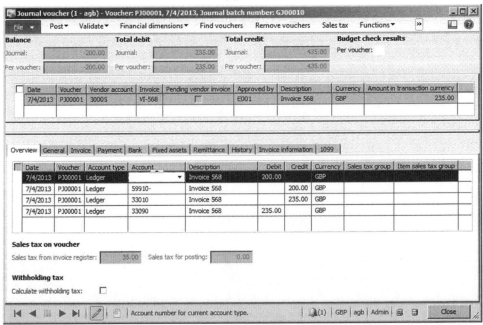

Figure 8-16:   The invoice approval journal lines after fetching an invoice register

The next steps depend on whether the approved invoice refers to a purchase order:

➢ **Not related to a purchase order** – In this case, select a ledger account – e.g. an expense account – in the lower pane of the invoice approval journal lines (first line in the lower pane of Figure 8-16). The expense amount does not include sales tax. If multiple expense accounts apply, enter several lines sharing the total amount. In order to finally post the approval, click the button *Post/Post*.

➢ **Referring to a purchase order** – In this case, click the button *Functions/Purchase order* in order to access the posting form for the related purchase order invoice. In the posting form, post the invoice as described in section 3.6.2.

8.3.3.7 Rejecting Invoice Approval

If you do not want to approve a vendor invoice, which has been posted in the invoice register (because it does not comply with applicable purchase orders or because of other reasons), you have to post a cancellation.

For this purpose, access the invoice approval journal lines, retrieve the applicable invoice register and click the button *Functions/Cancel*. Clicking the button *Post/Post* in the invoice approval journal posts the cancellation.

8.3.3.8 Invoice Pool Inquiry

All open invoice register approvals show in the form *Accounts payable> Inquiries> Invoice pool*.

For invoice register journals referring to a purchase order, the invoice pool inquiry provides an alternative to the invoice approval journal for posting the approval. For this purpose, click the button *Purchase order* in the invoice pool inquiry opening the posting form for the related purchase order invoice (like the corresponding button in the approval journal lines).

8.3.4 Payments

Posting an invoice creates an open transaction for the vendor liability or the customer debt.

8.3.4.1 Open Transactions

For viewing the open transactions, click the button *Settle/Settle open transactions* on the action pane tab *Collect* of the customer page (*Accounts receivable> Common> Customers> All Customers*) or on the action pane tab *Invoice* of the vendor form (*Accounts payable> Common> Vendors> All vendors*).

The button *Transactions* in the customer or vendor form opens the transactions form showing all transactions. Selecting the checkbox *Show open only* there applies a filter showing only open transactions.

In order to print open transactions, choose the report *Accounts receivable> Reports> Transactions> Customer> Open transactions* for customers and the report *Accounts payable> Reports> Transactions> Invoice> Vendor invoice transactions* for vendors.

8.3.4.2 Customer Payment

For registering and posting a customer payment, open the general journal or the customer payment journal (*Accounts receivable> Journals> Payments> Payment journal*).

If choosing the customer payment journal, insert a record in the journal header there and switch to the lines. In a new journal line, enter the payment with customer number, transaction text, payment amount, and offset account. If the customer has paid to your bank account, choose "Bank" for the offset account type.

If you want to apply an invoice when entering a payment line, select the appropriate invoice number in the column *Invoice* of the journal line (automatically inserting the invoice amount for payment).

Alternatively apply one – or more – invoice numbers to a payment line by clicking the button *Functions/Settlement*. In the settlement form, choose paid invoices by selecting the checkbox in the column *Mark*. After closing the settlement form (there is no separate button *OK*), recorded marking applies to the payment journal line.

As an alternative to manually entering payment lines, click the button *Enter customer payment* in the payment journal header in order to create and settle payment lines by selecting paid invoices. An option applying to direct debiting is the customer payment proposal in the payment journal lines (similar to the vendor payment proposal, see below).

Once you have finished recording payment lines, post the customer payment journal by clicking the button *Post/Post* in the header or lines.

8.3.4.3 Vendor Payment

Like customer payments, payments to vendors may be entered in a general journal or in a specific payment journal. The payment journal for vendors is available in the menu item *Accounts payable> Journals> Payments> Payment journal*.

Manually registering a vendor payment works similar to registering a customer payment – including the options for settlement. But in most cases, you need additional support and control of outgoing payments. In Dynamics AX, the payment proposal and the payment status are available for this purpose.

If you want to prevent paying a particular invoice, clear the checkbox *Approved* or enter an *Invoice payment release date* on the tab *General* of the vendor transaction. The payment proposal does not include the invoice until you mark the approval-checkmark in the transaction again or the release date has passed.

8.3.4.4 Vendor Payment Proposal

The payment proposal supports selecting vendor invoices for payment. In order to run a payment proposal, click the button *Payment proposal/Create payment proposal* in the journal lines of a vendor payment journal.

In the dialog box of the payment proposal, choose the *Proposal type* (due date or cash discount) and a date range for including invoices (*From date, To date*). Clicking the button *Select* allows entering a filter on vendor and transaction data. In order to actually generate a proposal, the checkbox *Generate* has to be selected.

Depending on the proposal type, the proposal defaults the invoice due date or the cash discount date in the posting date for payment. If this date is in the past or before a future date entered in the *Minimum date*, today (or the *Minimum date*) applies as default.

After closing the dialog box by clicking the button *OK*, the payment proposal form displays for checking and editing the payment proposal. The lower pane of the payment proposal form for this purpose shows suggested payments. After selecting a payment line in the lower pane, edit related invoices in the upper pane as necessary (removing invoices from payment or editing the payment amount). The tab *Cash discount* in the upper pane enables editing the cash discount date. Finally clicking the button *Transfer* in the action pane strip of the payment proposal form transfers the proposal to the payment journal.

The payment proposal marks a settlement for the selected invoices. Depending on the method of payment in the particular invoices, there is one payment line for several invoices or a separate payment line per invoice.

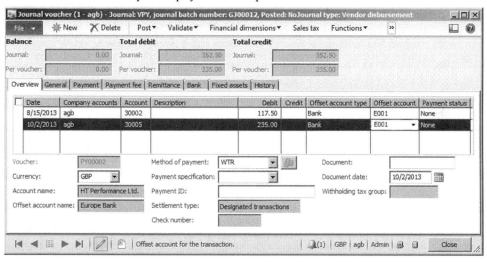

Figure 8-17: Registering lines in a vendor payment journal

Before posting the vendor payment, you can still edit the transferred proposal by clicking the button *Payment proposal/Edit payment proposal* in the journal lines.

8.3.4.5   Method of Payment

Methods of payment in the form *Accounts payable> Setup> Payment> Methods of payment* are an important setting for processing vendor payments.

Usually there are at least two methods of payment: One for manual transfers and one for electronic banking. In the field group *Posting* on the tab *General* of the methods of payment, optionally enter a bank (or ledger) account from which you want to pay. This account is the default for the offset account when selecting the method in a payment. If you want to support bank reconciliation by posting to a bridging account (see below), select the checkbox *Bridging posting* and enter the bridging account number.

For methods of payment related to electronic payment, you should select the status "Sent" or "Approved" for the *Payment status* in order to prevent posting a payment before generating a related payment export file. Further settings for electronic payments like the file formats are available on the other tabs.

In order to assign a default payment method to a vendor, enter it on the tab *Payment* in the vendor form. The *Method of payment* selected in the vendor record defaults to purchase orders, vendor transactions and the payment journal.

8.3.4.6 Generating and Posting Payments

Before generating and posting a payment, optionally print the payment journal for control purposes by clicking the button *Print/Journal* in the header or lines.

In order to generate an export file for electronic payment, click the button *Functions/Generate payments* in the payment journal lines once the lines contain the appropriate method of payment. If you need an export file, make sure to generate it before posting the payment.

When generating the payment, Dynamics AX sets the payment status of the journal lines to "Sent". If required, change the payment status manually by clicking the button *Payment status*.

In order to finish the payment procedure, click the button *Post/Post* in the payment journal for posting the payment from the selected bank or ledger account.

8.3.4.7 Applying Bridging Accounts

If the payment does not directly post to a bank account, but to a bridging account as specified in the payment method, you need to post a transfer from the bridging account to the bank account when receiving the appropriate bank statement later.

For registering and posting this transfer, create a new journal in the general journals (*General ledger> Journals> General journal*). In the general journal lines, click the button *Functions/Select bridged transactions* in order to access the form for selecting and accepting the transaction concerned.

8.3.4.8 Centralized Payment

The functionality of centralized payments supports a company structure with a central company processing payments of an affiliated group. As a prerequisite for using centralized payments, set up intercompany accounting (*General ledger>*

Setup> Posting> Intercompany accounting) for the legal entities concerned. In addition, appropriate permission settings applying an organization hierarchy with the purpose "Centralized payment" are required.

Payment journals and payment proposals show the company in the column *Company accounts*. When posting a payment applying centralized payments, settle invoices in other companies as applicable.

8.3.4.9 New in Dynamics AX 2012

Payment features new in Dynamics AX 2012 include changes in the setup of centralized payments referring to organization hierarchies and shared data.

8.3.5 Reversing Transactions

In Dynamics AX, there are two different types of transaction reversals: Manually entered reversals (for corrections) and automatic reversals (for accruals).

8.3.5.1 Transaction Reversal

The transaction reversal, which is available for ledger, vendor and customer transactions (e.g. free text invoices), provides a simple way for correcting wrong vouchers in finance. It is not available for transactions referring to inventory, purchase orders or sales orders, however. In order to reverse these kinds of transactions, register an appropriate document in the original menu – for example a customer return order in the *Sales and marketing* menu.

If you want to reverse a financial transaction, access the transaction inquiry by clicking the button *Transactions* in the vendor page (*Accounts payable> Common> Vendors> All vendors*) or customer page (*Accounts receivable> Common> Customers> All Customers*). For ledger transactions, click the button *Journal entries/Posted* in the main accounts page (*General ledger> Common> Main accounts*).

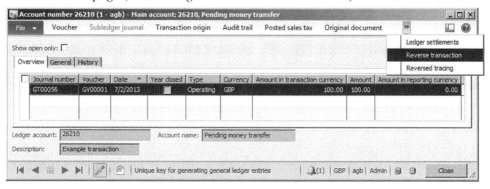

Figure 8-18: Reversing a ledger transaction

After selecting the particular transaction, click the button *Reverse transaction* showing a dialog for entering the posting date for reversal. If you want to reverse a settled vendor or customer transaction (e.g. a paid invoice), you have to cancel the settlement of the transaction (see section 8.2.5) for making it available for reversal.

Transaction reversal posts a new transaction, offsetting the original transaction. If required, reverse a reversal.

8.3.5.2 Automatic Reversal with Reversing Entries

Unlike manual transaction reversals, which apply to adjust incorrect transactions, reversing entries are transactions generated automatically in order to reverse accruals in a later period.

Reversing entries are available in general journals (*General ledger> Journals> General journal*). In order to generate a reversing entry, select the checkbox *Reversing entry* and enter a *Reversing date* in the rightmost columns on the tab *Overview* of the journal lines when entering the original transaction. In the general journal header, the checkbox *Reversing entry* and the reversing date are available providing a default for the lines.

When posting a general journal with automatic reversal, Dynamics AX in parallel posts a second transaction reversing the original transaction.

8.3.6   Case Study Exercises

Exercise 8.5 – Journal Names
You want to register the transactions of the exercises below in your own journals. For this purpose, create a journal name "G-##" (## = your user ID) with the type "Daily", a journal name "I-##" with the type "Vendor invoice recording", and a journal name "P-##" with the type "Vendor disbursement". Choose an existing number sequence for all of the journal names.

Exercise 8.6 – Segmented Entry in General Journals
You want to transfer GBP 50.00 from your main account "ZZ##" in "Area ## 1" to your petty cash account "111C-##" (both accounts entered in exercise 8.2).

Register an appropriate transaction in a general journal, choosing your journal name "G-##". Which segments apply to your main account "ZZ##"? Check the value lookup for the main account and the financial dimension.

Then post the journal and check the balance and the transactions on both accounts of the journal line.

Note: If a *Balancing financial dimension* applies, enter an appropriate value for this dimension in the applicable segment of the ledger account and the offset account.

Exercise 8.7 – General Journal
You want to withdraw GBP 100.00 from the bank account "B-##" entered in exercise 8.4 and put it to your petty cash account "111C-##" entered in exercise 8.2. Register the appropriate transaction in a general journal, choosing your journal name "G-##".

Check the balance and transactions of the bank account and of the petty cash account before posting. Then post the journal and check the balance and the posted transactions again.

Note: If a *Balancing financial dimension* applies, enter an appropriate value for this dimension in the applicable segment of the ledger account and – after clicking the button *Financial dimensions* in the journal lines – for the bank account.

Exercise 8.8 – Purchase Invoice

The vendor, which you have entered in exercise 3.2, submits the invoice "VI808" showing a total of GBP 50.00 to your company. The invoice refers to expenses, for which you have entered the main account "6060##" in exercise 8.2.

Record this invoice in an invoice journal with your journal name "I-##". The terms of payment and the cash discount entered in exercise 3.1 apply to this invoice.

Check the vendor balance, the vendor transactions, the ledger balance of your expense account, and the corresponding ledger transactions before posting. Then post the invoice and check the balances and the transactions again.

Note: If a *Balancing financial dimension* applies, enter an appropriate value for this dimension in the applicable segment of the expense account.

Exercise 8.9 – Vendor Payment

You want to pay the invoice "VI808" which you have posted in the previous exercise. Register the payment in a vendor payment journal applying your journal name "P-##". Pay from your bank account "B-##" entered in exercise 8.4 and withdraw applicable cash discount.

Check the vendor balance and the bank account balance before posting. Then post the payment and check the balances again, in addition controlling the voucher transaction and the transaction origin of the payment transaction.

Exercise 8.10 – Transaction Reversal

Your vendor of exercise 3.2 now submits the invoice "VI810" with a total of GBP 30.00 to your company. Register and post the invoice like you did in exercise 8.8.

Noticing that the invoice is incorrect afterwards, you want to reverse it. Check the vendor balance, the vendor transactions, the ledger balance of your expense account, and the corresponding ledger transactions before reversing. Then reverse the invoice and check the balance and the transactions again.

8.4 Ledger Integration

One of the main advantages of an integrated business solution like Dynamics AX is, that business transactions registered anywhere in the application are then available in all areas. For example, posting a sales order invoice does not only generate the required document, it also affects other areas generating following transactions:

> **Inventory transactions** – Reducing inventory value
> **General ledger transactions** – To revenue, COGS, stock and customer debt accounts
> **Customer transaction** – For the open invoice in accounts receivable
> **Sales tax transactions** – As applicable

Depending on the particular transaction, the invoice additionally for example posts transactions for commission, discount or cash payment.

8.4.1   Basics of Ledger Integration

Ledger integration – the integration of the general ledger in finance with the other areas of the application – is one of the core characteristics of an integrated business solution (ERP solution).

In Dynamics AX, transactions in all areas relevant to finance – like sales, purchasing, inventory, or production – automatically post transactions to the general ledger.

8.4.1.1   Basic Settings

A number of settings control, whether and which main accounts apply to the different transactions in business. For the areas of purchasing, sales, inventory, and production covered in this book, following settings are relevant:

> **Summary accounts for vendor liabilities and customer debts** – In the posting profiles for accounts payable/receivable
> **Main accounts for inventory transactions** – In the inventory posting setup
> **Main accounts for production transactions** – In resources, cost categories and production groups

In addition, specific settings are available for particular transactions like sales tax, cash discount, indirect costs, or miscellaneous charges.

8.4.1.2   Vendors and Customers

Vendor posting profiles control the assignment of vendor transactions to summary accounts in the general ledger. Customer posting profiles for customer transactions work similar.

More details on posting profiles are available in section 3.2.3 of this book.

8.4.1.3   Subledger Accounting

Subledger accounting in Dynamics AX provides the option to decouple posting to subledgers – like accounts receivables – from posting to the general ledger. Applying the subledger journal entry functionality, it is possible to run the transfer to the general ledger either synchronous or asynchronous, and either detailed or summarized.

Subledger accounting does not apply to all subledger transactions, but to specific document types including:

> **Free text invoice** – See section 4.6.3
> **Product receipt** – Purchase order receipt, see section 3.5.4
> **Vendor invoice** – Purchase order invoice, see section 3.6.2

In the general ledger parameters (*General ledger> Setup> General ledger parameters,* tab *Batch transfer rules*), settings for the subledger transfer are available at company level and per document type. The *Transfer mode* in the particular batch transfer rule controls, when a subledger transaction is posted to the general ledger:

> **Synchronous** – Immediately posting to the general ledger
> **Asynchronous** – Posting as soon as sever capacity is available
> **Scheduled batch** – In a separate batch job (e.g. in the nighttime), providing the option to view subledger transactions before transferring to the general ledger

For documents applying scheduled batch transfer, posted subledger transactions show in the form *General ledger> Inquiries> Subledger journal entries not yet transferred* before transfer. Clicking the button *Transfer entry* (for immediate transfer) or *Batch transfer* (for scheduled transfer) in this form posts the subledger transaction to the general ledger.

The button *Subledger journal* in the subledger transfer form and in applicable source documents (e.g. free text invoices) provides access to the complete accounting information including all applicable financial segments.

8.4.1.4 New in Dynamics AX 2012

In Dynamics AX 2012, the financial framework includes subledger accounting.

8.4.2   Ledger Integration in Inventory

When posting inventory receipts and issues to the general ledger, Dynamics AX distinguished two different types of transactions (see section 7.1.1):

> **Physical transaction** – Packing slip
> **Financial transaction** – Invoice

Physical and financial transactions refer to different main accounts.

8.4.2.1 Physical Transaction

Posting of physical transactions to the general ledger is optional, not compulsory. Relevant settings on this subject include following checkboxes:

> **Post physical inventory** (in the item model group)
> **Post product receipt in ledger** (Accounts payable parameters, tab *Updates*) or **Post packing slip in ledger** (Accounts receivable parameters).

In the production menu, a similar checkbox in the production control parameters applies. Physical transactions in production are picking list and report as finished transactions.

8.4.2.2   Financial Transaction

For financial transactions, the checkbox *Post financial value* in the item model group determines whether inventory transactions post to the general ledger.

If this checkbox is cleared for an item model group, ledger integration is not active for the assigned items. This is the appropriate setting for service items. Posting a purchase invoice in this case directly posts to the expense account for consumption. Inventory issues do not post ledger transactions.

8.4.2.3   Assignment of Main Accounts

In order to check the main accounts applying automatically when posting an inventory transaction, access the inventory posting setup (*Inventory and warehouse management> Setup> Posting> Posting*). The inventory posting setup form includes account settings for following transactions:

➢ **Sales order tab** – Packing slips and invoices in sales
➢ **Purchase order tab** – Product receipts and invoices in purchasing
➢ **Inventory tab** – Journal transactions in inventory
➢ **Production tab** – Picking lists, reporting as finished and costing of production orders
➢ **Standard cost variance tab** – Standard cost variances

Each of these tabs shows a list of available transaction types in the left pane. After selecting a transaction type in the left pane, the right pane shows the main accounts for this transaction type.

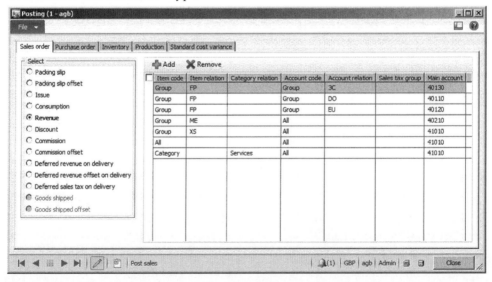

Figure 8-19:   The inventory posting setup, showing account settings for revenue

8.4.2.4 Transaction Combinations

The inventory posting setup primarily depends on the combination of two dimensions:

➢ Items or categories
➢ Customers or vendors

In addition, main account settings optionally are depending on the sales tax group and – for standard cost variance transactions – on the cost group.

For the item dimension and for the customer (tab *Sales order*) – or the vendor (tab *Purchase order*) – dimension, main account settings are available at three levels:

➢ **Table** – Individual item, customer or vendor
➢ **Group** – Item group, customer group or vendor group
➢ **All**

The *Item code* "Category" – an additional option for the item dimension in sales and purchasing – enables settings depending on product categories. The last line of the revenue settings in Figure 8-19 shows an example for such a setting.

When posting a transaction, Dynamics AX always searches for the specific setting ("Table") first, then for the group setting, and finally for the general setting ("All"). For example in a sales invoice transaction, settings for the customer and item number have the highest priority, followed by group settings. Settings in the field group *Posting* on the tab *Ledger and sales tax* of the accounts receivable parameters control, whether the search should prioritize the item or the customer dimension. A similar setting for purchasing is available in the accounts payable parameters.

Main account assignment is not only available in the inventory posting setup form. Alternatively access these settings by clicking the button *Posting* in the item group form, or the button *Setup/Item posting* in the customer group or vendor group form. When accessing the posting setup from a group form, it shows the ledger settings filtered on the selected group. In the item group form itself, the right-hand pane shows the main account settings filtered of the selected item group.

8.4.2.5 Available Combinations and Ledger Reconciliation

The transaction combinations form (*Inventory and warehouse management> Setup> Posting> Transaction combinations*) determines the dimension levels, which are available in the inventory posting setup.

Since reports for the reconciliation between inventory and the general ledger like the report *Inventory and warehouse management> Reports> Status> Inventory value> Inventory value* usually refer to the item group, the item group relation is active in a common setup scenario. The setup for the inventory value report is available in the form *Inventory and warehouse management> Setup> Costing> Inventory value reports*.

8.4.2.6 Example – Transactions Referring to Sales Order Processing

As an example for automatic ledger transactions, the lines below show the transactions in sales order processing with activated ledger integration for packing slip and invoice posting (physical and financial transactions).

When posting the packing slip for the sales order, Dynamics AX posts a ledger transaction to the main accounts specified for *Packing slip* and *Packing slip offset* in the inventory posting setup. When posting the invoice, Dynamics AX reverses the ledger transactions of packing slip posting, and posts a ledger transaction to the account *Issue* against *Consumption*. In parallel, a customer debt to the summary account (specified in the posting profile) posts against the account *Revenue* and – if applicable – the sales tax account.

If the inventory posting setup includes settings in the option *Discount* for the line discount, the discount posts to this account. Otherwise, the discount does not post separately, but reduces the revenue amount.

8.4.2.7 Standard Cost Price and Moving Average

For items assigned to an inventory model "Standard cost" (see section 7.3.1), there are important settings on the tab *Standard cost variance* of the inventory posting setup. This tab contains the main accounts applicable for posting differences between the actual cost price of the purchase invoice (or production costing) and the standard cost price, broken down by different posting types like *Purchase price variance*.

For items assigned to an inventory model with a fixed receipt price, settings for posting the price difference are available on the tabs *Purchase order* and *Inventory*.

For items assigned to an inventory model "Moving average", settings for posting the price difference (for quantities not on stock any more when receiving the invoice) and for revaluation are available on the tab *Inventory*.

8.4.2.8 Service Items and Non-stocked Items

Items like office supplies or consumables may be linked to the product type "Service", applying a specific item group and item model group. In the item model group, ledger integration for physical and financial transactions should be deselected. In sales orders, only a ledger transaction of the revenue account against the customer summary account is posted for these items. There is no transaction to an issue or consumption account.

Non-stocked items, which are not part of a bill of materials, may alternatively or additionally refer to an item model group with a cleared checkbox *Stocked product* (see section 7.2.1). This setting prevents inventory transactions and ensures that ledger integration for physical and financial transactions is deselected.

8.4.2.9 Change of Settings

In order to avoid issues when reconciling inventory and general ledger, you should not change integration settings in the item model group, in parameters and in the inventory posting setup for items, which are on stock or show open inventory transactions. This includes both, changing the setup itself, and changing the assignment of active items to item groups.

8.4.2.10 New in Dynamics AX 2012

In Dynamics AX 2012, settings for product categories enhance the posting setup for the item dimension.

8.4.3 Ledger Integration in Production

Unlike ledger transactions in purchasing, sales and inventory, ledger transactions in production have to include the cost of resource operations for calculating the inventory value of finished items.

8.4.3.1 Production Control Parameters

In order to comply with this requirement, production parameters (*Production control> Setup> Production control parameters*) controlling ledger integration contain following options in the lookup field *Ledger posting*:

➢ **Item and resource**
➢ **Item and category**
➢ **Production groups**

The setting in the general production parameters, which is not available in the production parameters by site, is the default for production orders. It is possible to override this default in particular production orders, for example if applying specific settings for prototype production.

8.4.3.2 Item and Resource

If choosing the option "Item and resource" in the *Ledger posting* parameter, the main accounts specified in the inventory posting setup apply to item transactions. For resource operations, the main account settings on the tab *Ledger* of the resource (*Organization administration> Common> Resources> Resources*) apply.

8.4.3.3 Item and Category

If choosing the option "Item and category" in the *Ledger posting* parameter, the main accounts specified in the inventory posting setup apply to item transactions again. But for resource operations, settings of the applicable cost category (*Production control> Setup> Routes> Cost categories*, tab *Ledger-resources*) apply.

8.4.3.4 Production Group

If choosing the option "Production group" in the *Ledger posting* parameter, main account settings in the posting group (*Production control> Setup> Production> Production groups*) apply.

Production orders show the applicable production group on the tab *General* in the detail form. In the released product form, a default for this production group of a finished product is available on the tab *Engineer*.

8.4.3.5 Ledger Transactions for Production

When processing a production order, following ledger transactions are posted to the main accounts (depending on the *Ledger posting* parameter, see above):

➢ **Picking list** – Account *Picking list* against *Picking list offset account*
➢ **Resource operation** – Account *WIP issue* against *WIP account* (WIP = "Work In Process")
➢ **Report as finished** – Account *Report as finished* against *Report as finished offset account*

When costing the production order, Dynamics AX reverses all these transactions and posts the final finished item receipt, component issue and resource issue transactions to the main accounts as specified in the *Ledger posting* parameter.

9 Core Setup and Essential Features

The organization of an enterprise determines the setup of the ERP system. Before starting to work in Dynamics AX, there needs to be an implementation project setting up the enterprise organization and other core parameters.

9.1 Organizational Structures

An instance is an independent installation of Dynamics AX, which contains its own database and application. Since instances are independent from each other, modifying configuration settings and programmable objects in one instance does not affect other instances. You may physically install one Dynamics AX instance on one or more database and application servers. But it is also possible to install several instances on one server.

In a business environment, there is usually at least one instance for development and tests, which is separate from the operational ERP system in order to avoid affecting daily business.

Within one Dynamics AX instance, data partitions in Dynamics AX 2012 R2 enable independent data for enterprises working in a common Dynamics AX database without sharing business data.

Within a data partition, the organization model shows the structure of the enterprise and its business processes. The organization model therefore has to be configured according the specific operational and statutory structure.

Depending on the type and the size of an enterprise, there may be different organizational structures. These organizational structures show following types:

> **Statutory organization structures for legal reporting** – Hierarchies according to regulations of public authorities (e.g. for tax purposes)
> **Operating organization structures for management reporting** – Hierarchies according to requirements of the internal management for controlling and improving business processes (e.g. divisional structures)
> **Informal structures** – Not showing organizational hierarchies

In order to comply with the different reporting requirements, large enterprises may show different organizational structures and hierarchies in parallel. Applying parallel hierarchies, one of the hierarchies for example matches the structure and purpose of legal entities, another hierarchy supports the divisional structure, and a third hierarchy complies with regional structures.

For other enterprises, one simple hierarchy without the need for different organizational structures may be adequate.

9.1.1   Data Partitions

Dynamics AX 2012 contains multiple areas of shared application data – e.g. parties, addresses, products, currencies, resource capabilities, or employees. Depending on the specific requirements, enterprises either want to share these data across multiple or all companies, or to keep company data isolated.

Data partitions in Dynamics AX 2012 R2 enable independent data for enterprises working in a common Dynamics AX instance (database and application).

9.1.1.1   Architecture of Data Partitions

In each relevant table, the column *Partition* is a key field containing the applicable partition of the records. Within a partition, the key field *DataAreaId* in tables with company-specific data determines the company of the particular record.

Companies working in different partitions only share the application code – therefore using the same program functionality and customizations – and basic shared system data including database settings, AIF ports and batch jobs. Dynamics AX users, permissions, and shared application data like parties or currencies are not shared across partitions.

When deciding on the setup of data partitions, keep in mind that some features in Dynamics AX like the intercompany functionality (for automatic purchase and sales processes between companies) require working in a common partition.

9.1.1.2   Creating and Using Partitions

Installing Microsoft Dynamics AX creates the default partition "Initial". If you do not need multiple partitions for separating data, you can set up all companies in this partition then.

In case you want to create an additional partition, access the menu item *System administration> Setup> Partitions* and create a new partition as required. Once saved, you cannot delete a partition. The system administrator creating a partition must then create the users and permissions in this partition. Next you can create companies, organization units and hierarchies, and other setup data as applicable.

When logging on to Dynamics AX, you are accessing a particular data partition and company. This partition usually is the default partition as specified for your user in the user administration (*System administration> Common> Users> Users*, checkbox *Current partition is default partition* in the detail form). You cannot switch partition in a client session. If you want to access another partition, create or choose a client configuration with the appropriate partition for starting the client.

Depending on your user options, the status bar and the title bar of forms show the current partition.

9.1.1.3   New in Dynamics AX 2012 R2

Data partitions are new in Dynamics AX 2012 R2.

9.1.2 Organization Model Architecture

The flexible organization model in Microsoft Dynamics AX supports the requirements of different organization types. Depending on these requirements, the organization setup alternatively includes multiple organization hierarchies in parallel, decoupling the operating organization from the statutory organization, or only one simple hierarchy used for all purposes at the same time.

9.1.2.1 Organization Types

The organization model in Dynamics AX includes following organization types:

➢ **Legal entities** – Showing the statutory organization
➢ **Operating units** – Showing the operating organization
➢ **Teams** – Showing informal structures

Only organization units of the type "Legal entity" and "Operating unit" are applicable elements for setting up organization hierarchies in Dynamics AX.

Since organization units of the type "Team" are an informal type of organizations, they are not included in hierarchies. Teams apply to several areas of Dynamics AX, for example as a basis for restricting access to the global address book.

9.1.2.2 Using the Organization Model within Dynamics AX

Following areas apply the organization model within Dynamics AX:

➢ **Company structure** – Legal entities are linked to companies in Dynamics AX, which is why you have to set up legal entities for creating companies.
➢ **Financial dimensions** – Since legal entities and operating units are available as financial dimension, they may be used for financial reporting.
➢ **Data security** – Based on the organization hierarchy purpose *Security*, access of users to organizations may be configured independently from the structure of legal entities.
➢ **Business policies** – Business rules for areas like approval processes and centralized payments may apply to a structure which is different to the hierarchy of legal entities.

Legal entities and operating units are not only part of organizational hierarchies, but they are also included in the global address book (see section 2.4). Therefore, features of the global address book like address and contact administration apply to these elements of the internal organization.

9.1.3 Organization Units

The organization model includes organization units of the type "Legal entity", "Operating unit" and "Team". Legal entities and operating units are the basic elements in the organizational hierarchies of an enterprise.

The list page *Organization administration> Common> Organization> Internal organizations* shows an overview of all organizations with their type. Forms tailored to the specific requirements of the different organization types are available in the folder *Organization administration> Setup> Organization*.

Internal Organization		
Legal Entities	**Operating Units**	**Teams**
Statutory organization (Companies)	*Operating organization* ➢ Departments ➢ Cost centers ➢ Business units ➢ Value streams ➢ Retail channels	*Informal organization*

Figure 9-1:   Organization units in the organization model

9.1.3.1   Legal Entities

Legal entities (*Organization administration> Setup> Organization> Legal entities*) are company accounts in Dynamics AX (see section 9.1.5 below), constituting the basic level for legal reporting. Tax reports and financial statements like balance sheets and income statements are based on legal entities.

Since a data partition in Dynamics AX may contain several legal entities, you can manage the relations between these legal entities. Depending on your requirements, following features are available:

➢ **Financial consolidation** – Managing financial consolidation of companies in an affiliated group
➢ **Intercompany** – Automating business processes between the legal entities of a multi-company organization
➢ **Organization hierarchies** – Applying legal entities in the organization model (e.g. for setting up data security or approval processes)

9.1.3.2   Operating Units

Operating units (*Organization administration> Setup> Organization> Operating units*) are there for management reporting, supporting internal control of business processes. Depending on the enterprise, it includes different types of operating units like divisions or regions.

A standard Dynamics AX implementation contains following operating unit types:

➢ **Department** – Representing functional categories, also used in human resources
➢ **Cost center** – For budgeting and expenditure control
➢ **Value stream** – Referring to production flows (lean manufacturing)
➢ **Business unit** – Controlling strategic business objectives (e.g. divisions)
➢ **Retail channel** – Referring to retail management

When setting up a new operating unit by clicking the button *New* in the action pane strip of the operating unit form, select the *Operating unit type* first. Then enter additional data like name, addresses and contact data in the detail form.

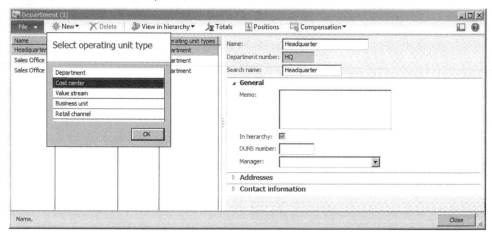

Figure 9-2:   Creating a cost center in the operating unit form

Once an operating unit is assigned to one or more hierarchies, clicking the button *View in hierarchy* enables checking the positioning within organizational structures. Linking operating units to financial dimensions (see section 8.2.3) allows reporting on their performance.

9.1.3.3 Teams

Teams (*Organization administration> Setup> Organization> Teams*) represent the informal organization of an enterprise. Teams are groups of people, without a hierarchical organization structure between different teams.

Team types, accessible by clicking the button *Team types* in the action pane of the teams form, may restrict team membership to different kinds of people – e.g. Dynamics AX users, employees, or sales contacts.

When creating a new team, you have to select the team type first. Then click the button *Add team members* on the tab *Team members* of the teams form for assigning persons to the team. Depending on the team type, available members are for example Dynamics AX users, or vendors, or employees.

Teams are applicable to different areas of the application, e.g. collections (select the responsible team in the accounts receivable parameters) or access restriction to the global address book (see section 9.2.4).

9.1.3.4 New in Dynamics AX 2012 and in AX 2012 R2

The organization model is a new element in Dynamics AX 2012. Compared with the initial version of Dynamics AX 2012, the R2 version additionally contains the operating unit type "Retail channel".

9.1.4   Organization Hierarchy Structures

Organization hierarchies show the relationship between different organization units in a particular perspective towards your enterprise. An organizational hierarchy of legal entities for example shows the legal structure.

Depending on the requirements of your enterprise, there are several hierarchies in parallel. The purposes of a hierarchy determine its functional areas. Hierarchies of the type *Security* for example apply to data security.

9.1.4.1   Organization Hierarchies

For accessing organization hierarchies, choose the form *Organization administration> Setup> Organization> Organization hierarchies*. If creating a new hierarchy by clicking the button *New*, you have to enter the hierarchy name first. Then click the button *Assign purpose* on the tab *Purposes* of the hierarchies form for assigning one or more hierarchy purposes to the hierarchy.

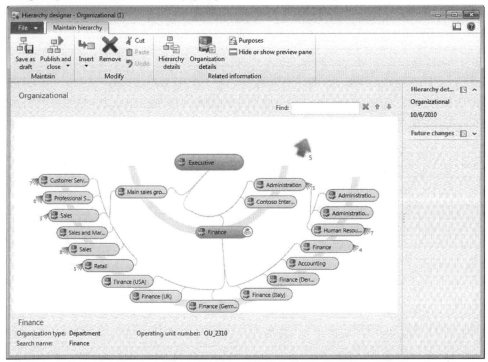

Figure 9-3:   Editing an organization hierarchy in the hierarchy designer

Clicking the button *View* in the action pane strip provides access to the hierarchy designer for viewing the hierarchy. In the hierarchy designer, navigate within the hierarchy, or switch the focus by clicking the icon 🌀 on the right of the nodes.

After switching to the edit mode by clicking the button *Edit* in the action pane of the hierarchy designer, insert or remove organization units from the hierarchy as applicable by clicking the appropriate button in the action pane or choosing the pop-up menu (right-hand click on an organization unit). The buttons *Cut* and *Paste* provide the option to move a unit including subunits within the whole organization hierarchy.

The organization structure applies validity periods, which is why you have to enter an effective date when publishing the hierarchy after editing.

9.1.4.2 Organization Hierarchy Purposes

The organization hierarchy form may include several hierarchies in parallel, applying different perspectives – or purposes – to the individual hierarchies.

Organization hierarchy purposes are available in the form *Organization administration> Setup> Organization> Organization hierarchy purposes*. Since hierarchy purposes refer to functional features, available purposes – like *Centralized payments* or *Security* – and the allowed organization types per purpose are determined by the Dynamics AX standard application.

Clicking the button *Add* on the tab *Assigned hierarchies* of the hierarchy purposes form enables assigning organization hierarchies to purposes. Depending on the requirements, assign several hierarchies to one purpose or one hierarchy to several purposes.

9.1.5 Legal Entities (Company Accounts)

When logging on to Dynamics AX, you are accessing a particular company account (legal entity) which is the current company for the session. The default company applicable when starting the client is specified in your user options or in the client configuration.

Depending on your user options, the status bar and the title bar of forms show the current company. If you want to switch from one current company to another, choose the command *File/Tools/Select company accounts* or click the company field in the status bar.

9.1.5.1 Managing a Company

The company management (legal entity administration) in Dynamics AX is available in the form *Organization administration> Setup> Organization> Legal entities*. If you want to create a new company, click the button *New* or push the shortcut *Ctrl+N* and enter the company name, the company ID (with up to 4 digits), and the country/region (specifying applicable country-specific Dynamics AX features) in the *Create new legal entity* dialog.

Before you can start entering and posting transactions in the new company, the setup of the company has to be done in all applicable areas and modules (like general ledger, accounts payable and accounts receivable). A checklist of basic settings is available in the appendix of this book.

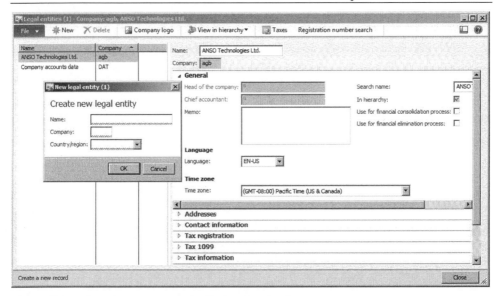

Figure 9-4: Creating a company in the legal entity form

In the legal entity form, setup data include the company name (which prints on all documents and reports) and further settings like the primary address of the company on the tab *Addresses*. If the company has got additional addresses for purposes like invoicing or delivery, add them by clicking the button *Add* on tab *Addresses*. An example of an additional address is a default delivery address which is different to the primary company address. This delivery address is the default for purchase orders then (if no address from a site or warehouse applies).

Contact data of the company are available on the tab *Contact information*. Legal entities in Dynamics AX apply to the global address book, which is why company addresses and contact data are included there.

Further important settings in the legal entity form include the primary bank account and registration numbers (like the *Routing number* for tax reporting) on the tab *Bank account information*. Companies located in the European Union enter their VAT registration number (exempt number) on the tab *Foreign trade and logistics*.

9.1.5.2 Companies in the Data Structure

One data partition may include multiple company accounts. Except for shared application data (like parties or and products), company accounts hold their separate set of data within the partition. The key field *DataAreaId* in all relevant Dynamics AX tables then determines the company of the particular record.

A specific company included in all data partitions is the company "DAT". Dynamics AX automatically generates this company, which holds system data, when installing the system. You cannot delete it and you should not use it for a test or operational company in order to clearly distinguish company data from non-company specific data.

9.1.5.3 New in Dynamics AX 2012

In Dynamics AX 2012, the concept of legal entities replaces the structure of company account settings in former releases. The legal entity form now includes the former company information, moving the company currency to the ledger form (see section 8.2.2).

9.1.6   Virtual Company Accounts

Dynamics AX 2012 contains several functional areas sharing data across legal entities – e.g. parties, address books, charts of accounts, or shared products.

In addition, virtual company accounts enable a joint management of data, which are not included in these areas, but nevertheless are common to several companies within one partition. Depending on the requirements, applicable areas of common data include delivery terms, tax setup, bills of material, or any other table.

9.1.6.1 Setup of Virtual Companies

Virtual companies are available in the form *System administration> Setup> Virtual company accounts*. For creating a virtual company account, insert a new record on the tab *Virtual company accounts* with an ID and a name there. Dynamics AX internally applies the virtual company account ID instead of the regular company account in the key field *DataAreaId* for all tables of the table collections assigned to the virtual company. Therefore, it is not possible to choose a code which already exists for a regular company in Dynamics AX.

Once the new virtual company account record is saved, switch to the tab *Company accounts* and assign companies to the virtual company as applicable by moving them from the right pane to the left pane (either dragging and dropping with your mouse or by clicking the arrow buttons ⬚ and ⬚).

For specifying the tables which are common to these companies, switch to the tab *Table collections*. You cannot specify individual tables on this tab, but only table collections representing a group of tables. Creating and editing table collections is only possible in the development environment.

Virtual company accounts are a basic setup, which needs to be configured at the very beginning of an implementation project. If adding virtual companies or shared tables once data are already stored in the tables concerned, you have to manage data consolidation directly in the database. Without data consolidation, these tables do not show former data of the companies concerned.

9.1.6.2 Working in Virtual Companies

Unlike regular company accounts, virtual companies do not provide a direct access. In order to access virtual company data, log on to a regular company and insert, modify and delete records of shared tables like you do in tables with company-specific data. Changes of data in tables of a shared table collection are immediately available in all companies of the virtual company account.

9.1.7   Sites

Unlike company accounts, which comply with legal entities, sites represent subsidiaries within a company. Being an inventory dimension (storage dimension), sites are available in all areas of supply chain management within Dynamics AX.

In order to distinguish subsidiaries in finance and cost accounting, optionally link the inventory dimension "Site" to a financial dimension. Applying a filter on the financial dimension allows for example printing an income statement per subsidiary.

9.1.7.1   Multisite Functionality

The multisite functionality for managing subsidiaries in Dynamics AX includes the following options:

➢ **Operations planning** (master scheduling) – Per site or for the entire company
➢ **Bills of materials** and **Routes** – Per site or for the entire company
➢ **Production control parameters** – Per site or for the entire company
➢ **Item data (Released products)** for order management and planning – Per site or for the entire company
➢ **Transactions** – Sites in all inventory transactions, sales orders, purchase orders and production orders
➢ **Financial reports** – Optionally for sites (if linked to a financial dimension)

9.1.7.2   Setup of Sites

Sites are available in the form *Inventory and warehouse management> Setup> Inventory breakdown> Sites*. Apart from the ID, the name and the address, a site includes the assigned financial dimension on the tab *Financial Dimensions*. This setting is mandatory if the dimension link is activated.

The dimension link between the inventory dimension "Site" and a financial dimension is specified in the form *Inventory and warehouse management> Setup> Posting> Dimension link*. If applicable to your enterprise structure, activate and lock the link there. Figure 9-5 for example shows the site form in a company linking the financial dimension "Department" to sites.

Since sites are a mandatory storage dimension, they are automatically activated in all storage dimension groups. Appropriate dimension values therefore have to be entered in every inventory transaction. In addition, each warehouse has to be linked to a site.

If sites do not apply to the organization of your enterprise, set up Dynamics AX in a way that a single site defaults to all transactions (e.g. applying appropriate defaults in the *Default order settings* of released products). More information on inventory dimensions is available in section 7.2.2.

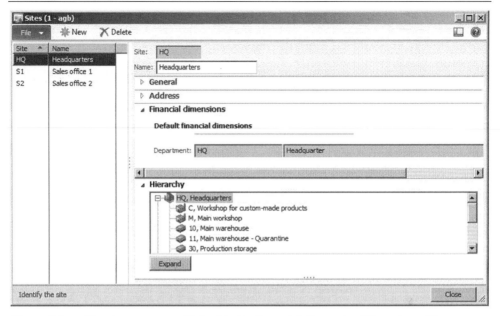

Figure 9-5:   Sites in a company (linked to the financial dimension "Department")

9.1.7.3 Production Units

Whereas material management applies *Sites* as a storage dimension for establishing a structure level below legal entities, capacity management applies *Production units* for structuring resources and resource groups. Each production unit is linked to a site and represents a plant in operations planning.

9.1.7.4 Linking Sites to the Organization Model

It is not possible to directly include sites in the organization model. But you can link sites to a financial dimension and financial dimensions to organization units, which in the end provides the option to use sites in the organization model.

In order to apply sites to Dynamics AX finance and organization administration, perform following implementation steps:

➢ **Set up operating units** for the individual sites choosing a common operating unit type (e.g. *Department* or *Business unit*)
➢ **Set up a financial dimension** linked to this organization unit type
➢ **Apply an account structure** in the company containing this financial dimension
➢ **Link the storage dimension** *Site* to this financial dimension

Choosing the same name for the organization unit and the related site visualizes sites in the organization hierarchy. Through the organization model, security settings are available at site level. If the link between site and financial dimension is activated in the dimension link, financial reporting is available at site level.

9.1.7.5   New in Dynamics AX 2012

In Dynamics AX 2012, sites are mandatory.

9.2   Security and Information Access

Business applications like Microsoft Dynamics AX contain confidential data. In order to protect sensitive information, access to the application has to be limited depending on the needs of the specific enterprise.

9.2.1   Access Control

Access control in Dynamics AX is based on two elements:

➢ **Authentication** – Identification of users
➢ **Authorization** – User permissions

9.2.1.1   Authentication

As a prerequisite for authenticating you in Dynamics AX, system administration has to create and enable a Dynamics AX user linked to your Windows user ID.

Usually you do not notice the authentication and logon procedure, since it happens automatically in the background applying your Windows user ID. But if you are not set up as a valid Dynamics AX user, Dynamics AX rejects to grant access.

User authentication is not only required for permission control. It is also the basis for logging your transactions and for tracking your editing of table data. Further settings linked to your Dynamics AX user include the favorites, the user options, and the usage data, which enable a personalized workspace in Dynamics AX.

9.2.1.2   Authorization

According to the role-based security concept in Dynamics AX, information access within Dynamics AX depends on the permission settings of the roles attached to your Dynamics AX user.

Your roles are linked to duties and privileges, limiting data access to read or write permission. Access control in this functional context is based on menu items, forms, tables and fields.

Extensible data security policies in addition enable limiting access to table records depending on record data – for example setting a restriction, that a particular user may only access customers of a particular customer group.

9.2.2   User Management

As mentioned above, each person accessing Dynamics AX has to be set up as a Dynamics AX user.

Apart from Active Directory authorization, Dynamics AX user management may also include users with claims-based authentication – especially for users only accessing the Enterprise Portal. Claims-based authentication refers to a trusted identity provider in SharePoint for authenticating the user

9.2.2.1 User Accounts

For manually creating a Dynamics AX user, access the list page *System administration> Common> Users> Users* and click the button *New/User*. After inserting the *User ID* for a Dynamics AX user with the *Account type* "Active Directory user", enter the Windows user ID in the field *Alias* and the Active Directory domain in the field *Network domain*. In addition, the checkbox *Enabled* has to be selected for enabling the user to log on to Dynamics AX.

As an alternative to manually inserting, import Dynamics AX users from the Active Directory through the import wizard, which is accessible by clicking the button *New/Import* in the action pane of the users form.

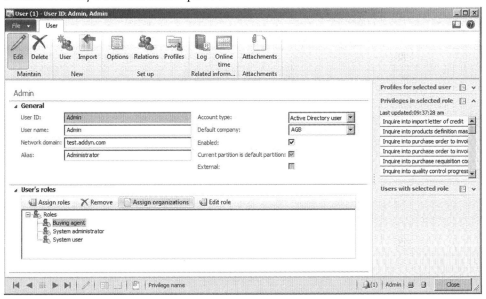

Figure 9-6: Managing a user in the user detail form

9.2.2.2 Assigning Security Roles

If you want to specify the permissions of a particular user, access the tab *User's roles* in the user detail form and assign appropriate security roles. Alternatively choose the form *System administration> Setup> Security> Assign users to roles* for linking users to roles.

Security roles of a particular user also display in the appropriate FactBox of the users list page. If a user is assigned to multiple roles, the permissions of all selected roles are effective. In case permission settings for an object overlap, the higher access level applies.

9.2.2.3 Assigning Permissions on Organization Level

After assigning a security role to a user in the user detail form, access of this user applying this role may be restricted at organization level.

For this purpose, select the particular role on the tab *User's roles* of the user detail form and click the button *Assign organizations* in the action pane strip. In the *Assign organizations* form, grant access to the user in the selected role either in all organizations or only in specific organizations. If selecting specific organizations, choose either legal entities or elements of organization hierarchies with the purpose *Security*. After selecting an organization in the upper pane of the *Assign organizations* form, click the button *Grant* in the action pane strip of the lower pane for actually assigning the permission.

9.2.2.4 User Options

Clicking the button *Options* in the action pane of the users form provides access to the user options of the selected user. In case the user got appropriate permissions, he may also access his user options by selecting the command *File/Tools/Options*.

Accessing the user options from the user management may be useful, if the administrator wants to predefine settings like the language or the start company.

9.2.2.5 User Profiles

Clicking the button *Profiles* in the action pane of the users form provides access to the user profiles for assigning the user to a role center (see section 2.1.4).

Profiles and role centers are independent from security roles. In order to ensure that data access required in a particular role center is granted to the users concerned, assign the users to appropriate security roles.

9.2.2.6 User Relations

Apart from being a user, persons who are accessing Dynamics AX may be employees, contractors or external parties (e.g. customers). Master data for workers (employees and contractors) on the one hand, and for external parties on the other, are stored in separate tables within Dynamics AX.

In order to assign a Dynamics AX user to his worker record or external relation, Dynamics AX requires a link. This link is available in the form *System administration> Common> Users> User relations*, alternatively accessible by clicking the button *Relations* after selecting the appropriate user in the users list page.

For linking a user to a worker record (or an external party), click the button *New* in the user relations form and select the person from the global address book in the lookup field *Person*. For searching a person in the value lookup of this field, apply an appropriate filter (e.g. a filter by field right-clicking the appropriate column in the lookup).

Worker records are required throughout the whole application of Dynamics AX. Examples of applicable areas are purchase requisitions, pallet transports, sales commissions, project accounting, human resources, case management, and sales prospect management. After linking a user to a worker record, the worker ID applies to all areas concerned – e.g. automatically inserting it in the field *Employee responsible* when entering a new prospect (*Sales and marketing> Common> Prospects> All prospects*).

9.2.2.7 Workers (Employees)

The user form contains general user settings for persons accessing Dynamics AX. Independent from the user administration, the worker form is there to manage data of the enterprise personnel.

Workers include internal employees and contractors, Dynamics AX users as well as personnel not accessing Dynamics AX. Worker records are shared and included in the global address book. The employment of a worker determines his assignment to one or more companies.

For accessing worker records, open the list page *Human resources> Common> Workers> Workers*. In order to create a new worker, click the button *Hire new worker* in the action pane then. In the *Create new worker* dialog, enter the name, employing company (*Legal entity*), personnel number (if not deriving from a number sequence), worker type (employee or contractor), and employment start date.

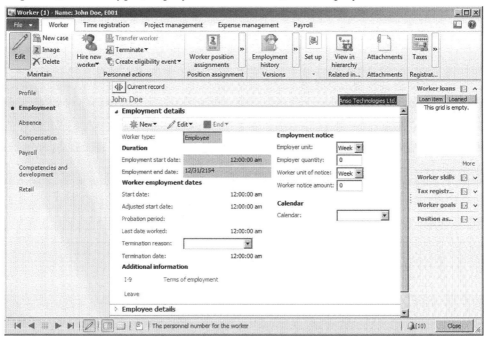

Figure 9-7:   Managing employment data in the worker detail form

The default for the employing company is the current company. If you want to change the employment later to another company or hire the worker in parallel in another company, access the tab *Employment* in the worker detail form and edit the existing or add a new employment.

Numerous data in the worker record are company-specific. If the employee got a current employment in more than one company, click the button showing the company name on the tab *Employment* ("Anso Technologies Ltd." in Figure 9-7) in order to switch the applicable company for company-specific data. In the worker list page, apply an advanced filter on the legal entity of employment if you want to view only workers employed in a particular company.

Required detail data in the worker record are primarily depending on the Dynamics AX modules used in your organization. If applicable, specific details are necessary for project accounting, human resources, and expense management.

Note: Employment and particular data in the worker record are date-effective. By default, the worker list page and detail form only show current data.

9.2.2.8 Online Users

If you want to know the users currently accessing Dynamics AX, open the form *System administration> Common> Users> Online users*. The inquiry shows all client sessions connected to the application. If you got appropriate administrator permissions, log off a user by clicking the button *End sessions* there if required.

9.2.2.9 User Groups

User group administration (including the assignment of users) is available in the form *System administration> Common> Users> User groups*. User groups do not refer to the role-based security concept, but they apply to specific settings.

You may for example open ledger periods, which are on hold, for a specific user group. In workflows or financial journals, optionally apply user groups for assigning workflow tasks and for approval and posting restrictions.

9.2.2.10 New in Dynamics AX 2012

Items new in Dynamics AX 2012 refer to the role-based security concept, assigning users to security roles (instead of user groups). Direct assignment of security roles to companies replaces the security domains available in Dynamics AX 2009.

Shared data for employees (workers) refer to changes in human resource management and the global address book.

9.2.3   Role-based Security

According to the role-based security concept, permissions are not directly granted to users, but to security roles.

9.2.3.1 Security Concept

The role-based security model in Dynamics AX contains the following elements:

➢ **Role** – Group of duties required for a job function (e.g. sales manager)
➢ **Duty** – Group of privileges to perform a task (e.g. approving product prices)
➢ **Privilege** – Contains permissions for individual objects (e.g. post price journal)
➢ **Permission** – Basic access restriction to data and features (e.g. tables, fields)

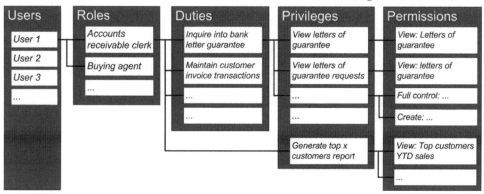

Figure 9-8:   Grouping levels for assigning users to permissions

These elements represent a hierarchical structure for assigning permissions to a user. As shown in Figure 9-8, a user may be assigned to one or more roles depending on his job functions.

Roles are linked to privileges preferably through duties, but it is also possible to directly assign a privilege to a role.

Usually, assigning one or more roles to a user – including the assignment of applicable companies – in the user form is the only task required for specifying permissions when setting up a new user.

9.2.3.2 Security Roles

A role is a set of access permissions required to perform a job function. In a Dynamics AX standard application, there are about 100 reference roles. Roles, which are depending on factors like size, culture, and industry, show different role types:

➢ **Functional roles** – e.g. buying agent
➢ **Organizational roles** – e.g. employee
➢ **Application roles** – e.g. system user

The role *System administrator* has access to all areas of the application. The access settings of this role are not editable.

For accessing role management, open the form *System administration> Setup> Security> Security roles*. The left part of the form shows the roles available in your application. After selecting a role, assigned duties and privileges are available on the tab *Role content*. The icon next to the individual elements shows, whether it is a duty (⬜) or a privilege (⬜). For adding duties and privileges to a role, click the button *Add* in the role content pane.

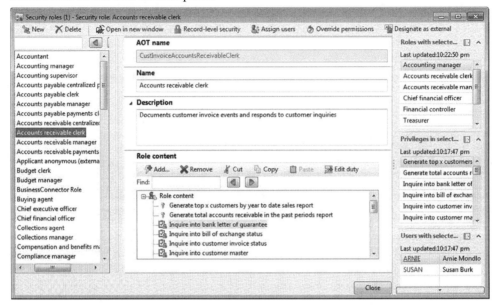

Figure 9-9:   Security roles, showing duties and directly assigned privileges

For a duty selected on the tab *Role content*, the FactBox *Roles with the selected duty* on the right of the form shows all roles containing the particular duty.

9.2.3.3 Duties and Process Cycles

Duties represent a group of privileges required for a particular task, e.g. maintaining customer invoice transactions. A Dynamics AX standard application comprises about 1000 reference duties which are updated when hotfixes and releases cause changes to data structure, functionality and permissions.

For accessing duties, click the button *Edit duty* in the role content pane of the security roles form. Duties are alternatively accessible through the menu item *System administration> Setup> Security> Security privileges*.

The security privileges form shows a tree structure applying process cycles. A process cycle in this context is a grouping according to high level processes like the revenue cycle.

In order to access a particular duty, expand the process cycle tree or search for the duty using the search field located above the process cycle section. Expanding a duty as shown in Figure 9-10 (example: "Approve BOMs") shows assigned privileges.

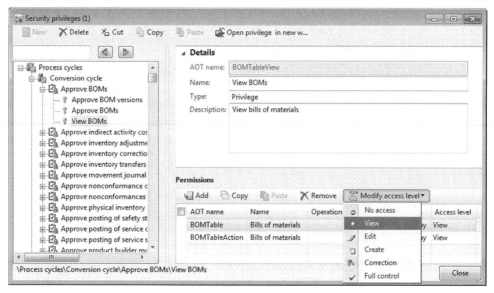

Figure 9-10: Managing duties and privileges in the security privileges form

For editing an element or for assigning privileges and permissions, click the buttons *New*, *Delete*, *Cut*, *Copy* or *Paste* in the action pane strip at the top of the form (or drag and drop elements with your mouse). Depending on the hierarchy level of the element selected in the privileges tree, you are managing a duty or a privilege.

9.2.3.4 Privileges and Permissions

A privilege contains all permissions required for an individual application object. The example in Figure 9-10 shows the privilege "View BOMs" with assigned permissions on the tab *Permissions*. If required, add or remove permissions from a privilege by clicking the appropriate button in the action pane strip of this tab. Clicking the button *Modify access level* enables changing the access level of an assigned permission.

Permissions set access restrictions at the lowest level, based on individual features and record data (like tables and fields). The permissions available in the security privileges are determined by application development.

9.2.3.5 Adjusting Security Settings

Setting access restrictions usually starts by assigning users to roles of the reference model. If required, adjust existing or create new roles, removing duties or adding additional duties.

Since reference duties in Dynamics AX are updated with hotfixes and new releases, it is preferable to adjust existing duties for grouping standard features rather than creating new duties. New duties are applicable to individual functionality developed additionally.

Although it is possible to directly assign privileges to roles (see Figure 9-8), maintenance of permissions is easier if privileges are only assigned to roles.

9.2.3.6   Segregation of Duties

If your organization requires ensuring segregation of duties, manage the rules applicable for the segregation of duties in the form *System administration> Setup> Security> Segregation of duties> Segregation of duties rules*. Creating one or more sets of duties, which may not be assigned together to the same user, supports compliance with segregation of duties policies by logging conflicts for approval or rejection.

Compliance with the segregation of duties in business processes is supported by business policies and workflow management (see section 9.4).

9.2.3.7   New in Dynamics AX 2012

Roles in the role-based security concept of Dynamics AX 2012 replace the user groups of Dynamics AX 2009. Instead of directly assigning user groups to permissions, permission settings for roles in AX 2012 involve duties and privileges.

9.2.4   Securing the Global Address Book

The core usage of the role-based security framework is to restrict access to functional roles. But the global address book, containing all parties within a Dynamics AX partition, is required by nearly all roles.

In order to control access to different party and address data depending on address associations, there are security options for the global address book. These options refer to two groupings:

> ➢ **Address books** – Grouping different parties
> ➢ **Teams** – Grouping different people

9.2.4.1   Security Setup

Address books (see section 2.4.2) are available for assigning a party when entering the party record. A party may be assigned to one or more address books. Since address books are a basis for security settings, keep required access restrictions in mind when setting up address books (e.g. creating a separate address book holding employee records).

Teams (see section 9.1.3) are a flexible option for setting up organization units independently from a hierarchical structure. Referring to the global address book, set up specific teams according to the requirements for access restriction to the global address book (e.g. a separate team for users accessing employee addresses).

9.2.4.2   Security Options

On the tab *Security policy options* of the global address book parameters (*Organization administration> Setup> Global address book> Global address book parameters*), select the checkbox *Secure by address book* if you want to control access at address book level.

After clicking the button *Assign teams*, select one applicable address book after the other in the lookup field *Address book* of the assign teams form. Then select the teams which can access the selected address book. Another option for assigning teams is to click the button *Assign teams* in the address books form (*Organization administration> Setup> Global address book> Address books*).

The checkbox *Secure by legal entity* in the global address book parameters restricts access to parties depending on party roles (e.g. vendor or customer). If this checkbox is selected, users may only access parties assigned to a role in the current company.

9.2.4.3   Applying Address Book Security

If the global address book parameter *Secure by address book* is selected, only users belonging to a team, which is assigned to a particular address book, may access parties of that address book.

A party in the global address book assigned to several address books is available to all users, who have the permission to access any of the address books concerned.

Access restriction does not only apply to the global address book list page itself, but also to other list pages and forms containing party data (like vendors or customers). In addition, the restriction includes related information such as orders or invoices.

9.2.4.4   New in Dynamics AX 2012

Global address book security options are new in Dynamics AX 2012.

9.3   General Settings

There are a number of settings, which are required before an enterprise can start to use Dynamics AX operationally. These settings include:

➢ **Organization management** – See section 9.1
➢ **Security management** – See section 9.2
➢ **Finance settings** – See section 8.2

Each module used by your enterprise also needs to be configured according to the specific requirements (e.g. setting up effective terms of payment in purchasing and sales). In addition, some basic general settings apply to all areas of the application. You can find a short description on core general settings below.

Explanations regarding the setup of individual modules are available in the chapter referring to the particular module. An overview of the basic settings for a Dynamics AX installation is included in the appendix of this book.

9.3.1   Number Sequences

Number sequences control the allocation of numbers throughout the whole application. They are in particular used for following kinds of data:

> ➢ **Master data** – For example assigning vendor numbers
> ➢ **Journals (including orders)** – For example assigning purchase order numbers
> ➢ **Posted transactions** – For example assigning invoice numbers

Dynamics AX 2012 provides number sequences common to all companies within a partition. The scope parameters of a number sequence then control whether it is shared or specific to a company (or other organization unit). In addition, number sequences optionally refer to a fiscal calendar period.

9.3.1.1   Creating and Editing

For editing number sequences, open the list page *Organization administration> Common> Number sequences> Number sequences*. In the number sequences list page, the FactBox *Segments* immediately shows the company and other segments of the selected number sequence as applicable.

For creating a number sequence, click the button *New/Number sequence* or push the shortcut *Ctrl+N* in the number sequence form. After entering a unique *Number sequence code* and a *Name*, expand the tab *Scope parameters* of the detail form in order to specify whether the number sequence is shared or restricted to a company or organization unit.

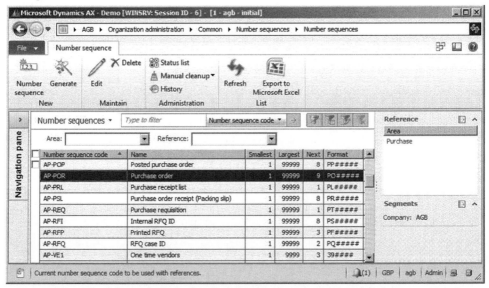

Figure 9-11:   The number sequences list page

9.3.1.2   Segments

On the tab *Segments* of the detail form, specify the format of numbers referring to the number sequence. Segments of a number may show different types:

➤ **Alphanumeric** – Number increasing every time the number sequence is used by replacing the number signs (#) in the format with the next number. The length of the alphanumeric segment has to comply with the largest number.

➤ **Constant** – Segments for prefixes (e.g. for a format "INV#####" or "12#####") and for suffixes (e.g. a format "#####-INV"). In general, prefixes are preferable since they are easier to use (e.g. for filtering).

➤ **Other types** – Segments of the type *Company, Legal entity, Operating unit* or *Fiscal calendar* are available, if included in the *Scope* of the number sequence.

9.3.1.3 Number Sequence References

After setting up the number sequence itself, the number sequence references determine the assignment of a particular number sequence to master data or transactions. For editing number sequence references, switch to the tab *References* in the number sequence detail form. Alternatively, access the number sequence references on the tab *Number sequences* of the parameters form in each module.

In order to ensure easy tracking of transactions within the whole application, it is preferable to use unique document and transaction numbers without overlapping.

A single number sequence may be assigned to several number sequence references at the same time – for example if you want to apply a common number sequence to invoices and credit notes. This setting does not generate duplicate number, but alternately assigns numbers to invoices and credit notes depending on the chronological order of the transactions.

9.3.1.4 General Settings of a Number Sequence

The numeric first (*Smallest*) and last (*Largest*) number of the number sequence are specified on the tab *General* of the number sequence detail form. The field *Next* there shows the number, which the number sequence applies to the next number. You can change the next number, but you have to make sure to avoid duplicate keys and gaps in continuous numbers.

Another option controls if users can change a number automatically assigned from the number sequence to a higher or lower number. Selecting the checkbox *Manual* determines a purely manual entry of numbers.

The checkbox *Continuous* prevents gaps in a number sequence. Considering server performance, select this checkbox only in number sequences actually requiring continuous numbers. Continuous numbering frequently applies to voucher numbers, since it is a statutory requirement in many countries.

9.3.1.5 New in Dynamics AX 2012

In Dynamics AX 2012, number sequences are shared across legal entities.

9.3.2   Calendars

As a prerequisite for posting any transaction in Dynamics AX, an open ledger period covering the posting is required.

9.3.2.1 Ledger Calendar

Ledger calendars (*General ledger> Setup> Ledger*, button *Ledger calendar*), which refer to the fiscal calendar associated with your company, determine the periods open for posting transactions (see section 8.2.1).

9.3.2.2 Other Calendars

Apart from calendars in finance, additional period and calendar definitions apply to other areas within Dynamics AX.

The form *Organization administration> Common> Calendars> Working time templates* contains default settings for the weekly working times, which is a basis for setting up calendars in the form *Organization administration> Common> Calendars> Calendars* (see section 5.3.1). These calendars apply to supply chain management – including operations planning, production, purchasing, sales and inventory management.

The project accounting module has a separate calendar in the form *Organization administration> Common> Calendars> Period types*, required for estimates, invoice subscriptions and employees. This calendar is a basis for project invoicing.

9.3.2.3 New in Dynamics AX 2012

In Dynamics AX 2012, the concept of accounting periods has changed, now providing shared fiscal calendars also replacing fixed asset calendars.

9.3.3   Address Setup

Address setup is a prerequisite for entering and printing addresses correctly. For accessing the address setup, open in the form *Organization administration> Setup> Addresses> Address setup*.

9.3.3.1 Address Parameters

On the tab *Parameters* of the address setup, checkboxes provide the option to determine whether *ZIP/postal code*, *District* or *City* are validated when entering an address. If selected, you cannot enter an address with – for example – a new ZIP code before inserting the new ZIP code in the ZIP code main table.

9.3.3.2 Address Format

The address format on the tab *Address format* determines how street, ZIP/postal code, city and country display in the address field of addresses. In order to comply with the regulations in different countries, an individual format per country is possible. For this purpose, the column *Address format* in the country management (tab *Country/region* in the address setup) controls the address format per country.

If you want to set up a new format, click the button *New* in the upper section of the address formats. In the lower section, enter the way address components (including *Street* and *City*) should show on printed documents. The component selection also applies to editing addresses: When entering an address, only address fields included in the address format of the particular country are available.

When setting up address formats, take into account that Dynamics AX stores the formatted address in addition to the individual fields of the address. If you change the format after entering addresses, update the existing addresses by clicking the button *Update addresses* in the address format setup.

9.3.3.3 Country/Region

Microsoft Dynamics AX provides a standard list of countries, which you may view on the tab *Country/region* of the address setup. For entering additional countries, click the button *New* there.

9.3.3.4 New in Dynamics AX 2012

In order to support the global address book, components like address formats and countries are shared across all companies in Dynamics AX 2012.

9.3.4 Parameters

Parameters are basic settings, enabling to select the business process version, which fit best to your organization, from the options available in Dynamics AX.

Setting parameters is a core task when implementing Dynamics AX. Depending on the individual parameter, later changes are – or are not – easily possible in a working environment. Before changing any basic setting in an operational environment, be sure you are aware of all consequences. Depending on the circumstances, read the online help or ask an expert to avoid data inconsistency or other problems.

9.3.4.1 System Parameters

The system parameters in the form *System administration> Setup> System parameters* contain global parameters like the system language (default language for language texts in shared data, e.g. product descriptions), or the default basic currency.

9.3.4.2 Module Parameters

In addition, a parameters form controlling company-specific settings is available in each module of Dynamics AX. For accessing the parameters of an individual module, open the menu item *Setup> Parameters* – for example the accounts payable parameters in *Accounts payable> Setup> Accounts payable parameters*.

9.4   Alerts and Workflow Management

A workflow is a sequence of operations in a routine business process, containing necessary activities to be performed on a document. Typical examples of workflows are approval processes, e.g. for purchase requisitions.

Microsoft Dynamics AX provides functionality for configuring and processing workflows, including the option of automated processes. You can apply this functionality for example for automatically approving low-value purchase requisitions while requiring manual approval for high-value requisitions. If you need a workflow not included in standard Dynamics AX, a workflow development wizard in the development environment enables creating additional workflows.

Alerts within Dynamics AX are automatic notifications based on alert rules, which are triggered by selected events (e.g. inserting a record). Compared to workflows, which support a sequence of activities including automatic actions, alerts are simple notifications without further options.

9.4.1   Alert Rules and Notifications

Alerts do not require a complex setup, but only creating an alert rule in any Dynamics AX form in order to automatically notify users.

9.4.1.1   Alert Rules

Depending on your permission settings, create alert rules as required. You can for example set up a rule to notify the responsible person when an agreed delivery date passes, or when a new vendor is entered.

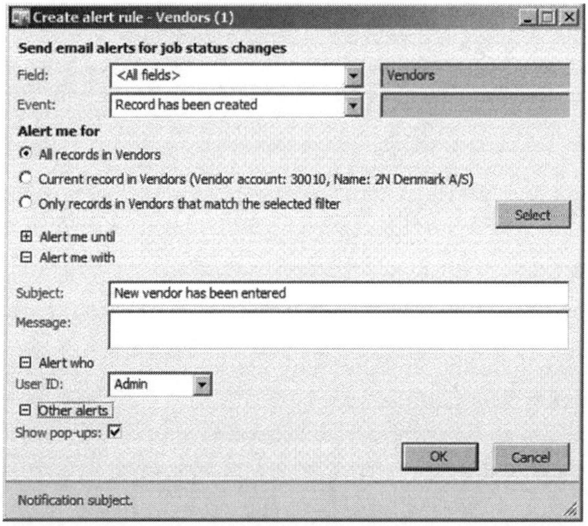

Figure 9-12:   The dialog box for creating an alert rule

For setting up alert rules, choose the option *Create alert rule* in the pop-up menu (doing a right-hand click) or the command *File/Command/Create alert rule* in every detail form or list page (in case of a field-based rule after selecting the appropriate field). Dynamics AX then shows a dialog box for editing the alert rule.

In the field *Event* of the alert rule dialog, select the trigger for the alert – e.g. creating or deleting a record, or modifying the content of a particular field. If the basis of an alert rule is a date field, the field *Event* in addition provides the option to generate alerts when the date is due.

Figure 9-12 shows the example of entering an alert rule which applies when a new vendor record is created. In order to limit alerts, optionally enter a filter by clicking the button *Select* in the alert rule dialog (for example if you only want alerts for vendors of a particular vendor group).

9.4.1.2 Settings for Alert Management

If you want to edit existing alert rules, choose the command *File/Tools/Manage alert rules* in the jewel menu, or access the menu item *Organization administration> Setup> Alerts> Alert rules*. Apart from editing existing rules on the tab *General*, the alert rule administration form also provides the option to create new alert rules (based on alert templates). Alert templates are regular record templates (see section 2.3.2), which are created in the alert rule administration form.

Alert notifications only show after executing the periodic activity *System administration> Periodic> Alerts> Change based alerts* and/or *System administration> Periodic> Alerts> Due date alerts*. These activities are usually periodic batch jobs, but you can run them online for testing purposes manually.

On the tab *Alerts* of the system parameters (*System administration> Setup> System parameters*), specify the period which Dynamics AX should process for due date alerts like exceeding an agreed delivery date.

9.4.1.3 User Options

In your user options, the tab *Notifications* contains a setting specifying the period for receiving notifications. Optionally select there in addition, if you want alert notifications as email message or in a pop-up window.

In parallel to the notification settings for alerts, the user options also include settings for workflow notifications.

9.4.1.4 Working with Notifications

Once an event triggers an alert, the appropriate notification will show. Depending on alert rule settings and your user options, alert notifications and workflow notifications display in the status bar, in a pop-up, or in an e-mail message.

When receiving an alert notification, display the alert in the notification list by double-clicking the alert icon in the status bar, or by selecting the command *File/View/Notifications*. In the notification line, click the button *Go to origin* in the action pane strip for accessing the alert origin.

For deleting alert notifications not required any more, push the shortcut key *Alt+F9* or choose the command *File/Delete Record* in the notification list. Alternatively, set the alert notification status to "Read" by switching to the tab *General* or by clicking the button *Change status*.

9.4.2   Configuring Workflows

Workflows are available in many areas of Microsoft Dynamics AX, including but not limited to:

> Financial journals
> Purchase requisitions
> Purchase orders
> Invoice posting
> Time and attendance

9.4.2.1   Workflow List Page

In each applicable menu, the setup folder contains a menu item for the workflows in the particular module. When selecting this menu item, the workflow list page displays the workflows configured in the particular module. The list page *Procurement and sourcing> Setup> Procurement and sourcing workflows* for example allows editing workflows in the procurement module.

9.4.2.2   Graphical Workflow Editor

After selecting a particular workflow in a workflow list page, double-click the workflow line or click the button *Edit* in the action pane for accessing the graphical workflow editor.

By default, the graphical workflow editor shows three panes:

> **Canvas** – Space for designing workflows (drag and drop elements and connections)
> **Toolbox** – On the left, containing available workflow elements
> **Error pane** – Displays error messages and warnings below the canvas (not shown in Figure 9-13, display by clicking the button *Error pane* in the action pane)

In the toolbox, workflow elements are grouped by different types like *Approvals* and *Tasks*. Depending on the selected workflow, different elements are available. In order to hide or show the toolbox, click the button *Toolbox* in the action pane.

If you want to add a workflow element to the workflow, click it in the toolbox and drag it to the canvas. For editing the properties of the element, choose the option *Properties* in the pop-up menu (right-hand click on the element) or click the appropriate button in the action pane group *Modify element*.

Apart from basic settings like the element name, enter responsible persons – belonging to different assignment types – for *Notifications* and for *Assignment*.

Applicable assignment types include participants (referring to user roles and user groups), hierarchies (referring to the position hierarchy in human resources), workflow users (user starting or owning a workflow), or specific user names.

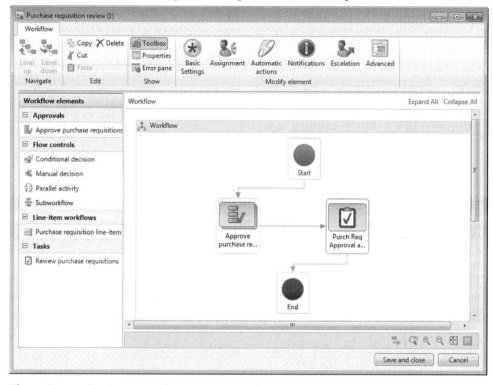

Figure 9-13:   Graphical workflow editor showing the purchase requisition workflow

In the *Escalation* settings, set up automatic reassignment of a work item once the time limit for the assigned user is exceeded. On the tab *End action* in the escalation settings, an automatic action is specified in case the escalation path fails.

Settings for *Automatic actions* provide the option to automatically take an action if the condition entered for the automatic action is met – e.g. approving a requisition if the invoice amount is below a particular value.

The *Advanced settings* determine allowed actions for the workflow element.

Workflow elements of the type "Approval" contain a lower workflow level with the approval steps. For accessing the approval steps, double-click the particular approval element or click the button *Level down* in the workflow editor. In order to view the upper level again, click the button *Level up* or click the link *Workflow* in the path shown in the header line of the canvas.

9.4.2.3 Workflow Properties

For accessing the properties of the workflow itself, do a right-hand click or click an appropriate button in the action pane group *Modify workflow* after selecting an empty space in the canvas. Important settings include the *Owner* of the selected workflow.

9.4.2.4 Work Item Queues

A specific option for assigning workflow elements is "Queue" (e.g. applicable for tasks). The assignment to queues refers to work item queues entered in the form *Organization administration> Setup> Workflow> Work item queues*.

Work item queues are there to pool activities originating from a workflow, assigning an activity to a group of people instead of a single person. If a work item is assigned to a work item queue, all members of the queue may claim the work item and work on it.

When setting up a new work item queue, select the workflow type in the lookup field *Document* determining the workflows in which the work item queue is available. After setting the status of the work item queue to *Active*, it is available for assignment in the appropriate workflows.

As an alternative to manually adding users to a work item queue, choose an automatic assignment based on filter criteria through clicking the button *Work item queue assignment* or selecting the menu item *Organization administration> Setup> Workflow> Work item queue assignment rules*.

9.4.2.5 Workflow Versions

When saving a workflow by clicking the button *Save and close* in the workflow editor, Dynamics AX creates a new version. A dialog box asks whether to activate the new version or to keep the previous version activated.

If you want to check and edit the versions of a workflow, click the button *Versions* in the workflow list page. In the workflow versions form, optionally set a new or old version as active if applicable.

The active version applies to workflows submitted after activation. Work items of workflows in progress finish on their original version.

9.4.2.6 Create Workflows

The button *New* in the workflow list page for creating a workflow opens a form, where you have to select the applicable workflow *Type* – e.g. "Purchase requisition review". Clicking the button *Create workflow* after selecting the type then opens the graphical workflow editor as described above.

If there are two workflows of the same type in the workflow list page, specify a default by clicking the button *Set as default* in the action pane of the list page.

9.4.2.7 Basic Settings for Batch Processing

Processing of workflows is an asynchronous batch job, which is why the next step in a workflow is not available immediately, but only after batch processing of the specific workflow element has been completed. Depending on the batch configuration, this may last some time.

In order to initially set up the workflow infrastructure, a wizard is available in the menu item *System administration> Setup> Workflow> Workflow infrastructure configuration*. This wizard generates three batch jobs, which show in the form *System administration> Inquiries> Batch jobs> Batch jobs* (see section 2.2.1). As a prerequisite for using workflows, these batch jobs have to be processed repeatedly.

In the system service accounts (*System administration> Setup> System> System service accounts*), an account for workflow execution has to be specified.

9.4.3 Working with Workflows

If workflow processing is required in a particular Dynamics AX form, a yellow workflow message bar shows at the top of the form. This message bar reminds the user entering a transaction that workflow processing is necessary, providing the option of submitting the workflow immediately.

When working with workflows, keep in mind that the workflow system processes workflow tasks in a batch process. Work items therefore are not available before the batch process has processed the submitted workflow.

9.4.3.1 Submitting a Workflow

After creating a record which requires workflow processing, submit the workflow clicking the button *Submit* in the yellow workflow message bar (see Figure 9-14).

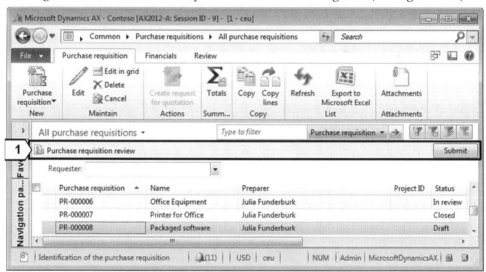

Figure 9-14: Submitting a workflow for a purchase requisition

Submitting a workflow actually starts it, generating work items for processing corresponding workflow elements.

Once the workflow is submitted, the workflow message bar shows the button *Actions* instead of *Submit*. Depending on workflow settings and the current status, there are different options in the *Actions* button.

For checking the current status of workflow processing, click the button *Action/View history* in the workflow message bar.

9.4.3.2 Approving Work Items

Depending on the settings of the related workflow element, work items are either assigned to a work item queue, or to individual users (including assignments by definitions like participant or workflow user). The work items assigned to a user show in his work item list (*Home> Common> Work Items> Work items assigned to me*).

The options available in the workflow message bar at the top of the work item list are depending on the workflow element (Actions allowed in *Properties/Advanced settings*). If applicable, approve a work item by clicking the button *Actions/Approve*.

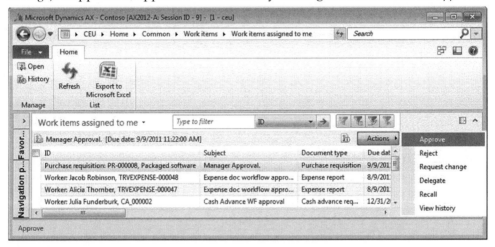

Figure 9-15:   Approving a work item

Depending on the settings for workflow notifications in your user options, a notification shows in case a new work item is assigned to you.

9.4.3.3 Working with Work Item Queues

If a work item is assigned to a work item queue, it shows in the list page *Home> Common> Work Items> Work items assigned to my queues*. As a prerequisite, you have to be member of the work item queue referring to the work item.

In the work item queue, claim a work item by clicking the button *Actions/Accept* in the yellow workflow message bar for working on it. This prevents other queue members to work on the same item. After claiming a work item, it shows in the work item list among the work items directly assigned to you as described above.

In the work item list, execute applicable workflow actions like approving or rejecting like you do for directly assigned work items. In addition, the option

Reassign is available for reassigning the work item to other persons and the option *Release* for releasing it back to the queue.

9.4.3.4 New in Dynamics AX 2012

In Dynamics AX 2012, the workflow framework has been significantly enhanced including the graphical workflow editor resembling Microsoft Visio, line-item workflows, work item queues and a simplified installation architecture (avoiding workflow server components on an IIS server).

9.5 Other Features

Advanced features, available across the whole application, include document management, case management and the task recorder.

9.5.1 Document Management

In daily business, you are working with structured data available as records in your business application (e.g. customers). In parallel, important data referring to these records are available only in an unstructured format (e.g. files or mails).

Document management in Microsoft Dynamics AX supports solving this issue by assigning as many files as required to any table record. The files attached are accessible directly within Dynamics AX.

If you use document management to attach all notes and files referring to a particular customer in the customer form for example, Dynamics AX provides access to all relevant data on this customer – business data within Dynamics AX as well as related files – directly from the customer form.

9.5.1.1 Document Handling Form

The document handling form, accessible in any list page or form by clicking the button 📄 in the status bar or in the action pane (called *Attachments* there), provides the option to manage notes and documents in Dynamics AX. In the document handling form, edit existing or add new documents as applicable. These documents are attached to the record selected in the original form when opening document handling.

If you want to create a new document in the document handling form, insert a new line clicking the button *New* in the action pane strip or pushing the shortcut key *Ctrl+N*. The *Type* selected in this line determines if the document is a note, a file attachment, a URL, or a new Word document/Excel worksheet.

If you want to view an attached document in an existing line, click the button *Open* showing the attachment in a separate form. Alternatively, select the checkbox *Show file* in the document handling form displaying the file in the lower pane of the form.

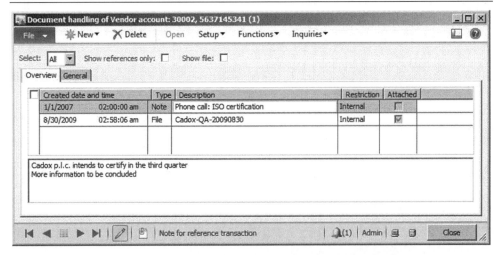

Figure 9-16: Document handling form showing attachments to a particular customer

As an alternative to the access from the individual tables, the document handling form is also available in the home menu (*Home> Common> Document management> Documents*). The document form there shows all documents which comply with the filter entered in the header pane, regardless of the table to which a document refers to.

9.5.1.2 User Options

As a prerequisite for accessing the document handling form through the document handling button, the checkbox *Document handling active* in your user options has to be selected. The checkbox *Show attachment status* in the user options controls, whether the document handling button is highlighted for records holding attached documents.

9.5.1.3 Document Types

Document management distinguishes between several types of documents:

➤ **Simple notes** – Not including an attached file. In the lower pane of the document handling form, optionally enter multiple lines of text.
➤ **File attachments** – Available for attaching any files.
➤ **Word documents** and **Excel worksheets** – Available for creating documents directly in the document handling form.
➤ **URLs** – Available for entering web links in the lower pane of the document handling form.

In order set up available document types, open the form *Organization administration> Setup> Document management> Document types*. Each document type refers to a particular class and group (fields *Class* and *Group*), specifying if assigned documents are simple notes, attachments or new documents. If entered, the setting in the fields *Location* and *Archive directory* overrides settings from the document management parameters. If selecting "Database" for the file location, Dynamics AX stores the files inside the database.

Note: The menu item *Document content types* in document management setup refers to unattached documents (*Home> Common> Document management> Unattached documents*).

9.5.1.4 Document Management Setup

Parameters for document management are available in the form *Organization administration> Setup> Document management> Document management parameters*. Basic parameters include the *Archive directory* (usually a separate shared directory on a file server) and a number sequence for documents. The archive directory in the parameters is not applicable for document types with a specific file location entered in the particular document type. Make sure to include the archive directories in backup procedures.

The tab *File types* in the document management parameters controls, which file types are available in document management – enabling to exclude possibly malicious file types like EXE-files.

If the checkbox *Use active document tables* in the parameters is selected, document handling is only available for tables included in the active document tables (*Organization administration> Setup> Document management> Active document tables*).

The document data sources (*Organization administration> Setup> Document management> Document data sources*) specify data sources available for the Microsoft Office Add-ins (see section 2.2.2).

9.5.1.5 New in Dynamics AX 2012

Items new in Dynamics AX 2012 document management include the document form in the home menu, the document type URL and the support of Office add-ins.

9.5.2 Case Management

Case management is available to centrally manage questions and issues. It does not only support customer service, but also applies to collections, purchase management, and human resources.

9.5.2.1 Case Configuration

There are two main items relevant for configuring case management:

➢ Case categories
➢ Case processes

Case categories (*Organization management> Setup> Cases> Case categories*) group cases by functional areas in a hierarchical structure. For setting up a case category, click the button *New* in the action pane there. On the tab *General*, choose defaults for the owner and the *Case process* of cases linked to the category.

Case processes (*Organization management> Setup> Cases> Case processes*) support performing necessary steps when processing a case. Depending on the different types of cases in your enterprise set up one or multiple case processes.

When setting up a new case process with *Name* and *Description*, assign steps (stages) for processing related cases by clicking the button *Actions/Create level* in the action pane strip of the right pane. In the field *Purpose*, enter the name of the stage. If required, you can create a multi-level hierarchy of stages.

For simple case processes, setting up stages may be sufficient. But if applicable, enter activities (including *Appointments* or *Tasks*) assigned to the stages by clicking the button *Actions* (or through a right-hand click on the appropriate element in the *Actions* area of the form). Activities referring to cases are in common with the activities in *Sales and marketing* (former CRM activities), also available in the *Home* menu (see section 2.1.4).

If you want to ensure, that particular activities are executed when working on a case, select the checkbox *Required* on these activities, and the checkbox *Check for required activities* on the tab *Exit criteria* of the related stage.

9.5.2.2 Processing Cases

For creating a new case, click the appropriate button in the action pane of any list page or detail form applying case management – e.g. in sales orders (*Sales and marketing> Common> Sales orders> All sales orders*, button *Cases/Create case* on the action pane tab *General*), customers, collections, vendors, or released products.

Cases created in a sales order are assigned to the order and to the customer. When creating such a case, enter the *Case category* and a *Description* in the *Create* dialog. Defaults for *Owner*, *Service level agreement* and *Case process* on the tab *Other* of the dialog are retrieved from the selected *Case category*. Clicking the button *Create* in the dialog then creates the case.

If you want to follow up on a case, open the list page *Home> Common> Cases> All cases* and switch to the detail form for editing the case. Assignments of the case (e.g. to a sales order) show on the tab *Associations*. If additional associations apply later, add them in the case form (e.g. assigning a return order in addition to the original sales order). The FactBox *Process* shows the planned case process stages and activities according to the configuration. The current status of the stages shows in the case process form (next to the *Name* field on the right after selecting a stage in the left pane), which you can access by clicking the button *Case process* in the action pane of the case form.

When starting to work on a case, click the button *Change status/In process* in the action pane (if this status has not been already selected when creating the case). When proceeding with the case later, click the button *Case/Change stage* and select the next stage of the case.

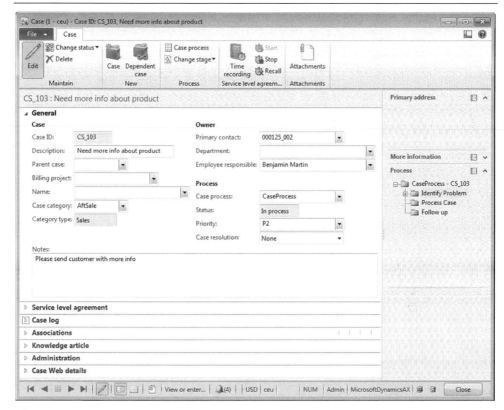

Figure 9-17: Editing details of a case

The tab *Case log* shows all interactions (e.g. receiving a product) referring to the case. Using the case log, other persons looking at a specific case may easily know the status of a case.

If the case is attached to a *Case process* enabling *Activities*, access the related activities through the menu item *Home> Common> Activities> All activities* (or by clicking the button *Activities/View activities* on the action pane tab *General* of the case form). Required activities of a case have to be completed by the responsible person.

If the case refers to a *Service level agreement* (tab *Service level agreement*), time recordings are enabled. Time recording starts when the case status changes (button *Case/Change status* in the action pane) or when clicking the button *Case/Start* or *Case/Stop*. For viewing the recorded time, click the button *Time recording* in the action pane of the case form. Time recordings in case management do not refer to time recordings in project management or manufacturing execution.

In order to close a case, click the button *Change status/Closed* in the action pane of the case form.

9.5.2.3 New in Dynamics AX 2012

Case management is a new feature in Dynamics AX 2012.

9.5.3   Task Recorder

The task recorder in Dynamics AX provides an easy option for automatically generating click-through instructions of procedures in Dynamics AX. After recording, you can directly publish the instructions in Microsoft Word.

The task recorder opens by choosing the option *File/Tools/Task recorder* in the jewel menu. For starting to record a sequence of activities, click the button ▣ in the task recorder dialog. Then execute the recorded steps in the Dynamics AX client. In order to stop recording, switch to the task recorder dialog and click the button ▣ there. In a separate dialog, enter a name for the recording then.

In order to access recorded tasks, click the button ▣ in the task recorder dialog. The recorded tasks form then shows all recording. For generating a Microsoft Word document or a PowerPoint presentation, click the button *Generate document* in the recorded tasks.

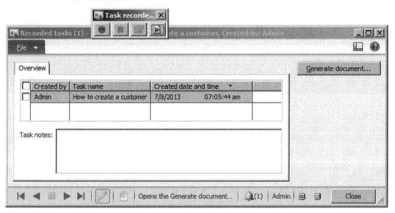

Figure 9-18:   Recorded tasks in the task recorder

Appendix

Setup Checklist

The checklists below show the most essential steps for setting up a new Dynamics AX database. You can use these checklists as a guideline for a basic setup of Dynamics AX.

The section "Basic Setup" contains necessary configuration steps for all functional areas covered by the book. They have to be finished before you can start to use any module. Master data and other essential settings of particular modules are shown in the section afterwards. Depending on the specific requirements of an implementation, additional setup is required in most cases.

Basic Setup

Table A-1:   Basic setup of a Dynamics AX database

No.	Name	Menu Item	Section
1.1	Partitions	*System administration> Setup> Partitions*	9.1.1
1.2	Configuration	*System administration> Setup> Licensing> License configuration*	
1.3	Parameters	*System administration> Setup> System parameters*	
1.4	Legal entities	*Organization administration> Setup> Organization> Legal entities*	9.1.5
1.5	Users	*System administration> Common> Users> Users*	9.2.2
1.6	Virtual company accounts	*System administration> Setup> Virtual Company accounts*	9.1.6

Table A-2:   Basic setup of a legal entity

No.	Name	Menu Item	Section
2.1	Operating units	*Organization administration> Setup> Organization> Operating units*	9.1.3
2.2	Dimensions	*General ledger> Setup> Financial dimensions> Financial dimensions*	8.2.3
2.3	Sites	*Inventory and warehouse management> Setup> Inventory breakdown> Sites*	9.1.7
2.4	Dimension link	*Inventory and warehouse management> Setup> Posting> Dimension link*	9.1.7
2.5	Warehouses	*Inventory and warehouse management> Setup> Inventory breakdown> Warehouses*	7.4.1
2.6	Fiscal calendars	*General ledger> Setup> Fiscal Calendars*	8.2.1
2.7	Currencies	*General ledger> Setup> Currency> Currencies*	8.2.2
2.8	Rate types	*General ledger> Setup> Currency> Exchange rate types*	8.2.2
2.9	Exchange rates	*General ledger> Setup> Currency> Currency exchange rates*	8.2.2

No.	Name	Menu Item	Section
2.10	Chart of Accounts	*General ledger> Setup> Chart of accounts> Chart of accounts*	8.2.4
2.11	Account structure	*General ledger> Setup> Chart of accounts> Configure account structures*	8.2.4
2.12	Ledger	*General ledger> Setup> Ledger*	8.2
2.13	Bank accounts	*Cash and bank management> Common> Bank Accounts*	8.2.5
2.14	Address setup	*Organization administration> Setup> Addresses> Address setup*	9.3.3
2.15	Address book parameters	*Organization administration> Setup> Global address book> Global address book parameters*	2.4.2
2.16	Number sequences	*Organization administration> Common> Number sequences> Number sequences*	9.3.1
2.17	Units	*Organization administration> Setup> Units> Units*	7.2.1
2.18	Unit conversion	*Organization administration> Setup> Units> Unit conversions*	7.2.1

Table A-3:   Basic setup for the general ledger

No.	Name	Menu Item	Section
3.1	Default descriptions	*Organization administration> Setup> Default descriptions*	
3.2	Accounts for aut. transactions	*General ledger> Setup> Posting> Accounts for automatic transactions*	8.2.4
3.3	Ledger posting groups	*General ledger> Setup> Sales tax> Ledger posting groups*	8.2.6
3.4	Sales tax authorities	*General ledger> Setup> Sales tax> Sales tax authorities*	8.2.6
3.5	Sales tax settlement periods	*General ledger> Setup> Sales tax> Sales tax settlement periods*	8.2.6
3.6	Sales tax codes	*General ledger> Setup> Sales tax> Sales tax codes*	8.2.6
3.7	Sales tax groups	*General ledger> Setup> Sales tax> Sales tax groups*	8.2.6
3.8	Item sales tax groups	*General ledger> Setup> Sales tax> Item sales tax groups*	8.2.6
3.9	Journal names	*General ledger> Setup> Journals> Journal names*	8.3.1
3.10	Parameters	*General ledger> Setup> General ledger parameters*	

Table A-4:   Basic setup for procurement and accounts payable

No.	Name	Menu Item	Section
4.1	Terms of payment	*Accounts payable> Setup> Payment>Terms of payment*	3.2.2
4.2	Vendor groups	*Accounts payable> Setup> Vendors> Vendor groups*	3.2.3
4.3	Posting profiles	*Accounts payable> Setup> Vendor posting profiles*	3.2.3
4.4	Accounts payable parameters	*Accounts payable> Setup> Accounts payable parameters*	
4.5	Procurement parameters	*Procurement and sourcing> Setup> Procurement and sourcing parameters*	

Table A-5:   Basic setup for sales and accounts receivable

No.	Name	Menu Item	Section
5.1	Terms of payment	*Accounts receivable> Setup> Payment>Terms of payment*	3.2.2
5.2	Customer groups	*Accounts receivable> Setup> Customers> Customer groups*	4.2.1
5.3	Posting profiles	*Accounts receivable> Setup> Customer posting profiles*	4.2.1
5.4	Form setup	*Accounts receivable> Setup> Forms> Form setup*	4.2.1
5.5	Accounts receiv. parameters	*Accounts receivable> Setup> Accounts receivable parameters*	

Table A-6:   Basic setup for product and inventory management

No.	Name	Menu Item	Section
6.1	Storage dimension groups	*Product information management> Setup> Dimension groups> Storage dimension groups*	7.2.2
6.2	Tracking dimension groups	*Product information management> Setup> Dimension groups> Tracking dimension groups*	7.2.2
6.3	Item groups	*Inventory and warehouse management> Setup> Inventory> Item groups*	7.2.1
6.4	Transaction combinations	*Inventory and warehouse management> Setup> Posting> Transaction combinations*	8.4.2
6.5	Posting	*Inventory and warehouse management> Setup> Posting> Posting*	8.4.2
6.6	Item model groups	*Inventory and warehouse management> Setup> Inventory> Item model groups*	7.2.3
6.7	Costing versions	*Inventory and warehouse management> Setup> Costing> Costing versions*	7.2.4
6.8	Journal names	*Inventory and warehouse management> Setup> Journals> Journal names, inventory*	7.4.1
6.9	Warehouse journals	*Inventory and warehouse management> Setup> Journals> Journal names, warehouse management*	7.4.1
6.10	Parameters	*Inventory and warehouse management> Setup> Inventory and warehouse management parameters*	

Table A-7:   Basic setup for production control

No.	Name	Menu Item	Section
7.1	Production units	*Production control> Setup> Production> Production units*	5.3.1
7.2	Working time templates	*Organization administration> Common> Calendars> Working time templates*	5.3.1
7.3	Calendars	*Organization administration> Common> Calendars> Calendar*	5.3.1
7.4	Resource capabilities	*Organization administration> Common> Resources> Resource capabilities*	5.3.2
7.5	Resource groups	*Organization administration> Common> Resources> Resource groups*	5.3.1

No.	Name	Menu Item	Section
7.6	Resources	*Organization administration> Common> Resources> Resources*	5.3.2
7.7	Journal names	*Production control> Setup> Production journal names*	5.4.1
7.8	Route groups	*Production control> Setup> Routes> Route groups*	5.3.3
7.9	Cost groups	*Production control> Setup> Routes> Cost groups*	5.4.1
7.10	Shared categories	*Production control> Setup> Routes> Shared categories*	5.3.3
7.11	Cost categories	*Production control> Setup> Routes> Cost categories*	5.3.3
7.12	Calculation groups	*Inventory and warehouse management> Setup> Costing> Calculation groups*	5.2.1
7.13	Costing sheets	*Inventory and warehouse management> Setup> Costing> Costing sheets*	5.4.1
7.14	Parameters	*Production control> Setup> Production control parameters*	
7.15	Parameters by site	*Production control> Setup> Production control parameters by site*	

Table A-8:　Basic setup for master planning

No.	Name	Menu Item	Section
8.1	Coverage groups	*Master planning> Setup> Coverage> Coverage groups*	6.3.3
8.2	Master plans	*Master planning> Setup> Plans> Master plans*	6.3.2
8.3.	Forecast models	*Inventory and warehouse management> Setup> Forecast> Forecast models*	6.2.2
8.4	Forecast plans	*Master planning> Setup> Plans> Forecast plans*	6.2.2
8.5	Parameters	*Master planning> Setup> Master planning parameters*	

Other Key Settings and Master Data

Table A-9:　Other key settings

No.	Name	Menu Item	Section
9.1	Workers	*Human resources> Common> Workers> Workers*	9.2.2
9.2	User relations	*System administration> Common> Users> User relations*	9.2.2
9.3	Terms of delivery	*Sales and marketing> Setup> Distribution> Terms of delivery*	3.2.1
9.4	Modes of delivery	*Sales and marketing> Setup> Distribution> Modes of delivery*	4.2.1
9.5	Cash discounts	*Accounts payable> Setup> Payment> Cash discounts*	3.2.2
9.6	Payment methods (Purchasing)	*Accounts payable> Setup> Payment> Methods of payment*	8.3.4
9.7	Activate trade agreements (Purchasing)	*Procurement and sourcing> Setup> Price/discount> Activate price/discount*	3.3.3
9.8	Vendor price/ discount groups	*Procurement and sourcing> Setup> Price/discount> Vendor price/discount groups*	3.3.3

No.	Name	Menu Item	Section
9.9	Item discount groups	*Procurement and sourcing> Setup> Price/discount> Item discount groups*	4.3.2
9.10	Trade agreement journal names	*Procurement and sourcing> Setup> Price/discount> Trade agreement journal names*	3.3.3
9.11	Price tolerance setup	*Accounts payable> Setup> Invoice matching> Price tolerances*	3.6.2
9.12	Activate trade agreements (Sales)	*Sales and marketing> Setup> Price/discount> Activate price/discount*	4.3.2
9.13	Customer price/ discount groups	*Sales and marketing> Setup> Price/discount> Customer price/discount groups*	4.3.2
9.14	Charges codes (Purchasing)	*Accounts payable> Setup> Charges> Charges code*	4.4.5
9.15	Charges codes (Sales)	*Accounts receivable> Setup> Charges> Charges code*	4.4.5
9.16	Return action (Purchasing)	*Procurement and sourcing> Setup> Purchase orders> Return action*	3.7.1
9.17	Disposition codes	*Sales and marketing> Setup> Sales orders> Returns> Disposition codes*	4.6.4
9.18	Category hierarchies	*Product information management> Setup> Categories> Category hierarchies*	3.3.1
9.19	Procurement categories	*Procurement and sourcing> Setup> Categories> Procurement categories*	3.3.1
9.20	Sales categories	*Sales and marketing> Setup> Categories> Sales categories*	4.3.1
9.21	Carrier interface	*Inventory and warehouse management> Setup> Sipping carrier> Carrier interface*	4.2.1
9.22	Document management parameters	*Organization administration> Setup> Document management> Document management parameters*	9.5.1
9.23	Document types	*Organization administration> Setup> Document management> Document types*	9.5.1
9.24	Workflow configuration	*System administration> Setup> Workflow> Workflow infrastructure configuration*	9.4.2
9.25	Batch-Server	*System administration> Setup> System> Server configuration*	2.2.1

Table A-10:   Master data

No.	Name	Menu Item	Section
10.1	Vendors	*Accounts payable> Common> Vendors> All vendors*	3.2.1
10.2	Customers	*Accounts receivable> Common> Customers> All customers*	4.2.1
10.3	Products	*Product information management> Common> Products> All products and product masters*	7.2.1
10.4	Released products	*Product information management> Common> Released products*	7.2.1
10.5	Bills of material	*Inventory and warehouse management> Common> Bills of materials*	5.2.2
10.6	Operations	*Production control> Setup> Routes> Operations*	5.3.3
10.7	Routes	*Production control> Common> Routes> All routes*	5.3.3

Commands and Shortcut Keys

Table A-11:   Basic commands and shortcut keys

Shortcut Key	Command	Description
Ctrl+N	*File/New*	Create a record
Alt+F9	*File/Delete Record*	Delete a record
Alt+F4	*File/Exit*	Close form or workspace
Esc		Close form (optionally without saving)
Ctrl+F5	*File/Command/Restore*	Restore record (Undo pending changes)
F5	*File/Command/Refresh*	Refresh (Save and synchronize record)
Ctrl+P	*File/Print/Print*	Print auto-report
	File/View/Show Favorites in Navigation Pane	Show/hide favorites pane
Ctrl+W	*Windows/New workspace*	Open an additional workspace
Ctrl+X	*File/Edit/Cut*	Cut (content of one field)
Ctrl+C	*File/Edit/Copy*	Copy (field or record)
Ctrl+V	*File/Edit/Paste*	Paste (content of one field)
Ctrl+F	*File/Edit/Find*	Find (opens the field filter window)
Ctrl+F3	*File/Edit/Filter/ Advanced Filter/Sort*	Open the window for advanced filtering
Alt+F3	*File/Edit/Filter/ Filter by selection*	Set a filter applying the content of the selected field
Ctrl+G	*File/Edit/Filter/ Filter By Grid*	Show the filter line
Shift+ Ctrl+F3	*File/Edit/Remove Filter/Sort*	Clear filter
	File/Command/Document handling	Document management
	File/View/Notifications	Show notifications
F1	*Help/Help*	Help on forms

Bibliography

Literature

Keith Dunkinson, Andrew Birch: Implementing Microsoft Dynamics AX 2012 with Sure Step 2012, Packt Publishing (2013)

Mindaugas Pocius: Microsoft Dynamics AX 2012 Development Cookbook, Packt Publishing (2012)

The Microsoft Dynamics AX Team: Inside Microsoft Dynamics AX 2012, Microsoft Press (2012)

Scott Hamilton: Discrete Manufacturing Using Microsoft Dynamics AX 2012, Visions Inc. (2012)

Scott Hamilton: Managing Your Supply Chain Using Microsoft Dynamics AX 2009, Printing Arts (2009)

Marco Carvalho: Microsoft Dynamics AX 2009 Administration, Packt Publishing (2011)

Microsoft Corporation [Ed.]: Help system in Microsoft Dynamics AX 2012 (2013)

Microsoft Corporation [Ed.]: Course 80300 – Introduction to Microsoft Dynamics AX 2012, MOC Courseware (2011)

Other Sources

www.microsoft.com

Index

6562631R00232

Printed in Great Britain
by Amazon.co.uk, Ltd.,
Marston Gate.